The Prospect of Lyric

STUDIES IN GENRE

Louise Cowan, General Editor

THE TERRAIN OF COMEDY

THE EPIC COSMOS

THE TRAGIC ABYSS

THE PROSPECT OF LYRIC

The Prospect of Lyric

Edited by
Bainard Cowan

With an Introduction by
Louise Cowan

THE DALLAS INSTITUTE PUBLICATIONS
The Dallas Institute of Humanities and Culture

Copyright © 2012   Dallas Institute Publications
All rights reserved. The Dallas Institute of Humanities and Culture, formerly known as The Pegasus Foundation

No part of this publication may be reproduced, stored in any retrieval system, or transmitted in any form or by any means, mechanical, photocopying, recording, via the internet or otherwise, without permission in writing from the publisher, except by a reviewer, who may quote brief passages in a review to be printed in a magazine or newspaper.

Cover art:
Paul Klee, Swiss, 1879–1940, Remembrance of a Garden,
1914 (150 Kb); Watercolor on linen paper mounted on cardboard,
25.2 x 21.5 cm; Kunstsammlung Nordrhein-Westfalen, Dusseldorf;
Walter Klein photography
Layout by O! Suzanna, Suzanna Brown

Owing to limitations of space, acknowledgments of permission to quote from previously published material can be found on pages 421-424.

Library of Congress Control Number: 2012931332

ISBN 978-0-911005-49-3

The Dallas Institute Publications
publishes works concerned with the imaginative, mythic,
and symbolic sources of culture.

The Dallas Institute of Humanities and Culture
2719 Routh Street   Dallas, TX 75201 USA
www.dallasinstitute.org

Contents

EDITOR'S PREFACE　　　　　　　　　　*Bainard Cowan*　　*vii*

INTRODUCTION: The Lyric Nostalgia　　*Louise Cowan*　　*1*

THE TRADITION

1　The Psalms: Spacious Places for Wrestling　　　　21
　with God　　　　　　　　　　　*Daniel Russ*

2　Greek and Roman Lyric　　　　*Karl Maurer*　　45

3　From Nothing to Being: Medieval Lyric　　　　77
　and Poetic Form as Entelechy　　*Gregory Roper*

4　Lyric Bearing: Shakespeare's Sonnet 116.12,　　95
　Virgil's *Aeneid*, and the Ship of Metaphor　*Scott F. Crider*

THE ENGLISH ARC

5　John Donne's Three Voices: Toward the Still,　　111
　Quiet Word at the Center of the Lyric　*Robert Alexander*

6　Keats's Pilgrimage: The Five Great Odes　　　135
　　　　　　　　　　　　　　　Louise Cowan

7　"And that is why my Garden lasts": *Emily*　　153
　Dickinson's Herbarium, Her Garden, and the
　Poems　　　　　　　　　　　　*Anna Priddy*

8　Word, Sacrament, and the Divine Lover:　　　171
　Gerard Manley Hopkins and Emily Dickinson
　　　　　　　　　　　Bernadette Waterman Ward

MODERN CRISES OF LYRIC

9 Lyric as Sanctuary: Yeats, Davidson, Ransom, and Frost — *Glenn Arbery* — 199

10 Wallace Stevens' Scrawny Cry — *Seemee Ali* — 217

11 Pound and Eliot: Tradition and the Co-opetitive Talent — *Robert Scott Dupree* — 241

12 The Symbolic Imagination: Allen Tate's Search for Analogy — *Larry Allums* — 269

13 The Harlem Renaissance: Identity and Poetic Redress — *Claudia Allums* — 291

14 Awake at the Top of the Mast: Elizabeth Bishop's "The Unbeliever" and Lyric Identity — *Mary Di Lucia* — 309

15 The Heart's Metronome: Dennis Scott and Jamaican Lyric — *Bainard Cowan* — 335

A MANIFESTO: THE CURRENT SCENE

16 Lyric and the Self — *Frederick Turner* — 359

WORKS CITED — 379

INDEX — 397

PERMISSIONS — 421

Editor's Preface

BAINARD COWAN

A quarter century ago the series *The Genres of Literature* began, examining Western literature from the point of view of the four great genres of Greco-Roman tradition. Despite its classical grounding and its reliance on Aristotle's *Poetics*, this undertaking was envisioned as a means of detecting and developing our understanding of a deeper imaginative life underlying works of literature across the centuries. In her introduction to the first volume, series editor Louise Cowan sounded a note that has run as a continuo throughout the essays to follow in this series: "In a sense a knowledge of genre might be thought of as a guide to the laws of the land, if one is willing to grant the existence of a territory of the imagination" (L. Cowan, "Introduction" 8). Surely, she reasoned, as beings of the same species, our profoundest experiences have so much in common that in them we traverse the same terrains, though each person's path through them may be unique. We treasure great poetic works not so much because of their cleverness or conceptual resourcefulness as because of their ability to condense these profound experiences and shed light on them. They reveal the contours of the terrain more brightly than any other form of writing can do.

An intuition of lyric as a real phenomenon of poetic and imaginative life unites the contributors to *The Prospect of Lyric*. In this we find Aristotle a useful aid. His *Poetics* has very little to say about "dithyrambic" or lyric poetry, but his philosophy as a whole serves as a reminder that it is entirely rational to view human action as proceeding from fundamental motions of the human spirit and that such motion is brought into the open by the work of art. Imitation to him did not mean copying or duplicating—he called music the *most* imitative of the arts, and what could music be said to replicate? Considering art an imitation of action, he saw it as revealing more clearly than ordinary description could the outlines of that purposive action that defines human character, *energeia*.

In our more cautious modern era, Mikhail Bakhtin in his studies of genre identified the existence of "a series of inner genres" that human consciousness possesses that underlie and to an extent determine the outer manifestation (Bakhtin and Medvedev 134); and he saw genre as possessing a life extending across time, beyond the individual work and author and period, growing and at the same time "*remember*[ing] its past" (*Problems* 106). It is that life that the essays in this volume go in search of, for we deem its uncovering and emphasis a more urgent matter than the cataloguing of the literary history of the genre or the taxonomy of its techniques.

In ordinary parlance the meaning of "lyric" denotes a heightened experience, a time apart from everyday action, musical, harmonizing the senses and the emotions. Literary criticism has tended to view lyric as a still moment, a private cry, a spontaneous overflow, or a meditation, approaching it quite readily with these formulations. Yet any serious consideration must penetrate beyond such beginning intuitions, for poetry itself is grounded more deeply in currents of being. Lyric, we might say, unites—it interweaves body, heart, and mind, harmonizing sound and sense. It is personal yet impersonal: in the lyric territory other becomes self and self becomes other, like the lovers in Donne's "The Ecstasy" or the speaker and the chorus in the Song of Songs. Bernard of Clairvaux maintained that in song one can experience the immediacy of the presence of God. In lyric performance, self/other dichotomies are broken down. This liberation amounts to an undoing of the usual bonds that constrict and define the self. In the authoritative examples from lyric's origin, this is a "joyful noise unto the Lord" (Ps. 100). In the lyric of the modern world, however, and especially in lyric poetry of the last hundred years, the expansiveness of this experience has become constricted to a private possession, a moment of consciousness, even a mental experiment, and the desired union has contracted to a distant wish or has finally been lost altogether in the attempt to make the self or language the ultimate microcosm.

What, then, is the prospect of lyric? Widely appreciated as even the simplest lyrics are for their intuitive appeal and power, in our time poetry seems to have lost touch with that intuition; and the critical theory of lyric has generated interesting and complex ideas on the modern lyric but offers no path toward a unitary understanding of its nature and importance. In view of this seeming impasse, we offer this collection of essays, to recall and renew the greatness of the lyric tradition and to ponder its present and future.

The ambiguous word *prospect* designates three definite aspects of our response. Most tangibly, a prospect is a point from which to view a beautiful scene at a certain remove. Louise Cowan's introduction to this volume conducts an open inquiry into what that scene is, the longed-for land that in some sense all lyric poems look toward. Like that "Pisgah view" (to use Melville's phrase) of the Promised Land, lyric poems look on a common realm of human longing. They are not, then, merely subjective utterances, but each illumines through its viewpoint part of the world that exists in our imaginations as a kind of birthright. However, though the lyric poem, like that prospect, is also itself a pleasant place, a *locus amoenus*, its distance from what it allows us to see is its reason for being and sparks its heights of virtuosity.

The cover painting for this volume, Paul Klee's *Remembrance of a Garden*, expresses a great painter's insight into the lyric moment. The painting is one of a series of watercolors Klee created in response to a visit to Tunisia he made in 1914—a visit he considered a turning point in his career, a "blessed moment" in which he could finally say, "Color and I are one. I am a painter." In this picture one might discern a kind of deconstructive transformation of a garden scene, taken apart and reassembled in the intensely colored retrospective light of Klee's experiencing the sheer gift of his calling. Both the subject and the title of the painting, then, witness to the essential object of lyric contemplation, and they acknowledge as well the essential *distance* necessary to create a work of imagination evoking it—a distance that is always a loss but that intensifies the erotic relation to that moment.

Lyric's emotive power persuades us of its immediacy, so that we may experience it as utterance, as an ecstatic overflow of being into its own testimony. As writing, as inscription, by contrast, lyric is forced to be something quite different; and the distance conferred by the almost sculptural concision of the written lyric is what makes its emotive power equaled by the insight it provides into the human condition. Some insightful studies have connected the figurative power and epigrammatic brevity of lyric to tomb inscriptions, the last word in finality and concision but also in acknowledgment of absence and loss.

As a view, a prospect is also an overview, and hence a second meaning of "the prospect of lyric" has to do with our attention to the long tradition of lyric. Lyric poems grow in meaning by association with other lyric poems; more than a dialogue, this mutuality is a veritable "conference of birds" (in Farid ud-Din Attar's mystical phrase) as poems amplify each other on the great lyric images and themes. Although its particular Western enunciation depends on a sense of tradition stretching back to the Babylonian Exile, lyric is a poetic mode that seems to appear wherever cultures have organized themselves. Recent research in anthropology and sociolinguistics has asserted with conviction "the universal, cross-language and cross-cultural reality of lyric epiphany" (Friedrich 217). That lyric springs forth so naturally from the soul means it is even more cross-cultural a phenomenon than epic. China has no known ancient epic; its earliest "classic" (so designated by Confucian tradition) is a collection of lyrics, called in English the *Book of Songs*, whose communal nature exposes what most modern lyrics hide, the requirement of a communal imagination for the soul to dream of its longed-for bliss.

Moreover, if read not synchronically as conference but diachronically as story, the history of lyric poetry in the Western tradition has its own significance as a profound record of consciousness, the emotions, and their relation to the invisible realms over time. Hence, in the sixteen essays constituting the brief tour of lyric history in this volume, we have remained within the line of descent of the English-language lyric. Unquestionably Ki no Tsurayuki, Joachim du Bellay, Osip Mandelstam, and many others would add substantially to our knowledge of the terrain if studied here (for these poets speak to us, and an acquaintance with their poems vouches that they are walking the same terrain). Yet English is our language—as it so happens, not a poor one for outstanding examples of lyric—and there is a special need for us to understand first the lyric voice in the language that we use most. A people builds itself on its lyrics. Lyrics show a people what it loves beyond all else, and love builds the city, as Augustine remarked with penetrating simplicity. We move toward what we admire; lyric, then, is not only our origin but our becoming.

This consideration leads to a final connotation. *Prospect* can mean also an assessment of the probable fortunes of something in the future; hence our title phrase takes on a note of urgency that runs variably through several of the essays collected here. A perusal of the history of lyric in the Western world cannot help uncovering that it has become less naturally graceful, less in touch with transcendent meaning, and less solidary with the people among whom it finds itself. Less musical, less communal, less enjoyable, many poems in recent years are framed more as strategies to awaken readers out of a kind of terminal apathy than as outpourings of any kind, spontaneous or otherwise. What does the future hold for lyric? One fears that the question is intertwined with the question of the human future itself. As the prestige of poetry has waned in the face of technology, it has become too easy to ignore or belittle the urgency of the question concerning whether our culture can rediscover a place of honor for lyric intuition and utterance beyond an ephemeral expression in popular music; yet the question is undoubtedly an urgent one, for it is in lyric that our ideals are framed most genuinely and taken to heart. Without a genuine rebirth of lyric, the future of our culture, if not our civilization, is at risk.

This is the thrust of the final essay in this collection, written by a poet. Frederick Turner's diagnosis of the state of poetry in the contemporary world is a clarion call to revitalize the place of poetry in our lives and in our culture. Poetry needs to be in touch with the world of human action, and the reverse is equally true. For reasons Turner and other contributors make clear, there can be no genuine culture in a society without the lyric, and the lyric itself cannot exist without a lively sense not only of this world but of that other, invisible world as well. We take this position with careful consideration and think of the lyric of any age in terms of its communal testimony, its embodiment of the sense of transcendence, its lament for the lack of these elements, or its attempt to compensate through means such as subjectivity and fragmentation. By careful attention to the poetry of the Psalms, Alcman, William the Troubadour, Shakespeare, John Donne, Emily Dickinson, William Butler Yeats, Allen Tate, Wallace Stevens, Langston Hughes, Elizabeth Bishop, and others, we hope to outline a new understanding of the vital role of lyric in our culture.

The Terrain of Comedy, *The Epic Cosmos*, and *The Tragic Abyss* all had their point of combustion in the award-winning summer institutes for teachers offered at the Dallas Institute of Humanities and Culture for nearly the past thirty years. By contrast the lyric has had no special syllabus of study; typically, rather, poems insinuate themselves readily into any course on literature, for doubtless some lyric poet somewhere has expressed insight on every literary topic in the world. The genesis of this series goes beyond those summer programs to *their* origin, however, that is, to Louise Cowan, her vision of literature, and her passion to teach it and share it with others. A conference she hosted brought together many of the contributors to this book to discuss its ideas. In addition, Joanne Stroud, director of the Dallas Institute Publications, deserves special thanks for her support of this series and of the production of this book. Larry Allums and Robert Scott Dupree offered helpful discussion and advice. This book owes much, finally, to Christine Cowan, for her careful editing of the manuscript and compilation of the index, and to Elizabeth Reyes for her generous help in compiling the notes, references, and List of Works Cited.

Introduction:

The Lyric Nostalgia

Louise Cowan

"Ah, Sun-flower! weary of time," William Blake writes, his eyes on the visionary territory toward which the great yellow flower turns as it follows "the steps of the Sun,"

> Seeking after that sweet golden clime
> Where the traveller's journey is done....

In contrast, A. E. Housman begins one of his bittersweet lyrics with a nostalgic rather than prophetic gaze:

> Into my heart an air that kills
>   From yon far country blows:
> What are those blue remembered hills,
>   What spires, what farms are those?

These two slight little poems establish the poles of the lyric cosmos. They leave, however, a perplexing and unanswered question: does the lyric long for something lost or for something never found? Throughout its history run the two strains: a nostalgia for those "blue remembered hills" and a yearning for "that sweet golden clime," each a desire for a territory that the heart considers its rightful domain. For the heart knows that something is amiss in the present, in whatever land it finds itself. Whether it conceives of the right order of things as in the "dark backward and abysm of time," as Prospero says, or in some Tennysonian "divine far-off event," its cry is most frequently that of the displaced person.

The land for which the lyric yearns, looking back, overtly or not, is usually taken to be the Garden of Eden, the misty site of origins. The home toward which it aspires, straining forward, is symbolized by the New Jerusalem, the ultimate consummation for which all creation groans. Between these two poles, the retrospective and the visionary, lies the third ground of lyric, the garden, less encountered but in atmosphere no less intense, an affirmation and celebration of the present moment. This is the realm of consummation and joy, expressed in such lines as Hopkins' "The world is charged with the grandeur of God./It will flame out, like shining from shook foil," or Donne's "O my America! my new-found-land," Keats's "Thou still unravish'd bride of quietness," or even Robert Frost's single-sentence testimony:

The way a crow
Shook down on me
The dust of snow
From a hemlock tree

Has given my heart
A change of mood
And saved some part
Of a day I had rued.

But such contentment is brief. Throughout all lyric utterances, whether or not openly acknowledged, runs the threat of the lyric enemy, Time. Love is the natural dwelling ground, the "garden" of the lyric, and time is its chief adversary. For time leads inevitably toward mutability, and behind change and loss lurks the spectral image of extinction. Above all else, the lyric is motivated by the desire to overcome obliteration. *Eros* versus *thanatos* is its constantly recurring concern, and it strains to be able to say, with the Song of Songs, "Love is stronger than death." Shakespeare's entire sonnet sequence is concerned with the menace of temporal ravages: "O how shall summer's honey breath hold out/Against the wreckful siege of battering days...?" (Sonnet 65), his speaker queries, as does Andrew Marvell's urgent lover in his *carpe diem*: "at my back I always hear/Time's winged chariot hurrying near." Time's end, death, is an affront, an intrusion, an interloper. "Back from my trellis, Sir, before I scream!" says the lady to the "gentleman in dustcoat" in John Crowe Ransom's "Piazza Piece." So great an antipathy toward time and

Introduction: The Lyric Nostalgia

loss stems from an apparent conviction that death should not be part of the human contract. Indeed, the lyric emerges from a region of the soul convinced of its rightful immortality. This archetypal intuition is reinforced in Western culture by the Book of Genesis story of creation and fall, the doctrine that death came into the world as a divine afterthought, a punishment on an otherwise immortal creature.

But despite its reluctance, the lyric has had to face its endings: "*Timor mortis conturbat me*," as the fifteenth-century Scottish poet William Dunbar wrote in a time of plague. Poets throughout the ages, while ostensibly refusing, like Dylan Thomas, "to mourn the death, by fire, of a child in London," have composed endless elegies, epitaphs, and lamentations to children of all ages. "Now no matter, child, the name:/Sorrow's springs are the same," Hopkins declares, recognizing that whatever the immediate occasion, "it is Margaret you mourn for." Forced by their very sensibility to remember mortality, poets have written eloquent and moving protests against it, lamenting the grim and callous destruction wrought by the inexorable chronological process. "How with this rage shall beauty hold a plea?" Shakespeare questions in Sonnet 65, proffering his answer with little apparent hope:

> O none, unless this miracle have might:
> That in black ink my love may still shine bright.

Throughout the ages lyric poets have protested "in black ink" the affront of mortality, writing sometimes frantic *carpe diems* with their pretended hedonism as though reacting to a primal wrong. None of the other genres confronts death quite so openly as an affront. Tragedy sees obliteration as a necessary outcome and almost a welcome relief. Comedy merely pretends to believe in death's existence and overcomes dying with love and images of resurrection. Epic fights extinction as a dreaded adversary, as Achilles battles it all through the *Iliad*, finally confronting death en masse at the river's edge, filling the stream with corpses. But lyric is taken aback by mutability, grieves over it, views it as something amiss, not as the necessary course of events. "Do not go gentle into that good night," Dylan Thomas advises from deep within the lyric territory; "Rage, rage against the dying of the light." And Andrew Marvell ruefully reminds his coy mistress, "The grave's a fine and private place,/But none, I think, do there embrace." Death is so contrary to our nature, lyric poets would say, that, as Ransom puts it in "Bells for John Whiteside's

Daughter," our minds are staggered, we are affronted—"vexed"—at the little lady, formerly so busy, now "lying so primly propped":

> There was such speed in her little body,
> And such lightness in her footfall,
> It is no wonder her brown study
> Astonishes us all.

The brutal contrast between life and death is so absolute as to astonish its viewers, to turn them, in the original sense of the word, to stone.

The lyric's real hope for overcoming death, then, is not just ceremony or, as Shakespeare would have it, "black ink," but beauty, through what Jacques Maritain, following St. Thomas, has called "ontological splendor," achieved form (*Art* 28n). And though the other genres also strive to achieve this form, they are able to attain its heights only when their language reaches lyric intensity. For beauty has its own energy that propels it to the peak of mortal awareness, toward the dark "cloud of unknowing" within which life meets its enigmatic beginnings and endings. The viewer of the tireless little lady in Ransom's poem has to remember her as vitally alive and then transform those images into a fairy-tale-like eternity:

> Her wars were bruited in our high window.
> We looked among orchard trees and beyond
> Where she took arms against her shadow,
> Or harried unto the pond
>
> The lazy geese...
> Tricking and stopping, sleepy and proud,
> Who cried in goose, Alas,
>
> For the tireless heart within the little
> Lady with rod that made them rise
> From their noon apple-dreams and scuttle
> Goose-fashion under the skies!

It is only by immortalizing the busy little girl as a kind of fairy princess and thus transforming her image into the beautiful, that we, as witnesses, can bear the raw contrast between life and death.

But beauty is not to be found in a mere appeal to the senses. Beauty is the splendor of form, the radiant ontological breakthrough in which flesh encounters spirit. Thus lyric seeks the place where human nature encounters immortality, the obscure realm where the *imago dei* still resides. This region is the source of thinking and feeling, communal not only in that each is connected to the other by a kind of empathy but in that, at least momentarily, each is the whole human race.

Small and fragile as it is, the lyric achieves this universality. But because of its extensive territory and multiple forms, it has been difficult to define as a literary genre. Most handbooks speak of it as the short subjective musical utterance of a single voice, but none of these qualifications is absolute. Although Aristotle mentions lyric as one of the four kinds—tragedy, comedy, epic, and "dithyrambic poetry"—he omits any discussion of lyric in the notes constituting the *Poetics*. His basic distinction concerning the different kinds is helpful, however, in focusing less on their external characteristics than on the general interior action each enacts. And though literary critics have mastered and extended Aristotle's remarks on tragedy and epic and have apologized for his inadequate dismissal of comedy, they have made scarcely any attempt to apply his insights to lyric. Nor have they accepted the fundamental implications of his basic system of four major kinds, each the *mimesis* of a different *praxis*, not the plot, but an underlying "action," interpreted by the drama critic Francis Fergusson as something like "movement of spirit" (29).

If we investigate what Aristotle might have meant by the praxis of the different genres, it is easy to see that the basic inner movement of tragedy is loss, that of comedy, restoration. It may not be quite so simple to discern the action of epic, which in general concerns a people's farewell to an old way of life and its struggle to achieve something new. As for lyric, though no one has really tried to ascertain its determining praxis, the fundamental action at its base seems quite obviously to stem from eros. But genre determines more than thematic characteristics; in fact, the four kinds are so ontologically distinct that they seem to exist in separate worlds, so to say, where the laws are different and particular standards of behavior are required. For instance, the daughter figure is at risk in both tragedy and epic but cannot be harmed in comedy; one can commit adultery with more or less impunity in comedy and lyric but not in epic or tragedy.

To understand the completeness of the perspective from which each genre views human experience, one has to resort to a geographical metaphor. What country, what territory is inhabited by each? What are its laws? What kind of land are we in when we step into its bounds? It seems important to understand this virtual territory of the several genres since the images evoked by each are governed to a large extent by the terrain in which the action, the fundamental movement of the human spirit, takes place. For instance, tragedy occurs largely within the family in a symbolic time when the *oikos* is giving way to the *polis*, a time, however, when the fatal obligations of honor require immediate and violent redress. Comedy depicts the intricacies of community behavior, enduring and finally prevailing from within the imperfect city, where patience and hope enable fortune, rather than fate, to work her benevolent tricks. Epic, looking back on an exhausted order, speaks from within a devastated land and works toward the founding of a new order that is more an ideal than a possible achievement.

But as for lyric, where is its territory? Since its basic action is eros, a yearning for limitless freedom, its virtual fictional territory seems to be prior to the city, in an innocence prior even to marriage and the family. The great traditions of love poetry seek not so much to possess the lady as to declare devotion to her and praise her beauty. And, admittedly, though lyrics are many times written from within a city, ostensibly celebrating or lamenting specific actual occurrences, their true location, their nostalgia, is for some sort of original freedom, the realm of unfettered love and timelessness, outside and prior to the city's laws. The lyric comes from a place in the soul stubbornly convinced that we were born not for law but for love, not for death but for innocence and clarity. Metaphorically, then, lyric arises in a psychic realm that could be called the garden, that place that was our home before the fall and that we attempt to replicate as enclosed places within the city. Ignoring every scientific argument to the contrary, the lyric persists in reverting to this original time of blessedness. Czesław Miłosz, commenting about our enduring fascination with the story of the expulsion from the Garden of Eden, writes: "In our deepest convictions, reaching into the very depths of our being, we deserve to live forever. We experience our transitoriness and mortality as an act of violence perpetrated against us. Only Paradise is authentic; the world is inauthentic, and only temporary. That is why the story of the fall speaks to us so emotionally, as if summoning an old truth from our slumbering memory"(*ABC's* 9). As Miłosz points out, the lyric persists in remembering some sort of divine origin, some blessed time,

Introduction: The Lyric Nostalgia

lost through human fallibility but still possibly available, perhaps in the beloved, perhaps in the song of a bird, perhaps in the very language that comes unbidden to a poet.

Thus lyric wants always to remind us of something forgotten and to conduct us to the "way we were," the dazzlingly bright original blessedness and the way our hearts still are in their innermost recesses. But what we really want is what Frost desires in "Birches": to climb "*Toward* heaven, till the tree could bear no more,/But dipped its top and set me down again,*" for lyric is intimately concerned with incarnation. Thus we want no fate to "wilfully misunderstand" us and turn us into pure spirits. Indeed, as he concludes, "Earth's the right place for love:/I don't know where it's likely to go better." The lyric is privy to a secret about even divine love: it longs for incarnation. So the paradise toward which lyric poetry leads is eminently earthly, a memory of the original blessedness embedded in matter.

This Earthly Paradise is the region to which Dante climbs at the summit of Mount Purgatory, an image instilled in the limbic core of the brain, unreachable by scientific probing. Dante envisions it as the ultimate goal of earthly life. Virgil (his poetic predecessor, his tradition) leads him to this original garden, and it is here that he encounters the beauty his heart has been seeking. Beatrice's radiant but forbidding presence enables the pilgrim to know himself and thus be cleansed of his flaws. It is of this realm that T. S. Eliot speaks when he describes "a condition of serenity, stillness, and reconciliation" into which poetry conducts us "and then leave[s] us, as Virgil left Dante...when that guide can avail us no further" (*Poetry and Drama* 44). And indeed the poetic ancestors, the Virgils, cannot take the poet on into the celestial regions; Dante requires different mentors for that perilous journey: Beatrice and St. Bernard, beauty and spiritual wisdom. But to come this far into the poetic region seems, on the contrary, to be going back, back to primal innocence. The pilgrim regains the wholeness of the original human race, becoming like Adam and gazing at Beatrice, his Eve, with the fullness of love.

Many poets write about this earthly paradise, but Frost's entire body of poetry is an exploration of the psychic space just outside the garden, where the memory of blessedness is a constant reproach. His poems exist in a moment before civilization, when humankind and nature are still close, man and woman are still blaming each other for the loss of the garden, work is just beginning to be turned into a blessing and not a curse. The line of dark trees hiding unknown territory, the presence of evil in the new design (white spider on a white leaf), the sound of Eve's voice echoed by the birds: all these speak of a fallen world, an exile. Frost attests to this fall quite overtly in his play on words in the poem "The Oven Bird." This solitary singer, a "mid-summer and a mid-wood bird," tells us that "for flowers/Mid-summer is to spring as one to ten" and prophesies the coming of "that other fall we name the fall."

> The bird would cease and be as other birds
> But that he knows in singing not to sing.
> The question that he frames in all but words
> Is what to make of a diminished thing.

The oven bird, remembering spring, is aware in midsummer of diminishment. He would cease singing entirely except that he has mastered the art of not singing when he sings, for his entire song is not praise but disparagement. He sings in order to testify to the beauty and fullness he has known and to contrast it with what is before him. His song is a question much like that of the psalmist: "How shall we sing the LORD's song in a strange land?" (Ps. 137). How do we celebrate something that has lost its luster? All that is left of the original garden is Eve's voice in the song of the birds and, as Frost writes in "Directive," a broken chalice taken from a children's playhouse and the language that, though now halting, once sprang spontaneously from Adam's mouth as he named the animals. It is in that original language, which can be recovered only with effort, that any kind of heart's ease is to be found for the lyric poet.

Sometimes, however, in this remembered realm of innocence within the city, the poet himself is the false note. Sometimes he brings with him the serpent, as Donne says in "Twicknam Garden," and the tone becomes bitter and often cacophonic. For, either harshly or gently, the lyric rebels against the heart's violation everywhere to be found in civilization, where structures continue to expand like a Tower of Babel that confounds the common language of the heart.

So the lyric poet tends to be miserable in the city. One thinks of Blake's harsh castigation of London in which he finds the streets "chartered" for industrial purposes. In this bleak world even a natural thing like the river is harnessed for commercial use, with the soldier's blood staining government walls and child labor casting a pall on the church. Everyone in the city is weakened, with lives made miserable by

Introduction: *The Lyric Nostalgia*

the unnatural regimentation and mercantilism of daily life. Love itself is bought and sold: in "midnight streets" one can hear

> How the youthful harlot's curse
> Blasts the newborn infant's tear
> And blights with plagues the marriage hearse.

The organic center of social life, the family, is afflicted by the damage done to the city's feminine victims and their consequent moral and physical disease.

By the early twentieth century, the lyric is lonely and unheeded in the barrenness and alienation of urban life. Eliot writes, in "Preludes":

> The winter evening settles down
> With smell of steaks in passageways.
> Six o'clock.
> The burnt-out ends of smoky days.

Yet looking beyond the tawdry images of the city, the poet confesses,

> I am moved by fancies that are curled
> Around these images, and cling:
> The notion of some infinitely gentle
> infinitely suffering thing.

Something of the lyric nostalgia can be discerned underneath the apparent sordidness. In fact, the city itself, as a human community, is "infinitely gentle," suffering patiently its degradation. Allen Tate is more bitter and passionate in his castigation of the modern city: in his poem "Aeneas at Washington," Aeneas, who endured such hardships to found the New Troy, views what has become of that civilization engendered by his struggles and remembers the destruction of the mother city:

> I stood in the rain, far from home at nightfall
> By the Potomac, the great Dome lit the water,
> The city my blood had built I knew no more
> While the screech-owl whistled his new delight
> Consecutively dark.

> Stuck in the wet mire
> Four thousand leagues from the ninth buried city
> I thought of Troy, what we had built her for.

Its roots going even further back in memory and prophecy, lyric recalls its origins in the brilliant original pattern of being and grieves at what is not right in the city. Recalling the way things were in the garden before the fall and the promise of eternity, it can only cast accusations at the present scene, grieve for it, or withdraw completely. Within the modern urban environment, poets necessarily feel unwelcome; for their lament and their prophecy testify against the abstraction and narcissism of urbanized life. This testimony is a constant witness to the richness and depth of matter, with which all of us in our childhood were in touch. Thus the lyric is never really at home in the structured and restricted—and abstract—city. For the things of the body and of the heart will never be right in the city: there will always be wars and rumors of wars, greed and corruption, broken homes, deserted children, lovers betrayed, public scandal, cities like Troy and Dresden and Hiroshima destroyed, and, always and everywhere, destitution. The poor we will have with us always, and there will always, apparently, be strife and violence.

The lyric's mission, then, is how to sing "of a diminished thing." As Donne writes in "The Canonization,"

> Soldiers find wars, and lawyers find out still
> Litigious men, which quarrels move,
>   Though she and I do love.

Thus, he declares, even though we two as lovers have withdrawn from the world, we have gained its essence:

> [We] did the whole world's soul contract, and drove
>   Into the glasses of [our] eyes
>   (So made such mirrors, and such spies,
>   That they did all to [us] epitomize)....

If we love, he insists, we ourselves can be the voice of the lyric in a disharmonious world and bring to it a pattern of love that is peace, a small replica of the garden ensconced in human hearts and minds.

The stages of the lyric voice are determined by this envisioned blessedness, each tending to express itself in one of three moments, all related to the beloved object: anticipation of its coming, consummation in its presence, and lamentation at its absence—desire, fulfillment, and loss. The mood of anticipation has been expressed throughout history: in many of the Psalms, in the traditional medieval *aubade*, in some of Donne's finest songs and hymns, Shelley's "Ode to the West Wind," and, in the twentieth century, such poems as Yeats's "Sailing to Byzantium" and Wallace Stevens' "The World as Meditation," among many others. One of Sylvia Plath's best poems, "Black Rook in Rainy Weather," exhibits the intense desire of anticipation within this first stage of lyric:

> On the stiff twig up there
> Hunches a wet black rook
> Arranging and rearranging its feathers in the rain.

The expectation, she makes clear, is not for a miracle "to set the sight on fire." It is just that the rook, "ordering its black feathers," can "haul/My eyelids up, and grant//A brief respite from fear/Of total neutrality":

> ... Miracles occur,
> If you care to call those spasmodic
> Tricks of radiance
> Miracles. The wait's begun again,
> The long wait for the angel,
>
> For that rare, random descent.

That "rare, random descent," here longed for but not witnessed, is most often portrayed, when it does occur, as the second stage, the stage of consummation, the momentary fullness of joy in the presence of the beloved or the revelation of supernal vision, glorious but fleeting. This "miracle" is what one discerns in such poems as the Twenty-Third Psalm, Donne's "The Canonization," Marvell's "The Garden," Keats's "Ode on a Grecian Urn," Hopkins' "God's Grandeur."

The third stage, lamentation, is by far the most frequently encountered in the lyric realm: Wyatt's "They Flee from Me," Donne's "Nocturnal upon St. Lucy's Day," Hopkins' "I Wake and Feel the Fell of Dark," Yeats's "The Wild Swans at Coole," Tate's "Ode to the Confederate Dead," Richard Eberhart's "The Groundhog." This dark lyric awareness of loss may be terrifying. Hopkins' exclamation "O the mind, mind has mountains" expresses the depth of this interior incompleteness, as does Theodore Roethke's "In a dark time, the eye begins to see." Jorie Graham's "San Sepolcro" combines all three lyric moments, compressing them into a composite lyric insight: an anticipation of the recurrence of a blessed time, a celebration of its remembered fullness, and a lamentation for its absence.

In each of these stages the lyric voice speaks as though privately, from one soul to another with plaintive urgency. In fact the public role for lyric poetry, it is to be feared, will never be very much in evidence in our society. Poets can be featured, as a kind of decoration, as they are sometimes used in presidential inauguration ceremonies; but one fears that to overemphasize the public role of poetry is to risk losing the heart of what poets are for. So what, finally, are they for? The philosopher Martin Heidegger raises this question, following the challenge posed by Friedrich Hölderlin some century and a half earlier in querying the role of poets in a destitute time. Responding to several poems on this theme by the twentieth-century poet Rainer Maria Rilke, Heidegger forms his response: poets are the only ones who can enter the abyss, he says, and bring back a wholeness into the Open, so that others may apprehend it. But, we would add, poets must suffer the secret longings of the human community and express its grief or delight in strange and unfamiliar words that strain to find the original tongue. Such a language is of the soul and viscera, not the abstract mind. It abhors sentimentality; worldly platitudes are foreign to it. Such a language records our nobility, remembers our wisdom, ties us to immortality. But it reminds its hearers that they are displaced persons.

As it turns out, however, the lyric voice is surprisingly sturdy, its apparent frailty belied by an ability to move minds and hearts. As William Butler Yeats wrote, "I am certainly never sure, when I hear of some war, or of some religious excitement, or of some new manufacture, or of anything else that fills the ear of the world, that it has not all happened because of something that a boy piped in Thessaly" ("Symbolism" 158). The "piping" of the lyric brings sound and sense together in a single utterance, accomplishing a kind of hypostatic unity that Ransom has called "a miracle of harmony" ("Future"). It addresses itself not so much to a rational faculty as to a kind of bodily intuition which, though

Introduction: The Lyric Nostalgia

ultimately cognitive, depends upon a sensitivity keenly aware of the underlying reverberations of language. Its symbolic territory is outside the polis, away from the arena of argument; and, though uttering itself from within a marred and fallen status, it longs for unfettered freedom, the state of the pilgrim in Dante's earthly paradise, where he is told he is free to follow pleasure because he now desires only the good. From this yearning issues a heightened awareness of bondage and of longing, giving voice to the multiple impulses that shape a culture, keeping alive a memory of home. Psalm 137 is a poignant expression of this aching sense of exile and its intimate connection with song, awakened in the poet's homelessness:

> By the rivers of Babylon, there we sat down, yea, we wept,
> > when we remembered Zion.
> We hanged our harps upon the willows in the midst thereof.
> For there they that carried us away captive required of us a song...
> How shall we sing the LORD's song in a strange land?

But as lyric poets throughout history have discovered, the very singing of loss and exile brings heart's ease and hope of recovering home. In the midst of the forgetful city, poets recall the garden.

Significant as the recollection of the original garden is, however, it is still not the primal lyric memory. The lyric retains still a dim awareness of the way things were before time was, in the original pattern of being. Metaphorically we could say that underneath all its temporal concerns, in the deep current of its underground stream, is a yearning for the moment of creation, when the form of things existed in the divine mind, imprinting matter with the supernally joyous stamp of form. It is not the earthly garden, then, that the poet intuits as the lyric's ultimate aim but a pre-earthly realm, one that Plato envisions with his concept of the forms, one that Dante enters in the *Paradiso* when he "transhumanizes" himself, one that the author of Proverbs writes about as participating in creation:

> The LORD possessed me in the beginning of his way,
> > before his works of old.
> I was set up from everlasting, from the beginning,
> > or ever the earth was.

> When there were no depths, I was brought forth; when there
>   were no fountains abounding with water.
> Before the mountains were settled, before the hills was I
>   brought forth:
> ...
>
> ... and I was daily his delight, rejoicing always before him;
> Rejoicing in the habitable part of his earth; and my delights
>   were with the sons of men.
>
> (8:22-25, 30-31)

The "sons of men" are thus included in Wisdom's scope and are called constantly to her voice:

> Unto you, O men, I call; and my voice is to the sons of man.
> O ye simple, understand wisdom: and, ye fools, be ye of an under-
>   standing heart.
> Hear; for I will speak of excellent things; and the opening of my lips
>   shall be right things.
> For my mouth shall speak truth; and wickedness is an abomination
>   to my lips.
>
> (8:4-7)

It is the figure of Wisdom that is speaking here, the Word that participated with the Creator "in the beginning." This Wisdom, the true Sophia, the form of things, calls out to "the sons of men," beckoning them to truth, to "excellent things." This is the highest reach of the lyric, its true insight into the being of the world, whether it expresses itself as aspiration or loss.

And it is this memory implied within the lyric that contains the seeds of all the poetic kinds. As the center of poetic energy, lyric is a primary element of formation in the other genres. To go one step into the darkness beyond its lamentation is to enter the region of tragedy; to accept and work with its homelessness is to make do in the realm of comedy; to strive to reestablish the lost garden is to respond to the stirrings of epic. Further, the language of all these other genres remains at their height unmistakably lyric, as though these great forms were mere enlargements of the lyric insight.

As individual poem, however, focusing on what Aristotle lists as the least important parts of tragedy—*melos* and *opsis*, music and image—

the lyric continues to yearn for wisdom, connecting that primordial yearning with its memory of the unfallen garden. For, ultimately, the lyric reveals the secret at the heart of poetry: that, as Dante has made us see, it seeks not only the face of Beatrice but the blindingly bright visage of the Supreme Being. Coleridge discerned this lyric insight at the beginning of the poetic act, designating it as the primary imagination, "the repetition in the finite mind of the eternal act of creation in the infinite I AM" (*Biographia* Chap. 13). Its mark is eros, desire, and behind that desire is the hunger for insight, for the wisdom that is the invisible reality of being. This is the kind of knowing that Jacques Maritain has spoken of simply as "poetry," finding it to be the basis of all the arts. "Art continues in its own way the labor of divine creation," he writes (*Creative Intuition* 65). He speaks of "an immense and primal preconscious life," resembling the primal diffused light first created before God made the lights in the firmament to divide the day from the night. In its essence, then, perhaps we can maintain, the lyric imaginal world is the primordial, the moment of creation, of fullness of being, of joy. In Bede's account, the fabled poet Caedmon had been unable to sing until a stranger appeared and commanded him. And on Caedmon's question "What shall I sing," the visitor, his angel, responded, "Sing creation."

And the lyric does indeed sing creation. We could have no perceivable world without the lyric. It is the "jar" around which, as Wallace Stevens puts it, the "slovenly wilderness" arranges itself. Its chief importance for the human community is its ability to engender a sense of both immanence and transcendence. It goes beyond the boundaries of ordinary thought. Did it not descend so deep, it could not rise so high. At its peak the lyric process implies more than can be encompassed by the senses, or even the ratiocinative powers, suggesting an invisible order, though one dependent upon sensation for its realization. Shelley is so greatly overcome by this very real dimension (which he addresses as "intellectual beauty") that he makes the mistake of yielding to it on its own terms and abandoning human limits. The temptation to enter the transcendent realm, to become in a sense an angel without connection to matter, is the dislocation Tate has designated the "angelic imagination" (*Essays* 401-23). What keeps the poet firmly rooted in the finite yet still in touch with the cloud of unknowing that envelops physical phenomena is the symbolic imagination, or rather, as Tate's own writing suggests, the sacramental imagination. Without the lyric to testify to this invisible order of being, an entire age gradually becomes insensitive to the numinous.

The loss is expressed first in the poets themselves, who utter their disillusion and disgust with the present order, calling the epoch to a new, entirely secular world view. The other genres then begin to reflect the lyric negativity, the culture gradually losing touch with the invisible world, its religious impulses going in two radically different directions: one headed toward a kind of moralistic narcissism, the other toward a fanatical fundamentalism in an attempt to preserve the otherworldly aspects of faith. This, alas, seems increasingly to characterize our present state.

There can be no genuine sacramental life for a society, no genuine culture, without the lyric; and the lyric itself cannot exist without a lively sense of the transcendent. In our time we seem to have arrived at the place that the modernist poets predicted—where, in T. S. Eliot's words, "the dead men lost their bones." Ours is an age of disrobing. Lyric poets, having divested themselves of the old garments of another age, are now tearing away at the body beneath. Many recent poets resort to a long listing of names and objects in an attempt to regain the "thinginess" of things. Others continue their frantic search for the wholeness of the garden state.

It is tempting to say that the lyric impulse can never completely disappear from the human community, that someone among us will always be called to utter "the LORD's song in a strange land"; and certainly early twentieth-century Russia seems to have borne out this optimism. Tyranny and oppression may perhaps make the lyric flourish, even if it has to be composed in concentration camps, with only memory as preservation. But then one recalls eighteenth-century England, where reason and good sense harnessed the lyric impulse for its own purposes, where the lyric gifts of such poets as Prior, Dryden, and Pope were used to pave the way for the triumph of ratiocination rather than sacramentality. England was deprived of the true lyric voice for more than a hundred years at a time of crucial development for Europe. As Tate's poem "Mr. Pope" suggests, in a time "strict [with] the glint of pearl and gold sedans," Pope, the deformed genius, was able to conform to the strictures of poetic diction. But he who "dribbled couplets like a snake/ Coiled to a lithe precision in the sun" possessed more poetic genius than the age could permit. "One cannot say," Tate's poem continues, what prompted his "wit and rage"; but "Around a crooked tree/A moral climbs whose name should be a wreath." Pope's poetic genius was used for moral instruction rather than for lyric song. When the lyric resurfaced, half a century later, the English language had been fatally split; poets began writing in an unmitigated language of feeling that would eventually issue in what T. E. Hulme termed a "wet" style, as if treacle had been spilled on a table (259). In the twentieth century, the disappearance of the poet from the general assembly of voices determining the common destiny is dangerous indeed.

Like the canary in the coal mine, the lyric is a fragile indicator of whether the air in a society is fit to breathe. Lyric's languor may be, like the canary's, an indication of hopeless pollution. "'Hope' is the thing with feathers," Emily Dickinson remarks in one of her lyrics, making overt the subliminal connection of the bird with that eternal spring within the human breast. Throughout the ages the persistence of bird imagery in lyric poetry—Hardy's freezing little thrush uttering its unlikely affirmation, Keats's nightingale redeeming an entire history of inequality and grief, Frost's crow, Plath's black rook, Hopkins' ecstatic windhover—these point to that genre as an indicator of society's most constant, if fragile, optimism. More than its erotic drive, more than its celebration of beauty, the lyric's expectation for some sort of blessedness underlies even its most poignant laments. For the lyric utterance is a response to the gift of life, the first joyous cry celebrating existence. Adam's voice when he sprang upright from the dust, Eve's when she found herself separate and entire—these utterances before the fall are the intonations underlying the lyric voice, whatever its purported expectations, its chosen stance. Lyric remembers wholeness, longs for it, and hopes in its return.

So when the canary stops singing, we know things are really ominous. And, frighteningly enough, that seems to be a possibility for the lyric in our society today. It seems to have become totally committed to what Donald Davidson called the "guarded style," guarded from any expression of feeling or faith or hope, available only to intellectuals and not the general populace. To be sure, lyric may once again blossom, as it gives signs of doing in popular culture. Its high form, however, requires readers who can understand the obliquity of its language, hear its hidden music, and be moved by its plaints. For lyric is dissatisfied with the way things stand and, as I have maintained, is either apocalyptic or nostalgic, the latter hearkening back to "the way we were," to a subliminal memory of a virtual garden state, the former to a final consummation. But whatever the condition of the community, the lyric poet is enjoined to sing, as W. H. Auden exhorts the poet, "of human unsuccess/In a rapture of distress."

So, though lyric remains virtually impotent in the practical affairs of society, it is necessary to human culture, a protection of the channel between word and thing, between heaven and earth, elevating the human to the workings of the spirit. As poet and artist, the lyricist is on our side, against the terror of the numinous, calming the pounding heart as we approach the burning bush, whereas the mystic and prophet are on the side of the holy, against us, reviling our sins and our failings. The lyric cry is the last thing we have between ourselves and annihilation; and as such it is the cornucopia from which human culture issues. It was in Adam's voice when he named the animals, in Eve's when she lamented the loss of Eden, in Mary's when she accepted the annunciation of the angel. It encompasses our joys and our griefs. It is our *nostos*, the story of our exile and homecoming. It is our word, which will stand with us at the last day. And in the meantime its task is to keep our inner being in touch with the cosmos. As Howard Nemerov writes in his poem "The Blue Swallows,"

> ... poems are not
> The point. Finding again the world,
> That is the point, where loveliness
> Adorns intelligible things
> Because the mind's eye lit the sun.

THE TRADITION

I

The Psalms:
Spacious Places for Wrestling with God

DANIEL RUSS

The Psalms are a living body of universal lyric poetry that has remained vibrant after more than 2,500 years. Constituting a book within the Book, they have marked the Jewish people—the people of the Book, the Law, and the Prophets—powerfully and indelibly with their song. They are themselves traditionally divided into five sections, or books, echoing, some scholars believe, the structure of the Pentateuch. Even more, though this rich collection of 150 common prayers is first and finally the source and expression of worship, longing, and lament for the Hebrew people, through Jews and Christians the Psalms have come to articulate the yearnings of all human beings for transcendence, wholeness, and justice.

Even their enemies and oppressors asked of the Israelites while in exile, "Sing to us one of the songs of Zion," spreading the lyrics outward from Israel. From ancient Egypt to modern Europe, through the Diaspora enemies would cause the songs of Zion to be sung on every continent. Christians would take up the Jewish Psalter as their own hymnbook, and wherever the Gospel was spread, so too were the Psalms. Through both of these religious traditions, the Psalms have retained their vitality and have been a source and resource shaping the imaginations and cultures of countless peoples.

Like all great lyric poetry, the Psalms invoke a timeless place of encounter with the depths and heights of being human. They do not merely give expression to this range of human experience; rather, they recover its depths and, in them, a sense of origins and destinies. Some serious thinkers, not least among them Plato, have dismissed the lyric as immature and even dangerous, arousing passions best left under rational control. In the spirit of Plato, the novelist Milan Kundera writes, "A lyric poet is the most exemplary incarnation of man dazzled by his own soul and by the desire to make it heard." He concludes, "I have long seen youth as the lyrical age—that is, the age when the individual, focused almost exclusively on himself, is unable to see, to comprehend, to judge clearly the world around him" (40). He asserts, of course, that the novelist, by contrast, no longer thinks and speaks like a child.

While most of Kundera's critique of the lyric poet and "lyricism" is wrong-headed and even a bit self-serving, one must grant that there does exist in the lyric a recovery of a childlike apprehension of the self and the world. It sets out, in the words of Caedmon's angel, to sing "the beginning of created things" or, in the words of the psalmists, "to sing to the Lord a new song." Contemporary songwriter/singer Paul Simon also connects song to soul and one's beginnings, intoning, "This is the story of how we begin to remember/This is the powerful pulsing of love in the vein/...These are the roots of rhythm/And the roots of rhythm remain." The lyric poet gives mature expression to childlike apprehensions about the ways the world is or should be connected, whole, and joyful. The body/soul, humanity/nature, and immanence/transcendence dichotomies of those who "judge clearly the world around them" are alien to the lyric vision, which sees that blood pulses love and, more, that human creatures are at the same time deeply connected to the rest of creation and God-imaged.

The particular contribution made by Hebrew poetry to the lyric tradition arises from its reliance on and elaboration of the relationship of Yahweh with Israel. Many have understood this relationship as founded first and foremost in the Law of Moses. There is some truth to this conception, but as the Jewish scholar Abraham Heschel asserts, "Before the Torah, the covenant was" (2:10), indicating that the lyric tradition, while taking much from the Torah, transcends it to reach the original connection between God and man. Theological abstractions about God's omniscience, omnipotence, and omnipresence express an understanding of God alien to the Jewish mind and were derived, Heschel argues, by later Jewish and Christian thinkers from Greek ideas such as Aristotle's "unmoved mover." The ancient Israelites instead understood that God is holy, just, and loving, but they also praised him for his pathos: comprehending his passion for his people and all creation works as a central insight in Judaism and its poetry. As Heschel explains, "The divine pathos is not conceived of as an essential attribute of God, as something objective, as a finality with which man is confronted, but as an expression of God's will" (2:11). Not constrained by the fact that he created things, God instead freely chooses to love his creation, particularly human creation, with pathos. This passion for his creation is what makes Walter Brueggemann say of the God of the Israelites that he is "the strangest thing about the whole Bible." Brueggemann elaborates: "And his strangeness is in this. He is with his people. He is for his people" (*Bible* 61). However enigmatic and silent he may sometimes appear to them, the God of the Bible loves his people with unabashed pathos, and the people express their longing, praise, and complaints with equal passion, nowhere more than in the Psalms.

What are the distinctive qualities of Hebrew poetry? This question could not be fully answered until fairly recently. As David Noel Freedman maintains, "The rediscovery of the poetry of the prophets is a major contribution of modern scholarship, as is the recognition of the poetic tradition behind the earliest prose narratives" (5). Freedman contends that the neglect of biblical poetry stems from three causes, all of which relegate poetry to a secondary position: first, the Pentateuch, a prose narrative that is "the first and great prose classic of antiquity," sets the tone for all Scripture; second, the scribes copied poetry as prose; third, the Bible's sacred character caused translators to reduce all words to exact meanings, and thus "poetry was leveled out as prose" (16). Most scholars date the rediscovery of the Bible's poetic dimension from the work of Robert Lowth in the late eighteenth century. Lowth's successors then combined enlightenment rationalism with archaeological discoveries to recover the distinguished character of Hebrew poetry as art, allowing the clear and integral truth it embodies to emerge.

Interestingly enough, the original discovery of parallelism made by Lowth in 1753 remains, with some refinements, the only certain distinctive technique of Hebrew poetry. Parallelism is simply the device of saying the same things in two ways. Scholars use the term *stich* (*stichos*) for the separate lines of poetry that make up the couplet, or colon, in which parallel structure inheres. The Psalms are replete with examples of this poetic device, beginning with the opening of Psalm 1:

> 1 Blessed is the man
> > that walketh not in the counsel of the ungodly,
> > nor standeth in the way of sinners,
> > nor sitteth in the seat of the scornful.

2 But his delight is in the law of the Lord;
    and in his law doth he meditate day and night.
3 And he shall be like a tree planted by the rivers of water,
    that bringeth forth his fruit in his season;
    his leaf also shall not wither;
    and whatsoever he doeth shall prosper.[1]

The three verbs ("walketh," "standeth," and "sitteth") in verse 1 form parallel actions that further develop the notion of what the good man doesn't do. The parallelism in verse 2 elaborates on law ("delight is in the law" and "in his law doth he meditate"), and verse 3 provides a simile (he is "like a tree planted by the rivers") to broaden the understanding of goodness. Later in the lyric the psalmist provides a parallel to the opening line ("The ungodly are not so," 1:4) and examines the nature of the ungodly thereafter, just as he earlier examined the nature of the blessed. These forms of parallelism were discovered by Lowth (the three varieties a, b, and c, below) and by later scholars who agreed upon a few additional varieties: (a) synonymous, "in which the second line of a couplet more or less repeats the thought of the first line in different words" (Ps. 1:1; see also 51:1); (b) antithetical, "in which the second line of a couplet (colon) presents the opposite of the thought in the first" (Ps. 1:6; see also Prov. 11:2); (c) synthetic, in which "the second line develop[s] or complet[es] the thought of the first" (Ps. 1:2; see also 27:6); (d) emblematic, in which "one of the lines presents as a simile the thought in the other" (Ps. 1:4; see also Prov. 25.14); (e) stairlike, in which "part of one line is repeated in the second" but then developed further (Ps. 29:1-2); and (f) introverted, in which the members of the lines are in the order of the chiasmus (Ps. 124:7) (Thompson 18-19).

    Most biblical critics do not venture beyond these categories of parallelism because of the danger of fabricating an analytical structure and distorting the poetry. But parallelism need not be exhibited in endless varieties to be one of the most profound and most translatable of poetic devices. Thus Albert Cook agrees with Lowth that a "sublimity inheres in the very simplicity of the utterance, a simplicity that cannot readily be discussed in any normal category of 'high' or 'low' or 'middle' style, at least partly because the verse style rests on so single a convention, that of the statement doubled in parallelism" (34). R. K. Harrison asserts that "Every other stylistic or rhetorical feature of Hebrew poetry...must now be regarded as being consistently subordinate to the parallel expression of thought forms." Harrison and others warn against the dangers of speculating on meter and stanza in Hebrew poetry, since these are at best subservient to parallelism, the rhyming of ideas (968).

Aside from its distinctive parallelism, Hebrew poetry shares many of the themes, devices, and tropes of the lyric poetry of many nations, enjoying (and partly having created) a continuity across cultures, languages, and time. Hence a modern English-speaking reader may closely and confidently read ancient Hebrew poetry in an English text. In doing so he or she must rely heavily on Hebrew scholars and translators, but this reliance can be accepted with greater confidence in Hebrew poetry than in other translated verse. As scholars such as Norman Gottwald attest, it is "astonishing...that the formal structure of ancient Hebrew poetry was transmitted through the centuries generally intact" despite, as Gottwald points out, the "lack of poetic format" (830). Ruth apRoberts exalts the stubborn structure of Hebrew poetry as "more self-conserving than prose, whether evangelical or historical, because the Hebrew genre unit is the form unit." It is on the conviction that they translate well that one can approach the Psalms in English and, further, that their language and rhythms have been woven into English poetry over the centuries, though they have largely been considered an arena of study reserved for Semitic scholars and theologians. With due respect for their highly specialized work, I must second apRoberts in her concern: "Secular culture loses when it leaves these great texts [Hebrew poetry] to the theologians" (1002).

I would add two further observations, one speculative and the other practical. I suspect that the reason parallelism came to characterize Hebrew poetry is that the vision and understanding of the Hebrew Scriptures run parallel. These Scriptures introduce and celebrate a reality in which a transcendent deity has created a world and crowned it with a creature made in his image—a world and creature that he continues actively and passionately to love. These acts presume two analogous realms of reality, the invisible and the visible, that are parallel to one another from the beginning to the end of history. Indeed, history is the work of the transcendent God redeeming fallen humanity so that what goes on in the visible world has origins and implications in the invisible.

Many biblical scholars who take biblical poetry seriously fail to distinguish between any poetry written in verse and the lyric genre, using the term *lyric* simply as a designation of exterior form. The Homeric epics and most of the Book of Job, for example, are written in verse, but neither could be called lyric. In short, these scholars generally fail to grasp the ancient understanding that all imaginative literature is poetry, that much narrative poetry is written in verse, and that what distinguishes lyric poetry from tragic, comic, and epic poetry is its vision and inner form, what Aristotle calls the movement of spirit within the work.

Each kind of poetry, each genre, imitates a certain dimension of human action and tends to express itself in particular themes, conventions, and stances toward the world observing that action. The lyric grows out of the poet's symbolic longing for, celebrating, or lamenting the moments of love, as Louise Cowan has argued. Indeed, Cowan has asserted that the anthology constituted by the Psalms affords the fullest expression of the imaginative range of lyric poetry, which she describes as "the place of origins and sources, the land of heart's desire, symbolized by the garden" ("Introduction" 10). She suggests that the large sweep of the lyric moves through three stages: from anticipation of the wholeness and joy to be found in union with the beloved, on to consummation of that joy, and finally to lamentation of its loss. Or as the psalmists would express it, both the individual soul and Israel (and with these two, all creation) express hope in God's fulfilling his promises, cry out when he seems to be silent, and worship him with praise when *shalom*, the right order of things, exists, whether in the soul, the Temple, or the whole of creation.

Although love is not the exclusive theme of the lyric, it predominates and constellates the other major concerns. For the lyric remembers a time of pure love and wholeness, a *shalom* characterized by the joy and delight of all life flourishing. C. Day Lewis hints at this remembrance when he distinguishes the lyric as "a poem written for music," whether actual music or "music at the back of the poet's mind" (3). When we consider the classical notion of the music of the spheres, we cannot help but realize that even this simple definition contains profound support for the connection of the lyric to cosmic order. The simplest model, however, is probably the prelapsarian Garden of Eden. There, man, woman, work, and nature existed in perfect integrity, each in and for the other, and all in harmony and union with God. Although other notions of wholeness have contributed to the lyric tradition, none is more complete or richer than Eden, and none more clearly elucidates the species of lyrics: hymns, love songs, ballads, odes, and elegies. Lyric poetry, more than epic, tragedy, or comedy, enables one to know what is and ought to be by remembering what was and might be. The lyric never leaves the meeting place between worlds: between gods and mortals, man and woman, human and nature, body and spirit, thoughts and feelings. It may render only flashes of hope, joy, and grief, but its nature is such that it will not relinquish the dream of singing to the Lord a new song, expressing and creating anew that primal unity. And though its expression of this longing is interior and personal, the nature of the lyric is essentially communal, not private, because it voices the shared hopes of the human spirit.

It is no wonder, therefore, that lyrics direct themselves toward the audience, the listeners in the world outside the poem. The tension between personal longing and communal nature is found in the language of the lyric, which necessarily reflects some ambiguity, more, perhaps, than the language of any other "kind," as Aristotle would put it. Words are used symbolically, the poet expressing his vision in what Northrop Frye calls the "rhythm of association": "most of it below the threshold of consciousness, a chaos of paronomasia, soundlinks, ambiguous senselinks, and memorylinks very like that of a dream." Out of this, Frye concludes, "the distinctively lyrical union of sound and sense emerges" (270-72). While this lyrical union is personal and particular, the sense or meaning it contains is accessible to common reason; it is not private. Yet the lyric does not allow the idea to be separated from the physical reality; its expression through meter, fiction, and tropes forces the listener (or reader) to recover the remarkable power and meaning of the thing, the event. These poetic devices are, in a very real sense, rhetorical devices as well, for they give the lyric poet a dual stance: at the same time he has a concern for an audience, he also "turns his back on his listeners," letting them overhear his outpourings (Frye 250). Further, a sense of community is present because lyric poets speak of those moments in life in which their feelings, like Adam's, are inseparably involved with all humankind. In this sense, they write psychologically prior to the split between poet and audience so characteristic of the other genres. Even Barbara Hardy, who celebrates the lyric's "undiluted attention to feeling and feeling alone," adds that the lyric transfers this feeling "from privacy to publicity" (2). Lyric poets, whether David or Donne, Wordsworth or Auden, presume their passionate expressions are those of the watching world, which listens in on the poetic voice as if it were hearing its own voice echoed back to it. Both biblical and non-biblical lyrics enact this drama of the soul, universal in its particularity: the longing for and remembrance of wholeness, expressed for and on behalf of the community, through intensely personal love.

The Psalms, the first of the lyrics, invoke timeless places to encounter God and his creation, including human beings in myriad ways. I say "invoke" because the Psalter does more than remember or describe. Most, if not all, psalms call God into the presence of his people, call creation into the presence of God, and call the soul to reflect on itself in the presence of God and his creation. But the psalmists do more than invoke these presences; through language, image, and song they make "spacious places" where human creatures are bold to speak passionate love, deep sorrow, and scathing criticism to the creator. Whether read devotionally as Scripture, sung worshipfully as hymn, or recited rhetorically as poetry, the Psalms take us to places that transcend yet encompass the mundane and the temporal.

One can see this in the face of impish choirboys and portly choir members, both of whom enter into the music and the music into them in such a way that they are transported to a spacious place, larger than any sanctuary or earthly garden. Toni Morrison captures this transformative nature of the lyric in her novel *The Bluest Eye*. In one scene, the narrator, Claudia, looks back to when she was a young girl who hated those days when her bitter and angry mother could stand at the kitchen sink in a tirade all day, enraged at everyone from her no-account children to President Roosevelt. But, Claudia recalls, "If my mother was in a singing mood, it wasn't so bad. She would sing about hard times, bad times, and somebody-done-gone-and-left-me times. But her voice was so sweet and her singing eyes so melty I found myself longing for those hard times, yearning to be grown without 'a thin di-i-ime to my name.'...Misery colored by the greens and blues in my mother's voice took all of the grief out of the words and left me with a conviction that pain was not only endurable, it was sweet" (25-26). What Claudia describes is not an escape from reality but a transformation of reality. Her mother's blues changed that ramshackle house from a prison that Claudia longed to escape into a sanctuary of sweet lament. Not only did that lament transform this bitter mother and this battered child, but it militated against the prosaic, sociological realities that would reduce this suffering and noble mother and daughter to mere victims of racism and poverty.

Likewise, the Psalms enabled the Israelites to walk the earth and see themselves differently; their new songs transformed even "the wilderness into a standing water, and dry ground into watersprings" (Ps. 107:35). Through the covenant with Yahweh and the Scriptures that made the covenant present to the people, Israel remembered the presence of God's past faithfulness. They cultivated in word and song what Brueggemann has aptly called a "historical imagination," an "openness and sensitivity to the pulses of meaning that can be discerned in reflection upon historical experience preserved in an historical community." By means of the historical imagination, "'Pharaoh' comes to be a symbolic reference to every form of oppression. 'Bread' comes to refer to the strange gift of nourishment, which happens in the desert....This community, like every vital community, has its own energizing repertoire of images which give life and direction" (*Bible* 32).

Such a historical imagination does not oppose the literal facts of history to the symbolic expressions of poetry. The events of history can be both factual and symbolic. Jews and Christians can believe in both the historical crossing of the Red Sea or the Jordan River and the symbolic crossing that we all experience in passing from wandering to home and from death to new life. The psalmists were steeped in that history and presumed that communal memory could be a bountiful resource of images, similes, and metaphors for their songs.

With this background in mind, I want to reflect here on how understanding the Psalms as lyric poetry illuminates their meaning and, conversely, how these masterworks of biblical poetry enrich our understanding of the lyric. I begin these reflections with what Louise Cowan has called lyrics of consummation, because praise, worship, and singing "to the Lord a new song," which constitute the normative vision of the psalmists, are expressions of the ultimate intersection of human with divine. Just as Donne might understand the love of man and woman as the consummate experience of wholeness, and Wordsworth would dream of human oneness with nature as that consummation, the Hebrew psalmists were focused on the glory and grace of God as the fulfillment of earthly desire.

What the greatest lyric poets of all traditions hold in common is the highest expression of lyric utterance as praise.[2] They differ in what or whom they praise and in how they express that praise. For Israel and her poets, to praise God is inclusive of all good things in the universe. Thus, though there are other forms of praise in a few psalms, in the Song of Songs, Job, and the Prophets, they all constellate around and find their glory in the God who alone is worthy of the highest praise. And most important here is the freedom of the poet in recognizing this fact. There is no sense in the Hebrew imagination of being forced to fulfill this task of praising. Nor is there a sense that worshipping God is a form of enslavement, any more than the love poet feels enslaved by the beloved or the nature poet feels diminished and controlled by the flight of the bird that captivates his heart. The psalmist praises God because of the manifestations of beauty and truth in all of creation and because of the revelation of truth and goodness in God's word.

While this dual expression of creation and revelation resonates throughout the Psalms, the clearest expression is found in Psalm 19, which opens with a kind of strophe to the creation story of Genesis, where God speaks creation into being. Here creation speaks back, telling of the glory of its creator.

> 1 The heavens declare the glory of God; and the firmament sheweth his handiwork.
> 2 Day unto day uttereth speech, and night unto night sheweth knowledge.
> 3 There is no speech nor language, where their voice is not heard.
> 4 Their line is gone out through all the earth, and their words to the end of the world.
> In them hath he set a tabernacle for the sun,
> 5 Which is as a bridegroom coming out of his chamber, and rejoiceth as a strong man to run a race.
> 6 His going forth is from the end of the heaven, and his circuit unto the ends of it: and there is nothing hid from the heat thereof.

The primary metaphor in the opening six verses is that of a language of creation that speaks forth the presence of the creator day and night, everywhere in heaven and on earth. Indeed this generative language is a tent from which the sun emerges each morning to radiate further the glory of God. The psalmist personifies this solar circuit that encompasses the earth as a bridegroom and a strong runner, a reminder that creation originates in a personal creator who brings not only light but warmth to all things.

Then, in an antistrophe, the next verses juxtapose creation, which proclaims God's glory, to God's revelation to humanity, which proclaims his perfect law:

> 7 The law of the Lord is perfect, converting the soul: the testimony of the Lord is sure, making wise the simple.

8	The statutes of the Lord are right, rejoicing the heart: the commandment of the Lord is pure, enlightening the eyes.
9	The fear of the Lord is clean, enduring for ever: the judgments of the Lord are true and righteous altogether.
10	More to be desired are they than gold, yea, than much fine gold: sweeter also than honey and the honeycomb.

The words describing the law ("testimony," "statutes," "commandment," "fear," "judgments") would sound harsh to the ear were it not for the concluding verse that declares God's law to be more desirable than gold and sweeter than honey. To the Hebrew mind, in a world that is too often dangerous, lawless, and unjust, God's law is precious and sweet, reminding us that the ruthless do not have the final word and, like the sun that circumscribes the earth, the law of God speaks to all creatures in all creation. There is no place to hide from its light and heat.

Finally, since the psalmist knows that we are among those creatures that need the warmth of the sun and the truth of the law, he turns that heat and light on himself, realizing that his words and even the unuttered meditations of his heart are meant to declare the glory of God, informing him with wisdom, joy, enlightenment, and reverence:

11	Moreover by them is thy servant warned: and in keeping them there is great reward.
12	Who can understand his errors? cleanse thou me from secret faults.
13	Keep back thy servant also from presumptuous sins; let them not have dominion over me: then shall I be upright, and I shall be innocent from the great transgression.
14	Let the words of my mouth, and the meditation of my heart, be acceptable in thy sight, O Lord, my strength, and my redeemer.

In short, God speaks all creation into being, and all creation echoes his glory; God speaks the law to the crown of his creation. Man, recognizing his temptation to error, requests the aid of God and responds by acting, speaking, and thinking like the image of God that he is created to be. Here we achieve the right order of things.

For similar but very distinct reasons, Psalm 8 offers God unabashed praise for the *shalom* of creation. Like Psalm 19, which begins with the macrocosm of natural revelation, Psalm 8 begins by proclaiming the majesty of God, "O Lord our Lord, how excellent is thy name in all the earth! Who has set thy glory above the heavens," and continues, praising the "work of [God's] fingers." In contrast to the second part of Psalm 19, which presents the microcosm of God's revelation to humanity through the law, however, the psalmist here asks a direct and searching question: "What is man, that thou art mindful of him?" Having gained our attention, he then explores how God has "crowned [man] with glory and honor," putting "all things under his feet." The psalm thus celebrates a cosmic interchange of mutual glory, beginning with the glory of God. At first, it seems the poem will follow much the same pattern as Psalm 19: the heavens glorify God and God's law is perfect. But here we are told that while God's glory is above the heavens, nonetheless babes and sucklings testify to God's majesty in the face of enemies and avengers. At the point that Psalm 19 and others elaborate on the glories of creation reflecting the glory of God, Psalm 8 arrests us with this mystery, that in the midst of suns and moons so vast the mind cannot comprehend them, the creator has not only crowned humanity with his glory but subjected all things to the dominion of this puny glory called man. Why should human beings be so chosen and so endowed among all the glories of creation? The psalm deepens the inscrutable reality that gives rise to that question: the majestic and glorious creator has poured his glory into his creation, above all crowning humanity with glory, causing us in turn to glorify the creator in and through creation.

Psalm 8 does not pose a question to be answered or a problem to be solved; rather it celebrates an ecology of love, rendering a universe in which glory is shared with the creation. Although the psalm begins and ends with the same proclamation of God's majestic glory, the final lines, like all refrains in lyric poetry, are not mere repetition. After a contemplation of the beauty of the cosmos and the surpassing glory of even the most helpless human creatures, the psalm ends by celebrating God's glory as not less but more glorious.

If one has not yet been convinced that the essence of the Psalms' lyric quality lies in their being "inherently worshipful," then Psalms 146 to 150 can leave no room for doubt. Biblical scholars debate questions concerning the five books of the Psalms and the significance of their order, but almost no dispute has arisen among scholars concerning the significance of these last five psalms. In placing them at the end of the sequence, the Hebrew editors of this collection make the passion for praise that rings throughout the Psalms reach a crescendo. Indeed, the progression in these five poems recalls a spectacular fireworks display that fills the night sky with such breathtaking beauty that one cannot imagine anything more splendid, until the finale begins, taking up the most magnificent explosions of beauty, compressing them together, and magnifying them to unimaginable heights.

These brief and explosive songs of praise and joy do not merely repeat the theme of "hallelujah: praise the Lord." Rather, each calls us to praise God for different reasons and in diverse ways. For example, in Psalm 146, the poet utters praise from his soul, not because of a desire for inner peace or personal salvation, but because God, "Which made heaven, and earth, the sea, and all that therein is" (146:6), defends and cares for the hungry, the prisoner, the blind, the orphan, and the widow. God is praised because of what he is doing in the harshest of human circumstances among the least of us. The next psalm picks up this same theme of praising God who "healeth the broken in heart, and bindeth up their wounds" (147:3). The image, however, is not simply one that opposes a redeeming God to a deistic creator designing the universe but staying aloof from it. The psalmist is after something different entirely. The next line after the reference to God's healing broken hearts and wounded bodies is "He telleth the number of the stars; he calleth them all by their names" (147:4). God is praised not only because he is intimately present to those who suffer but also because he is intimate—and we might even say personal—with the stars that he set in the heavens. This passion of God for all creation is why Psalm 148 summons all creation in turn to praise God: angels; sun, moon, and stars; dragons and deeps; fire and hail; snow and vapor; stormy winds; mountains and hills; fruit trees and cedars; beasts and cattle; creeping things and flying things; kings and the people; princes and judges; young men and maidens; old men and children. All things in creation are inspirited with personality that they might join with humanity in praising the creator.

Then the penultimate psalm rings in with a call: "Sing unto the Lord a new song," a theme that resonates from early in the Psalter as well as in the rest of Hebrew Scripture. Indeed, the essence of the lyric of consummation is that the song is always new, no matter how many times it has been sung or recited. If one asks why lyric poets are always attempting to give original expression to our deepest and oldest passions, the answer from the biblical tradition is that we live in a world continually being created by a God who is about new things, from "In the beginning God created" to the prophets proclaiming to Israel and the nations, "Behold, the former things are come pass, and new things do I declare" (Isa. 42:9) or "I will give them one heart, and I will put a new spirit within you; and I will take the stony heart out of their flesh, and will give them an heart of flesh" (Ezek. 11:19). While most lyrics are not psalms and holy sonnets, all lyric poems, especially those celebrating the moment of consummation, sing a new song. "The beginning of created things" is always beginning.

Psalm 150 completes the Psalter by repeating "Hallelujah," or its translation "praise ye the Lord," in every verse. The hallelujahs are called for in his sanctuary in the opening stanza, but they spill out quickly in a cornucopia of praise to the sky, where God dwells over the whole earth. He is to be praised not for his divine attributes, in some abstract philosophical sense, but "for his mighty acts" that give witness to "his exceeding greatness." Then the psalm calls for a symphony of praise from every instrument, accompanied by dance and loud-clashing cymbals. This is no classical symphony but a swelling up of every earthly and heavenly sound before God. The psalm concludes with the call to all who have life and are inspirited with God's breath: "Let every thing that hath breath praise the Lord, Hallelujah."

Two observations round out the discussion of these psalms of consummation, of unabashed praise. First, they are few in number among the songs in the Psalter. While they are the alpha and omega of the lyric vision, it seems that the psalmists capture that highest and most radiant vision less often than they express a vision of longing or lamentation. I suspect this has to do with the brokenness of human nature and the concomitant corruption of all creation with sin and death. Second, psalms of consummation tend to be brief because fallen humanity receives only glimpses of the joy and wholeness that was, that will be, and that is when we are given the grace to see that "The world is charged with the grandeur of God," as Gerard Manley Hopkins expresses it.

Although few capture it, a large number of psalms express a longing for and anticipation of "the new song," the new reality. If life is "vanity of vanities" and there is "nothing new under the sun," if life is a tale "full of sound and fury, signifying nothing," if the world "Hath really neither joy, nor love, nor light,/Nor certitude, nor peace, nor help for pain," as Matthew Arnold laments, then is this Psalmic anticipation of wholeness, of *shalom*, of God, just an escapist fantasy? What is the source of this longing for wholeness, for a reality that is promised but not usually present? Are Plato and Kundera correct about the lyric longing as irrational and childish? The lyric poets across cultures and centuries would surely answer in the negative. Most anticipation lyrics were conceived by mature poets who understood on every level the suffering of creation and the affliction of humanity. Indeed, many of the greatest expressions of such longing are to be found in lyric interludes of tragedies, such as Sophocles' "Ode to Man" in *Antigone* or God's creation catalogue to Job: "Where wast thou when I laid the foundations of the earth?" David, Dante, Donne, Wordsworth, Coleridge, Yeats, not to mention those often anonymous poets and singers who fashioned the Negro spirituals, were people "of sorrow, acquainted with grief."

Deeply acquainted with sorrow and grief throughout their history, the Hebrews, like people of so many other human cultures, longed for a new reality, a new song. In fact, they did not merely long for and anticipate *shalom*. They expected, often presumed, and even demanded it of God. For God had promised them in his covenant and demanded of them in his law that there can be a place in this world where they will flourish as he created them to flourish. He had demonstrated through his historical faithfulness to Abraham, Isaac, Jacob, Moses, and now David that he is with them. Therefore, he expects them to expect him to fulfill that promise. Moreover, he does so in the language of a father to his children, of a mother eagle to her eaglets, of a lover to his beloved. This is not just a legal arrangement or a desire of a holy God to create a moral people. As Heschel reminds us: "There is no dichotomy [for God] between pathos and ethos....It is because God is the source of justice that his pathos is ethical; and it is because God is absolutely personal—devoid of anything impersonal—that his ethos is full of pathos" (2:5). So David and the other psalmists expected, presumed, and demanded of God that he be true to his passion, to his word, to his people.

Perhaps no other verse in the Psalms captures this passionate relationship of the people to God more than one in Psalm 17: "Keep me as the apple of your eye;/hide me under the shadow of your wings" (17:8, BCP). This parallel structure probably originates in the poet's imagination from this very familiar passage in Deuteronomy:

9 For the LORD's portion is his people; Jacob is the lot
   of his inheritance.

> 10   He found him in a desert land, and in the waste howling wilderness; he led him about, he instructed him, he kept him as the apple of his eye.
> 11   As an eagle stirreth up her nest, fluttereth over her young, spreadeth abroad her wings, taketh them, beareth them on her wings:
> 12   So the LORD alone did lead him, and there was no strange god with him.
>
> (Deut. 32:9-12)

As the psalmist takes up these images of God's relationship with his people, he emphasizes two contrasting nuances of the one covenant relationship. First he focuses on God's passionate love for his people in the image of the eye, so beautifully expressed later in John Donne's "My face in thine eye, thine in mine appears" ("The Good-Morrow," l. 15). This is the intimate image of the lover and his beloved gazing so closely into one another's eyes that the eye of the other becomes a mirror. The image in Hebrew is of the pupil "in which the saint knows himself to be so near to God, that, as it were, his image in miniature is mirrored in the great eye of God" (Keil and Delitzsch 5:238). So on the one hand, God's people are the beloved bride who is reflected as the apple of God's eye. On the other hand, in the second line, God is the feminine presence, the mother eagle whose fierce love and strong wings protect the nestlings from harm. For this is the second aspect of humanity's relationship with God: his people are vulnerable and need divine protection. The metaphor is apt; when nestlings are fed by the mother, the little ones expect food. They do not appear the least bit grateful when they receive it but rather expect more again and again.

This along with other revealing images in the Psalms indicates how the Psalter represents the heights and depths of the lyric realm. While the people of Israel are taught to fear the Lord—the beginning of wisdom—this fear apparently does not preclude telling God of their disappointments in him. When the psalmist praises God for delivering him from his enemies, he adds without embarrassment, "He brought me out into a spacious place; he rescued me because he delighted in me" (Ps. 18:19, NIV). How differently, the Psalms suggest, one walks through life knowing that he is God's delight, the apple of God's eye. But the apple of his eye seems always inseparably bound to the shadow of his wings. Something hidden within the human person longs for intimacy with the divine. This longing is nowhere more poignantly expressed than in the opening of Book Two of the Psalms:

> 1   As the deer pants for streams of water,
>   So my soul pants for you, O God.
> 2   My soul thirsts for God, for the living God.
>   When can I go and meet with God?
>
>   (Ps. 42, NIV)

There is here not only a visceral and soulful longing for the living God. There is also the expectation that God should fulfill that longing, as we hear in the refrain:

> 5   Why are you downcast, O my soul?
>   Why so disturbed within me?
>   Put your hope in God,
>   For I will yet praise him,
>   My Savior and my God.
>
>   (Ps. 42, NIV)

This dialogue in the soul between the self enlightened by memory and revelation and the self lost in its own shadow rings throughout many of the Psalms. The psalmist reminds his darkened soul that this moment of God's silence must be experienced in light of God's past faithfulness and the expectation of his keeping his promises. This is a song not "of myself" but to oneself, to pull oneself together through memory and hope.

    For all their intense gaze into the individual soul, the Psalms of expectation are not about some inward longing, either of the ancient mystical sort to be found in many Eastern religions or of the modern narcissistic kind to be located in much poetry and psychology since the romantic period. Israel's poets longed for the God who reveals himself in history. That is why so many Psalms recall the Patriarchs, Exodus, the settling in the Promised Land, and the glories of King David. They long for the God who has revealed himself to the world through a "peculiar people," Israel. They expect to meet him in his law: "I will run the way of your commandments,/for you have set my heart at liberty" (Ps. 119:32, BCP). God is as good as his word, and God's law is freedom. Indeed those laws are as much poetry as commandment: "Your statutes have been like songs to me/wherever I have lived as a stranger" (Ps.

119:54, BCP). In the Psalms there is no split between the Apollonian and the Dionysian, between *nomos* and *physis*. Rather, these aspects were fused in Israel's expectation and anticipation of meeting God in worship. For example, the Psalms of ascent (120-34) are thought to have described the journeys of pilgrims to Jerusalem for the great festivals. The Hebrews reconceived time around their sacred events, celebrating God's work in creation and salvation, building into the very fabric of their existence the anticipation of meeting God around the Sabbath table, in Jerusalem, in the Temple, and later in exile in the Synagogue, where they sang the songs of Zion.

While praise and wholeness are at the heart of the lyric vision expressed in the Psalter, psalms of both anticipation and consummation are outnumbered by those of lament. Psalmists seem to compose songs more readily about broken hearts, broken relationships, and a broken world. I suspect that this is probably true of most cultures because one of the central and most pervasive human experiences is that of loss. However, any reading of lyric poetry from other traditions indicates that the Hebrews held a view of the human condition at once higher and lower than that encountered in other cultures: they envision man in complete union with the divine, not subservient but beloved, and they recognize the profound loss of that relationship—a loss that exiles man from the garden and reduces him to dust and ashes.

Some sixty psalms that may be classified as laments allow one to describe the lyric terrain east of Eden. All have to do with manifestations of death, of loss, and of suffering. One of the most familiar laments, Psalm 137, I alluded to earlier:

> 1 By the rivers of Babylon,
>   there we sat,
>   sat and wept,
>   as we thought of Zion.
> 2 There on the poplars
>   we hung our lyres,
> 3 For our captors asked us there for songs,
>   our tormentors, for amusement,
>   "Sing us one of the songs of Zion."
>   ...
> 8 Fair Babylon, you predator,
>   a blessing on him who repays you in kind

	what you have inflicted on us;
9	a blessing on him who seizes your babies
	and dashes them against the rocks!

(Tanakh)

Much is rightly made of the final stanza of this so-called imprecatory psalm that calls God's wrath down on the Hebrews' enemies: an eye for an eye, a tooth for a tooth, a dashed baby for a dashed baby. The cruelty against the inhabitants of Jerusalem and Judah was unspeakable, but the poet spoke it, not to command God to take vengeance, but to offer, as Brueggemann says of the prophets, "symbols that are adequate to the horror" (*Prophetic* 49).

But the larger grief about which the psalm speaks is the loss of home. One of the great laments in the Bible is that human disobedience stripped all humanity of a permanent place, from the beginning, with Adam and Eve being barred from the Garden, to Cain becoming a wanderer who builds the first city, which remains a place of displaced and lonely humanity, to the Patriarchs wandering the land until the exile of Egypt, then the wilderness, and so forth, all these moments together forming an unsurpassable history of loss and longing. The same is true, moreover, of other cultures as their bards tell of the homelessness and homesickness of Gilgamesh, Odysseus, Oedipus, Aeneas, Beowulf, Dante, Don Quixote, and Melville's Ishmael, not to mention the millions of displaced people in the modern world from native Americans to countless persecuted refugees. We celebrate home, whether or not we ever enjoyed one; we long for home, where we can again hear "the songs of Zion"; and we lament our homelessness, so that we can move beyond the paralysis of repressed grief.

The Psalm of Moses, Psalm 90, takes up homelessness from a different perspective: "Lord, thou hast been our dwelling place in all generations" (90:1). Traditionally thought to have been written by Moses toward the end of the wilderness wanderings, this psalm acknowledges the deep mystery that God not only created but also in some mysterious sense inhabits time and space and that human beings can dwell in that sacred time and spacious place.

The imaginative source of this vision of time and space probably arises out of Israel's experience of God symbolically moving with them from Sinai to the Promised Land in the form of the Tabernacle, this sacred and beautiful goat-hair tent. It was carried in their midst from place to place and, when they camped, was always set up east of the tribe of Judah to remind them of God's redemptive presence in time and space every time the sun rose over Judah, the tribe assigned that spot, the tribe from whom the Messiah would come. With Israel still lacking a permanent home, the psalmist goes on to lament that "all our days are passed away in thy wrath" (90:9) and cries out to God to relent. In the midst of this petition is the request that recognizes that the ordering of their hearts is the means to the home they are searching for: "So teach us to number our days, that we may apply our hearts unto wisdom" (90:12).

Wandering in the wilderness and unused to the rhythms of God's presence and God's will, the people grieve over being placeless and timeless. In the end, though, they do not ask for the Promised Land or even that God's anger be removed. They ask for dual blessings: "And let the beauty of the Lord our God be upon us: and establish thou the work of our hands upon us; yea, the work of our hands establish thou it" (90:17). In other words, they grieve over the loss of God's beauty (which also can be translated "favor"), and they fear that the work of their hands, as co-creators in God's image, will leave nothing permanent. They want once again to worship God in his glory and cultivate the creation he has bequeathed to them. This is a most transcendent and at the same time mundane image of the biblical lyric vision of the meeting of God's glory and man's work, the meeting of heaven and earth. We want our presence on this earth to be remembered, and only God's memory transcends the wilderness of death.

The lamentation expressed in Psalms 137 and 90 is communal; other psalms focus on the existential grief of the individual. Among the best known of these are Psalms 22 and 51, personal laments that render with unique beauty and power the outcry of the God-forsaken person. The first has great prominence among Christians because its opening lines are uttered from the cross by Jesus: "My God, My God, why hast thou forsaken me?" This is the outcry of the afflicted who, like Job and Jesus, have done nothing to deserve their suffering, yet God is silent. Although the last section affirms that God "hath not despised nor abhorred the affliction of the afflicted" (22:24), there is only the promise based on God's past faithfulness—only a word *about* the Lord, not a word *from* the Lord. No other ancient grief can compare with the existential grief of the Hebrew poets, because unlike the gods of the gentiles, Yahweh has declared his love and delight in his people. The widow of the husband who has loved her faithfully and passionately all her life grieves more deeply than the widow of the unfaithful abuser. Like Job, like Lamentations, such psalms as these dare to ask the Creator, "Why, O Lord?" and "When, O Lord?"

Psalm 51, however, represents a more common lament, one in which the psalmist knows why he deserves to be God-forsaken. Here David, that lying, adulterous, murdering "man after God's own heart," cries for mercy for his sin and confesses: "For I acknowledge my transgressions: and my sin is ever before me. Against thee, thee only, have I sinned, and done this evil in thy sight" (51:3-4). David knows that the ultimate reason he committed adultery with Bathsheba and conspired to murder her husband was that he had forsaken God, preferring the prerogatives of a king to follow his own desires. He also knows that the ultimate consequence of such sin is greater even than the death of Uriah and of the child Bathsheba conceived with David; he faces, as did his predecessor Saul, the death of his walk with Yahweh. Unlike the innocent afflicted ones found in Job and Psalm 22, David is guilty and can only throw himself on the mercy of God, begging him to "Create in [him] a clean heart," to "renew a right spirit" in him, to "restore...the joy of [Yahweh's] salvation," and to "uphold" him with God's spirit (51:10-12). David was not groveling to get something he longed for; he was asking to be renewed and restored to a joy he had once known and had thrown away in his lust and pride. He knew in his earlier experience that, as Heschel describes it, "Man is rebellious and full of iniquity, and yet so cherished is he that God, the Creator of heaven and earth, is saddened when forsaken by him" (2:5). In this sense, David understood that the origin of sin, suffering, and death is not in his being God-forsaken but in that God has, again and again, been man-forsaken.

Yet God remains not only steadfast but passionate in his love for his creation, and especially for that creation in his image, and it is their knowledge of that passion that enables the Hebrews to voice their deep grief to God. The mystery of a God who is so passionately in love with his creation that he would enter into its sufferings and weep for its afflictions is the mystery that enables Hebrew poets to range from the heights of the one transcendent creator of all things to the depths of the human soul, fashioned in the image of God.[3]

Hebrew lyric poetry in general and the Psalms in particular afford a unique access to the lyric realm. The lyric is born out of a communal and yet highly personal vision of the human enterprise that is "crowned with glory" by God. It yearns for a *shalom* in which all things flourish, and it laments and complains to God to restore the glory and bring about the *shalom*. While it does so using the many figures of speech common to lyric poetry, it finds normative expression in parallelism, a poetic form that reflects an intuition that two realms of reality are constantly in dialogue with each other, interpenetrating without either losing its distinct identity. The Psalms explore the heights and depths of the lyric vision because they hold such a high view of the Creator God, who was in the beginning, and such a glorious view of human beings, created in the image of God. Preoccupied with such glory, however, they do not explore the breadth of lyric wisdom that we find in the more nuanced lyric poetry of the broader Western tradition.

The Psalms, nonetheless, belong to a greater audience than Jews and Christians. They have informed and continue to inform the poetic traditions of world cultures. They do so because the Jews, too often for tragic reasons, have read, recited, and sung them in almost every culture on earth. Likewise, Christians in every culture have incorporated them into their worship and imagination. Whether as part of the Tanakh, early Christian hymnology, the songs of Caedmon, Gregorian chant, the Book of Common Prayer, the Bay Psalms of Colonial America, the Gospel songs of African American slaves, or the compositions of John Coltrane, the Psalms, unlike so much fine lyric poetry of other cultures, have never ceased being a living tradition. They have even entered and enlivened the global media culture in the lyrics of U2:

> I waited patiently for the Lord
> He inclined and heard my cry
> He brought me up out of the pit
> Out of the miry clay
>
> I will sing, sing a new song…
> How long to sing this song…
>
> He set my feet upon a rock
> And made my footsteps firm
> Many will see
> Many will see and hear.

"The Psalms thus propose to speak about human experience in an honest, freeing way," writes Brueggemann. "This is in contrast to much of human speech and conduct, which is in fact a cover-up" (*Praying* 17). What Brueggemann says of the Psalms can be said of all authentic lyric poetry. Not only does it free us to hear the truth, but it is itself a revelation of truth. The Psalms, though, constitute a special revelation, for they seek an intimacy between human and divine, to remember and reestablish a relationship that was lost and seems ever just beyond our grasp. In voicing our deepest longings and fears, they create an interval in which all time is present and all space is here, in which man wrestles with God, weeps with God, walks with God, and at last is embraced in his arms.

Notes

1. Except where noted parenthetically (BCP = The Psalter of the 1979 Book of Common Prayer; NIV = New International Version; Tanakh = The Tanakh, New Jewish Publication Society translation), quotations of the Psalms are taken from the King James Version of the Bible because of its unsurpassed poetic expression.

2. In my research and reflection on the Psalms, I have incorporated the insights of biblical scholars, seasoned preachers, church musicians, and lovers of poetry about their understanding of lyrics in general and the Psalms in particular. My son Harry, who reads and loves poetry from David to Homer to Robert Lowell, as well as contemporary popular music, points out insightfully how language is used in the Psalms: "My overwhelming feeling about lyric writing is that it is language of worship. I believe this is the fundamental strength of poetry. Even poetry that primarily purposes to criticize rather than praise draws upon the inherent understanding people have of the lyric to incite feelings of conflict. I think the fact that poetry is inherently worshipful is the reason that poetry of lament is so powerful. It uses the language of praise to grieve" (Email, Harry Russ to Dan Russ, 6 March 2007).

3. Cornel West, in a lecture entitled "Christ Matters," at a conference on the images of Christ in contemporary cultures, used the difference between Socrates, who is never reported to have wept, and the prophets (as spokesmen for Yahweh) and Jesus, who are recorded as weeping for the people, to explore this mystery of a sympathetic God.

2

Greek and Roman Lyric

Karl Maurer

In our time the word *lyric* has an oppressive vagueness; it has come to mean, and the thing itself has come to be, almost everything and nothing. The cause is partly I think a general ignorance of lyric verse's Greek origins, and equal ignorance of a certain subtle but deep change that happened as early as the Romans. So I shall try to show something of this, that is, some of the most striking traits it had in Greek and Roman antiquity.

But 'Greek and Roman Lyric' means seven whole centuries, from Hesiod to Horace, and two closely interwoven but quite distinct poetic cultures. In order to avoid dissolving it into a 'lyric' mist, I decided on two coarse devices, for which I hope I may be forgiven: (a) to quote only a very few poets, who seem sufficiently memorable and pithy, even in briefest quotation; and (b) to divide the whole into four sections, each having a different main theme.[1]

I. About 'Verse' Ancient and Modern

... τᾶς ἀκούει μὲν βάσις, ἀγλαΐας ἀρχά,
πείθονται δ' ἀοιδοὶ σάμασιν,
    ἁγησιχόρων ὁπόταν προοιμίων ἀμβολὰς τεύχῃς ἐλελιζομένα.

(O phorminx) whom the footstep, the beginning of splendor, hears;
and singers obey your signals, whenever,
humming, you build the preludes of choir-guiding overtures.

(Pindar, *Pythian* 1.2-4)

Formal verse is often thought to be a convention, as 'arbitrary' as any rhyme-scheme, which a poet today may choose to avoid; but to Greeks and Romans alike, it seemed poetry's essence; for it alone weaves, steadily, into language the *rhythm* of the human footstep, breath, and heartbeat. By analogy we discern rhythm in larger movements that enlarge heartbeat and footstep and give them context: a dance's circles, or see-sawing; the circle of the seasons; the circling of the earth by sun or moon and stars.[3] In various ways, for example in the stanza-forms of choral lyric, verse easily, brilliantly mimes those also.

Thus the word *verse* (Lat. *uersus*) means a 'turning': that of a plowman at the end of a field, or of dancers, or of the sun circling in zig-zags through the zodiac; and a verse's 'feet' (*pedes*) are its footsteps.[4] By this very simplest act of mimesis verse performs the first, and perhaps most important, of all its many offices: that of *purifying* all thoughts and emotions, even the most terrible, by linking their expression in language to the simple heartbeat, footstep, and breath, which are much the same in all humans, and by linking those to the quiet 'rhythms' of the world.

These simple facts were seen clearly by the Greeks. Let us go as far back in time as we can, to the clumsy, powerful verse of Hesiod:

> But they (the Muses) went to Olympus, glorying in their sweet voice,   68
> in ambrosial dance, and all about them the dark earth reechoed
> as they sang, and a lovely beating rose beneath their footsteps
> as they went to their father, who is king in the heavens, who
> himself holds the thunder and the flashing lightning.
> ...
> And if a man has anguish in his newly-troubled soul   98
> and a heart stupefied with grief, yet, when a singer,
> the servant of the Muses, chants the glorious deeds
> of men of old and the blessed gods who inhabit Olympus
> at once he forgets his anguish and remembers nothing
> of his griefs; for the goddesses' gifts soon turn him away from these.
>   (*Theogony* 68-72, 98-103)

This excerpt pinpoints a trait of Greek verse in particular, which is that, whether epic or lyric, it was always *sung*. Greek meter is quantitative and *musical*.[5] Because it is musical, it has a beauty, subtlety, suppleness, and boldness that other, stress-tied or tone-tied meters cannot match. But for this it pays a heavy price, which is that it is more like song than living speech and more like a dancing step than a simple footstep. That Greek verse is song is the source, for instance, of Pindar's amazingly various and always astounding 'musical' images for verse, as in that quoted above, or for example *N.* 8.14-15, where verse is "a Lydian headband embroidered with ringing flute-sounds" (φέρων/Λυδίαν μίτραν καναχηδὰ πεποικιλμέναν). This musicality is also why it is hard to hear the very voice, the living speech, of Pindar or Alcman or Simonides, and why there is a certain deep stateliness even in Homer or in the dialogue of Greek tragedy.

By contrast English meter is based on mere stress accents. As Robert Graves once said, in words that apply both to iambs and to alliterative Saxon verse, English has "the meter of the tugged oar and the marching footstep." It is thus a barbarous thing, compared with Greek meter; but it can get much closer to naked living speech. Only English can have a Shakespeare, a Frost, or a Hardy.

Midway between the two is Latin, which is in some ways the most beautiful. Romans could use the complex, musical Greek meters because they too were sensitive to the quantities of syllables (we see this, for example, in their oratory, in the fastidious *clausulae*, the carefully measured sentence-ends). But like English, and unlike Greek, Latin had always a strong stress accent; and that its verse does incorporate this is shown by the following fact. Normally, in the first half or two-thirds of any Latin verse, whether epic or lyric, the metrical *ictus* seems to ignore the stress accents of daily speech; but at the ends of lines, the two systems coincide with striking consistency. To take for example (to choose purely at random) the first five lines of Vergil's *Georgics*: in the phrases I italicize, the everyday stress accents coincide with the meter, so that if it were read aloud by someone quite ignorant of the meter, that would still be heard perfectly:

> Quid faciat laetas segetes, *quo sídere térram*
> *vertere*, Maecenas, ulmisque *adiúngere uítis*
> conueniat, quae cura boum, *qui cúltus habéndo*
> sit pecori, apibus quanta *experiéntia párcis*,
> hinc canere incipiam. *uos, ó claríssima múndi*....

Thus, because it incorporates two patterns so unlike, Latin verse has a prodigious range, greater than that of Greek or English. In the hands of a Vergil, it can attain a scarcely credible musical density yet cling to the poet's own voice and speech and footstep, register the tiniest emotions, and mime the gropings of his thought. It has an incomparable freshness. In the *Georgics*, we seem to see the very movements of thought itself, palpating the world; yet at the same time each verse is as taut as a cello string and 'sings' with an astonishing depth and purity of sound.[6] And thus also Ennius, the first Roman imitator of Homer and the father of Roman epic verse, whom Vergil knew by heart, described himself in this way in his epitaph, very musically yet prouder of his living speech:

> nemo me lacrumis decoret nec funera fletu.
>   faxit cur? uolito uiuu' per ora uirum.
>
> Nobody ever adorn me with tears nor weep at my burial.
>   Why do that when I flit live in the mouths of men?

Key is the charming word '*uolito*' (flit, flutter, hover, dart); apart from Pindar (who as we shall see could say absolutely anything) it would never be used by a Greek poet.[7]

II. The Intimate 'Public Voice' of Choral Lyric

> The Muse thus stood beside me
> as I found a new-shining way
> to fit to the Dorian sandal the voice //
> that gives splendor to the feast. For garlands joined to tresses
> exact from me this god-imposed debt,
>   to mingle the word-embroidering phorminx and the cry of flutes
>   (Pindar, *O.* 3.4-9)
>
> The Aeolian flute went its way/On the Dorian path of songs.
>   (Pindar fr. 180 [191 Sn.], trans. Bowra)

It was partly Greek verse's alliance with music, with dance and song, that gave it, from Homer and Hesiod to Pindar and Greek tragedy, a public presence that today rather astonishes and partly the fact that it seemed a link between men and the gods, that is, a revelation of the order of the world. *Revelation* is a rather pompous word, but the Greek poets themselves, and their audience, well knew that their best verse came to them from God.[8] The result of both things was that poetry had an authoritative public presence, so unforgettable that the Romans, and then later poets, would remember every smallest aspect of it but never recover it. The entire later history of poetry is a kind of *grieving* for this loss and an attempt to understand it. As we shall see later, longing for it made the Romans invent and shape, with astonishing skill, our own more wistful conception of poetry. The present section will only be a sort of collage of quotations, chosen carefully to give an adequate glimpse of the omnipresence of lyric verse in Hellas and of the implicit depth of its 'authority.' I shall quote only three Dorians—Polybius, Alcman, Pindar—who seem to let us glimpse the essence of choral lyric, that mother of all lyric.

Polybius of course was not a poet but an austere historian. But in Book IV, chapter 20 and following, he pauses briefly to explain *why* the citizens of Cynaetha, a town in Arcadia, had behaved with abnormal cruelty and treachery. Unlike other inhabitants of the Peloponnese, they had strangely neglected music:

> We should not think that the ancient Cretans and Lacedaemonians to no purpose introduced the flute and the measured tread, instead of the bugle, into war, or that the early Arcadians to no purpose filled their whole public life with music, to such an extent that not only boys but even young men up to the age of thirty had to study it constantly, although otherwise their lives were most austere. For everybody knows that only in Arcadia, first, the boys from earliest childhood are trained to sing in measure the hymns and paeans in which the people of each place, by tradition, hymn their local heroes and gods; later, learning the nomes of Philoxenus and Timotheus, every year in the theater they compete keenly in choruses at the Dionysiac flute-competitions, the boys in the boys' contests and the youths in what is called the men's contest. And through their whole lives, in social gatherings they entertain themselves not with hired performers but by themselves, calling for song from each in turn. And though they are not ashamed to deny acquaintance with other studies, song they can neither deny knowing, since all are compelled to learn it, nor, since they admit that they know it, can they excuse themselves; for among them this is thought shameful. Besides this, the young men practice marching tunes with the flute and in formation, and perfect themselves in dances, and each year perform in the theaters for their fellow citizens, all at the public expense....

> (The ancients) also accustomed both men and women alike to frequent festivals, and sacrifices, and dances of men and women, and used every possible device to mollify, by such customs, the extreme hardness of the natural character. The Cynaetheans neglected these institutions, though in special need of them, as their country and climate is the most rugged in Arcadia; and by devoting themselves to their mutual frictions and animosities, finally became so savage that in no city of Greece were greater and more constant crimes committed.[9]

Polybius, proud of his own country, Arcadia, exaggerates its uniqueness: we know from a hundred sources that all Greece was like this.[10]

But what he says of boys and men was quite equally true of girls. Girls' festivals included keen choral competitions, which the whole town watched. In fact the loveliest Greek lyric verse that we still possess, apart from Pindar, is that of Alcman (fl. 630 B.C.), written for *partheneia*, or choral songs sung and danced by young girls. His verse is now in mere fragments, for example these four, which I quote first because they all address the Muse in what could be choral preludes. Because they are fragments, often we cannot discern who is the speaker, the poet or (as for example certainly in the last I quote, fr. 3) the girls, who certainly did perform the main body of each ode:

> Muse, come, Calliope, Zeus's daughter,[11]
> begin the lovely words; make our hymn
> full of charm and our dancing have grace.
>
> (fr. 27 = 76D)
>
> Muse, come, clear-voiced Muse,
> O many-toned singer forever, a new song[12]
> begin, for the maidens to sing.
>
> (fr. 14 = 7D)
>
> The Muse, the clear-voiced Siren, has cried out....
>
> (fr. 10D)
>
> ...Olympian [*Muses*], me in my heart...
> [*then some lines missing; then:*]
> ...[*? the song*] will scatter sweet sleep from [*?their*]
>   eyelids
> ...leads me to the contest
> where I will shake my yellow hair...
>   [*then 50 lines missing; then:*]
> (61)...with limb-loosening desire, but more meltingly
> than sleep or death she looks (at one),

> but not a bit in vain [? *is*] she sweet.
>   But Astyméloisa answers me nothing,
> but having the wreath,
> like some star through the brilliant
> sky shooting
> or (like) a golden shoot, like a soft feather
>   [*then a line missing; then:*]
> ...she passed through on slender feet.
> The dewy grace of Cyprian perfume
> rests on maidens' long hair.
>   Astyméloisa amidst the crowd
> ...a care for the people
>
>   (fr. 3)[13]

In wondering what to make of this, a reader should bear in mind two things. First, the reason a hymn must "be full of charm, our dancing full of grace" is that it is performed at a religious festival, for a goddess; or in other words, for all its boldness and intimacy, each song is also a prayer. Second, each ode was probably part of a public competition between competing choruses, at which the whole town was present. This makes rather astonishing the intimacy of the fragment last quoted (fr. 3): as if a fit subject for such art were the vanity and daydreams of a young girl and her 'crush' on another!

For a long time such scraps as these were all that we possessed of Alcman. But by good luck, in 1855 in Egypt a long papyrus fragment, which is now in the Louvre, was discovered by the French Egyptologist Auguste Mariette, containing about half of an entire *partheneion* by him. It probably had ten stanzas of fourteen lines each. Stanzas I-V are too badly damaged to translate; but V-X are nearly intact (lacking only the last four lines) and I will translate them here.

Among scholars there are fierce disputes about every detail. It seems best not to tax the reader with these but to summarize what we seem to see for certain. The poem was a song sung and danced to by a chorus of ten girls (l. 98; see also the names in stanza VIII) in a rite just before dawn (ll. 40-43), probably at a spring harvest festival, perhaps for a dawn goddess (the names 'Orthria,' l. 61, and 'Aotis,' l. 87, both seem cognate with Greek words for dawn). The 'speaker' is either the whole chorus of ten girls or various members of it or perhaps two halves of it singing in alternation.[14]

Of the lost first five stanzas we have only scraps, enough to show that, probably after a 'prelude' very like those quoted above, they related a myth about Heracles and earliest Spartan history.[15] This ended at line 35 (omitted from my translation) with the words "dreadfully they suffered, who plotted evil." Briefly a moral is drawn (below, ll. 36-39); then the poem enters, curiously, the little world of the chorus itself.

Apparently they are competing with another chorus (ll. 60-65, where, because of ambiguities in the Greek, one cannot tell if "the Doves" is the name of this chorus or another chorus). But they rely on the grace and beauty of their chorus leader, Hagesichora, and their principal dancer, Agido.[16] But the whole chorus seems to have a sort of schoolgirl crush on both girls and are not afraid to talk about it:

VI[17]

Vengeance from the gods there is. 36
O happy is he who calmly
Weaves his daylight to the end
Not weeping! But I am singing
 Ágidó's own light. I see 40
Our Ágidó like the sunlight
 She herself now summons up
To shine for us! All the same, I
Neither blame nor praise: // our famous Chorus Leader
Tolerates no peer: // for *she* it is who must be 45
 Most conspicuous, as when someone
 Through the cattle leads a handsome
Prize-winning filly, whose hooves full of thunder each
Heart can but dream of, in winged dreams.

VII

 Don't you see? One girl a steed: 50
Venetian! The mane of the other—
 That, I mean, of my best kin
Hagésichorá—oh, blossoms
 Golden just like purest gold.
Her star-lighted face is silver. 55
 See? Why must I make it plain?
Hagésichorá is with us.
Still, a girl who'd race // our Ágidó for beauty

> Like a steed from Scythia // races an Ibenian.
>> See? the Doves, as now we bear the   60
>> Sacred *pharos* to Orthría,
> Rising up, hovering through the ambrosial
> Nighttime like Sirius, fight for all.

VIII

>> No abundant scarlet cloth
>> Suffices now to defend us,—   65
>>> No, no golden serpent bright
>> With inlay, and not the Lydian
>>> Headband that makes violet-eyed
>> Girls appear even lovelier,
>>> No, and not our Nanno's locks,   70
>> Not Áreta like a goddess,
> Sýlakís? Not her. // Not our Kleésiséra.
> No. You would not even // at Ainésymbrota's
>> Say, "Can Astáphis take my side?" or
>> "Let Philýlla just be with me,"   75
> "Let Demaréta" or "Let pretty Iánthemis,"
> No! Just "Hagésichorá makes me suffer so!"

IX

>> For is not the fair-of-foot
>> Hagésichorá beside us?
>>> Stays she not near Ágidó?   80
>> Commending our feast together!
>>> What we offer you, O gods,
>> Take from us. For with gods our
>>> Ends are. Leader of our Choir,
>> I have to confess I did once,   85
> Like a tiny hoot-owl // hooting from the rafter,
> Sing to no good purpose! // O but now, Aotis,
>> You I most would please. In troubles
>> Only the goddess is our doctor.
> Still, from Hagésichorá we the maidens have   90
> Gotten the peace that is all that we love.[18]

>   X
>   See how by the trace-horse we
>   Are schooled in the ways of turning.
>   Each good vessel's captain has
>   A voice to which all must hearken.
>   True, she cannot outperform   95
>   The sirens, if they are divine, and
>   We are not eleven, no,
>   But only ten children singing.
>   Swan-like, though, as on the // currents of the Xanthus
>   Sings she! And her lovely // yellow hair is flowing...   100

What on earth should we say about this? Certainly we can say first, in the good words of C. M. Bowra: "The scanty remains of choral song before Pindar indicate that it used certain devices that belong to its very nature and were its instruments for securing variety and surprise and the distance from the immediate scene which was necessary to attain dignity and detachment" (*Pindar* 198).

But how strange the method used for "securing...distance from the immediate scene": that of entering *very* deeply into it! How intimate, this voice of a public festival! Fresh silly gossip, fresh silly emotions of young girls, imitated with depth and exactness, are thought worthy of a first-rate poet's close attention and carefully preserved against the tooth of time by a sealed time capsule of sturdy, graceful, well-made verses. Equally surprising, a quite complete unity between what we ourselves tend to separate into the religious and the secular, the serious and the frivolous. The prayers are plainly real prayers; just as plainly, the girls are real girls, intensely alive, and not walking (or rather dancing) solemnly.

And what may we conclude, then, about the figure of the poet? Not very much; and that is itself significant. On the one hand, Alcman was honored by all Hellas, and by Peloponnesians in particular, as one of their greatest poets.[19] On the other, in what is apparently a fairly typical poem by him, he is a transparent presence, a recording ear, an omnipresent eye, a music maker, a simple maker of songs. He seems a person so secure of his worth to the community that, in a poem like this at least, he has no more self-importance than a Greek potter or a Parthenon marble carver.

All this is plain; but I exaggerate just a little. In the extant fragments he does sometimes speak of himself. I end with five in which he does so; to me they seem not to contradict but to prove my larger point. The tone in which he speaks of himself is unself-conscious, is that of a man at home and happy in Sparta:

> Male halcyons are called κήρυλοι and in old age are carried on the wings of the female birds; so when Alcman declares that he is old and feeble and cannot join in the girls' song and dance, he writes:
> Not any more, you honey-toned, holy-voiced maidens
>   can my limbs carry me. Would, O would that
>   I could be a kingfisher
>   flying just over the flowering wave in the
>   midst of the halcyons,
> keeping a fearless heart, a sea-purple, happy bird.
> (fr. 26)[20]

> Whoever of us are children, praise the lyre-player.
> (fr. 20D)

> And some day I shall give you a great cauldron on a tripod,
> and in it you may gather food of every kind.
> Now it is unfired, but soon it will be full
> of porridge, such as Alcman, who eats everything,
> loves hot after the solstice.
> For he does not eat what is well confectioned,
> but, like the people, seeks the common fare.
> (fr. 20D, trans. Bowra)

> I know the tunes of all the birds....
> (fr. 40)

> Words and tune Alcman
> invented, by putting in speech
> the voices of partridges.
> (fr. 49)

III. Pindar's Intimate 'Panhellenic' Voice

πολύφατον θρόον ὕμνων δόνει/ἡσυχᾷ.

Agitate the many-voiced din of songs/quietly.
(Pindar, *N.* 7.80-82)[21]

Alcman, then, was an intimately Laconian poet. His verse embraced heaven and earth and, surely, charms even today, yet it is so rooted in the occasion, the tiny local festival, that often we can scarcely penetrate the allusions. His great successor Pindar (c. 518-438 B.C.) is quite equally intimate (as will be seen in every one of my quotations) and often terribly obscure from a similar cause. But Pindar, whose extant complete poems glorify athletes at the Panhellenic games, is acutely conscious of a much wider world. He knew how many and how various his listeners were; he even *says* that his song is not 'local' and, in a typically bold image, compares it to merchandise sent across the sea:

> I am no sculptor, to make statues resting, standing on the same base!—
> no, but on every merchantman, sweet Song, in every skiff,
> leave Aigina, to announce everywhere that/Lampon's son Pytheas....
> (*N.* 5.1-4)

> (*To Hieron, winner in the chariot—and as if the ode were nearly over:*)...
> Farewell! Like Phoenician merchandise this
> song is sent over the foaming sea.
> But the Castor-song in Aeolian chords, please,
> look out for and greet, for the sake of the seven-stringed phorminx.[22]
> (*P.* 2.67-71)

For this same reason—his acute awareness of all Hellas listening—often he boldly personifies his song as a messenger bringing 'news' or as a herald at the games. For example, at *O.* 13.97-100: "(*This family's victories*) at the Isthmus and at Nemea I shall make plain instantly in brief; and for me, truthful,/bound by oath, heard sixty times in either place, will be/the sweet-tongued cry of the noble herald." Or: "To you (Syracuse) I come from gleaming Thebes, bearing/this song, news of the earth-shaking four-horse chariot" (*P.* 2.3-4). Or: "But I bearing willingly on my back a double burden, have come as a herald,/to bellow that this is (this family's) twenty-fifth//vow (discharged) after contests" (that is, that the family has won twenty-five victories) (*N.* 6.59-61).

In two places this image of the herald is sharper and deeper and has the radiance that is peculiar to Pindar's best verse:

> Me as her chosen
> herald of knowing verses
> the Muse has set in charge of Hellas of the beautiful choirs.[23]
>
> (fr. 61 [70b Sn.] 18-20)
>
> Now spur your comrades,
> Ainias, first to sing Hera, the goddess of maidens,
> then to know if, in very truth, we have escaped
> the old reproach, "Boiotian pig"! For you are an exact messenger,
> a scroll-wand (σκυτάλα) of the fair-tressed Muses,
> a sweet mixing-bowl of loud-sounding songs.[24]
>
> (O. 6.87-91)

Still more boldly, in three passages the poem, that loveliest of all heralds, brings its good news even to the dead!

> And now to the black-walled house
> of Persephone go, Echo, bearing glorious news to [*the victor's*] father,
> Kleodamos, in order having seen him to say that his son
> in the famed vale of Pisa
> crowned his young locks with the wings [*i.e., the winged wreath*]
>   of ennobling victory.
>
> (O. 14.21-24, end of poem)
>
> And deeds of excellence,
> in (the form of) soft dew
> sprinkled in the outpourings of festivals,
> they hear with underground minds.[25]
>
> (P. 5.98-100, about the dead kings of Cyrene)
>
> He in fact forgets Hades—/the man who has done well.
> But I must awaken Memory, to tell
> of the victorious glory of the hands of the Blepsiada[*i.e., the
>   victor's family*],
> who have now been wreathed with their sixth wreath from the games.
> For even the dead have a share/of rites duly performed,
> and dust does not bury/the noble grace of their kinsmen.
> Iphion [*i.e., the victor's dead father*] hearing Hermes' daughter,/

> Tidings, may perhaps tell Kallimachos [*i.e., the victor's dead uncle*] of the shining
> adornment at Olympia, which Zeus has given their race!
>
> (*O.* 8.72-84, near end of poem)

I here dare any reader to name any poet who moved so freely as this one between Heaven and Earth and Hell! or any so at ease and sure of his authority, while remaining so intimate, so playful, in every verse. He knows, as Alcman did, that Hellenes have quick ears that catch even the most lightning-like allusion and that they will notice the subtlest simile.

Of course by quoting only brief passages, I do terrible injustice to Pindar. Some odes are several hundred lines; all are organized fascinatingly; each is as well-shaped as a Greek vase. But since I have little space here, it seems best to try to give some impression just (a) of his boldness and prodigious range and (b) of his conception of the place of lyric poetry.

I end with three more of his astounding images of poetry. In the first (*O.* 7 init.), the song is a mixing-bowl. That image appeared in *O.* 6.91, quoted above, but here it is denser, so dense that it begins to radiate light:

> As someone having taken from a rich (man's) hand a mixing-bowl
> bubbling inside with the vine's dew/shall give it/
> to a young bridegroom, toasting him from a home to a home—
>   (a bowl) pure gold, crown of possessions,
> grace of the drinking party—and so honors the new kinship, and   5
>   before the friends
> present makes him envied for his bridal bed's harmony,
> so I, by sending flowing nectar—gift of the Muses, sweet
> fruit of the mind—to prize-winners in games,/ask blessings,/
> for victors at Olympia and Pytho. Happy is he who is held in   10
>   good report!
> Now at one man, now at another Grace (Χάρις) gazes, giving
>   life by the sweet-melodied
> phorminx and the many-toned instruments of flutes.
>
> (*O.* 7.1-12)

In the second, it becomes a shower of arrows and an eagle:

Many are the swift arrows beneath my arm/inside the quiver,
that speak to the knowing *(sophoi)*: but for the crowd they need
interpreters. Knowing is he whom nature teaches much; the
        self-taught are boisterous
in their chattering, like daws, and in vain the pair of them babble
against the holy bird of Zeus.
Now at the mark aim the bow! Come, heart—whom are we hitting,
letting fly arrows from a kindly heart? We aim at Akragas....[26]

(*O.* 2.83-92)

In my last passage, the poem is again a herald, then a plow, then a treasure house impregnable to the wind and rain. I quote this in part because there is an exact echo of it in Horace, which I shall later contrast with it. *Pythian* 6 was composed for the winner of the chariot race at the Pythian games in 490. Xenocrates was the brother of Theron, tyrant of Akragas in Sicily. The Emmenidae are their clan; Thrasyboulos, Xenocrates' son and Pindar's friend, probably drove the chariot. The initial word "Listen!" (ἀκούσατε) imitates the cry of a herald:[27]

Listen! Is it bright-eyed Aphrodite's
or the Graces' field that now
we plow[28] again as we near the shrine
that is the navel of the deep-thundering earth?—
where, for the prosperous Emmenidae and Akragas on her river,   5
and above all for Xenocrates, in Apollo's gold-filled glen
has been walled in
a Pythian victor's treasure-house of songs:

Which neither the beating of in-driven winter rain—
the deep-thundering clouds'   10
pitiless army—nor the wind will drive,
struck and knocked by the all-bearing gravel,
into the gulfs of the sea! Listen: its pure bright brow,
Thrasyboulos, in Crisa's chasms announces
your father and his race   15
to be in the speech of mortals
renowned for a chariot victory.

(*P.* 6.1-17)

The poem's "pure bright brow" means (a) the bright facade shining afar of Apollo's Delphic temple, or his treasury, and (b) the opening, the prelude, the "pure bright brow" of his song itself, which, in its entirety, is that same temple.[29]

IV. The Roman Poets' "Ignoble Arts of Quietness"

The history of lyric poetry is often badly distorted, in a way illustrated by these remarks from Edward Mendelson's otherwise excellent book on W. H. Auden:

> The romantics inverted the ancient poetic hierarchy that saw dramatic and epic poetry as superior to lyric....Romanticism, hearing epic resonance in the personal voice, glorified the lyric as the highest mode of poetry, and made it the vessel for philosophical and historical subjects few earlier ages would have tried to force into it. The large forms of literature and the arts left the service of specific audiences and social occasions, and became their own sufficient reason for being. Art declared its independence from local settings, and established itself instead in the neutral context of the museums and concert halls that sprang up as its temples, bastions of its newly won autonomy. (xvi)

Three things seem amiss. First, the "ancient poetic hierarchy" is not so ancient; Pindar, for example, never had the least impression that his art was in any way inferior to epic! Second, he sets up a historically false antithesis between the 'personal' and the epic or public. We saw that even the most 'personal' choral lyric, like Alcman's or Pindar's, was always closely tied via music to public festivals and to local settings, and this is true of *all* lyric, both archaic and classical. In Archilochus, Solon, Alcaeus, Sappho, and Theognis, private and public united, and those very terms did not exist.[30] Third, glorification of "lyric as the highest mode of poetry" was first done not by the romantics but, tentatively, by Callimachus (c. 305-240 B.C.)[31] and, unmistakably, by the Romans, above all by those seemingly most public Romans, Vergil and Horace.

To prove this last point will be the burden of the following pages. Mendelson's error is common and forgivable, because the Romans made this inversion—a queer subversion of epic and a mirage of lyric 'autonomy,' which still oppresses us—with such immense, subtle skill that one can fail to see it even when it stares one in the face.

Let us look, briefly, at a famous Roman 'didactic epic,' Vergil's *Georgics*. It is ostensibly an agricultural handbook, giving advice to farmers; it often closely imitates, on the one hand, epic verse such as Hesiod's *Works and Days* and, on the other, real Roman farmers' manuals, which still survive.[32] But the poem's first readers would instantly have noticed oddities. First, most passages that masquerade as advice, or as objective description, have a kind of lyric wildness that startles. Second, the poem's overall structure, though clear in its main outlines, is so whimsical in details that one can never guess what is coming next. So many passages have both traits that to illustrate both I can take one almost at random. For example, Book III is about the care of livestock; in one passage Vergil is ostensibly advising us about the needs of sheep (3.295-304) and goats (3.305-21) but launches two sudden, wanton, beautiful digressions: a tiny one about goats (314-17), followed by more 'instruction' (318-21), then a longer digression, describing a herdsman's summer day (here the first word, "they," refers to goats):

> They graze in forest, on Lycaeus' ridges,
> on bristly shrubs, on steepness-loving thorn-trees.   315
> At dusk they lead their kids and come unsummoned
> and their full udders barely clear the doorsill.
> With greater trouble, then, since they give less trouble
> to men, you shield them from the snow-filled wind
> and happily bring inside their twiggy fodder,   320
> and never lock them from midwinter haylofts.
>   But when the West Wind, breathing sappy summer,
> calls both kinds into field and glade, O let us
> run to the chill fields, where the Dawn Star sparkles,
> when day is freshest, when the turf is white,   325
> and dewy young grass sweetest to the herd.
> But when four hours of sun have gathered thirst,
> when the cicadas' din bursts out of thickets,
> I want them near deep wells, near ponds, or drinking
> the wave that rustles in the holm-oak trough.   330
> Then, in the noon heat, seeking shade-filled valleys,
> wherever Jove's great oak with ancient strength
> spreads immense boughs, or if a black grove dense
> with holm-oak sleeps in its own sacred shadow.
> Then once more lightly water, pasture lightly,

> till sun sets and the Twilight Star drops coolness,   335
> and the red dewy moon refreshes glades
> and banks ring with kingfishers, thorns with finches.

Lines 322-36 provide a rounded perfect whole, dawn-star to dusk-star, daybreak dew to dew of dusk, one perfect summer day! Surely, this is what we ourselves loosely call 'lyric.' Such wild passages, each autonomous, dense with a music of its own, are so many that the *Georgics* is a bead-chain of them. And always the scraps of 'instruction,' from which these 'digressions' depart, are no instruction at all. The imperatives and jussive subjunctives (here "You shield them...O let us/run...I want them near deep wells," and so on) have at heart nothing in common with those of the farming manuals they imitate.

Third, at moments we hear unmistakably the too-quiet, anti-epic, anti-public voice and bias of Callimachus. For example, in the third book, after an especially long and wanton digression about love (3.237-83), Vergil returns to the ostensible topic, the care of flocks, with these words:

> But meanwhile Time flies, flies, beyond recovery,
> while we near details hover, caught by love.[33]   285
> Enough of herds! Ours now that other worry
> of herding woolly flocks and shaggy she-goats.
> Real work, this, farmers. Food for a hope of glory!
> I know how immense my own task is: to master
> such humbleness in words, that find it honor.   290
> But up the desert steeps of sweet Parnassus
> love lifts me!—joy in heights, where sloping grass
> falls to a Spring, where no one's wheel-tracks are.
>
>   (*Geo.* 3.284-93)

Well, this spring "where no one's wheel-tracks are" does show the *footprints* of Hesiod. But whereas in Hesiod's *Theogony*, lines 1-114, *all* emphasis is on the truth of the vision that the Muses give him, here it is on the glory, and the feelings, of the person singled out. Further, the self-oblivious Hesiod is never conscious in his *Works and Days* of dignifying, with his attention, "humble things"; to him the right way to farm seemed as important as anything else on earth.

The poem's fourth, perhaps most important, un-epic trait is a deep ambiguity in the poet's attitude toward all of it: on the one hand, as in the passage just quoted, a bold claim of glory;[34] on the other, a strange deep fear that this glory is actually nothing. In the haunting eight verses that conclude the work, Vergil puts it this way (by "Caesar" is meant Augustus):

> Haec super arvorum cultu pecorumque canebam
> et super arboribus, Caesar dum magnus ad altum   560
> fulminat Euphraten bello victorque volentes
> per populos dat iura viamque adfectat Olympo.
> Illo Vergilium me tempore dulcis alebat
> Parthenope studiis florentem ignobilis oti,
> carmina qui lusi pastorum audaxque iuventa,   565
> Tityre, te patulae cecini sub tegmine fagi.
>
> Thus of the tilth of fields I sang, of herds,
> of trees, while mighty Caesar by the deep   560
> Euphrates thundered war, gave willing peoples
> a victor's laws, and found paths to Olympus.
> Me, Vergil, in that time sweet Naples nourished,
> I blossomed in the ignoble arts of quietness,
> and played at shepherd song, and bold in youth,   565
> Títyrus, sang you in deep beech-tree shadow.
>
>   (*Geo.* 4.559-66)

What is the secret of these verses? Even today they are piercingly beautiful. First, a very subtle irony. The "mighty Caesar," Octavian, has four verses; our ignoble, nearly invisible poet, also four. In those depicting Octavian, each phrase has rhetorical power but is subtly false. He was in fact in the East, but not "by the deep Euphrates," that is, not in Parthia.[35] He did not "thunder," that is, make war; he merely threatened it. The laws he gave "to willing peoples" were in fact, precisely, a "victor's laws": the whole phrase is superb oxymoron. And though he was called *Divi filius*, son of Divine Caesar, it was not he but Julius Caesar who earned that. Palpably, he was not becoming an Olympian god! Yet anyone could overlook those facts; the praise is convincing because it is given with baroque tact and a subtle humor, and for another reason that I shall analyze in a moment. And Vergil himself? Part of him knew well that his "arts of quietness" were not "ignoble." Latin *ignobilis* means literally 'unknown' or 'unworthy to be known,' but these verses conclude what he certainly knew was an immortal poem, one of the very greatest of the ancient world.

I call the irony subtle, and beyond that even beautiful, because it catches *all* of the exact situation of any great *Roman* poet. Unlike their Greek predecessors, Vergil and Horace seemed, as we would say now, marginal, because both the Roman ideal, which the poets themselves helped to articulate (as Vergil does in the very verses quoted below), and Roman reality, which followed that ideal, were deeply un-Greek and deeply anti-artistic. Again, the most telling text is one by Vergil. This place too is piercingly beautiful, but it lacks the subtle humor of the other and strikes one as still more sad. But here we see in much clearer focus the peculiarly *Roman* problem:

> excudent alii spirantia mollius aera
> (credo equidem), vivos ducent de marmore vultus,
> orabunt causas melius, caelique meatus
> describent radio et surgentia sidera dicent: 850
> tu regere imperio populos, Romane, memento
> (haec tibi erunt artes) pacisque imponere morem,
> parcere subiectis et debellare superbos

> Others will mold bronze gentlier till it breathes
> Or, no doubt, lead live faces out of marble,
> Plead causes better, paths of the night sky
> With compass mark, and sing the rising stars: 850
> You, Roman, study to rule the tribes by empire,
> Your "arts" will be to impose the habit of peace,
> To spare the beaten, and outwar the proud.[36]

(*Aen.* 6.847-53)

To "others," plainly the Greeks, belong, as if it were their vocation, all that Vergil himself most loved, namely, all the "arts." We discern that by this he means also the sciences.[37] He specifies plastic arts (847-48), oratory (849, but one senses that this is shorthand for all works of language), astronomy (849-50, hence implicitly also philosophy). Roman is only the strange "art" of governing and of "imposing" a victor's peace!

Presumably this is the master art that makes all the others possible. But in this Roman ideal, at least as Vergil puts it, one senses something amiss. To "*impose* the habit of peace" verges on oxymoron, very like that in the *Georgics*: "gave *willing* peoples/a *victor's* laws" (4.561). Either phrase, I think, should make a reader uneasy because in each hides an *untruth* of which Vergil himself seems aware (hence the bold, startling language) but perhaps never saw clearly. I have no space here in which to explore this,[38] but we can now, I think, at least summarize a Roman poet's peculiar dilemma.

Vergil and Horace have a *Greek* poetic heritage; that is, the Roman poet has learned from the Greeks that the poetic vocation is sacred, that all good verse comes from—and only from—the Muses, messengers of God, revealers of truth about the order of the world.[39] Thus he knows that a singer is the equal of kings (as, for example, in Hesiod or Pindar);[40] the only bestower of immortality (Homer, Theognis, Pindar); the *sole* source of knowledge of the distant past (Homer); the sole 'theologian' (Hesiod);[41] the person at the center of any city's festivals (e.g., Alcman, Pindar, the Attic tragedians, the comedians, all composers of hymn and dithyramb); and even a person of such stature that, because of his wisdom, acknowledged by all, the city's very constitution should be entrusted to him (Solon).[42]

The Roman poets knew all this; they often proclaimed it more loudly than did the Greeks themselves. But they faced the hard facts of Roman reality, where, compared with any general 'thundering' in a province, a poet was quite as marginal, if not yet quite as unimportant, as he is in our own democracies.

I say "not yet quite as unimportant" because the Roman upper class was still cultured, aristocratic, Hellenized and because of the accident that Augustus, unlike most autocrats, was astute enough to sense the worth to himself and his regime of enlisting the best poets; and Horace and Vergil were astute enough to reciprocate. They prized the challenge thus given to make sense of the new regime, to find in it a sense deeper than the obvious one, that it brought a longed-for tranquility. But because of this tentative, groping 'endorsement' and from other causes, there is a widespread misimpression that these were essentially 'public' poets.[43] But the sadness of the passages that I have quoted, and of those that I will quote, is, though a subtle thing, so palpable that behind the urbanity one sees the truth, which is that of a great solitude.

Out of this impasse—the sacredness of the poet's vocation, made clear by the Greeks, set against the marginality of any poet's place in Rome—there were two possible routes,[44] and the Romans tried both. The first, poetically less convincing but still of immense later consequence, is that of solitude and defiance: "The vulgar crowd I hate and keep at bay," and so on.[45] The second path, also of huge later importance, is that of irony; but in Horace, just as in Vergil, the irony is often many-sided, nuanced, moving, and very beautiful. We have space only for several poems; I here quote one of Horace's greatest, the little one he put at the end of his first three books of *Odes*:

>   Exegi monumentum aere perennius
> regalique situ pyramidum altius,
> quod non imber edax, non aquilo impotens
> possit diruere aut innumerabilis
> annorum series et fuga temporum.   5
> non omnis moriar multaque pars mei
> vitabit Libitinam; usque ego postera
> crescam laude recens, dum Capitolium
> scandet cum tacita virgine pontifex.
> dicar, qua violens obstrepit Aufidus   10
> et qua pauper aquae Daunus agrestium
> regnavit populorum, ex humili potens,
> princeps Aeolium carmen ad Italos
> deduxisse modos. sume superbiam
> quaesitam meritis et mihi Delphica   15
> lauro cinge volens, Melpomene, comam

> I made a tombstone that will outlast bronze,
> higher than royal dust of pyramids,
> which no fierce winter rain and no North Wind
> enraged can topple, nor the chains of years
> that have no measure, nor the flying age.   5
> I will not all die. Many pieces of me
> will evade Libitina, for forever quickened
> by new praise I shall grow, so long as pontiff
> and silent virgin climb the Capitol.
> I shall be said where fierce Aufidus roars   10
> and Daunus poor in water once was king
> of rustic people, from the humblest origin
> to have been first to shape the verse of Italy
> out of Aeolic song. Put on the pride
> that merit searched for, and with leaves from Delphi, 15
> Melpomene, descending, wreathe my hair.

(*Odes* 3.30)

Notice first in verses 1-5 a prolonged, sharp, clear echo of the beginning of Pindar's *Pythian* 6, quoted at the end of part III, and the depth of its difference from that. We are in a different world! Both poets imagine immortality in 'song,' which is a fortress impregnable to wind, rain, and the passage of time. Yet for all his pride Pindar is self-oblivious. His "Pythian treasure-house of song" does not belong to him but to a youth who won a race; it came not from Pindar but from the gods, and it is a radiant, fluid, floating web of voices, a dancing chorus, at the heart of a Greek *polis*! Further, Pindar's song is merely a messenger announcing "to the speech of mortals" (or as he says in *O.* 11, announcing "to later stories") a boy and his family who are to be "renowned for a chariot victory"! Horace's pyramid is lonely, concrete, static, self-conscious: not a living, breathing creature, but a dead thing among dead things; and the image's emphasis, unlike that of Pindar's radiant treasure-house, is on "I...I...I...I...."

And yet Horace's are very great and moving verses.[46] Why is this? For one thing, like those last eight lines of the *Georgics*, they radiate humor and the subtlest irony. First, the pyramid 'works' precisely because it is massive, static, mute, and in short the exact *opposite* of what it represents: fluid poems in Greek meters, made to hold the imprint of a passing hour! It has 'humor' (if that word were not too heavy, the quality too subtle), yet at the same time it thrills by the power of its description of the passing of time.[47] Next, when he says, "I will not all die," we *know* that he *knows* that he will wholly die; worms will crawl in his eye-sockets! We know this from the way he puts it: "many pieces of me/will evade Libitina," for Libitina is not Death; she is only the patron goddess of the guild of Roman undertakers.

When Horace says, "for forever quickened/by new praise I shall grow" (6-7), there too is a subtle humor, for he means that literally. He is again subtly echoing Pindar, who in many places likens a man's posthumous fame to a plant, watered by the dew of a poet's praise.[48] Again, 'humor' is scarcely the right word. This image of verse growing, sprouting 'fresh' leaves every time it is praised again, has truth and depth.

But subtlest, greatest, most alive of all are the last seven lines (10-16). The Aufidus is a rough little river in Horace's native Apulia; Daunus, a legendary king of that place. My translation here is very literal. Horace says that *there*, where the Aufidus roars, people will say something of him. One suspects that they will not! In that rustic, sparsely peopled, unfamous province, scarcely anyone will even know what

'Aeolic' meter is.[49] This, too, is subtlest irony. I say 'subtlest' because his larger claim is simply, movingly true: his verse *will* last far longer than even the Roman empire, and for exactly the reasons he names.

What, exactly, are these reasons? That he was first "to shape the verse of Italy/out of Aeolic song." Or more literally "first to lead out" (*deducere*, as if founding a colony) Aeolic song to Italian meters. This poem has half a dozen brilliant transferred epithets,[50] but this double transfer is the most astonishing, for what he really means is the opposite: Aeolic meters, Italian song. But the bold reversal 'works' because, in the last analysis, it means the same and is more beautiful, for it makes us see how utterly his love has knit the two unlike things.

This is a strange sort of supreme climax: that he was the first Italian to imitate Greek meters![51] But when done with the rapt, minute attentiveness of a Horace, imitation is a form of love. As Joseph Brodsky said once, "The more you steal, the more you have!" 'Greek meters' are a figure for Horace's love of all that Greek poetry stood for. For when love (not merely a 'taste' for something but rapt love) imitates what it seems to see, the result is always wholly original. The more raptly an Italian imitates a Greek, the more palpably Italian he will seem.

This is why the poem touches us; why in spite of its "I...I...I..." it too, like Pindar, is self-oblivious. More real than Horace, more important even than his skill, is simple love, which after all is a thing much greater than poetry.

The subtle humor, or irony, of Vergil and Horace, though often it seems not noticed by modern readers, is magical because it does full justice to *both* truths, truths that are in tension and might even seem irreconcilable: (a) that poetry is a sacred thing and the poet sacred, a Greek insight that they could not forget and could not give up; and (b) that in Roman reality, compared with a general or an Augustus, a 'great poet' is rather absurd, merely someone who "blossoms in the ignoble arts of quietness."

So it seems fitting to end this quietly, by quoting *Ode* 4.3, the most 'private' poem ever written by Horace or perhaps any other Roman. It dates to c. 17 B.C., two years after the death of Vergil. It is true that one seems to discern in it the results of public success,[52] yet that is less important than an antithesis that the poem quietly makes between *all* public honors or functions, even the greatest, and the intense, mysterious privacy of the poetic gift. One senses that Horace felt scarcely worthy of that gift; the poem is touching because, rather strangely in this normally agnostic poet, it seems a real prayer. Here I shall quote the English first so as to end with the beautiful, beautiful Latin verses:

> Whomever, Melpomene,
> in his hour of birth your quiet eye has watched
> no Isthmian toil exalts
> as boxer, nor can swift Greek horses lead him
> to victory in a chariot 5
> nor will a deed of war, because he crushed
> the swollen threats of kings,
> display him, as a general laurel-wreathed,
> to the high Capitol;
> but the wild waters of abundant Tivoli 10
> and dense leaves of the forests
> will shape him noble with Aeolic song.
> At Rome, the prince of cities,
> the people think me worthy to belong
> to the dear choirs of prophets 15
> and Envy's tooth already bites me less.
> Pierian girl who quietly
> temper the sweet din of the Golden Shell,
> and even to mute fish
> could give at will the deep voice of a swan, 20
> all that I am *you* made,
> and that each stranger's finger points at me
> as the harp-player of Rome
> inspired to please, if I please, is from you.[53]

Quem tu, Melpomene, semel,
   nascentem placido lumine videris,
illum non labor Isthmius
   clarabit pugilem, non equos inpiger
curru ducet Achaico 5
   victorem neque res bellica Deliis
ornatum foliis ducem,
   quod regum tumidas contuderit minas,
ostendet Capitolio:
   sed quae Tibur aquae fertile praefluunt 10
et spissae nemorum comae

> fingent Aeolio carmine nobilem.
> Romae principis urbium
>   dignatur suboles inter amabilis
> vatum ponere me choros 15
>   et iam dente minus mordeor invido.
> o testudinis aureae
>   dulcem quae strepitum, Pieri, temperas,
> o mutis quoque piscibus
>   donatura cycni, si libeat, sonum, 20
> totum muneris hoc tui est,
>   quod monstror digito praetereuntium
> Romanae fidicen lyrae:
>   quod spiro et placeo, si placeo, tuum'st.

Notes

1. All translations are mine unless otherwise noted. Abbreviations of their titles: *Aen.* = *Aeneid*; D. = Diehl (i.e., Alcman fragment number assigned by Diehl, other Alcman numbers those of Page); fr. = fragment; *Geo.* = *Georgics*; *I.* = *Isthmian*; *N.* = *Nemean*; *O.* = *Olympian*; *Od.* = *Odyssey*; *P.* = *Pythian*; Sn. = Snell (i.e., Pindaric fragment number assigned by Snell, *Pindari Carmina*, other numbers those of Bowra, *Pindari Carmina*).

2. On my epigraph see West 122: "The preliminary notes of the lyre serve as a signal and guide to dancers and singers." He compares Homer, *Od.* 1.155, 8.266, 17.261-63.

3. The seasons thrillingly *are* men's footsteps at Vergil, *Geo.* 2.403-4: "redit agricolis labor actus in orbem,/atque in se sua per uestigia uoluitur annus" ("Their labor done returns to farmers, circling/As the year turning steps in its own footprints").

4. Lewis and Short s.v.: "*uersus*...a turning round, i.e. of the plow"; hence a furrow; hence a line of writing; a verse; and "IV. *A kind of dance*, or a *turn, step, pas* in a dance, Plaut. *Stich.* 5, 7, 2." Greek *strophe* meant a 'turning' of the dancing chorus (it came to mean 'stanza' because each such turn was a metrical unit); and curiously, Pindar compares this with the turning of a plowman in a field! (See, e.g., *N.* 6.33 "plowmen of the Pierian Muses" and Maurer, "Index" I.10.)

5. 'Quantitative' refers to the 'lengths' of syllables, i.e., how long it takes to say each syllable.

6. In the last two lines of his poem to Vergil, Tennyson calls him "Wielder of the stateliest measure/ever moulded by the lips of man." This is moving because it catches both things: in "stateliest measure" his music, and in "wielder" and "moulded by the lips" his living speech. Academics, less astute, tend to imagine Vergil inventing his verse cerebrally, as they do their papers; but he wrote with his hearing. There is an ancient anecdote about this, which seems authentic, in Donatus's *Vita Vergiliana*, Chap. 22: "It is said that when he wrote the Georgics, his habit was to dictate very many verses which he had pondered in the morning, and in revising them throughout the day, to reduce them to a very small number, saying wittily that he give birth to his poem as a mother bear did, that he shaped it just by licking it (ursae more...et lambendo demum effingere)."

7. Ennius's epitaph was imitated by later Roman poets, e.g., Vergil, *Geo.* 3.8-9: "temptanda via est, qua me quoque possim/tollere humo uictorque uirum uolitare per ora" ("to find a path, by which I too may fly/from earth and flit, victorious, through men's mouths").

8. The Muses are daughters of Zeus. The *locus classicus* is Hesiod, *Theogony*, 1-90; but even for someone as late as Pindar, the 'Muse' was not a mere figure of speech. Apropos of the much later antithesis between Reason and Revelation, Eric Voegelin has a good remark worth quoting: "Throughout the entire ethnic history of the Hellenes, from the time we have literary records—that is, since Hesiod—every Hellenic thinker was aware that what he had to say came, not from his natural reason, but from divine revelation. Further, he was aware that he lived in the tension of seeking and receiving, that is to say, in the dual movement of the godly and human type, in which a human *responsio* takes place in answer to a movement that originates in God. All of Hellenic culture, from Hesiod to Plato and Aristotle, is conscious of this revelatory moment....The assertion that it was a matter of natural reason is a crude and inadmissible falsification of the historical documents" (388).

9. On this passage, see Snell 281-82.

10. On Greek public festivals and choral lyric, see especially Fränkel 159-70 (on Alcman); see also Bowra, *Greek Lyric Poetry* 16-73 (on Alcman). Less sound, yet pithy, are Calame's *Les Choeurs* and *Alcman*. Of ancient sources the most revealing seems Plutarch's *Life of Lycurgus*.

11. Alcman elsewhere, in a cosmogonic poem now lost, made the Muses daughters of Ge and Ouranos (Earth and Sky). Fränkel thinks he did this so that they could witness the events in his cosmogony. Perhaps, but such importance given to the Muses is not peculiar to Alcman; according to Plutarch's *Lycurgus*, the Spartans had public shrines to them and even sacrificed to them before battle.

12. The Greek word μέλος, which I translated 'song,' might also mean 'tune' or 'tone'; Fränkel thinks he refers to the flute melody.

13. From a papyrus fragment published in 1957 (P. Oxy. 2387). Fränkel 169, n. 26: "The much-mutilated text allows us less to see than to guess at some very remarkable things." The whole poem apparently had fourteen stanzas, or 126 lines, and was apparently a *partheneion*, perhaps for a festival for Hera. The girl's name, Astymeloisa, means 'a care for the people.'

14. Uncertainty about the speaker haunts all Greek choral lyric, even Pindar and the choral odes of tragedy. For surveys of the evidence, see e.g., Lefkowitz, "Who Sang Pindar's Victory Odes?" and *First-Person Fictions*.

15. About how "Heracles slew the sons of Hippocoon, a usurper of the Spartan throne, and restored it to its rightful tenant, Tyndareus, who may have helped in the slaughter" (Podlecki).

16. The name Hagesichora also *means* 'chorus leader.' Many scholars (e.g., Nagy) rashly deduce from this that the name is fictional. But *most* Greek names were like this; so Demosthenes = "having force with the people," Pericles = "illustrious," Socrates = "sane strength," and so on.

17. My translation, using stressed syllables for long ones and unstressed for short, closely imitates the complicated Greek meter.

18. How is the goddess a doctor? And in what sense have they got, through Hagesichora, "longed-for peace"? Calame and Gentili think that this means sexual satisfaction! But probably it means simply that in the past with Hagesichora's help they won some longed-for prize; cf. a similar place, the bewitching first verses of Pindar, *Nemean* 4 (for a victorious wrestler): "Of troubles [i.e., the toil and trouble of contests] that have been decided, the best doctor is good cheer; and songs, those wise (σοφαι) daughters of the Muses, massage and soothe! Even warm water melts the limbs less than does praise (εὐλογία) linked with the lyre." "Good cheer" is *Euphrosyne*, the victory celebration, personified as if it were a goddess, which is very like Alcman's "lovely Peace."

19. He was honored of course especially by Spartans. See, e.g., Plutarch's *Lycurgus*: "And...when the Thebans made their invasion into Laconia, and took a great number of the Helots [i.e., in effect, Spartan slaves], they could by no means persuade them to sing the verses of Terpander, Alcman, or Spendon, 'For,' said they, 'the masters do not like it'" (121).

20. Quoted by Antigonus of Carystus, *Mirabilia* 23; its meter is dactyllic hexameter, and it is probably again from a prelude, sung by the poet himself before a girls' choral performance (Campbell 217). Bowra thinks that since "bird dances were not uncommon in Greece" these verses refer to a chorus of girls who actually imitate halcyons (*Greek Lyric* 24). One could suspect this too in the partridges of fr. 49. Choral mimesis seems described also in the *Homeric Hymn to Apollo*: "The tongues of all humans and their clattering speech/they [the girls' choruses] imitate as they sing: each would say that he himself/were speaking, so close to him is their sweet song" (162-64).

21. Pindar is addressing the chorus trainer.

22. The "Castor song" is probably another poem, which the poet promises to send later (see Burton 122-23). But some think that it was "an old Spartan battle song, the rhythm anapaestic...the mood Doric, the accompaniment the flute" and that "P. uses it as a [horseman's song] in honor of victory with horse and chariot...the mood is Aiolian, and the accompaniment the [phorminx]" (so Gildersleeve ad loc.; in brackets are my translations of the Greek words he quotes).

23. ἐμὲ δ' ἐξαίρετον/<u>κήρυκα</u> σοφῶν ἐπέων/Μοῖσ' ἀνέστασ' Ἑλλάδι καλλιχόρῳ·

24. Aineas is an Athenian chorus trainer. A scroll-wand was used by the Spartans for coded messages. As Mullen says, around it "a commander winds slantwise a leather strip; the letters of the dispatch are then written vertically, so that only a commander with a baton of exactly the same thickness will be able to match the letters up...and read the message. This is an intricate metaphor for an exarchon standing in the midst of a band of dancers that 'winds about' him; because he is an exact equivalent for the poet himself, the audience can interpret the evolutions of the dance and 'read off' from them correctly the meaning of the poet's words" (36). But plainly, the image *also* means that Pindar himself transmits the *Muses'* intentions exactly.

25. "Underground minds" (χθονίᾳ φρενί), i.e., "with such mind as the dead possess" (Gildersleeve ad loc.).

26. For other places where verses are arrows, see Maurer, "Index" IV. 1-2, esp. *O.* 9.5-14. *O.* 2.83 ff. was loved and movingly imitated by Osip Mandelstam at the end of stanza 7 of his "Slate Ode" (my translation):

> For the firm instant's right I write,
> Trade a steep noise for arrows' singing,
> Trade order for an eagle's winging.

27. The herald reappears in lines 15-18. The poem is a messenger, announcing this victory "to the speech of mortals." Compare *O.* 11.4-8 (italics mine): "If anyone fares well from toil, sweet-tongued songs,/*those beginnings of later tales* (ὑστέρων ἀρχὰ λόγων),/a trusty pledge of excellence, are given!/As praise beyond envy for Olympic victory/they are stored away."

28. Why "plow"? Because a man's posthumous fame is a tender plant, of which Pindar is now about to plant the seed. See Maurer "Index" I.2-4 and 9-10; and cf. Horace *Ode* 3.30.8 discussed in section IV of this essay.

29. See Burton 18-19. He compares *O.* 6.1-4: "Even as by setting up pillars of gold for a well-built forecourt,/men make a courtyard wondrous, so, when beginning any work,/one must make its brow far-shining." Curiously, this passage too was dear to Mandelstam. In his "Horseshoe Ode" (subtitled "A Pindaric Fragment") he beautifully, probably unconsciously, combined it with the headband of *N.* 8.14-15 (quoted earlier) to get: "Thrice blest is he/who puts a name in his song. A song adorned with a name/lives longer than others. She is marked among

friends by the fillet on her brow/that saves her from fainting, from any overstrong, stupefying scent/whether from a man's nearness/or from the fur of a strong animal, or simply the smell of savory rubbed between the palms" (trans. Brown, in Clarence Brown 290).

30. Words like ἴδιος and δημόσιος were never, so far as I know, applied to works of art.

31. See Snell, Chaps.12 and 13. In Callimachus the change is still inchoate and tentative; it becomes unmistakable only in his Roman imitators.

32. I.e., Cato, Varro, Pliny, Columella. We can discern from exact echoes that Vergil often consulted the first two; Pliny and Columella came after him and quote him but are in the same tradition. See also the Greek passages quoted at length in Mynors' edition of the *Georgics* (Vergil 325-33).

33. Lines 284-85 could be a motto for the entire poem, or even for poetry itself: "sed fugit interea, fugit inreparabile tempus/singula dum capti circumvectamur amore." The phrase "singula...circumvectamur" is scarcely translatable; he has in mind, I think, a bee or a butterfly hovering over a flower.

34. Cf. 2.475-93, a similar but more complex, more famous passage; also 1.41-42.

35. The *Georgics* were published in 29 B.C. In 30 B.C., by *threatening* war, Augustus negotiated the return to Rome of the standards that the Parthians had taken from Crassus at the battle of Carrhae (53 B.C.). See, e.g., Suetonius, *Augustus*, 21.3, and Syme 301-2. For a view similar to mine both of this passage and of *Aen.* 6.847-53 quoted later, see Griffin 65, 72-73.

36. "Others" (847) plainly means the Greeks. "Sing stars as they rise" (850) could mean not astronomy (that is in the preceding phrase) but the changing of the seasons (since each constellation 'rises' at a different time of year). "Study" (851) = "memento"; one could also translate that as "remember."

37. For a union, in Vergil's imagination, of art and science, see also, e.g., *Geo.* 2.475-92.

38. The source of trouble is that this 'art' of empire is *not* the art of politics, which, one senses, it here wants to be; and it did not, in fact, nourish the other arts. Every art without exception was born and blossomed in tiny, warring city-states; and the long imperial peace made a barren wasteland of every one of them. For a striking *Roman* analysis of this, and even a sadness akin to Vergil's, see Tacitus, *Dialogue on Oratory,* chaps. 39-41. See also Syme, on the so-called Augustan poets: "Their genius was not the creation of the Augustan Principate. They had all grown to manhood and to maturity in the period of the Revolution; and they all repaid Augustus more than he or the age could ever give them" (465).

39. For a *Roman* on the sacredness of a poet's vocation, see Vergil, *Geo.* 2.475ff.; also Horace, *Odes* 4.3 (quoted at the end of this essay), 3.4 (esp. 9ff.), 2.13, and 4.2 (which also reveals the depth of his love of Pindar); also Snell, Chap. 13.

40. See, for example, the clumsy, powerful passage in Hesiod, *Theogony* 80-97, where the same Muses who instructed Hesiod also instruct just kings. And Pindar, in passages too many to cite, simply took his own regal authority for granted.

41. θεόλογος, a word used of Hesiod by Aristotle (*Metaph.* 1000^{a}9; 1071^{b}27; 1026^{a}19).

42. See Aristotle, *Ath. Pol.*, Chaps. 5-12, and Fränkel 220-27. Horace often imitates Solon, especially fr. 1 (= 13W, the Hymn to the Muses), e.g., in *Odes* 1.1 and 3.1.

43. Very influential has been, e.g., Syme 461-62: "The new Roman literature was designed to be civic rather than individual, more useful than ornamental. Horace...exerted himself to establish the movement upon a firm basis of theory....The New State had [in Horace] its lyric poet, technically superb....More naturally came the moral, rustic and patriotic vein to the poet Virgil." This, I think, is superficial and deeply misleading.

44. Both suggested by hints in Callimachus. See Snell, Chaps. 12, 13.

45. Horace, *Odes* 3.1: "Profanum vulgus odi et arceo..." (see the discussion of Snell, 303-4). Similar is Vergil, *Geo.* 2.475: "Me uero primum dulcem ante omnia Musae/*quarum sacra fero* ingenti percussus amore" ("But me, you Muses, sweet above all things!/w*hose rites I carry*, pierced with immense love"). On the poet's solitude, see also Horace, *Odes* 2.20 and *Epistle* 1.19.20-48, and Maurer, "*Notiora Fallaciora*" 155-56.

46. There is a brazenly open, yet very great, imitation of them at Ovid, *Met.* 15.871-79.

47. Notice also that in 7ff. Horace can imagine the death of the Roman empire, even though it would last for centuries more, whereas Pindar seems never to imagine that archaic Hellenic culture could utterly vanish, though it did within decades of his death. The reason for the difference is that Horace, unlike Pindar, lived in what Voegelin called "the Ecumenic Age" and had seen or sensed the fall of world-empires, Persian, Greek, Carthaginian, Egyptian, Parthian (cf. Vergil, "regna peritura," *Geo.* 2.498).

48. See Maurer "Index" I.2-4 and 9-10.

49. 'Aeolic' were the meters of Lesbos, i.e., of Alcaeus (Horace's favorite Greek poet) and Sappho. Compare *Odes* 1.1.33-34 *Lesboum barbiton* (Horace's 'Lesbian lute'); 1.26.1 *Lesbio plectro* (Lesbian plectrum); 1.32.4-5 *barbite Lesbio*; 4.3.12 *Aeolio carmine* (Aeolian song).

50. E.g., 2 *regali* ('royal' should logically modify pyramids); 4 *innumerabilis* ('not numberable' should modify years); 8 *recens* ('fresh' should modify praise); 11 *pauper* ('poor' should modify people).

51. See above all *Epist.* I, 19, 19ff. where first he expresses maximum scorn for the "servile tribe" of his own imitators and then, in words that it would

be impossible to strengthen, boasts of his own complete originality—which consists precisely of *imitating* Greek meters! E.g., 23ff. "I first showed Latium/the iambs of Paros," i.e., the meters of Archilochus. See Maurer "*Notiora Fallaciora*" 154-55.

52. Lines 22-23 seem to refer to an honor he won in 17 B.C., of writing the *Carmen saeculare* for the city's *Ludi saeculares*. On this see the stirring description of Lanciani (73ff.).

53. The bewitching Latin meter is a mix of Glyconic (short lines) and major Asclepiad (long lines). "Isthmian toil" (2) echoes Pindar (as any Roman would notice instantly). See, e.g., *O.* 11.3, *N.* 4.1 both quoted earlier. "Tibur" (10), modern Tivoli, was near Horace's Sabine farm; he loved it partly for the waterfalls of the Anio (as did Propertius; cf. Prop. 3.16.4 "et cadit in patulos nympha Aniena lacus" ["and the nymph Anio falls in spreading pools"]). "Golden Shell" (18): the tortoise shell from which Hermes made the first lyre. "Temper the sweet din" (18) echoes many places in Pindar, who loved describing the 'cry' of the flutes and the din, boom, hubbub (θόρυβος, θρόος, etc.) of the many-voiced hymn; see Maurer, "Index" V.3. My translation here is literal, but one could also take *dulcis* predicatively: "temper sweet (i.e., into a sweetness) the din of the Golden Shell."

3

From Nothing to Being:
Medieval Lyric and Poetic Form as Entelechy

GREGORY ROPER

In the typical story of Western literature, lyric is reborn after the loss of ancient Roman poetry through the work of the troubadour poets writing in Provence in the eleventh century.[1] It is not a terribly accurate picture, for lyric poetry survived the fall of Rome in many places and in many modes.[2] But the strong sense remains that *something* important happened when Provençal poets gathered influences and poetic modes from Arabic Spain and carried them across the Pyrenees to the courts of a newly prosperous and (more or less) stable Christian Europe. Part of that sense comes from the undeniable fact that these poets' subject matter and lyric modes became the most influential across Europe for the next three (and one might even say six or more) centuries. The language, the subject matter, and, equally important, the lyric forms of *fin amours* became the poetic *lingua franca* of medieval Europe, eventually forming the essential foundation of the work of Dante, Petrarch, and, through the latter, the entire English early modern lyric tradition. The poets of their own time considered those who wrote in this tradition, among them Bernard de Ventadorn, Jaufre Rudel, Marcabrun, and Arnaut Daniel, to be the finest of their time, and critical opinion today still agrees. In these poems, often love and poetry intertwine, for as there is an art of poetry, so is there an art of love: there are rules of behavior, forms of conduct and address, that give shape to and refine one's experience of love. "Ieu sui Arnautz, q'amas l'aura/E chatz la lebre ab lo bou,/E nadi contra suberna," Arnaut writes at the end of his poem "En cest sonnet coind'e leri": "I am Arnaut, who gathers the wind, and hunts the hare on oxback, and swims against the rising tide" (Press 184),[3] and it is difficult initially to know whether he is writing about his pursuit of love or his writing of the poem. It only takes a second more of reflection to realize he assuredly means both. Love and language, the formless and the formed, passion and reason, love as that which makes one mad and love as that which ennobles, form the poles of so much of this verse and give the poets such remarkably fertile fields in which to test their poetic skill and create more complex forms in the competitive worlds of the court poetry of this day.

But it is a poem not so specifically about the persona's love interest that fascinates me the most in this tradition, a strange poem by one of the earlier troubadour poets, the nobleman William IX:[4]

Farai un vers de dreyt nien:	I'll make a poem of sheer nothingness;
Non er de mi ni d'autra gen,	it will not be about me, or about any other;
Non er d'amor ni de joven,	it will not be of love, or of youth,
Ni de ren au;	or of anything else;
Qu'enans fo trobatz en durmen	it was, rather, composed while sleeping
Sobre chevau.	on a horse.
No sai en qual guiza.m fuy natz:	I know not in what way I was born;
No suy alegres ni iratz,	I am neither gay nor downhearted,
No suy estrayns ni sui privatz,	neither a stranger nor a familiar friend,
Ni no.n puesc au;	nor can I do aught else,
Qu'enaissi fuy de nueitz fadatz	for thus was I charmed by night,
Sobr'un pueg au.	on a high hill.
No sai quora.m suy endormitz,	I know not when I sleep, or when
Ni quora.m velh, s'om no m'o ditz.	I wake, unless someone tells me so;
Per pauc no m'es lo cor partitz	by very little has my heart not broken
D'un dol corau.	With a deep sorrow.
E no m'o pretz una soritz,	And I care not a mouse for that,
Per sanh Marsau!	By Saint Martial!
Malautz suy e tremi murir,	Sick I am and fear to die,
E ren no sai mas quan n'aug dir;	and know nothing but what I hear tell of it;
Metge querrai, al mieu albir,	I'll seek a doctor, of my way of thinking,
E no.m sai tau;	and I know not such a one;
Bos metges er si.m pot guerir,	he'll be a good doctor, if he can cure me,
Mas ja non, si amau.	but never, if I grow worse.

Amigu'au ieu, no sai qui s'es,	I have a loved one, I don't know who she is,
Qu'ance non la vi, si m'ajut fes!	For I've never seen her, so help me by my faith!
Ni.m fes que.m plassa ni que.m pes,	She has done nothing to please me or to grieve me,
Ni no m'en cau,	nor am I bothered about it,
Qu'anc non ac Norman ni Frances	for I never had Norman or Frenchman
Dins mon ostau.	in my house.
Anc non la vi et am la fort,	I've never seen her and I love her dearly;
Anc no n'aic dreyt ni no.m fes tort;	I've never had right from her, nor has she done me any wrong;
Quan non la vey, be m'en deport,	when I do not see her, I get along quite well,
No.m pretz un jau,	I don't think it's worth a rooster!
Qu'ie.n sai gensor et bellazor,	For I know one more noble and more lovely,
E que mais vau.	and who is worth more.
Fag ai lo vers, no say de cuy;	I've made this poem, I know not of what;
E trametrai lo a selhuy	and I'll send it to him
Que lo.m trametra per autruy	who will send it on for me by another,
Lay vers Anjau,	yonder, towards Anjou,
Que.m tramezes del sieu estuy	that he might send it back to me, from his own wallet
La contraclau.	the key to it.

(Press 15-16)

What could such a poem be doing? What is the point of this riddle of a text? And how can we call it worth reading, since it is, as the speaker himself declares, about nothing?

Scholarly criticism has consistently seen this poem as one it must engage even when surveying the entirety of the troubadour tradition; it has been a crucial case study for historical, psychosexual, formal, feminist, and other forms of criticism.[5] To do justice to all of the critical history is beyond my space and purpose here, but clearly on one level "Farai un vers" is a parody of so many features of *fin amours* lyric that were, it would seem, already conventions in William's time. He opens by stating not the topic of the poem, as so many of these poems do, but that it has no topic; he announces that unlike conventional poems, his is not about the speaker or his love. Youth, that fundamental subject matter of love poetry, he sets aside along with anything else. The very act of composition and its occasion, so often the first mention in these lyrics, he mocks.[6] It is not May or spring, and he is not in a garden but asleep and riding on his horse.[7] In the second stanza he denies any biography for the speaking persona; in the third he denies that fundamental *topos* of the *fin amours* lover-poet, the broken heart and great sorrow that provide the motivation and energy for so much compositional effort.[8] The poem continues throughout in this vein, even mocking the traditional *envoi* by sending it to "whomever." He ends not by promising the key to this most closed of *trobar clus* lyrics but by proclaiming that someone else will have to send it to *him*. But the poem seems to go beyond mere mocking parody; it is, it declares, about nothing ("de dreyt nien"), it was composed while the poet was asleep and thus conveys no intention ("Qu'enans fo trobatz en durmen/Sobre chevau"), and the poet does not even know what it is made of ("Fag ai lo vers, no say de cuy").

A pedagogical digression will help me develop my argument at this point. When I teach this poetry in my classes in medieval literature, I explain to the students that, as far as medievalists have been able to determine, no real historical person ever acted in the way the *fin amours* poets repeatedly describe. That is, earlier historians who took *fin amours* texts as describing what actual eleventh-century humans did in their courts, their gardens, and their bedrooms were, we now know, quite wrong.[9] What a *fin amours* lyric describes, it would seem, is a set of literary conventions perhaps vaguely resembling reality but, more important, powerfully shaping the possibilities for subject matter, persona, imagery, diction, and more. The abject lover; the distant, cool, yet demanding woman as a love object; the time of spring, May, gardens, birds singing, flowers blooming; the speaker's desire to become worthy of this woman who disdains him in his current state; the need to take all of this frustrated psychic energy and turn it into finely chiseled verse—this is the stuff, not of life, but of powerful poetic conventions that both give artists a field in which to play and establish standards by which audiences can measure formal, artistic accomplishment.

The closest analogue we might have, I tell the students, is the *noir* detective film, whose conventions they all know intimately (though upon being questioned many admit they have not seen the great initial examples of the genre or read any Dashiell Hammett): the world-weary detective, his worn shoes propped on a beaten wooden desk and a revolver and a bottle of whiskey in the bottom right-hand desk drawer, facing the "gorgeous dame" (conventions go all the way down to particular diction, I remind them) who claims to be in terrible, terrible trouble yet is, all of the students know, ultimately going to prove treacherous. All of them know the conventions superbly well, though they cannot tell where they learned them, and all of them know just as well that no real detective actually lives like this or does any of these things. And they know that the pleasure in watching the films that play on these conventions (for instance, *Blade Runner* or *L.A. Confidential*) lies precisely in recognizing the artful way the writer and director have inhabited and played with the conventions.

This is the world of *fin amours*: a set of clearly defined conventions that allow the poets to compete in displaying their poetic skill. And they did compete, either as nobles with one another in more-or-less friendly after-dinner play or as traveling *minnesänger* hoping to achieve positions at court. Consequently in the *fin amours* lyric tradition there was an enormous focus on form. This was one of the great periods of formal inventiveness in Western verse: the villanelle, the sestina, and the sonnet were all invented by these poets and their successors. Any artistic field with careful and strict conventions lends itself to irony and parody, surely (many of the students, upon reflection, realize they learned *film noir* conventions from the Muppets or children's animated comedies), but such an artistic world also creates a marvelous focus upon artistry, upon *techne*, form itself, and upon the shaping imagination.

Seen in this light, "Farai un vers" becomes not the exception to the *fin amours* lyric tradition, or just a parody of it, but a kind of extension of it, taking its premises to their limits. If *fin amours* lyrics are not about reality but about their own conventions, William seems to suggest, if they point not outward but to themselves, then what might be the challenge of stripping all content from the poem, of making a poem about *nothing*? So William tries, providing us with no content whatsoever: "Non er de mi ni d'autra gen,/Non er d'amor ni de joven,/Ni de ren au" ("it will not be about me, or about any other; it will not be of love, or of youth, or of anything else"). The poem denies the speaker any personal history ("No sai en qual guiza.m fuy natz": "I know not in what way I was born"), emotional content ("No suy alegres ni iratz": "I am neither gay nor downhearted"), or relation ("No suy estrayns ni sui privatz": "neither a stranger nor a familiar friend"). He cannot do anything else, it would seem, but write, an act to which he was "charmed," so that writing seems to be the whole of his being ("Ni no.n puesc au;/Qu'enaissi fuy de nueitz fadatz/Sobr'un pueg au": "nor can I do aught else, for thus was I charmed by night, on a high hill"). The poem continues in this vein for four more stanzas before the speaker announces, as I noted earlier, that he has made the poem but does not even know of what the poem is made, that he has not the key to unlock or explain it, and that he would be happy for someone else to provide it ("Que.m tramezes del sieu estuy/La contraclau": "that he might send back to me, from his own wallet, the key to it").

The poem is, one could say, William's deliberate attempt to frustrate our attempts to find *meaning*, content, extractable statement. And what does it offer in return? The brilliance of its formal play, which even those without a full knowledge of Provençal but perhaps just a smattering of other Romance languages can see throughout the poem or in the lines just quoted; the meter and rhythm and end-rhyme so artfully handled, of course, but also plays on "trametrai"/"trametra"/"tramezes"; the notion that "Anjau" might be a key to the "contraclau" with yet the suspicion that Anjou is a blind, a red herring; the brilliant play of pronouns and their referents—all these in a musical verse that itself plays across the sounds and rhythms of the words. This formal excellence is not just a feature of the last stanza; it is fundamental to the stunning, playful accomplishment throughout. It is, I must say, a masterful lyric.

I should say that students in my classes sometimes begin to look at me at this point not just in disbelief or dismissal but in anger, and once even real outrage: how could I be praising a poem about nothing? Should not great art be about great questions and themes and human problems? Surely Homer, Yeats, Shakespeare, Milton, wrote about *some*thing; and that they wrote about something significant, and said something significant about those topics, is what makes their art great, they argue. "Farai un vers" might be clever, even technically accomplished, they say, but not great art.

But can't something just be beautiful? I ask. Can't there just be a beautiful line, a leaf, a streak of clouds, and it not mean anything, just be beautiful? What about my tie? I ask (for I now make sure, as I dress before this class, to wear a tie with a non-representational pattern). Don't you like it? Don't you say, "what a nice tie you have on today!" referring not to its content but its formal beauties? Don't you say a dress is beautiful when you like its cut, its color, its pattern, and you do not ask what it means? Is Beauty really a second-rank transcendental, running behind the True and the Good? Is Beauty worthwhile only if it leads us to the other two? That is, is the good of Beauty only instrumental?

We are deep into the fundamental questions of Western aesthetics here, I tell them, and the answers are not so simple. And is this not, I say to them and I suggest now, what lyric always does, and what it does best? Lyric is that genre which highlights form most of all, which, in its brevity and focus on the speaker, the moment, the emotional state, sees that the poet's main job is *poiesis*, making, that is, shaping and forming in order to create beauty and, yes, meaning—yet the meaning is in the formed matter, *is* the forming of the matter.

To see meaning in the forming of the matter, one can do worse than consider one of the great lyric poets of the latter half of the twentieth century attempting for her only time the villanelle, a form invented in the hothouse of medieval Provençal's poetic competition:

One Art

The art of losing isn't hard to master;
so many things seem filled with the intent
to be lost that their loss is no disaster.

Lose something every day. Accept the fluster
of lost door keys, the hour badly spent.
The art of losing isn't hard to master.

Then practice losing farther, losing faster:
places, and names, and where it was you meant
to travel. None of these will bring disaster.

I lost my mother's watch. And look! my last, or
next-to-last, of three loved houses went.
The art of losing isn't hard to master.

I lost two cities, lovely ones. And, vaster,
some realms I owned, two rivers, a continent.
I miss them, but it wasn't a disaster.

—Even losing you (the joking voice, a gesture
 love) I shan't have lied. It's evident
the art of losing's not too hard to master
though it may look like (*Write* it!) like disaster.

(Bishop, *Complete Poems* 178)

One could admit, perhaps, that the subject matter is not all that terribly original: Elizabeth Bishop is writing about the problem—the subject of Oprah Winfrey talk-show sessions and self-help books by the score—of "letting go," of enduring grief and the consonant emotional wreckage subsequent to loss of any kind. Poets have written about grief and grieving innumerable times. What makes it a marvelous poem, so heartbreaking, so moving, so painful, and yes, so beautiful, of course, is the beauty of the formed way, the villanelle, through which Bishop brings us this knowledge. I will not attempt a full and complete reading of the poem, but gesturing at a few of its excellences should make my point.

The first stanza seems to state simply and clearly its intentions, its content, as if she is laying out a thesis, which the villanelle structure then shades and deepens throughout the poem, contradicting the easy confidence of this statement not through further statement but through inference and shape and subtlety. The second stanza seduces us into more of this confidence, as the speaker changes to the imperative with a simple four-word sentence: "Lose something every day." The odd contrast of "door keys" and the less concrete, more troubling "hour badly spent" hints at more than the structure seems to be letting on, but the end of the stanza confidently returns to assurance in the smartly stated refrain. Yet as each of the two refrain lines gets repeated, and as the list of things lost gets larger, even fantastic—two cities, a continent—the desperation with which the speaker asserts that losing "isn't hard to master" becomes evident. And her balancing of end-stopped and enjambed lines produces the unsettling effects Bishop intends: a simple statement like "I lost my mother's watch" at first seems innocent, a claim of the possession's insignificance, until it contrasts and then echoes the loss that spills over the end of that line, not of any house, but the specific "next-to-last" of "three loved houses," and we readers discover the depth of meaning of both watch and too-casually mentioned house. By the fifth stanza, the refrain allows the speaker to admit "I miss them" yet defensively assert that "it wasn't a disaster." All of this sets up the astonishingly well-crafted final stanza, where the speaker shifts back from the global to the personal and local, from continents to a particular voice and gesture. The pain of this final loss echoes throughout the poem, giving the lie even before the final line's forced interjection "(*Write* it!)" and the stuttering repetition of "like" show the desperation with which the speaker is trying to convince herself of the double refrain's serene conclusions.

It is the villanelle structure, that is, conveying as it does the pain and effort of containing grief—and the failure and effort of denying that pain and effort and failure—that gives the poem its power and poignancy and beauty. We know what Bishop is saying, not as extractable content journalistically murdered in other settings, but as something new, because of the way of knowing through and in the poem's form. And her title cements this in our mind, for by comparing the art of poetry to the art of grieving, she shows that mere *techne* is irremediably consigned to failure: art is not merely a question of mastery of technical means; form comes from seeing deeply into the nature of things that "seem filled with the intent/to be lost."

Since lyrical *content* is not so much the point, then, the lyric is always moving in one way toward "nothing," toward a kind of purity and away from reference, toward an emphasis not on its subject matter but its form, toward, that is, the condition of music, which itself is always tending away from content. (I take it as axiomatic that even program music, the most representational kind of music evoking birdsong or horses' hooves or devils dancing on a mountain, is always moving toward the condition of pure song, pure sound.) One might even say that it is the essence and *task* of lyric as a genre to strip down, pare down, until what is left is form, sound, voice, meter, syntax, rhythm, so that we see the essence of *poiesis* as a mode of thought and not just frills on the more important content. Lyric envies music in this way, and in its own explorations of the sounds, rhythms, and play of words, it wants to become what its etymological roots say it should be: the sound of the lyre.[10] In this way, "Farai un vers" becomes, not just a great lyric, but a kind of *ur-lyric*, pointing to the radical (I mean the adjective in all its senses) nature of lyric. At another time, for instance in the early twentieth century, the movement in lyrical radicalism was toward the visual, toward the *image* stripped of all content, as in William Carlos Williams's poem "The Red Wheelbarrow" or Pound's haiku "In a Station of the Metro." More recently we have seen the attempts of the L*A*N*G*U*A*G*E poets to strip even the image and leave us with the barest realities of language itself, nouns and verbs and syntactical structures, in order to highlight this purity. This notion of the lyric, that at its core it is about nothing but the forming action, is unsettling, I will admit, yet it seems to me inescapable.

To attempt different language: Lyric, I am trying to argue, is like all literature an imitation. But instead of imitating an action, lyric attempts to imitate forming itself; it is about giving substantial form to prime matter. Or I think much better: *discovering* the substantial form of the poet's prime matter. This is the only way, it seems to me, to get beyond merely mechanical or technical or even artfully craft-based Kantian or Coleridgean notions of form: by seeing form as entelechy. A poet does not come up with a subject—the loss of a friend to death—and then decide upon a pretty way to say it or even, as a Kantian might suggest, self-create the grounding for its being. Instead, Bishop sees into the metaphysical reality of her subject's entelechy and finds in shaping her thoughts to that reality that only one form—the villanelle form, perhaps—most deeply discovers the pain generated in one's soul by the old self-deception that "the art of losing isn't hard to master." It is only in this way, I would suggest, that poetry is a way of knowing and not merely a pretty covering on other (philosophical, mathematical, scientific?) ways of knowing. And so, as one can often see most clearly in these moments of rebirth, like the eleventh century in Provence or the twentieth century in Europe and America, lyric has always pushed toward the limits of pure form, into nothingness, to ask deeply how one knows poetically and to answer: through form, through discovering the entelechy.

But there is a problem with this striving for nothingness in lyric poetry—a problem that does not trouble music or even painting: whether one likes it or not, *words have referents*. Unlike a G-sharp sixteenth note or a splotch of red pigment, a word refers to a thing or an action or an emotional state. And when the troubadour poets said or sang or wrote "love" or "lady" or "desire," reference—and thus the person, relation, and yes, politics and history and psychology and metaphysics—came rushing in, no matter how much they might have preferred to display only their technical prowess and forming imagination in their double sestinas.

And it was, in the Western tradition, Dante who recognized this. What reader of the *Vita Nuova* has not sensed the odd disconnect, one I think he intended, between the content of the love poetry and his seemingly mind-numbing formal analyses of the verse? Dante is the one who turns from the Italian *fin amours* tradition, the *dolce stil nuovo* his own masters had taught him, to say something more significant about the lady he leaves at the end of the *Vita Nuova*. After breaking off that poem, Dante turns to philosophy, not as a depressed rejection of poetry, but as an apprenticeship to Being so he may return. For Dante the lyric (and the *Commedia* is of course a lyric, the greatest in our tradition) must not be about Nothing but about Being—it must sing the Ground of All Being as well as the multifarious life created by and sustained by that Being.

From Nothing to Being: Medieval Lyric and Poetic Form as Entelechy   87

I am not the first to argue that this return to Being from Nothing is clearly the subtext of Dante's initial admiration for, and nevertheless ultimate rejection of, his master Brunetto Latini in the circle of the sodomites. In this canto, Dante has discovered how, despite his beautiful formal mastery, Brunetto's *poetry* is not fecund; the *fin amours* tradition had become a dead end, unable to produce progeny because its pleasures were all directed at a kind of self-pleasure of the poet's love of empty form. It is a cliché to say that Dante found love the subject of his song, but it is worth our continued thought and meditation to consider how he found in, or learned from, the stripped-down emphasis on Nothing, on form, on art for art's sake, the desiccated, formalized, conventionalized-into-nonentity subject of love between man and woman, that subject he would discover as his entelechy, the en-forming soul, the forming power of the cosmos: Love as a Being, as Being Itself. For the *Commedia* is above all the lyric poem which recognizes that one must strip back to Nothing as the only way to come to Being, that without the lyric risking Nothingness one can never scale the heights of, and come to sing, the core of all Being.

Only in this way, by moving from Nothing to Being, can Dante's poem take a true delight in the fecundity of God's creation, a world full of forms and shapes and beings created and shaped in their forms out of love. Karl Maurer has pointed me to the Peruvian poet Carlos Germán Belli, whose comments on form from the introduction to his collection *Asir la forma que se va* (Taking Hold of Form That Moves) I find particularly congruent with my thinking:

> Some believe in Divinity solely through fear in the face of a possible nothingness. In the same way some adore artistic form in the face of their fear of what will end by disintegrating forever. But in this case anguish is not the only cause, for there is also a tacit devotion of the senses as old as the aesthetic objects themselves. That is the faith in form, not from fear of the void, but from the pure pleasure of enjoying it. This happens in the same way in which Divinity is adored for itself, and even if it does not exist. In truth it is not spurious and does not come from baroque or Parnassian decadents. There must be no shame on account of it. It must not be made to abase itself. To work in that way is

> nothing but disowning our container. For the bodies in which we dwell possess a contour, also a structure, where the secret vital organs are found in perfect order and agreement. Let us hold fast to it, as we hold fast to our bodily form in the face of inevitable death. (155, trans. Karl Maurer)

That is, the reason form is so crucial is not merely to hold back the abyss of Nothingness: it is in their nature that things are *formed*—our beloved's cheekbones, a rose, the hind shank of a bull, a stone on the beach. In lyrical stripping down we can see the edge of the abyss and only then return to, perceive, be startled by, the beautiful forms. Czesław Miłosz reminds us that the real opponent here is abstraction, with its deadening refusal to acknowledge the richness and beauty of formed things:

> It has happened that we have been afflicted with a basic *deprivation*, to such an extent that we seem to be missing some vital organs, even as we try to survive somehow. Theology, science, philosophy, though they attempt to provide cures, are not very effective "In that dark world where gods have lost their way" (Roethke). They are able at best to confirm that our affliction is not invented. I have written elsewhere of this deprivation as one of the consequences brought about by science and technology that pollutes not only the natural environment but also the human imagination. The world deprived of clean-cut outlines, of the up and the down, good and evil, succumbs to a particular nihilization, that is, it loses its colors, so that grayness covers not only things of this earth and space, but also the very flow of time, its minutes, days, and years. Abstract considerations will be of little help, even if they are intended to bring relief. Poetry is quite different. By its very nature it says: All those theories are untrue. Since poetry deals with the singular, not the general, it cannot—if it is good poetry—look at things of this earth other than as colorful, variegated, and exciting, and so, it cannot reduce life, with all its pain, horror, suffering, and ecstasy, to a unified   tonality of boredom or complaint. By necessity poetry is therefore on the side of being and against nothingness. (Introduction xvi)[11]

Edward Hirsch notes how Polish post-war poetry came to these strengths. Blasted by the mid-twentieth-century experience of their country, these poets "could never believe in the future again," but neither could they "revert to traditional forms [or to] the aesthetics of elaborate, ornamental, or sonorous language." For them, "*it was as if poetry had to be reinvented again from the ground up*" (174, emphasis mine). Once again poetry was stripped back to nothingness in order to build back to being. Hirsch quotes Tadeusz Różewicz's poem "In the Midst of Life," and in it we see the stripping back to nothingness, the discovery of the entelechy of simple objects, and a poet holding fast to both as he would to his body in the face of death:

> After the end of the world
> after death
> I found myself in the midst of life
> creating myself
> building life
> people animals landscapes
>
> This is a table I said
> this is a table
> on the table is bread a knife
> a knife is to cut bread
> people live on bread
>
> Man must be loved
> I studied night and day
> what must be loved
> I answered man
>
> (174)

In this poem, Hirsch notes, one can see the poet enacting "what it means simultaneously to doubt poetry itself, and to put one's faith in it" (174), to strip the lyric all the way to the edge of nothingness in order to affirm faith in being: a table, a knife, man. And to realize the form, the entelechy, of one's knowledge of those things is poetic.

It was out of this ambition, this ability to see the breadth and expansion of the lyrical impulse to form, all the way to fullness of Being, that Western lyric became a dominant mode, if not *the* dominant mode, for the next six hundred years of literary history. From Petrarch, one of Dante's great early readers, the lyric tradition spread throughout Europe, such that the poetry seen as most important, the kind most esteemed, was lyric poetry, and love, that first subject of the lyric's rebirth in the eleventh century, maintained a central place in subject and form. (One might also essay the idea that Petrarch in transmitting Dante also sowed the seeds of lyric's downfall, for he suggested that love of Laura might reach to Platonic forms, but he never followed Dante so far as to leave Laura for the divine; thus this love poetry loses its ultimate ground in Being itself. His Platonic vision loses the physicality of Dante's sacramental world—he loses Różewicz's knife, bread, table—and in so doing loses the full extent of Dante's cosmic lyric ground in both directions.)

The problem with lyric poetry today is not a lack of technical practitioners, of even beautiful and interesting subjects, but, as Donald Hall wrote some years ago, a lack of ambition.[12] We have come through an age, as I already indicated, of another clearing out and paring down, from the Imagists to the L*A*N*G*U*A*G*E poets, a return to the stripping of content to lay bare the structures of form and the forming of structure. But we await the full return. The lyric has conceded too much ground to the novel and has been too content to display its technical mastery and form in tidy, even admittedly fascinating poems that do not risk a great deal. Not that the achievements here have not been wonderful in their quiet and masterful ways—I would trade Elizabeth Bishop on my bookshelves for few other writers, not just poets, and the Irish poets, not just Heaney and Boland but including them, are splendid—but it has been a long time, it seems to me, since we have had a lyric poet of really enormous scope and ambition. There is a hint of a return through the Eastern European poets, in their political situation impatient of a formalism content to occupy a safe middle ground between nothing and being, or through Walcott and the Caribbean poets, stripping poetry back to slave work songs and fundamental modes in building a new idiom for English verse. In a poet such as Jorie Graham one gets the ambition to gather philosophy, theology, and scientific learning into the lyric. Our current cultural situation, refracted, fragmented, deconstructing itself and its own literary culture, makes the rebirth difficult, but there are some promising signs. Perhaps we will soon see another great one arise soon, not necessarily from the centers of high literary culture, but perhaps a merchant's son coming from a relative backwater just about to explode, as Florence was when Dante was born in 1265. He will not likely compose while riding on a horse—or not riding on one—but I suspect he will, in one way or another, write about "the love that moves the sun and the other stars."

Notes

1. This erroneous view held for quite some time, along with the view (see n. 10 below) that *fin amours* poetry described real behaviors, in many a popular and standard literary history. Perhaps one of the more well-known is C. S. Lewis's *Allegory of Love*.

2. Perhaps the best and soundest refutation of the view that lyric was "reborn" in the eleventh century has been accomplished by the work of Peter Dronke, in a series of studies: *The Medieval Latin and Romance Lyric to AD 1300*, *Medieval Latin and the Rise of the European Love Lyric*, and *The Medieval Lyric*.

3. I use Press's edition and translations throughout for their simplicity and directness and the literal nature of the translations, which, though not conveying the lyric brilliance, at least gives one a clear sense of the poems' meaning. A strange choice perhaps for an essay on the lyric as forming, but I prefer to let the original speak for its own brilliance (for those who will give it a try) and to allow the translation to handle the less spectacular but more ponderous task of conveying the literal for the general English reader.

4. I have chosen to render the poet's name as the English equivalent, rather than the French Guillaume or, the most accurate, the Occitan Guilhem, simply because in most Anglophone histories of this period this is how he is referred to, so he will be more familiar to more readers. Duke of Aquitaine and Gascony and Count of Poitiers, he is often referred to as the "first troubadour." He lived from 1086 to 1127, went on the Crusade of 1101, and was Eleanor of Aquitaine's grandfather.

5. The scholarship on this poem, on the troubadour poets, and on *fin amours* poetry in general is vast. I wish to convey only one line of thought through that cosmos here but with enough suggestion of its variety and fecundity to stimulate those who might wish to pursue the subject further. One might begin by recalling it is Gaston Paris who invents the term "*amour courtois*" in 1888, consider Pound's and others' appropriation of Provençal lyric for their modernist project, leap ahead to Lewis's already-mentioned *Allegory of Love* as fueling a mid-century scholarly study, and see this stage as reaching its end in a book that answered Lewis in part, Valency's *In Praise of Love*. The next stage, at least in Anglo-American criticism, appears to have taken place with the publication of three anthologies: Goldin; the Press anthology I am using; and Hill and Bergin. Just before these, Zumthor created a new level of excellence in his *Essai de poétique médiévale*, where as a late formalist he asserted the impersonality of the verse and as a kind of precursor to postmodernism asserted the *mouvance* that characterizes, he argues, all medieval poetry. The explosion of new critical paradigms late in the century found fertile ground in these lyrics, featuring as they do

sexuality and gender, power relations and personal tropes, history and its erasure, psychology and the resistance to personality. A small sampling of these might include the following: Ferrante; Paterson; Kendrick, whose book is centrally concerned with "Farai un vers," praised for its brio and brilliance but not for its persuasiveness; Frank; Harvey; Cholokian; and Léglu. A really full bibliography could and should run to many pages, but my attempt here is to use the poem as a test case or limit case in notions of the lyric, not to offer a full answer to this large universe of scholarly conversation.

6. William's own poem V in this collection begins in this manner: "Farai chansoneta nueva/Ans que vent ni gel ni plueva" ("I'll make a new little song, before the wind and the frost and the rains come") (Press 20-21). Or try Arnaut Daniel's opening lines of poem III in Press's anthology: "En cest sonnet coind'e leri/Fauc motz, e capuig e doli,/Que serant verai e cert/Qan n'aurai passat la lima" ("To this light and graceful little air I fashion words, I carve and plane them, so they'll be true and sure when I've given them a touch with the file") (182-83).

7. See for instance Jaufre Rudel's classic beginning, so conventional and so standard: "Lanquan li jorn son lonc, en may,/M'es belhs dous chans d'auzelhs de lonh;/E quan mi suy partitz de lay,/Remembra.m d'un'amor de lonh" ("When the days are long, in May, I'm pleased by the sweet song of birds from afar; and when from that I've turned away, I remember a love from afar") (Press 32-33)

8. Continuing in the same poem by Rudel: "Vau de talan embroncx e clis,/Si quen chans ni flors d'albespis/No.m valon plus qu'iverns gelatz" ("I go, with longing somber and bowed down, so that neither song nor whitethorn blossom avails me more than icy winter") (Press 32-33). Arnaut Daniel makes the connection between the lady's disdain and the poetry that results: "Q'Amors marves plan'e daura/Mon chanter, que de liei mou/Qui pretz manten e governa" ("for Love soon smoothes and gilds my song which is inspired by her who maintains merit and guides it") (III, 5-7; Press 182-83).

9. The attack on the idea that real people actually behaved the way we encounter them behaving in the *fin amours* poems has been thorough and its victory complete. Donaldson succinctly attacked "The Myth of Courtly Love" in an article with that title. Before that, Robertson had mounted a sustained assault on the reality of *fin amours* in *A Preface to Chaucer*. A very fine exposition of the problems and historical realities can be found in the volume edited by F. X. Newman.

10. In this way, the fundamental opposition to the lyric is epic, which tries to encompass everything about a culture and thus is about human experience: history, politics, society, economics. And lyric is opposed to tragedy and comedy, two modes emerging out of epic that show the sides in which language, culture, and the person find their teleology through human choice. But tragedy and comedy in their focus on human choice bring us back to the forming imagination and the choices of the poet to shape form; and human choice leads us back

to the history, politics, society, and economics humans construct through their choices. It was Louise Cowan who taught me to reflect upon how the genres' separate concerns or emphases lead to one another.

11. It seems to me that Belli's and Miłosz's are the full answer to Giorgio Agamben's far-reaching critique that sees (and sees quite well) the Nothingness but cannot then come back to Being and the forms into which being is shaped.

12. This argument runs throughout Hall's *Poetry and Ambition*.

4

Lyric Bearing:
Shakespeare's Sonnet 116.12, Virgil's Aeneid, *and the Ship of Metaphor*

SCOTT F. CRIDER

> *L'acqua ch'io prendo già mai non si corse....*
>
> I set my course for waters never traveled....
> (Dante, *Paradiso* 2.8)

Shakespeare's Sonnets have not held the place in our understanding of lyric that his plays have held in our understanding of drama.[1] While few doubt that his plays in some fashion inaugurated modernity, one critic going so far as to argue that they have fashioned us as recognizably human,[2] many have doubted that his sonnet sequence did, and its critical reception has been, until the last century, uneven. Coleridge's litotes is my own favorite dismissal: "Shakespeare...is never *positively* bad, even in his Sonnets."[3] Perhaps this uneven reception is due to the transgressive sexuality of the sonnet sequence; perhaps, to an apparently insatiable appetite for biographical readings that are, to be generous, speculative. The uneven reception is surprising, nonetheless, since the English language's greatest poet appropriated and transformed not only *the* early modern poetic form, that of the sonnet (a form that has endured since in the most important moments of lyric history), but also its favored genre of anthology, the sonnet sequence, which established the precedent of narrative relation, if not obvious unity, across disparate lyrics collected.[4]

The unity of Shakespeare's Sonnets is hardly easy to discern. After all, the conventional division of the sequence into Fair Youth sonnets (1-126) and the Dark Lady sonnets (127-52), a division I accept,[5] still has difficulty accommodating the final two Cupid sonnets, and the fact of the sequence's *two* beloveds is hardly the norm: Petrarch had one Laura; Sidney's Astrophel, one Stella; and Spenser in the *Amoretti*, his one fiancée. Although I will concentrate upon the Fair Youth sonnets—indeed, upon one line in the most famous, Sonnet 116—I believe that the sequence has its own unity and that such unity can only be comprehended by taking seriously, in that poem, the speaker's poetics of love—a poetics that is, for reasons I will make clear, the poetics of modernity. Borrowing from Bloom, I shall argue that when we love the beautiful one during the lyric occasion and compose poetry in response to it, we are most like Shakespeare's speaker in the Sonnets. This is especially so in 116, the most famous, yet still not fully understood, sonnet.

Critical consensus often forgets its own consensual character, the history of an increasingly strong agreement that an interpretation is so, especially within texts so well known that they are difficult to discern freshly. Such is the case with our one line, line 12, from Sonnet 116: "[Love] beares it out euen to the edge of doome."[6] "[B]ears it out" can mean "endures," as Stephen Booth points out in his masterly edition (386).[7] To the best of my knowledge, all other contemporary editions follow Booth.[8] It is a perfectly legitimate gloss of the line, but it should not exclude other possible readings, two of which I will argue ought to be included in our commentaries and our understanding of the entire poem and its sequence: "bear" can also mean "carry" and/or "sail."[9] Let me interpret the poem and examine a thus far unremarked intertext, a moment in Virgil's *Aeneid*: Palinurus's death at sea and his encounter with Aeneas in the underworld (5.827-71 and 6.337-83). This intertextual moment helps both to bind the poem's three, positive definitions of love together and to provide two figures for the narrative of the sonnet sequence's lyric action: 1) the sequence as a ship, and the speaker as its pilot; and 2) that ship as a floating tomb for the Fair Youth. Lyric metaphor here suggests narrative action, and though some Shakespeareans are understandably reluctant to discuss narrative in the sonnets, doing so carefully allows us to understand more clearly the speaker's, and perhaps Shakespeare's, conception of lyric itself.[10]

Although the poem is well known, it is helpful to linger upon it before discussing it:

> Let me not to the marriage of true mindes
> Admit impediments, loue is not loue
> Which alters when it alteration findes,
> Or bends with the remouer to remoue.
> O no, it is an euer fixed marke
> That lookes on tempests and is neuer shaken;
> It is the star to euery wandring barke,
> Whose worths vnknowne, although his higth be taken.
> Lou's not Times foole, though rosy lips and cheeks
> Within his bending sickles compasse come,
> Loue alters not with his breefe houres and weekes,
> But beares it out euen to the edge of doome.
>
> > If this be error and vpon me proued,
> > I neuer writ, nor no man euer loued.

This is a sonnet of metaphoric definition,[11] and its definitions of love are both negative and positive, and they are multiple, exhibiting the rhetorical figures, respectively, of *horismus* and of *systrophe*.[12] In his *Garden of Eloquence*, Henry Peachem defines the latter thus: "*Systrophe*...is when an Orator bringeth in many definitions of one thing, yet not such definitions as do declare the substance of a thing by the general kind, and the difference, which the art of reasoning doth prescribe, but others of another kind all heaped together" (qtd. in Joseph 313). Are the definitions in the poem simply "all heaped together," or does the series perhaps disclose a pattern, even a sequence? After its opening (1-2) but before its couplet (13-14), it has four negative definitions of love (2-3, 4, 9-10, and 11) and three positive (5-6, 7-8, and 12). If one wished to chart the definitions as a sequence of provisional definitions (-, -; +, +; -, -; and +), one would discover that there is a broken symmetry here: two negative definitions are followed by two positive, then two negative by one positive. The expectation of a final pair of positive definitions creates an abrupt, conclusive definition. As Tucker Brooke first noted, "The chief pause in sense is after the twelfth line" (qtd. in Shakespeare, *Sonnets*, ed. Rollins 294). Focusing on the three positive definitions—1) "an euer fixed marke/That lookes on tempests and is neuer shaken"; 2) "the star to euery wandering barke,/Whose worths vnknowne, although his higth be taken"; and 3) "beares it out euen to the edge of doome"—we can discern a pattern, perhaps even a fulfillment in their location, order, and character. The first two definitions are commonly recognized as nautical; though the last can be so as well, that possibility will be missed if one accepts the tradition of editorial commentary. Interestingly, the first two nautical definitions figure love as an object, first as a cultural object (a beacon), then as a natural, celestial one (a star); the third definition figures love as a human action of enduring, carrying, and sailing. The narrative pattern is clear: love's metaphor moves farther and farther from shore.

"Let me not to the marriage of true mindes/Admit impediments" (1-2). As Helen Vendler explains, the poem arises from "the fiction of an anterior utterance of another which the sonnet is concerned to repudiate" (*Art* 488). As well, it is addressing what has certainly been a response of many readers to the speaker's love life: "Now that you have discovered that the Fair Youth is beautiful but not true, why not leave him and leave off the poetic project of fashioning for him a new textual body that will outlive the death of his natural body? How can there be a 'marriage of true minds' when one of the minds is untrue? Why immortalize a beautiful but untrue beloved?" The answer is, of course, that *love* is constant: "loue is not loue/Which alters when it alteration findes,/Or bends with the remouer to remoue" (2-4). The speaker's truth to the poetic project on behalf of the Fair Youth must be maintained even once the latter reveals himself as "unworthy." In an encounter with moral and physical "alteration," the speaker maintains his own constancy because love does not alter or bend.

In the next quatrain, we get our first two positive definitions, both nautical metaphors. First, love is "an euer fixed marke/That lookes on tempests and is neuer shaken" (5-6).[13] Second, "[i]t is the star to euery wandring barke,/Whose worths vnknowne, although his higth be taken" (7-8).[14] The third definition of love is also nautical. The Virgilian intertext here is Palinurus's fall from Aeneas's ship in the *Aeneid* in Book 5 as the Trojans sail from Sicily to Italy. In *William Shakspere's Small Latin & Lesse Greeke* (2:495-96), T. W. Baldwin explains that, in his grammar school education, Shakespeare would have studied and translated the first six books of the *Aeneid*, drill sufficient for him to have known the Palinurus episode:

[Aeneas] bids all the masts be raised with speed and the yards spread with sail. Together all set the sheets, and all at once, now to the left and now to the right, they let out the canvas; together they turn to and fro the yardarms aloft; favouring breezes *bear* [*ferunt*] on the fleet. First before all, leading the close column, was Palinurus; by him the rest are bidden to shape their course. And now dewy Night had just reached its mid-goal in heaven; the sailors, stretched on their hard benches under the oars, relaxed their limbs in quiet rest; when Sleep, sliding lightly down from *the stars* [*astris*] of heaven, parted the dusky air and cleft the gloom, seeking you, Palinurus, and bringing you baleful dreams, guiltless one! There on the high stern sat the god, in semblance of Phorbus, and pours these accents from his lips: "Palinurus, son of Iasus, the seas of themselves *bear* [*ferunt*] on the fleet; the breezes breathe steadily; the hour is given to rest. Lay down your head and steal your weary eyes from toil. I myself for a space will take your duty in your stead." To him, scarce lifting his eyes, speaks Palinurus: "Me do you bid shut my eyes to the sea's calm face and peaceful waves? Me put faith in this monster? And Aeneas— why, indeed, am I to trust him to the treacherous breezes, I whom a clear sky has so often deceived?" Such words he said and, clinging to the tiller, never let loose his hold, and kept his eyes upturned to *the stars* [*astra*]. But lo! the god, shaking over his temples a bough dripping with Lethe's dew and steeped in drowsy might of Styx, despite his efforts relaxes his swimming eyes. Hardly had a sudden slumber begun to unbend his limbs when, leaning above, Sleep flung him headlong into the clear waters, tearing away, as he fell, the helm and part of the stern, and calling vainly on his comrades again and again. The god himself winged his way in flight to the thin air above. Nonetheless the fleet speeds safely on its course over the sea, and trusting in Father Neptune's promises, glides on unafraid. And now, onward *borne* [*fertur*], it was nearing the cliffs of the Sirens...when the sire found that his ship was drifting aimlessly, her pilot lost, and himself steered her amid waves of night, often sighing and stunned at heart by his friend's mischance. "Ah, too trustful in the calm of sky and sea, naked will you lie, Palinurus, on an unknown strand!" (5.828-71, emphases mine)

Palinurus pilots "a ship" or "wandering bark," and he does so by "keeping his eyes upturned" or "taking the height" of the stars, motivated by a Roman love of his leader, Aeneas, but destroyed by Somnus, a god who seduces him with forgetfulness and sleep; therefore, he is unable to "bear" their vessel toward its destination, the new Troy of Rome. (Interestingly, the passage de-emphasizes Palinurus's agency by having the sea and the breeze bear, or carry, the ship he is piloting.) We learn later from Aeneas's encounter with him in the underworld that Palinurus came ashore, only to be murdered by Italians, and now desires to be properly buried, a request the Sybil grants by promising him a tomb (6.337-383). There are two verbal echoes: Palinurus pilots the ship on the sea and the breeze that "bear" them, and he does so by watching the "stars."

The differences between the poem and its Virgilian intertext, though, are revealing. First, Palinurus pilots his ship by means of plural stars; the speaker writes from the love that is "a star." Shakespeare's speaker emphasizes the isolated, immobile integrity of love, but Virgil is multiplying sources of natural guidance. Second, the "stars" are not unequivocally serving human flourishing since, after all, Somnus descends from them to destroy Palinurus; however, the speaker's single star, the Northern Star (commentaries agree upon it as such), is a constant source of orientation. Even if its essence or worth cannot be comprehended, its capacity to orient is nonetheless sure. Virgil's cruel natural cosmos is transformed into a less hostile one, yet one still hostile to human aspirations, since the speaker is writing to save the Fair Youth from a very natural decline as "wastfull time debateth with decay" (15.11). As we are to remember, "rosy lips and cheeks/Within [time's] bending sickles compasse come" (116.9-10). Third, Somnus attempts to seduce Palinurus by saying that "the seas of themselves bear on the fleet" (5.844). The speaker's love itself will "bear it out even to the edge of doom" (12) through his own poetic power, yet he will guide himself by means of a star. Fourth, Palinurus fails, though with divine "assistance," to fulfill his navigational duty, while at least at 116 the speaker's poetic project is reaching its achievement, though after Sonnet 126 he will experience his own failure.

What does the poem gain by the Virgilian intertext? What is gained is the recognition of a metaphor suggesting that the speaker's lyric love is an epic enterprise. When the metaphor shifts from love as a beacon to love as a star, the nautical metaphors prepare us for the final metaphor for love, which is also nautical: "Loue alters not with his breef houres and weekes,/But beares it out euen to the edge of doome" (11-

12). The trochaic substitution of the third foot of line 12 ("euen to"), especially following a medial caesura, emphasizes the extraordinary extent of the accomplishment: "But **bears**/it **out** // e'en to/the **edge**/of **doom**."[15] "[B]eares it out" is a verbal phrase always defined in editions of the sequence as "endure." It can mean "endure," but I think the intertext and the sequence of positive definitions provide a field of metaphoric possibility that allows "bear" to mean, as well, both "carry" and "sail." If one defines "out" as a preposition meaning "forth,"[16] then "bearing out" can be defined as "carrying forth" or "sailing forth." The object of the verb—the "it"—is equivocal, as we will see.

Let's examine "bear-as-carry" first: "Love bears [carries] it out even to the edge of doom." The *OED* defines "bear" as "carry" (I.1), and there is precedent in the first of the speaker's sonnets: "His tender heir might bear his memory" (4).[17] The speaker's love carries the Fair Youth's beauty within his own lyric love. Poetry's essence is metaphor, and thinking of its Greek roots, one remembers that metaphor is a "carrying across": in Greek, *meta* means "across" and *pherein*, "to bear or to carry." (The Latin for *pherô* is *fero*, the very word in the Virgilian text for "bear.") A metaphor transports, as George Puttenham remembers when he renames metaphor "transporte" (189-90).[18] The "procreation" sonnets (1-17) yield to the "creation" or "re-creation" sonnets, during which the speaker's poetry becomes the new textual body for the Fair Youth's beauty. The speaker has any number of metaphors for this transportation.[19] What matters is that these may here be discussed as a carrying-across, as *the* carrying-across of lyric metaphor itself. For the speaker, love is essentially the activity of fashioning the lyric metaphor that carries. The object carried is "it," of course, not "you": the Fair Youth's beauty is the object of love, and the speaker's desire is the experience of it. Love is both object and experience, and experience itself is altered by the re-productive process of writing poetry (yet another sense of "bearing"). The speaker's "sweet love's beauty" is both the Fair Youth's and the speaker's:

> For such a time do I now fortifie
> Against confounding Ages cruell knife,
> That he shall neuer cut from memory
> My sweet loues beauty, though my louers life.
> His beautie shall in these blacke lines be seene,
> And they shall liue, and he in them still greene.
>
> (63.9-14)

What is borne is equivocal: the Fair Youth and the speaker; the former's beauty and the latter's love for it. As the speaker explains, "O know sweete loue I always write of you,/And you and loue are still my argument" (76.9-10).

The speaker's third metaphor for love comes from the second; he is imagining himself as the poet who orients his poetic journey by means of love, then becomes that love. Vendler Christianizes the metaphor as it develops: "[A] love first described in transcendent vertical terms as a secular Petrarchan fixed star subsequently takes on the immanent horizontal Christian Pauline form of stoic fidelity in endurance" (*Art* 491). This is a fine reading, and the "edge of doome" certainly can figure Judgment. Even so, the nautical metaphor endows the temporal dimension of eternity with both the spatial character of the world's limits and the psychic character of the poet's.[20] As Booth points out, "doome" can mean "doomsday" or "death" (Shakespeare, *Sonnets* ed. Booth 386). It can also mean "the faculty of judging; judgement, discrimination, discernment" (*OED*, 3.b). The speaker is fashioning a lyric love that carries both him and his beloved all the way out to the utmost limits, those without and those within.

One sees the speaker, then, sailing to the end of the world and the limit of his understanding within the vessel of his poetry, a poetry that somehow carries his love.[21] A reader of the sequence will have seen "bear-as-sail" before. In one of the Rival Poet sonnets, the speaker indicates that his poetry is a kind of ship:

> But since your worth (wide as the Ocean is)
> The humble as the proudest saile doth beare,
> My sawsie barke (inferior farre to his)
> On your broad main doth willfully appeare.
> Your shallowest helpe will hold me vp a float,
> Whilst he vpon your soundlesse deepe doth ride,
> Or (being wrackt) I am a worthlesse bote,
> He of tall building, and of goodly pride.
>
> (80.5-12)

The "sail" of his verse "doth bear," or carry, the "worth" of the Fair Youth as it sails upon that worth. "Bear" here is a pun: the verse carries as it sails. The explicit metaphor in Sonnet 80 is implicit in Sonnet 116:

"[Love] bears [sails] it out even to the edge of doom." The *OED* provides a fruitful definition of "bear" as "sail[ing] in a certain direction" (37.a), and one need only remember the lines from *Othello* that Hilton Landry points out: "If that the Turkish fleet/Be not ensheltered and embayed, they are drowned. It is impossible to bear it out" (2.1.18-20).[22] In Shakespeare's Sonnets the "it" being sailed is now the ship of poetry, which itself houses the Fair Youth's beauty, here preserved from the decay and death that the Fair Youth himself will not escape. Indeed, the poetry is a floating tomb (unlike the tomb on shore that the Italians will build for Palinurus, Capo Palinuro), an immortal monument borne by the speaker upon the tempest.[23] An enduring speaker carries the Fair Youth across the annihilation of death by means of a lyric sailing: this is the ultimate figure for Sonnets 1-126. All of the earlier formulations of the project of immortalization are now given, if not a final, then an encompassing metaphor, a meta-metaphor, one that makes it impossible to extricate love from lyric or lyric from love.

This final definition of love as lyric mimesis is borne out by the couplet: "If this be error and vpon me proued,/I neuer writ, nor no man euer loued" (13-14). The reasoning here is surprisingly sane.[24] The antecedent to "this" may be the general sense of all three quatrains; then again, it may be the last definition of love. If his bearing—"enduring," "carrying," "sailing"—has been an error, then he has not written. But he has; hence, lyric proves the love that was its occasion. To bear is also, of course, "to sustain, support or uphold" (*OED*, II), including to support or confirm an argument. Lyric upholds and sustains the love that upholds and sustains lyric, even when that love is not what one imagined at first. That the speaker began to desire increase of his beautiful rose (1.1-4) when he presumed it had the "sweet odor" of truth and beauty (54.3-4) alters not when he discovers that it may be a cankered one (54.5-8) without such a perfume. This is the exact point where the speaker discloses the virtue of his pen. The speaker is defining love as a lyric enterprise requiring epic, Virgilian virtues of endurance and will—virtues Palinurus did not exhibit because he could not stay awake. As our speaker tries to carry his immoral friend over the sea of finitude into an immortality of print, he too fails through human weakness. Shakespeare's Sonnets do not end with 126, the last of the Fair Youth sonnets, in which the speaker reminds his friend that without the "craft" of the speaker's verse, the friend will be the empty space delimited by parentheses (126.13-14).

Rather inconstantly, the speaker turns to another beloved (Sonnets 127-52). That failure indicates, not that the speaker's vision of lyric love was itself necessarily an error, but that he did not have the will to bear it out to the edge of doom; instead, he fell into the tempest of another love and another poetry. As he confesses in the sequence's last line, "Love's fire heats water, water cools not love" (154.14). An epic romance of lyric love becomes, instead, a tragedy of sexual despair, one in which the character of the speaker's metaphors and his understanding of metaphor itself become quite other.

The speaker's vision of lyric love is, I would suggest, distinctly modern since its experience, self-understanding, and art are wholly and only human. To trace only one line from Shakespeare's Sonnets to modern poetry, one need only think of Keats's "Bright Star," a poem written in Keats's copy of the Sonnets. Vendler points out that Keats imagined Shakespeare as his "Presider" (*Art* 37). The Keatsian speaker forsakes the steadfastness of the bright star for that of a human love:

> No—yet steadfast, still unchangeable,
> Pillowed upon my fair love's ripening breast,
> To feel for ever its soft fall and swell,
> Awake for ever in a sweet unrest,
> Still, still to hear her tender taken breath,
> And so live ever—or else swoon to death.

We are here not very far way from Stevens' Sunday-morning lady and her post-Gospel response—"The tomb in Palestine/Is not the porch of spirits lingering"—to a beauty that is always already dying yet can be saved by the love of lyric mimesis, "[d]ownward to darkness, on extended wings." The speaker's lyric bearing is ours: his epic romance of lyric love should give us hope, yet his tragedy of sexual despair should give us pause. Shakespeare's invention of a speaker who encompasses both should dispose us, as do Falstaff and Hamlet, to recognition, wonder, and gratitude. In this, as in so very much, Shakespeare is our Presider.[25]

Notes

1. Shakespeare wrote in all three of the fundamental genres of imaginative literature—narrative, drama and lyric. Even so, his talent is dramatic and lyrical, not narrative. As Genette explains (10-14), this threefold division is not an Aristotelian system because the lyric as such is outside his concern in the *Poetics*.

2. In *Shakespeare and the Invention of the Human*, Bloom specifies the titular claim even further: "When we are wholly human, and know ourselves, we become most like either Hamlet or Falstaff" (745).

3. Qtd. in Edmundson and Wells, whose chapter on "The Critical Reputation of the Sonnets" (131-44) provides a good introduction. See, as well, Schiffer 3-71.

4. On the sonnet and the sonnet sequence, see Spiller. In English, earlier collections, such as *Tottel's Miscellany*, lacked the unifying principle of a single speaking voice. In Italian, of course, Dante and especially Petrarch may be credited with the invention in a modern language of the lyric *sequence*.

5. The most articulate defender of the division is Duncan-Jones, whose edition presumes it (Shakespeare, *Poems*); the most articulate critic of it is Dubrow, who complicates, without to my mind, however, undermining, the claim of unity and inner division between poems to a man and those to a woman.

6. All citations of Shakespeare's Sonnets are from Q in Booth. I have modernized only the long *s*. Booth's discussion of Sonnet 116 is extremely helpful; see Shakespeare, *Sonnets* ed. Booth 384-92.

7. The word was first defined as "survives" by Poole in 1918, according to Rollins (Shakespeare, *Sonnets*, ed. Rollins 295).

8. See, for example, Shakespeare, *Sonnets,* ed. Burrow 612; Shakespeare, *Poems* 342; and Shakespeare, *Sonnets,* ed. Evans 229. There is clearly editorial consensus on the question.

9. The first meaning has not, to the best of my knowledge, been noted; the second has been, but only twice, and commentators have yet to include it in their editions. Mahood notes "*bear out*...might mean 'steer a course'" (94); Landry argues that 116.12 "resumes the imagery of the second quatrain by comparing love to a ship which stays on course in spite of wind and sea and sails to the very edge of the flat world" (106).

10. For a thoughtful instance, again see Dubrow. I leave aside the question of irony with respect to the dramatized narrator; whether Shakespeare shares the speaker's claims in Sonnet 116 and throughout the sequence or treats them with irony is very difficult to determine. The rhetorical category of *ethos* or *persona* is present throughout, but it does not allow us to determine irony with any certainty.

11. In an illuminating reading (*Art* 487-93), Vendler argues that the poem's opening establishes it not as a definition poem but as a "dramatic refutation or rebuttal" (*Art* 488). Her reading and mine are not necessarily mutually exclusive.

12. Joseph points out that defining through negation is an instance of *horismus* (108), and she offers Sonnet 116 as an example and then explains the other figure, *systrophe*, "the heaping together of many definitions of one thing" (109). Joseph's remains the most thorough treatment of Shakespeare's art within the rhetorical culture of early modern England. For discussions of Shakespearean figuration, see, as well, Vickers, esp. 294-339; McDonald, esp. 51-88; and Freinkel, esp. 159-236.

13. For a reading of the sonnet that focuses on this definition, see Erne. The essay is very interesting, but I do not think he proves that "Shakespeare is not writing about a merely human but about a transcendental, God-given love" (295). In fact, that is exactly what the speaker is not writing about, though I do think that Shakespeare may at times elsewhere be ironizing the speaker by providing him with Pauline language, the consequences of which the speaker appears unaware. The Pauline language of several of the sonnets would be worth investigating. The "star" alone is insufficient evidence of divine presence, though. Erne presumes that the navigational metaphors of lines 5-6 and 7-8 do not continue in 11-12.

14. For a reading of the sonnet that focuses on this definition of love, see Trimpi. He too appears to presume that the last metaphor of love is not nautical.

15. Bolded syllables are stressed. For a metrical analysis of Sonnet 116, see Wright 84-88. He and I do not always scan the poem the same way, but I have profited from the book a great deal, and we do scan line 12 alike, including the trochaic substitution. Compare Sonnet 15.6, where the speaker uses the same construction, the trochaic substitution of "euen" coming in the third foot: "Cheered and checked ev'n by the self-same sky." See the same medial trochee with respect to "even" in Sonnets 56.6, 69.4, and 71.12.

16. See Abbott, entries 183, 121. See, as well, Hope, esp. his discussion of the prepositional phrase when "adverbial" (2.2.4), 176.

17. "Bear-as-carry" occurs numerous times in the sequence: Sonnets 1.4, 8.8, 10.1, 12.8, 13.8, 16.7, 36.4, 50.5-6, 51.1-2, 59.3-4, 77.3, 78.9-10 (with added meaning of "give birth to"), and 97.6-7. In Sonnets 34.12, 40.12, 68.3, and 88.14 "bear" also means "endure." Only in 116.2 and 80.5-6 does it also mean "sail."

18. For a brilliant discussion of metaphor within a Greek, esp. Aristotelian understanding, see Ricoeur, esp. 9-43 and 259-71. For metaphor in Shakespeare, see McDonald 51-69. Freinkel focuses on catachresis, not metaphor, as *the* figure of the sequence.

19. Examples: distilling (5.9-14 and 54.11-14); engrafting (15.13-14); breathing (18.13-14 and 81.9-14); printing (65.13-14); monumentalizing (107.13-4); and remembering (122.1-4). On the project of immortalization, see Leishman, esp. 102-18, and Ferry, esp. 1-65.

20. With respect to the first point, Roessner argues that "love's realm is spatially extended" (340). Her discussion of Sonnet 116.12 and the poem supports my reading of the poem and sequence as characterized by the "heroic determination to preserve love from its ruin" (346).

21. For a solid genealogy of nautical metaphors for poetry, see Curtius, esp. 128-30. Curtius points out that the metaphor of poetry as sailing arises as well in Virgil's *Georgics* 2.41 and 4.117. As Booth explains in his commentary on Sonnet 80, "The metaphor of the poet as sailor is traditional" (Shakespeare, *Sonnets* ed. Booth 274).

22. Landry 106. Interestingly, Honigmann, perhaps influenced by commentaries upon Sonnet 116, glosses "bear it out" as "hold out, survive it" (Shakespeare, *Othello* 162) but does not indicate that the Turkish fleet fails to endure because it can no longer sail. It is interesting that the nautical metaphor implicit in 116 is again explicit in the very next poem when the speaker admits: I have "hoysted saile to al the windes/Which should transport me farthest from your sight" (117.7-8).

23. Sonnet 116 does not explicitly employ the tomb language of the *Aeneid*. Other sonnets are clear that the poetry is a kind of counter-tomb to "the tombe/Of his [the Fair Youth's] selfe loue" (3.7-8). For other references to "tomb," see 4.13, 17.3, 81.7-8, 83.11-12, 86.1-4, 101.10-11, and 107.13-14.

24. The form of logic here is *modus tollens*: If P, then Q; not Q; therefore, not P. On syllogistic reasoning, see Joseph, 355-65. For an examination of the reasoning of the couplet, see Nelson.

25. This essay began as a paper for the 2003 meeting of the Shakespeare Association in Victoria, BC, in a seminar led by Paul Edmundson and Stanley Wells, "Interrogating *Shakespeare's Sonnets*," and I found the discussion very helpful. Several readers of this essay have provided valuable assistance: Kate Bluett, Michael Bolin, Bainard Cowan, Louise Cowan, Raymond DiLorenzo, Eileen Gregory, Peter Heyne, Theresa Kenney, Lance Simmons, Paul Voss, and Gerard Wegemer. I have presented versions of the argument to three graduate sections of a course on Shakespeare's Sonnets, to the fine students of which I dedicate the essay.

THE ENGLISH ARC

5

John Donne's Three Voices:
Toward the Still, Quiet Word at the Center of the Lyric

ROBERT ALEXANDER

John Donne's place in the lyric tradition rests on a number of extraordinary achievements. No poet before or since has produced as great a body of lyrics devoted to love. No lyric poet before with the possible exceptions of Dante and Petrarch has lavished more attention on the beloved. And no other lyric poet has so completely captured the full range of passions relating to love, from uninhibited lust at one extreme to the rare kind of joy and gratitude that come from loving and being loved in return at the other. Further, few lyric poets have done as much to make the connection between love and music explicit. Donne's ear and his genius for matching the movement, speed, and length of a line with the appropriate emotions are almost without equal among non-dramatic poets. Until his ordination, almost all he wrote was in verse: a great variety of quatrain forms, epithalamia, anniversaries, eulogies, sonnets, epigrams, meditations, and prayers modeled on Church rituals. Even personal letters were typically composed in running couplets, and a good number of his poems were actually set to music. Finally and perhaps most important, in their nearly exclusive attention to love, Donne's lyrics make clear or at least force on us the proposition that the motive spring of the lyric at its best and purest, no matter what its ostensible theme, is desire.

These achievements have firmly established Donne's place in the tradition, but because he wrote when he did, at a watershed moment in the development of the lyric, they have also left us with important questions. As heir to a variety of traditions and as one of the few early moderns to dedicate nearly all his work to love, Donne was a major influence in determining the direction of the lyric at a time when it was being transformed and passed on to the modern world. How are we to understand this legacy? What is the condition of the lyric as an instrument for exploring and giving expression to the whole range of sentiments concerning love? Equally important, what is the character of the sensibilities he helped form and pass on? More particularly, are Donne's early lyrics an expression of personal feelings, his own hidden interior, or are they expressions of a persona whom he uses to explore the range and depth of man's emotional, intellectual life?[1] Answers to these questions may throw some light on the nature of lyric; they may also tell us something of ourselves and of the sensibility we inherited from the Renaissance, particularly in its Reformation spirit.

For Donne, love was not only an expression of lovers' feelings but a metaphysical principle by which to interpret and make sense of the world. The tension behind his poems is the result not so much of "heterogeneous ideas yoked together by violence," as Samuel Johnson put it, as of Donne's openness to an underlying connection between things apparently unrelated. The most succinct positive expression of this principle may be the lines in "Love's Growth" in which love is presented as the motive force of *all* things in existence, the wills of lovers and even thought itself: "But as all else, being elemented too,/Love sometimes would contemplate, sometimes do."[2] The best example of the negative pole is fleshed out in "A Nocturnal upon St. Lucy's Day." There human beings are presented as having free wills and rational souls and being capable of assimilating the forms of other things, even other persons. Hence, they can know great joy; they can also know infinite loss. The poet, having lost his beloved, becomes "the grave/Of all, that's nothing." If he were any ordinary "nothing," her death would simply place him at odds with the rest of creation. But his loss cannot be reckoned in purely material terms. He is "by her death," "re-begot of absence," making him the "quintessence" of non-existence, "of the first nothing, the elixir grown." The whole poem, from the opening, "'Tis the year's midnight, and it is the day's,/Lucy's, who scarce seven hours herself unmasks," to the close, "This hour her vigil, and her eve, since this/Both the year's, and the day's deep midnight is," manages to convey an almost palpable stillness perfectly in keeping with the spiritual emptiness the poet feels at the loss of his beloved.

Between these two poles are poems treating love from a variety of perspectives and by means of a variety of tropes. In most of them Donne's typical method is to take a love situation and explore it through an extended conceit involving ordinary physical objects: a book, a map, a window, a blossom, twin compasses. At times, however, he uses a conceit taken from less tangible realities, such as space or light or shade, in order to call to mind some metaphysical aspect of love that ordinarily escapes the eye. In "A Lecture upon the Shadow," for example, Donne's light/shade conceit brings into focus the spiritually disordered love in which the lovers are trapped. According to the Platonic Christian tradition, which shaped much of Donne's thought, love *is* light. The poem begins with the poet interrupting the lovers' stroll to speak immediately to a revelation: at noon they tread their shadows, reducing all things to a "brave clearness." The orientation of the shadows becomes an occasion for the lovers to reflect on the secrecy of their love, a staple of the *amour courtois* conventions on which Donne casts a slanting light. The "infant loves" of the lovers required "disguises" and "shadows." But these expediencies kept them from attaining a love of "the highest degree." Standing in the direct light of the sun, the speaker sees that unless they remain as they are at this moment, with the sun directly above them—that is, in naked honesty—their course will produce shadows in the other direction, deceiving not only others but themselves. The light helps engender a realization: "Love is a growing, or full constant light;/And his first minute, after noon, is night." Any dishonesty from this point on will result not simply in the loss of sunlight but in a fall into "night."

This, in somewhat adumbrated form, is Donne's great theme. To read his poems this way, however, for principles or for what they are *about*, without regard to *mode*, their peculiar *personal perspective*, is to miss part of their meaning. Too often our understanding of mode is arbitrarily limited to technical elements or to tone or irony. But mode is an aspect of form; in truth the two cannot be separated. The lyric is primarily a *first-person* form of address, rendering *a person* speaking, the peculiar way he sees and feels things, all that suggests the person as *subject*, not object, with all that this implies of interiority, of what is unique to the poet and finds expression in his words. Joyce suggests something of this in the distinction he makes between poetic categories: "There are three conditions of art: the lyrical, the epical, and the dramatic. That art is lyrical whereby the artist sets forth the image in immediate relation to himself; that art is epical whereby the artist sets forth the image in mediate relation to himself and to others; that art is dramatic whereby the artist sets forth the image in immediate relation to others" (145). An artist can combine them to produce infinite modulations, but ultimately whatever their configuration, they are reducible to these three pure forms. In the lyric, the poet sets forth an image in *immediate* relation to himself, and as such the image is more directly expressive of his interior, the shadowed depths of his subjectivity, than is true of either epic or drama. Moreover, because of the lyric's affinities with the lyre, the image it offers is musical, a fact that should radically affect our understanding of mode.

It is necessary to see the lyric, then, no matter how objectified, how much focused on an object external to the poet, as expressing something of the poet's inward life and its seemingly musical character. Even if this is true, though, how are we to understand the lyric as a work of *poiesis*, an extra-mental reality distinct from the poet's interior? If Joyce is right and the lyric offers an immediate image of the poet himself, is its knowledge necessarily psychological, restricted to the poet's psyche? Or, as a "made-thing," wholly "other" from the poet, does it offer a meaning apart and yet still expressive of the poet's psyche at the same time? We are back to the question of how to read Donne and the significance of his voice.

If we consider Donne's poetry from the perspective of mode, I find three fairly distinct voices, each corresponding to a major phase of his life, early, middle, and late, and each giving rise to a subtly different kind of poetry. The three classes do not do justice, of course, to the differences in modulations of tone or sentiment that exist between them, but the advantage to approaching Donne in this way is that we may bring to light aspects of the lyric that remain in shade if questions of mode are neglected.

The First Voice

Almost all of Donne's early lyrics have as their subject, in one form or another, love and its relation to the intellect and passions. No matter what the vehicle, metaphors or conceits, or metrical structure he uses, love is their central motivating force: *love and its motions bring the lyric into being.* By virtue of the mode, the lyric "I," the self and love are made coterminous. The reason for this is not hard to find: Donne was simply putting into practice a belief inherited from the scholastics, that love is the originating voice of the "I Am," the cause and form of all things. According to this view, stated by Thomas Aquinas, the first principle behind all creation is love. Since God made all things good, their first motion is an inclination toward the good. Things lacking a rational soul move toward their good through the apprehensive power in their Creator; human beings do so through their own apprehensive power, by the choices they make based on their knowledge and desires (*Summa Theologica* 2:691-790; I-II, Q. 22-48). The affinity between all things by virtue of the Love that created them explains why Donne could treat the love between lovers in terms of so great a variety of things both physical and metaphysical. Things share the same inclination: they are all drawn to each other by ties of connatural sympathy. Whereas human emotions may seem chaotic because of the teeming reality arousing them, they in fact possess a nature with discernible stages and ends, both of which can be seen in two opposing trajectories, one tracing the soul's movement toward the good desired, the other, its movement away from anything threatening it. The two trajectories unfold in the following phases:

1	2	3	4	5	6
Love	Desire	Hope	Daring		Joy
				Anger	
Hate	Aversion	Despair	Fear		Sorrow

Love's natural motion is from desire to consummation, from the longing for something not possessed to the joy experienced in attaining it. The love awakened by the beloved may entail hope or daring or even anger, but it is meant finally to conclude in rest, the freedom from motion attained in possessing the object pursued. Set off against this primary trajectory is its opposite, the whole range of emotions called into play when the lover turns from any evil threatening the desired good. Donne's poems cover every major aspect of love along the paths of both trajectories.

Donne wrote few poems situated at the opening end of the arc where desire is pure and simple. "The Bait" is perhaps the poem closest to the beginning. Although its metaphors suggest some cleverness on the part of the poet (the beloved as both fish and bait), the sentiments behind "Come live with me, and be my love" are those of an innocent rustic, simple and direct, uncomplicated by the ingenuity that marks many of the other poems.

Farther along the primary arc are those poems dealing with hope or daring. "Song" ("Sweetest love, I do not go") and "The Dream" belong to this phase, though, interestingly, in these two poems hope is represented in metaphors suggesting illusion, that is, dream and sleep. In the other poems of this group, "Love's Growth," "Lovers' Infiniteness," "A Lecture upon the Shadow," and even "The Anniversary," the ground of hope is surer. Arguably, the last one could go with the poems on complete love; I place it here because while the poem celebrates a perfect love, the poet's awareness of a greater love beyond makes him hope for still more (in heaven the lovers will be "thoroughly" blessed). These poems realize a depth and fullness of hope that I find in no other poet. Taken in the strictest sense of a supernatural virtue, hope in these poems conveys a sense of assurance in a love already enjoyed but not yet to its fullest extent. "Lovers' Infiniteness" plays beautifully on this paradox: if the lover and beloved have given all—a Petrarchan commonplace—then they have not really loved, since in a mutable world, love by its very nature is infinite and always giving.

Exemplary poems at the close of the primary arc are "Negative Love," "The Ecstasy," "Air and Angels," "The Good Morrow," "The Sun Rising," and "The Canonization." The last three along with "The Anniversary" are among the most perfect expressions of joy in our language. Two qualities set these poems off from the others, both of them enhancing the experience of joy. The first is a near-epic treatment of a lyric desire: the love between the lovers unites them with the rest of creation, giving a grandeur and amplitude to their love that other lovers do not know. This situation is expressed in a number of different ways, among them: "All here in one bed lay.//She'is all states, and all princes, I,/Nothing else is" ("The Sun Rising"); and "For love, all love of other sights controls,/And makes one little room, an every where.../Let us possess one world, each hath one, and is one" ("The Good Morrow"). In every case the effect is the same: the completeness of the lovers' joy is felt to be greater, more encompassing for their being one with a universe in which they are at the center.

The second quality is the sense of boundless amplitude achieved by what is done with the joy itself. In "The Sun Rising," the emotion of joy is pure and unmixed, and it is impossible to separate its peculiar quality from the exhilaration and sheer delight expressed. In "The Good-Morrow" and "The Canonization" the joy is richer, more settled and mature, first because it is mixed with other emotions that are in themselves open-ended, leaving one with the impression that the joy is not bound by the constraints of form, and second because the fusion of emotions has been more fully worked out in the plots, as well as in the images and metaphors employed. In "The Good Morrow" the delight is greater than in "The Sun Rising" in being mixed with wonder, the feeling one has in the presence of things whose causes one longs to understand. The wonder has left the lover with a sense of happy incongruity, questioning what he and his mistress did before they loved and feeling at the same time that he is on a threshold promising more, open to whatever the future will bring: "and now good morrow to our waking souls."

The secondary trajectory consists of all those emotions the lover feels when faced with threats to the good he desires. The hate initiating the movement is followed by subtle shades of aversion, despair, fear, and anger against the threat (as opposed to anger *for* the good in the primary trajectory). This arc closes in sorrow either at the prospect of losing the beloved or at her actual loss. Donne produced no poem whose whole action expresses a hatred for the *right* reason. In those poems driven by hate, the aversion expressed typically arises from the speaker simply not having his way. "Song" is a perfect rendering of hate at its most innocent: the short, rapid lines, the wit, and the melodic effects convey a spirit of delight really belonging to the primary arc and completely at odds with the hatred expressed. From the opening, "Go, and catch a falling star,/Get with child a mandrake root," to the concluding,

> Though she were true, when you met her,
> And last, till you write your letter,
>   Yet she
>   Will be
> False, ere I come, to two, or three
>
> ("Song," 22-26)

the effect is pure fun, parody at its lightest. The tension between the tone and what is expressed, the fact that the poem carries the two arcs within itself, creates an irony so subtle, so mixed with delight and aversion as to be nearly irresistible. "Woman's Constancy" represents an advance along this arc, for there the element of parody is more complex, the contempt for women mixed with disappointment and spite.

In the remaining poems on the secondary arc, it is almost impossible to sort out emotions; they are less simple, more intertwined, more expressive of an adult sensibility caught in a state of intellectual cunning. Of the poems dealing with aversion and despair I would include as most representative "The Blossom," "Farewell to Love," "Love's Usury," "Love's Diet," "Love's Alchemy," and "The Will." The poems "Farewell to Love" and "Love's Alchemy" are pure cynicism untouched by the chastising effects of sorrow or loss. They are as fine an expression of the will determined *not* to be moved by love as any Donne wrote. In "Farewell to Love," finding no solace in indiscriminate sex, the speaker swears off "things which had endamaged me" and commits himself to avoiding beautiful women. If all else fails, he will apply "wormseed to the tail." The poem is a masterpiece of black, infernal humor, revealing the dark, rationalistic side of the intellect in reducing difficulties of male sexuality to the mechanical act of applying an anaphrodisiac. This poem is the male counterpiece to "Love's Alchemy," where the speaker concludes, against any illusions that women should be known for their minds: "Hope not for mind in women; at their best/Sweetness and wit, they are but mummy, possessed." Although Donne's surface is playful, it is impossible to miss the cumulative effect of all the references to alchemy and the darker implications of the conclusion: once enjoyed, women are little more than dead lumps of flesh. The range of emotions covered from "Song" to the last two poems, that is, from relative innocence in expressed aversion to a nearly savage cynicism, shows that Donne was as fully equal to the task of rendering the interior of revulsion as he was to that of joy.

Few poems render simple despair. The line ending "Love's Exchange" ("racked carcasses make ill anatomies") contains a note of glibness present from the opening ("Love, any devil else but you"). "The Legacy" comes nearer, with a note of genuine helplessness running through it. The one poem in which despair is closest to the center is perhaps "Love's Usury." There, the speaker makes a Faust-like bargain with the "Usurious God of Love," ironically offering to pay twenty times in old age what he "makes" now. Desperate to have his way, the speaker is willing to suffer any hardship or humiliation, on one condition: "Only let me love none." He asks the god of Love rather to "let [his] body reign...snatch, plot, have, forget...." The poem's brilliance lies in its turning inside out the traditional understanding of love as infinite: if the self-giving of love is infinite, how can it appear otherwise than as usurious to someone who wants to have no limits set on his appetites, who will make of his life an infinite, appeaseless taking? "Love's Usury" is a near-flawless exploration of a legalistic spirit hidden beneath the *amour courtois* conventions (desiring only with rewards in mind) and brought into the light by the essentially infinite and unconditional nature of love.

Those poems expressive of anger, like those expressing hate, show nothing rightful, only excess and perversion. Wanting only to hurt, the speaker chooses vengeance in the face of rejection rather than restraint or self-denial. Like all of the poems dealing with despair or hatred gone wrong, these are marked by a twisted intellect and venomous spirit. "The Will," "The Curse," and "The Apparition" are perhaps most representative of this group. In "The Apparition," the speaker plays on being killed by his mistress's refusal, treating her as his murderess and threatening her with a visit from his ghost. He satisfies a perverse thirst for vengeance by wishing she'd betray him and undergo a tortured repentance rather than be deterred with mere threats: "…and since my love is spent,/I had rather thou shouldst painfully repent,/Than by my threatenings rest still innocent."

The poems closing the secondary arc deal with sorrow, the end toward which all the emotions relating to loss have been tending. These include not only the valedictory ones but such poems as "Witchcraft by a Picture," "The Broken Heart," "Expiration," and "Break of Day." Perhaps the most representative are "Twicknam Garden" and "Nocturnal upon St. Lucy's Day." Unlike the rest of the poems on this arc (especially those dealing with hate where the good has been rejected), those that end it show the lover as carrying the good *with him* in his sorrow. Here, sorrow is chastening, making the poet better, more able to love, to offer himself without the persistent urging of a self-gratifying will. In two of the more eloquent poems, "The Relic" and "The Funeral," the sorrow expressed is rational; the speaker does not indulge his grief at the prospect of loss but restrains it, giving rise to a tone that is quiet, detached, and paradoxically suggestive of the joy of the poems closing the first arc. "The Relic" shows the lovers' love as having an innocence predating the fall. The quiet modesty of their feelings is exhibited in the exchange of kisses at greetings and partings "but not between those meals." They know no more of the "difference of sex" than their guardian angels. Surely, the finest touch of the poem lies in the lines "our hands ne'er touched the seals,/Which nature, injured by late law, sets free." The image of the "seals" implies a whole prehistory of love unlike anything known since the fall. It is in moments such as these that Donne displays his genius, taking a stock convention and extending it to reveal depths of meaning. The lovers, who exist in innocence, free of any temptations to indulge themselves or gratify mere sexual appetite, look back to the unfallen garden when all were free to love without taboo or danger.

It is almost impossible to come out of these early works, the Satires, Elegies, and Songs and Sonnets, without feeling Donne has explored the entire universe of emotional life. At the same time, it is equally impossible to read them without hearing a voice that is subtly different from those that follow. Three qualities set this voice off from the others. The first is that it is unmistakably Donne's. No matter what persona he adopts, all of his speakers have his distinctive genius, his "masculine force," his playful wit and energy; they all bear the marks of his vast and desultory learning, his love of punning and music; and they all exhibit his habit of couching passions in the form of arguments exploring correspondences between love and every possible facet of being.

The second is that Donne's first voice is rarely purely lyric. More often than not it is a lyric voice filtered through a dramatic or epic imagination. Its epic qualities rest in the fact that Donne never isolates his lovers. His typical method is to suggest how great love is by linking his lovers to the great chain of being in which they exist. A whole cosmos of kings, courts, angels, planets, all "the elements" and the "world's form," the beginning of time, Eden and the fall afterwards is called into being as a way of showing that the love between the lovers is never reducible to themselves; it is always greater than they are because love by its nature relates them to a universe conceived in love. The dramatic character of Donne's voice is rooted in the lover's struggles to be true to the first motions of his soul, thus placing him at odds not only with himself but with the social world around him, with courtiers, lawyers, statesmen, priests— the vast array of toadies who for reasons of fame or self-advancement seem to have no awareness of betrayal. Donne consistently takes situations that would expose characters in dramas and uses them to explore the lyric interior, to give its hidden obscurity intelligibility and order.

And most important, this first voice is self-consciously cultivated: we cannot read Donne's early works without being aware that the traditions in which he worked are being reflected through him. In his early poetry, it is nearly impossible to distinguish the poet or his persona from his influences. These fall into two broad categories. First, a whole medieval *cultus* involving angels, martyrs, and relics provides much of the material for his poetry (see "Air and Angels," "The Funeral," "The Relic," "The Canonization"). The orthodox belief informing this *cultus* held that matter is not evil but susceptible of grace, of being infused with a divine Spirit that gives an efficacy to the actions of martyrs and their relics.[3] The second broad influence was the poetic and philosophic traditions that gave him the formal means of organizing his materials. Ovid, the Roman satires (in the sense of *saturae* or the rough or uncomely), the Troubadours, Petrarch, the scholastics, the native English poets are all speaking through his poems and being answered simultaneously. These influences make it difficult to determine at times how much Donne is responding spontaneously to his beloved and how much he experiences his love through the alembic of his reading or through his habit of rationalizing the religious practices of the past.

Whether this confusion derives from self-conscious artistry or from other reasons, these early poems contain disproportions between thought and feeling that cannot be ignored. In a number of poems on complete love, the feelings that the poem enacts are at odds with the thoughts in which they are couched: the two are imperfectly fused. "The Good-Morrow," for example, presents feelings of sustained wonder for eighteen lines until they are broken by Donne's closing subjunctive: "If our two loves be one...." Some of the most memorable experiences are held by a thread of this same conditional mood: "*when* my grave is broke up," "*When* I am dead," "*What if* this present were the world's last night?" In each of these cases, the love that is the governing spirit or form of the poem is incompletely realized and presented at some point not as an actual experience but as an *intellectual possibility*.

Similar kinds of incongruities exist in poems on the secondary arc. In "Twicknam Garden," "Nocturnal," and most of the valedictory poems, the sorrow expressed is never at odds with reason; the two are nearly perfectly fused: reason is one with the emotions and their natural inclination toward the good. The lover never ceases loving the beloved, even in the face of an impending separation or actual loss. But in poems like "Farewell to Love," "Love's Alchemy," or "Love's Usury," that is, poems dealing with hate, fear, vengeance, and despair, the emotions rendered are not simply those called into play to resist an evil contrary to the good the will seeks; they are the result of the speaker *having chosen an evil and placing himself in opposition to the good and to the natural inclination of desire*. The result is a dissonant form in which a playful surface is at odds with its underlying spirit. The beauty of the form dignifies the emotions, so the poems are exquisite and pleasing; yet the emotions conveyed are in a state of moral arrest. Of reason we can say, with Donne, "a great prince in prison lies"; it is "captiv'd, and proves weak or untrue." If we assume the lyric speakers are Donne, he has attained a rare courage and truthfulness in laying bare his soul. If we assume Donne is taking on a persona or simply carrying on influences, then we have to see the lyric reaching a new stage of dramatic power and irony and Donne as a precursor to Baudelaire, Browning, and Eliot. From the perspective of the lyric interior we are not far away from familiar moderns caught in similar states of paralysis, as in Prufrock's "Do I dare" or Gerontion's "Think now...think neither...think at last....Tenants of the house, /Thoughts of a dry brain in a dry season."

The Second Voice

In the two *Anniversaries*, there can be no doubt about who is speaking. Donne is honoring a friend whose identity is known, and the death that is the occasion of the poem is real. Donne is not assuming a persona; the voice is his, and he believes what he is saying. In dealing with death, he is returning to a much worked-over theme of the songs and sonnets. But a change has taken place. Donne's view of the world has darkened. He speaks now as a man who has experienced the abyss of human evil; he knows it intimately, not just from readings, and he has internalized it. He is less naïve, less cavalier, more sober, and perhaps most important, he speaks as a public spokesman bringing a different kind of authority and purpose to the creative act.

Donne's purpose in writing the two *Anniversaries* is not only to eulogize Elizabeth Drury but to tell the world of its sickness. Both eulogies unfold in the form of two perspectives at odds with one another, one involving the utter depravity of this world, the other the complete and everlasting perfection of the next. The young girl is seen as the object by which the nature of both worlds is fully revealed. Alive, she was a pattern of virtue, intimating the perfection of the next world and thus exposing the infirmities of this one and helping by her example to preserve what little good it has managed to keep; dead, she is a call to the blessedness of the next life. Man's blindness to the world's corruption is almost complete, but the death of someone as virtuous as Elizabeth reminds the world of its actual state: "her death hath taught us dearly, that thou art/Corrupt and mortal in thy purest part" ("First Anniversary," 61-62). His praise is intended to show the world that its beliefs about the young woman's death are evidence only of its perverse blindness.

In the "First Anniversary," the reprise "She, she is dead, she's dead" gives a haunting, dirge-like quality to each of the many variations Donne plays on his primary theme. To know that Elizabeth is dead is to know "how dry a cinder this world is" (428). But Donne's focus is not simply the world's decay; it is also man's consequential blindness. Any attempt at understanding or seeing is doomed to fail, not only because what man attempts to "anatomize" will not survive his efforts, but because he refuses to face his condition. The human intellect is inherently clouded, most evidently so in that one sees only in terms of succession and parts, not as wholes or all at once:

> But as in cutting up a man that's dead,
> The body will not last out to have read
> On every part, and therefore men direct
> Their speech to parts, that are of most effect:
> So the world's carcass would not last, if I
> Were punctual in this anatomy.
>
> (435-40)

In the "Second Anniversary," Donne continues to explore death as a result of man's fall, this time, however, giving the corruption of the body and the world an even greater emphasis. In the "First Anniversary," he had described death as a release from the imprisonment of the body and the condition for a new birth (451-54). Here, the body is not simply a sign of the fall, a prison-house, little more than "a small lump of flesh"; it is associated with its cause: "My body, could, beyond escape or help,/Infect thee with original sin..." (166-67). Addressing his own soul and so reinforcing the poem's reflexive inward turn, Donne grieves that his body infected him as it did.

Moved by the thought that death has placed Elizabeth beyond the body and the experience of time and space as we know it, Donne approaches his second eulogy taking a completely different tack, one more Platonic and necessitating a new structure of metaphors. His conceptual framework has subtly changed. Instead of thinking in terms of sequence or succession, he is concerned primarily with a new way of seeing, with moving beyond an apprehension of the world through *ratio* (the power of seeing one step at a time) to an intuitive grasping of wholes through *intellectus* (an angelic way of apprehending, following Plato, only possible *outside* the body). Donne now imagines Drury's progress once her soul is released from its body: "But think that death hath now enfranchised thee,/Thou hast thy expansion now, and liberty" (179-80). No longer trapped in her body, she ceases to be bound by time or space: her soul "bates not at the moon, nor cares to try" (195) and passes through "the body of the sun" (201) until it comes to a point where "quick succession" is replaced by "one thing," her soul experiencing heaven with the same splendid nearness and concreteness as it would "colors" or "objects, in a room":

> But ere she can consider how she went,
> At once is at, and through the firmament.
> And as these stars were but so many beads
> Strung on one string, speed undistinguished leads
> Her through those spheres, as through the beads, a string,
> Whose quick succession makes it still one thing....
> Heaven is as near, and present to her face,
> As colors are, and objects, in a room
> Where darkness was before, when tapers come.
>   (205-10, 216-18)

The dark brooding of the poem surpasses anything in Donne's earlier work. The effect is not mere rhetorical exaggeration to underscore Drury's virtue; a near-Manichean spirit pervades the poem. Donne's Platonism and his Reformation belief in the *essential* corruption of man have removed the ground for any *natural* rational sight and pushed him to seek relief in the next life. The dark imagery has a deliberate aim: to give point to the kind of sight he essays through the poem's movement. He is attempting to cultivate a sight capable of penetrating beyond the experience of sequence or succession to an intuitive apprehension of the here and now of eternity. Where the focal point of the "First Anniversary" is the lyric self in a body, with its limited experience of time as succession of parts, the unifying point of view here is the soul moving beyond the body to an experience of rest and wholeness in an expanded, epic-like moment.

Two qualities set this second voice off from the first. In the early sonnets, Donne repeatedly offers dramatic renderings of the lyric self caught in a moment of love or one of its perversions. The action of the poems is always self-contained: the poems and the experience are one because of the immediacy of the first-person mode. In these poems he nowhere violates the lyric's autonomy. In the *Anniversaries*, however, a didactic element governs his voice. He is speaking *to* his people and *for* them, clearly hoping to cultivate a new way of seeing, a kind of vision that overcomes the subject/object dichotomy resulting, apparently, from the fall. Beholding God, man escapes the dualism under which he now labors: "...only who have enjoyed/The sight of God, in fullness, can think it;/For it is both the object, and the wit" (440-42).

Ironically, the condition of which Donne sings in the "Second Anniversary" is more fully realized in the sonnets because there the union of love is rendered *immediately*, in accord with the mode of the lyric: dramatic experience and the words expressing it are one. Here Donne is on earth speaking *about* a condition known only through an abstraction and from which he is removed; he sings of a union in which the object/thought dualism is overcome, but except for the brief moment when he *imagines* Drury's release from the body, such a union is never actually achieved. The didactic character of the poem prevents its realization.

The second distinctive quality of this voice is a new kind of authority taken on by Donne himself. In his early works, whether Donne speaks in his own person or as another, his voice reached the reader always in the mode of the lyric "I," and when he alludes to or invokes a transcendent power, it is typically figurative. In the *Anniversaries*, however, he speaks with an authority reminiscent of the ancient pagan seers and the Old Testament prophets. He intends to preserve Drury's honor ("First Anniversary," 473-74), but it is not enough that she be remembered in mere verse. To ensure that no one forget her, he writes a "song" like the one God had Moses write for his people: "because he knew they would let fall/The Law, the prophets, and the history,/But keep the song still in their memory" (464-66). The new kind of song requires a subtle and important shift to indicate its divine sanction. Donne is not expressing his private love through "influences"; he speaks as a "trumpet," an instrument of the Holy Spirit calling back a lost people:

> Since his will is, that to posterity,
> Thou shouldst for life, and death, a pattern be,
> And that the world should notice have of this,
> The purpose, and th'authority is his;
> Thou art the proclamation; and I am
> The trumpet, at whose voice the people came.
> ("Second Anniversary," 523-28)

The Third Voice

In his final voice, employed in the *Holy Sonnets* and his other explicitly religious poems, Donne no longer uses his genius to create fictional worlds rooted in shifting passions, his own or those of models. He takes his bearings from his belief as a Christian in an unchanging ground beneath them. Donne's reference point is no longer Roman or Italian or native English lyric traditions; it is the reality of the Christian experience enfolded in dogma. This shift utterly changes his voice in the lyric mode. If there is anything left of *cultivated* sensibilities, they have been subordinated to other ends. Donne speaks in his own voice here as he does in the *Anniversaries*. The difference is that now he places himself more consistently and directly before Christ and God the Father, doing all he can to keep alive the analogical ties between poetry and the immediate reality before him. His later poems typically arise from actual situations and in turn more immediately reflect them. They are less artificial, less given to rhetorical exaggeration. Donne's own personal passions are not less at stake, but instead of dealing with them through elaborate conceits, he renders them more simply, more directly.

There is nothing contrived about these poems, no assumed persona. In the *Holy Sonnets* Donne gives expression to actual personal anguish. Holy Sonnet XVII was almost certainly occasioned by the death of his wife in 1617. In "Good Friday, 1613. Riding Westward" Donne took the concrete realities of a personal journey and transformed them into a meditation on his failings and a plea to Christ: Donne asks the Savior to restore His image in the sinner, to "burn off [his] rusts," so that Donne can be recognized again as made in God's image and likeness and be able to "turn [his] face" back to Christ. In this last voice, Donne is more often a penitent, bent over and aware of death: "I am carried toward the west/This day, when my soul's form bends towards the east...." And the mood of his voice has changed. The conditional "if" or "when" that so often marks a turn in the songs and sonnets typically gives way to imperatives: "Seal then this bill of my divorce to all" ("A Hymn to Christ") or "Be this my text, my sermon to mine own" ("Hymn to God my God").

In his early lyrics, Donne gives full play to his ingenuity and the tensions contained in his beliefs, his this-worldly humanism and his otherworldly Platonic theology. The inveterate schism between body and soul that colors much of his early poetry is owed to this Platonic theology: Donne's tendency to do away with the sexual differences between men and women ("forget the He and She"); to see love in terms of ghosts, shadows, or apparitions, that is, of privations, of things lacking substance; or to treat love from the perspective of polar opposites, of perfections and "negations" or "dark eclipses." Some of the poems on complete love avoid the schism because in them the completeness envisioned reconciles body and soul. In the *Anniversaries,* this schism widens and may reach its critical breaking-point. There Donne's persistent idealization of Elizabeth Drury, even before her death, places her above the fall in which all other mortals participate: her sin, if indeed she had any, "was her first parents' fault, and not her own" ("Second Anniversary," 458); and she is presented as a disembodied spirit still hovering over the earth where "her ghost doth walk; that is, a glimmering light" ("First Anniversary" 70).

Some time around "La Corona" (1607-9), however, a poem predating the two *Anniversaries,* this dualism begins to wane. By the time of his final hymns (1613-23), if Donne has not fully accepted the body or the human person as a composite, he is close to doing so. In this last phase, Donne no longer deals with experiences envisioned in terms of intellectual possibilities or even Platonic idealizations; his lyric voice speaks from an immediate, personal identification with the Incarnation and its paradoxes and, even more important, with the unconditional love behind its mysteries. In the *Holy Sonnets,* palinodes give way to a spirit of devotion. Donne sings as a penitent holding himself accountable before a reality that neither his wit nor his passions can change. The change taking place is, significantly, from one kind of suffering to another: from Donne or his persona grieving because he does not get what he wants to Donne willingly suffering for his sins: "That sufferance was my sin, now I repent;/Because I did suffer I must suffer pain" ("Holy Sonnet III").

In the *Holy Sonnets*, Donne continues to present himself in terms reminiscent of the courtly romance lover, but the whole tenor of love, its nature and end, has changed. His object now is Christ and the Church:

> Dwells she with us, or like adventuring knights
> First travail we to seek and then make love?
> Betray kind husband thy spouse to our sights
> And let mine amorous soul court thy mild dove.
>
> ("Holy Sonnet XVIII," 9-12)

By this time, Donne can no longer maintain his dualisms without subtly undermining his belief in the dual nature of Christ, the fact of Christ's having descended into matter and glorifying the body along with all of nature. Donne's tendency to conceive of reality in terms of polar opposites and of the complex structures and dramas that these opened to him remains, but the language has changed and the tensions have relaxed as if more fully subsumed into Christian mysteries.

In "Good Friday, 1613," paradoxes are still present, but they are less precious in character:

> Hence is't, that I am carried towards the west
> This day, when my soul's form bends toward the east.
> There I should see a sun, by rising set,
> And by that setting endless day beget.
>
> (9-12)

Donne's journey westward on Good Friday brings him to meditate on his approaching death and Christ's redemptive mysteries. His soul having admitted "pleasure or business" for its "first mover," he is "whirled" by the world's material motions rather than impelled toward Christ, who as Son is linked to the "sun" as an active life-giving force at work within nature while resting beyond it. But here, in contrast to the *Anniversaries*, Christ is not left as an intellectual abstraction, his redemption not presented at a remove. Rather, his sacrifice is fully realized in the concrete workings of nature. Of Christ's death, Donne says, "It made his own lieutenant Nature shrink,/It made his footstool crack, and the sun wink." He then asks if he could bear to witness the very paradoxes he has formulated:

> Could I behold those hands which span the poles,
> And turn all spheres at once, pierced with those holes?
> ...
>   ...Or that blood which is
> The seat of all our souls, if not of his,
> Made dirt of dust, or that flesh which was worn,
> By God, for his apparel, ragged and torn?
>
>   (21-22, 25-28)

The fidelity of this passage to dogma combined with the remarkable compression of its details is a measure of how far Donne has come from his earlier voices. It is impossible for him to see his travels here except as simultaneously literal and metaphorical.

By the time of "La Corona," Donne is far more conscious of the transcendent source of words and also of the infinite analogies between the two. Earlier the link between words and some remote ineffable Word was implicit. Now it is out in the open; it is literal, metaphorical, and reflexive all at once, giving his treatment of words a much more fully developed metaphysical quality:

> The Word but lately could not speak, and lo
> It suddenly speaks wonders, whence comes it,
> That all which was, and all which should be writ,
> A shallow seeming child, should deeply know?
>
>   ("La Corona: Temple," 5-8)

Seen from this perspective, words are not simply signifiers making present a temporal reality outside themselves; they can also point to a transcendent order whose mode is silence, for "the Word...could not speak." Originating in the Word, they are part of a whole and imply it in all they do. Something of the mystery of words is contained in the paradox of God as Donne sees him in "La Corona," the "All changing unchang'd Ancient of days." In poetry words move through time, but in light of Donne's stance here (the source of words being the stillness and silence of the Word whose love is without desire), they also have a metaphysical power for bringing an action to its completion in the stillness of form. By form here is meant what the *mind* grasps when it sees the whole of the poem at once. Mario Praz has observed something of this same notion in his work on Donne:

> The poet's passionate argument does not allow for those stately, self-contained lines whose perfection redeems many a lifeless sonnet. There is hardly a line in Donne's poem which makes sense by itself, or can claim the power of emblazoning in a musical cadence a whole state of mind. The sense is rounded off only at the end of the stanza, or rather at the end of the poem: the unit is not the line, as in many sonneteers, and not even the stanza, but the entire poem....His main preoccupation is with the whole effect. (57)

The point bears repeating: Donne's poems have to be read and *seen* as wholes. He rarely simply describes or narrates; like the scholastics behind him, he is almost always making demonstrations, moving the mind to the grasping of a point. The typically argumentative character of his lyrics requires that we follow out their line of reasoning to determine whether their conclusions are warranted. His arguments are often specious, and he knows it, but even when they are, as in a poem like "The Flea," the emotions controlling the poem are pushing toward an end: he wants to get his mistress into bed (at least this is the fiction of the poem). The desire at work implies the rest or completion inherent in its end, its "point." In a comment reflecting on his own practices, Hart Crane said of the words composing a poem, "It is as though a poem gave the reader as he left it a single, new *word*, never before spoken and impossible to actually enunciate, but self-evident as an active principle in the reader's consciousness henceforward" (327). One ought to read Donne in this spirit.

Perhaps the most important change in Donne's voice occurs in his handling of paradoxes. The earlier poems seem to justify Johnson's censure of unlike things violently yoked. In the later poems Donne has matured; his vision is more steeped in faith and theological truths; oddities have slipped away and been replaced by genuine paradoxes. Some critics label his style throughout as witty; it would be more accurate to say that in this last phase, Donne is paradoxical, struggling to find words to do justice to his growing sense of the profound intelligibility at the heart of Christian mystery. One can yoke unlike things and not get close to a paradox; bringing together two apparently contradictory things that on the surface are antinomies suggests a greater ground of reason but one shrouded in mystery. "La Corona" and the later religious hymns are filled with such antinomies. In them, Donne continues to draw on his native ingenuity, but now it is more restrained, more nuanced. The syntax is rarely convoluted or complex; it is simpler, expressive of a calmer mind. His famous play on his name—the fact that he can enjoy a joke on himself with God—shows how far he has come in dealing with difficult passions:

> When thou hast done, thou hast not done,
>   For I have more....
> But swear by thy self, that at my death thy son
>   Shall shine as he shines now, and heretofore;
>   And, having done that, thou hast done,
>   I fear no more.
>   ("A Hymn to God the Father," 11-12, 15-18)

The play on "done" and "more" (after his wife Anne More), the creative link between the lyric self and the divine "self," and the efficacy of God that he counts on ("And, having *done* that..." [my italics]) show a mind steeped in realities that he wants to penetrate. There is nothing merely clever or ingenious here: the paradoxes go to profound mysteries having to do with the self and the mysterious depths of subjectivity. The shared activity of Donne's lyric "self" with the divine self and the parallel between them speaks of an immediate depth of intimacy far beyond anything hinted at in his earlier works.

Donne's lyrics are too dense in paradoxes to do justice to here, but I single out one now that is especially pleasing and profound. In "La Corona" Donne begins by offering his work to Christ, pleading that he be rewarded not with a "vile crown" but with one that will "flower always." This opening is followed by a more philosophical reflection on the nature of the act he hopes will take place: "The ends crown our works, but thou crown'st our ends...." (1.9). That neat antimetabole is followed by two of the most tightly constructed paradoxes in all of Donne: "For, at our end begins our endless rest" and "This first last end, now zealously possessed..." (1.10-11). "At our end begins" and "endless rest" are strange enough paradoxes, but how can we begin to put together the possible combinations of oxymorons and the mystery they point to in the opening of that third line? The words "first last end, now" sum up in legitimate grammatical order the whole order of earthly and heavenly realities of the "Corona" as well as most of Donne's later poetry.

The Enveloping Night

To the questions posed at the outset concerning Donne's legacy, it is now possible to venture an answer. The great range and variety of dramatic situations that Donne renders and the emotions underlying them give the impression of completeness. But a careful reading reveals unevenness and gaps, certainly if we read him with Dante and the scholastics in mind, two important influences in his life. Although Helen Gardner maintains that Donne is the only non-dramatic poet to give expression to the theme of the "rapture of fulfillment and of the bliss of union in love" (xvii), I can find nothing of rapture or even of bliss in anything Donne has written. I question whether the lyric can treat rapture effectively, whether it has enough length to make a place for the suffering or cost that is a necessary precondition of bliss, that intensifies and deepens bliss and takes it beyond mere happiness. In those poems dealing with a perfect union between lover and beloved, the emotion expressed is rather wonder and happiness. There is little of the ecstasy expressed in, say, Keats's "My heart aches, and a drowsy numbness pains/My sense....'Tis not through envy of thy happy lot/But being too happy in thine happiness....Already with thee! Tender is the night."

Several of Donne's poems on complete love and a few of those dealing with sorrow are among the most perfect in our language. Even in the best of the poems on joy, however, we are never made to feel the cost of joy, and in those in which sorrow is expressed, we are never allowed to experience a joy arising out of suffering. Donne is fully up to the task of giving dramatic expression to grudges, resentments, threats, to the feverish spinning off of will and mind into an imagined world where lust or revenge is carried out. Hints of the kind of love that comes from self-denial and unconditional self-giving are buried in the poems on complete love. But no poems render the state of patience, of the lover bearing with the infirmities of his beloved. Perhaps most important, given his beliefs, there are no poems in which Donne carries *back* to his beloved or the world about him all that he has learned to know and feel from his love of God.

In one of the palinodes written after the death of his wife and his ordination, Donne gives hints that as he aged, he found very little good in the world, at least as he had known it in his earlier life, and so turned his back on it:

> Seal then this bill of my divorce to all,
> ...
> Marry those loves, which in youth scattered be
> On fame, wit, hopes (false mistresses) to thee.
> Churches are best for prayer, that have least light:
> To see God only, I go out of sight....
> ("A Hymn to Christ," 25, 27-30)

A chasm exists between Donne's early poems on romantic love and those later poems expressing his love of Christ and God the Father. Whether it was the result of his Platonic cast of mind or of personal losses is hard to say. What can be said is that however much Donne took from the traditions in which he worked, the great achievement of Dante from the turn in the *Vita Nuova* all the way through the sustained and ever-deepening bliss of the *Paradiso* seems lost on him. Donne's great legacy may rest on other grounds. Although he is most likely to be remembered for his wit, for the exhilarating interplay between reason and passion, his greatest contribution may finally lie in the one area of the lyric that is the most obvious and so most easily overlooked—subjectivity.

An important truth of Thomas Aquinas is that the soul cannot be known as subject directly; it can only be known reflexively by what it knows. Following Thomas, Jacques Maritain describes the knowing self, the inner subjectivity of the soul this way: "Subjectivity as *subjectivity* is inconceptualizable; is an unknowable abyss....Subjectivity is not known, it is felt as a propitious and enveloping night" (*Existence* 69-70). One of the few means of access to this infinite abyss of the self, according to Maritain, is poetic knowledge. I would add that the genre most immediately expressive of it is the lyric. In the lyric we are brought closer to the thoughts and feelings of the poet in their original, unarticulated, unmediated form before they pass from a world of darkness into the world of contingency and the chains of causality that constitute a part of it, that is, before they pass into the city and the worlds of drama and epic. By accommodating situations usually confined to drama and epic to the lyric interior, Donne opened up this "abyss," not through concepts or the essences they make known to us, but in the only way possible, concretely and dramatically through poetic knowledge.

A distinctive quality of the lyric self, at least as it was received from Donne, is its power for assimilating other selves and then adopting them, in varying degrees of interest or disinterest, as its own. We are not yet at the grotesque interior of Browning's clergy or of "Prufrock" or even at the epic reaches of *The Waste Land*, but the ground for them has been laid. Donne's lyrics may have left us with uncertainties about how to read the self or speaker, but they have left little doubt about the means or ends of the lyric *eros*. In Donne especially, it yearns to unite the inward enveloping night of the speaker with an answering good outside himself, not only the beloved and the larger surrounding cosmos, but the "All changing unchang'd Ancient of days," still and wrapped in silence.

Notes

1. C. S. Lewis's criticism of Donne is "not that he writes *about*, but that he writes in, a chaos of violent and transitory passions" ("Donne" 80). His condemnation of Donne points up *the* critical issue and the importance of understanding genres: is Donne speaking in his own voice or adopting a persona? If the lyric is a direct expression of the poet's feelings, Donne is, as Lewis suggests, writing out of violent passions. The habit of academics to refer to "the speaker" illustrates the opposite inaccuracy. Donne makes use of both procedures, writing in his own voice and also adopting others. This fact requires careful adjustments in our reading of his lyrics.

2. I have consulted several editions of Donne's poems for this essay, most frequently *John Donne: The Complete English Poems*, ed. A. J. Smith; also *John Donne: A Selection of His Poetry*, ed. John Hayward, *The Songs and Sonnets of John Donne*, ed. Theodore Redpath, and *The Elegies and the Songs and Sonnets of John Donne*, ed. Helen Gardner.

3. Although Donne draws on this *cultus* for its language and dramatic situations, he nowhere makes a distinction between orthodox belief and its perversion, the superstitious belief in magic, charms, and talismans (cf. "A Valediction: of my Name in the Window" and "Witchcraft by a Picture").

6

Keats's Pilgrimage:
The Five Great Odes

Louise Cowan

Keats's "Ode on a Grecian Urn" marks the summit of the five great odes that, written in the spring of 1819, constitute a journey into the depths of lyric territory. This poem confronts and answers the questions raised in the three preceding odes, implicit in Keats's entire body of work. Near death, during this next-to-last year of his life, having in his own mind failed in his commitment to leave a lasting memorial to poetry, Keats began a fresh exploration of the meaning of beauty as it could be known through the imagination. "What the imagination seizes as Beauty must be truth—whether it existed before or not," he had written to his friend Benjamin Bailey (22 Nov. 1807). Now, during this time of illness and discouragement, Keats composed, among other masterpieces, the odes that may be taken as touchstones defining stages of the lyric moment. In this last suite of poems he has created a kind of divine comedy of the lyric order, plumbing its somber depths and scaling its paradisal heights. Together, the odes enact a process of transfiguration, unmatched since Donne's love poems and, before him, Dante's *Commedia,* even more than his *Vita Nuova.* The odes are not, then, mere experiments in craft; nor are they purely aesthetic investigations. For Keats, at this period of his life, poetry has become a spiritual exercise, like prayer. Here at the height of his powers, poised between life and death, he searches for the form of the primal wisdom, the underlying desire of the lyric mode. The odes become for him a probing of mortality, a quest for the metaphysical dimension lost to English poetry after the mid-seventeenth century.

The fourth in Keats's sequence, the "Ode on a Grecian Urn" is the crucial poem in the group, for its concern is incarnation itself. Confronting the urn's seeming imperviousness with the sad vulnerability of those who made it, the poet's imagination is given a glimpse of a dimension beyond the present in which the urn has its true existence. And though this vista provides no direct answers to his questions, it offers a witness that obliterates their need. The search for meaning in the Grecian Urn ode is so intense that in any serious attempt to ascertain the reach of lyric one is compelled to examine this enigmatic poem afresh, at the risk of repeating what numerous authorities have already said about it. For in its five ten-line stanzas of irregularly rhymed iambic pentameter, Keats has given form to the inner path of what in a letter written during this time he designated as "Soul-making" (to George and Georgiana Keats, 14 Feb.-3 May 1819). The Grecian Urn ode gathers the questions and insights of the preceding odes and, like an invocation, like a prayer, moves from a series of interrogations to a recognition of their irrelevance, from a somber reckoning of mortality to a celebration of transcendence. It makes this transition by shifting to a different plane of cognition, utilizing a voice that, by the end of the poem, the reader has recognized empathetically as the urn's, the poet's, and one's own. In thus tracing the path of lyric imagination, it accomplishes the miracle of raising a material object to immateriality and permanence.

Like the preceding poems of the sequence, the "Ode on a Grecian Urn" focuses on a feminine figure, a "Beatrice," to which the poet assigns the stature of divinity. In the first poem of the series, the numinous presence is the goddess Psyche, to whom the poet dedicates his efforts; in the next, Melancholy, then Philomela—the nightingale—and, later, Ceres, the goddess of harvest. In the crowning poem, the Grecian Urn ode, he addresses the urn as a kind of vegetation goddess such as Persephone might be, incarnate in a work of art, a "bride of quietness," carrying with her through time all the joys and pains of mortality, to be offered at the end—to Hades? The surface of the urn is "overwrought" with sculpted figures and vegetation. Its two sides represent the full scope of mortal experience, which, out of a long-lost time, it has carried forward to some sort of destination. Thus the urn represents, in a sense, the human essence as created and creating being. Where are the lives headed that we live with such passion?

The ode begins with an apostrophe to the urn, addressing it

in the first four lines as a goddess, then as divine progeny, as historian, and finally as itself artist, giving form to its own "flowery tale" of humanity:

> Thou still unravish'd bride of quietness,
>   Thou foster-child of silence and slow time,
> Sylvan historian, who canst thus express
>   A flowery tale more sweetly than our rhyme...

This is an invocation by a fellow artist, concerned as much about his poetry as his mortality. Here at the very beginning a contrast is set up, not only between present and past, but between word and thing, viewer and object, *melos* and *opsis*, sound and sight, present vocal sensibility and ancient mute testimony. Yet these antinomies remain covert, all the overt questions at the beginning of the poem having to do with the mystery of temporality. The urn presents to the modern viewer an uncharted reach of time. Something has washed up out of an unknown past, something that raises fearful questions for present viewers. To be or not to be? Where is the rest of the human drama that had to take place, behind the scene, for the urn to exist? Are mortality and its consequent subjection to the onslaughts of time worth nothing at all, to be brushed away like crumbs of clay when the design has been completed? Along with such somber musings arise questions that the rational mind considers genuine questions, matters of fact: the who, what, when, where of empirical inquiry.

One portion of the urn's surface celebrates an apparent *kômos*, a revel, a festive procession, out of which, according to Aristotle, comedy arose. The other portrays a sacrificial ritual, a variant of which, as some scholars say, produced tragedy. Who are the celebrators—men or gods? Where are they located—in Tempe or the dales of Arcady? To what god are they sacrificing—a kindly presence, as indicated by the joyous procession, or a vengeful force that demands blood offering? What kind of music are they playing? What is the legend the wild pursuit portrays? Was this joyous procession part of a ritual? Where is the little town? When and where did it all take place? Do we not need to ascertain the historical facts about these two scenes depicted on its alternate sides? The answers to these questions, if one could find them out, would constitute the archaeologist's "truth" about this particular artifact. But we cannot be certain of our facts, with no information available concerning the origins of the urn. The rational mind cannot know certain essentials about the urn; and our ignorance is frustrating. Further, acquiring any trustworthy facts about it, according to empirical standards, requires a distancing from its devastating impact.

And yet, as the speaker makes clear, we have the silent urn itself, preserved out of time, with its serene testimony, its mute message not spoken, a "still unravish'd bride of quietness." The musing poet probes its silent mystery. This striking Greek object, unmarred and intact, seems to have an intention of its own, as though it has been promised to someone, or has a message to deliver—but to whom? To an ultimate non-existence? In the next line the urn is designated as a "foster-child of silence and slow time," raising the question of how it can be both bride and foster child of the same entity. If bride, it has intentionality; if foster child, a past in which it has been sheltered. In the designations "bride of quietness" and "foster-child of silence," is there the implication that quietness and silence are different? Does quietness have to do with the urn's own existence, and silence with becoming? Further, if it is a foster child of both silence and time, then silence has adopted it, so to say, has paired with time—a force otherwise seen as destructive—to protect it. Since the urn is viewed as an orphan, then the viewer recognizes that its real parents are absent. Who, then, were they? Who really created it? And the answer implied in the speaker's musings—that is, the artist and his society—brings up the central issue of the poem. The solution to all our riddles is to be found in the enigma that now dominates the poet's speculations: time. But here we are told that in the long destructive stretch of the ages, contrary to what one would think, the urn has been "fostered," cared for by time, not diminishing but increasing in its worth.

The greatest mystery, however, concerns the ultimate destiny of this work of human craft. If the urn is still the intended bride of quietness, is that union directed toward some point beyond our view, to be celebrated only in the future? As we are pondering it, is it still on its way? When the consummation takes place, will the urn still exist in its present form? Or, in its wedding with quietness, will it be gathered into what Yeats calls "the artifice of eternity," a kind of nirvana—a clear stillness of the mysterious spiritual world, the all and nothing toward which it seems from the beginning to be headed? Then what is its significance to us who view it with such wonder? It is this agonizing question concerning intentionality, the *telos* discerned in the urn, that has been troubling the poet's mind. This work of art has not yet fulfilled its mission, though it has already gone long beyond its own day. Yet it appears to be destined for some sort of consummation—a wedding that seems, on the surface of it, to exclude mortal flesh and blood. As the poet-speaker views this lone survivor of another age and time, the dark question beneath all his interrogations concerns the value of human life itself. What is the meaning of mortal existence?

The poem, then, is a meditation on the mystery contained within a vulnerable material object that has a future, surprisingly having survived the temporal ravages of centuries. It is spoken by a viewer locked in the present, cut off from the artistry that produced the urn by layers of time enshrouding a past no longer accessible. And yet, as the speaker is aware, the purpose of this enigmatic witness has not yet been achieved; its message still remains to be delivered, its mission accomplished. It is pointed toward the future, remaining, in this sense, impervious to the viewer in its virginal integrity. The viewer characterizes himself as a poet, worshipful and at the same time envious of the urn's silent intensity: this "bride of quietness" can tell its visual story in a way "more sweetly than our rhyme." Here a further contrast is set up, not only between word and thing, but between the modern voice, the ancient testimony, and the visionary glimpse of the *parousia*, the time of fulfillment. How can we understand this emissary from the past, the poet implies, when it seems pointed beyond us, over our heads, so to speak, the royal bride of something beyond our knowing? The facts surrounding it—what we as moderns demand if we are seeking the truth of the matter—are missing. But most of all, we are excluded from any participation in the "wild ecstasy" portrayed on its surface.

But the urn's implicit message has not been obliterated. In the *kômos scene*, the lover or bridegroom pursues the maiden, leaning near but not touching; the pipers keep up their joyful music, the very flora and fauna rejoicing. But the music remains frozen, inaudible; the implicit kiss hangs in the suspended moment; the flowers bloom on without fading. The poet makes an attempt to cheer himself up at the prospect of time's permanent loss, for obviously, in actual life, the youth must have kissed the young woman, the melody would have been heard and enjoyed; yet nothing remains of those actual events. Time has destroyed the living pulse of consummation, so that fulfillment of desire seems to come to nothing, with the work of art preserving a lifeless entity. Is the urn a mere simulacrum—a meaningless design, an abstraction from the warm breath and beating heart? The poet makes an attempt to rejoice at the timelessness of the scene, celebrating its atemporal transcendence, with the imagined melody surpassing the actual, the prolonged moment before the kiss maintaining its intensity undiminished throughout the centuries.

Ironically, however, this celebratory scene induces sadness: the lover, immobilized at the highest pitch of desire, will never kiss the bride; the spirited music, though sweeter than any ever heard, remains, alas, inaudible. The past is dead, or so it seems at this point; frozen at a moment just before consummation, it remains sterile, beautiful but bloodless, to become a mere image in our minds. Yet "do not grieve," the speaker advises the youth:

> She cannot fade, though thou hast not thy bliss
> For ever wilt thou love, and she be fair!

The poet continues his reverie, still consoling the impotent lover; but his language rings a bit too hearty, giving rise to an undertone of wistfulness:

> Ah, happy, happy boughs! that cannot shed
>   Your leaves, nor ever bid the Spring adieu;
> And, happy melodist, unwearièd,
>   For ever piping songs for ever new...

In life, compared to art, passion, so fleeting in ordinary time, "leaves a heart high-sorrowful and cloy'd,/A burning forehead, and a parching tongue." But despite this contrast, the poet's meditations cannot obliterate the mortal truth: the reward of outlasting time is not, as he would want it, passion "For ever warm and still to be enjoy'd,/For ever panting, and for ever young." Rather, it is a stony lifelessness, even though "she cannot fade." The lyric joy has turned unobserved into a lament. In actual life, time destroys the most joyous and intense moments of happiness. In art, those moments are preserved in a cold and marble stillness. The urn has happened to catch and prolong one of those moments, but at the cost of draining it of its life. Other such moments have vanished without a trace.

There is a turn at this point, from the *kômos* of the revel to the other side of the urn, which portrays a darker side of the folk life. The sacrificial animal is a lowing heifer, fortunate here, since she will never reach the "green altar" on which her red blood must flow, an impossible goal toward which she is being led:

> Who are these coming to the sacrifice?
>   To what green altar, O mysterious priest,
>   Lead'st thou that heifer lowing at the skies,
>   And all her silken flanks with garlands drest?

The two sides of mortal life are thus caught on the urn; its creator was obviously aware, even in so idyllic a setting, of the two terms of life and death—of *eros* and *thanatos*. But both forces, subject to time, are caught as though suspended in a glass—or frozen in a block of ice.

If the viewer/poet is to imagine the scenes on the urn as having come from a warm and breathing life, however, he has to posit an entire community behind them. Thus, implied in the two rituals, though not overtly portrayed, is an invisible "little town," whose streets are permanently empty on this day that has projected its citizens into eternity, an incorporeal city preserved from decay. In opening to the implications of this further dimension, the meditative speaker now reveals an entire series of art forms proceeding from the life of the town, each elevating the already existent form into new form. Last in the series, the speaker—a lyric poet—raises them all not by abstraction but by actual images, through contemplation retaining their finite trappings. In this reverie lie "unconcealed" (as Martin Heidegger puts it in his essay "The Origin of the Work of Art," *Poetry* 57) several layers of artistic formalization: the designs of an urn-painter portraying the folk arts of song, dance, and the music of the pipe. Further, behind these celebratory rites, the poet speculates, must have been a lost "leaf-fringed legend" linking the community to its invisible sustenance in myth. Through the form he makes, the artist of the urn has given a further dimension to the ritual, the beauty of his art preserving a unique and particular human scene from the despoilment of time. And now the viewing poet must give this multilayered object a new incarnation, visualizing the deep *telos* of the urn and translating that form into language.

Who, then, was the urn made for? As the viewer contemplates this "historian" of woods long vanished, other questions present themselves. How can the urn wordlessly communicate its insight to an audience so far removed from the original scene? And if the urn is on its way toward an ultimate apotheosis, why does it have such intense meaning for us, the wayfarers that it will leave behind? The entire mystery of presence/absence is condensed on the face of the urn: a leaf-fringed legend that has been forgotten; a community ritual enacting the lost myth; a kiss that no doubt was consummated in actuality but soon vanished; the melodies that, once played, have ceased reverberating; the lowing of the no doubt sacrificed heifer; the flowers and vines long faded that provided the models for the scene-painter's art; the invisible town that, though not depicted on the urn, is caught now in the *mundus imaginalis* in all its emptiness, lacking its citizens, who will be forever truant.

These absences are made sharply present on the urn. Captured in one evocative form, the multiple layers of communal memory—what the Greeks called *kleos*, fame—are present, softening the hard outlines of the urn like encircling gauze. And the testimony of the poem is that we can know these entities better with all their absences vividly present to us (like the sweetness of the unheard melodies). The presence/absence evoked by the urn transcends mere mortality and leads the contemplator into the realm of something beyond life, something that transforms the urn, substantiating it into a unity, an "Attic shape," a concrete universal. In its journey through time the urn bears with it the whole of the human endeavor.

It is this coming together of the manifold layers of time that "teases" the viewer out of thought "as doth eternity." With no apparent narrative, the speaker has clothed his raptness in language that induces meditation, and in this process of musing he ponders the riddle of time, discerning that force to be at least selectively benevolent, since the urn, heavy with its significances, has survived time's assaults. The reach of temporality in the poem extends backward into the shrouded prehistoric mists and forward into the veiled future when the invoking voice will be silent. And with this change of perspective, the contemplation of a time beyond his own life (when the urn's "flowery tale" has become a significant form—an "Attic shape"), the tone of the poem changes.

> O Attic shape! Fair attitude! With brede
>   Of marble men and maidens overwrought,
> With forest branches and the trodden weed;
>   Thou, silent form, dost tease us out of thought
> As doth eternity...

Removed from the necessity of the immediate, the lyricist visualizes the urn no longer as an object but as a metaphysical form, the very shape of Attic life, "overwrought/With forest branches and the trodden weed." This is to view it as an incarnation—a hard, clear embodiment of an invisible and spiritual "attitude" that has nevertheless required life, the living presence of mortals, for its marble men and maidens.

The *peripeteia* is reached in the utterance that follows. In this exclamation the speaker comes to a recognition of the mission of the work of art, the answer to its questions, the solution to its riddle. In so doing he realizes the function of lyric in the paideia that constitutes what Keats calls "soul-making." And with the exclamation "Cold Pastoral!" the poet encounters a still moment in which time, that pressing concern, is suspended. It is at this point that the poem enters another dimension, with the speaker projected into a new and chilling perspective. He can see beyond his own death. He has been "teased out of thought" into a different mental and spiritual state: his rational faculties are for the moment stilled. He is in that condition of negative capability of which Keats wrote in his letter to George and Thomas Keats, when one is "capable of being in uncertainties, Mysteries, doubts, without any irritable reaching after fact & reason" (21 Dec. 1817). This "bride of quietness," this "foster-child of silence and slow time," has evoked a mystery far above "all breathing human passion." Its mission is beyond time. But though the urn transcends time, it will remain in time until the end of time, accessible to human beings, to whom it continues indefatigably, serenely, to extend the answer to the riddle.

> When old age shall this generation waste,
>   Thou shalt remain, in midst of other woe
> Than ours, a friend to man...

But all this is in the speaker's voice: the urn remains mute. The poet-speaker suddenly intuits the message of the silent urn as though it had spoken, and he is given the grace to declare it, still in his own voice; but now he is putting into words something which the urn's entire being signifies: "Beauty is truth, truth beauty." And in its embodiment of this oracle, as he now recognizes, the urn testifies by its presence that all our other questions are irrelevant: "that is all/Ye know on earth, and all ye need to know."

This raising of the visible into the *logos*—this understanding and speaking for the silent—is testimony to an incarnation and at the same time an *aporia* through which new light is shed on the mortal realities of love and death. In opening to the implications of this further dimension, the poet/speaker recognizes that in a process of *ekphrasis* he has given a new form to the already existent art object, as the urn's artist has done with the ritual, as the folk have done with the myth, as the myth has done with the raw materialities of life. He has elevated the urn into a less material medium, extending its embrace of matter into the most ethereal reaches of spirit. Removed from the necessity of the immediate, yet deeply submerged in the finite trappings of the urn, the lyricist ponders the timelessness of the "still unravished bride of quietness." He discerns its need for translation into language, from a spatial medium to a temporal one, from materiality into the invisible realm of the *logos*—a necessary step in the progressive spiritualizing process. His (the poet's) translation of the urn's meaning into a sibylline utterance reveals the ultimate secret: in the beauty of matter lies the metaphysical quality truth. It is for the lyric meditation, centuries away from the urn's origin, to reveal its significance, which must be put into language. As Rilke has written, earth longs to be made invisible ("Earth, isn't this/what you want:/rising up/inside us invisibly/once more?/Earth! invisible!/what is it/you urgently ask for/if not transformation?" 83:9.68-70). And the long journey of the urn in its embodiment in matter testifies to that truth. It has been looking for a poet. The wedding for which it has been intended takes place in the language of lyric.

What the urn testifies is that the work of art endures because of its beauty, its form, its incarnation of the *logos*. All its material elements are vehicles for this consummation: to be known, to be taken up, finally, by the spirit. The truth it reports to us, with its apparent conveying of history, is not to be found in specific facts but in metaphysical insight, expressed in a form invisible to any but the interior eye. It is a foster-child of silence and time, but the intended bride of the unspoken word. The truth about the urn then is beauty; art exists here among mortals as a witness to something unseen in their lives, beyond mortality. The destiny of art is elsewhere; but it is a bridge for us, a conveyor, a messenger, our friend. Its mission as a work of art is to "unconceal," to reveal the unnoticed significance in the passing show of life and to bear witness that beauty is a premonitory sign of something beyond us that we cannot see.

The ending to the poem is not melancholy, as it is usually interpreted to be. It is an affirmation: the speaker and we ourselves have been led by the urn into a region where we participate in the wholeness of being. We are lifted above "all human passion" to see into the ineffable beauty of matter. And it is through our most intimate medium, the one that represents most fully the human image—language—that we have been made to see and to understand. By this ability to raise human consciousness beyond itself and to utter it in language, thereby enabling us to speak the mystery, the lyric poet thus fulfills the implicit yearnings of human action, interpreting the community's deepest secrets and inserting their transfigured life into culture.

Keats thus accomplishes what Dante speaks of at the beginning of the *Paradiso*: a transhumanization, in which, through the celestial imagination, a person is turned inside out, with the invisible reverberations of physicality assuming a deeper reality than any empirical manifestations.[1] For a moment the poem removes the veil: we catch a glimpse of what it means to be in timeless time. And, like Dante in the *Paradiso*, we almost catch a glimpse of the divine visage. We have gone as far as poetry can take us.

Roman Ingarden, in *The Literary Work of Art*, argues that the most important function of poetic imitation is to reveal metaphysical qualities (290-93). These are qualities present in life but largely inaccessible to the conscious mind because manifested in times of stress when the analytical powers of the mind are in abeyance. In the Grecian Urn ode, the actual kissing of the bride and the sacrifice of the heifer are such engrossing moments that their metaphysical implications go unrecognized. The lyric poet, by an ability to bring into language multiple dimensions of reality, completes the fulfillment of life itself and moves creation nearer to its ultimate consummation. Keats's ode thus reconciles matter and spirit, time and eternity.

The "Ode on a Grecian Urn" may be seen, then, as a modern equivalent of a paradisal vision. In its place among Keats's four other odes, it takes on the radiance of a revelation. Like Dante, Keats gives form in this sequence to the stages of a psychic movement, addressing the large question of his life and commitment. Hence commentary on the Grecian Urn ode gains perspective and depth when the poem is placed within the group of poems that lead toward and away from its high reaches.

The sequence of these matchless odes begins with the "Ode to Psyche." In this lesser known but important work, the poet first finds himself, like Dante, "in a dark wood," where he encounters the lovers Cupid and Psyche, discerning in the pair the erotic longing between earth and heaven. The desire of Psyche to be part of eternity touches the poet's depths: in her eros he sees the yearning of the human soul for divinity, and in the lovemaking of the pair the possibility of transformation. Yet because Psyche as goddess is so lately come to her godhead, she remains unrecognized; no temples or shrines have been raised in her honor. In fact, as the poet declares:

> No voice, no lute, no pipe, no incense sweet
>   From chain-swung censer teeming;
> No shrine, no grove, no oracle, no heat
>   Of pale-mouth'd prophet dreaming.

He makes a pledge to the goddess to supply what is wanting:

> So let me be thy choir, and make a moan
>   Upon the midnight hours;
> Thy voice, thy lute, thy pipe, thy incense sweet
>   From swinged censer teeming....
>
> Yes, I will be thy priest, and build a fane
>   In some untrodden region of my mind,
> Where branched thoughts, new grown with pleasant pain,
>   Instead of pines shall murmur in the wind...

Keats had written to George and Georgiana Keats:

> You must recollect that Psyche was not embodied as a goddess before the time of Apuleius the Platonist who lived after their A[u]gustan age, and consequently the Goddess was never worshipped or sacrificed to with any of the ancient fervour–and perhaps never thought of in the old religion–I am more or thodox tha[n] to let a he[a]then Goddess be so neglected. (14 Feb.-3 May 1819)

His ode is a pledge not just to honor a late-come goddess but to venture upon a new territory, to recognize something mortal raised, like Beatrice, to the regions of eternity. But he knows that such an undertaking will have to take place in "some untrodden region" of his mind. Instead of the traditional trappings of piety, Psyche will have to be given "with pleasant pain" a heretofore unexplored portion of the poet's creative imagination. In his illness and, as he senses, near the end of his life, he vows to venture into new poetic territory:

> And in the midst of this wide quietness
> A rosy sanctuary will I dress
> With the wreath'd trellis of a working brain,
> ...
> And there shall be for thee all soft delight
>   That shadowy thought can win,
> A bright torch, and a casement ope at night,
>   To let the warm Love in!

This is a metaphorical description of the creative process itself, a pledge made to Psyche, the soul, to make a new poetry that will require a "working brain," "shadowy thought," and, above all, an openness to transcendence.

After this fateful commitment to Psyche Keats continues to the next stage of exploring the lyric region, recognizing that such service to the soul demands of him a transhumanization. For Keats, five centuries later, surrounded on all sides by what Allen Tate has called the "angelic imagination" (*Essays* 401-23), the process of self-realization requires going in the opposite direction, downward into a kind of primordial depths and speaking *de profundis*. Yet this descent demands a similar turning away from nature, forcing the poet to probe beyond joy into its underlying pain. Keats's search for passion and beauty must therefore be fraught with suffering. In the "Ode on Melancholy" he traces this process, this going against nature, the psychic pattern that must be the response of the lyric poet to any positive experience. "She dwells with Beauty," he declares, the "she" somewhat ambiguous: his raving mistress? Or Melancholy, the forbidding goddess of night? The next lines reveal that he is speaking of the goddess herself:

> Ay, in the very temple of Delight
>   Veil'd Melancholy has her sovran shrine,
>   Though seen of none save him whose strenuous tongue
>   Can burst Joy's grape against his palate fine...

In these primordial depths, if he is to write the new kind of poetry, the *dolce stil nuovo* that will raise the human soul (psyche) to the heights of the godhead, he must "burst Joy's grape against his palate fine." Thus "in the very temple of Delight," he will become a "cloudy trophy" of the goddess Melancholy. This transformation is drastic and permanent, requiring the lyric poet to live in a state of paradox, in which delight pursued to its depths not only becomes anguish, but is revealed in its essence to have been that contradiction all along.

In the next poem of the sequence, the oft-anthologized "Ode to a Nightingale," the poet, now "transhumanized," changed into a living oxymoron for whom pleasure fully experienced is pain, is in a state of numbness from being "too happy" at the burst of joy from a nightingale. His first impulse is to escape. On the natural level, the "ecstasy" of its beauty beckons him at first to a Dionysian celebration and revelry, toward "a beaker full of the warm South," following the normal human proclivity for sensual delight. But moved by his commitment to the dark goddess whose service requires melancholy, he follows the song of the bird into the shadowy obscurity, the "dark wood" of the creative imagination, where he again hears the bird's full-throated ecstasy. Listening in the mellow shadows of this earthly paradise, he detects the transformation he has sought: the profound melancholy that joy induces in its pull toward darkness:

> Darkling I listen; and, for many a time
>   I have been half in love with easeful Death,
> Call'd him soft names in many a mused rhyme,
>   To take into the air my quiet breath;
> Now more than ever seems it rich to die,
>   To cease upon the midnight with no pain,
>   While thou art pouring forth thy soul abroad
>   In such an ecstasy!

But the song, he realizes, is not plaintive; nor is it deathbound. Joyous and affirmative, it is universal and timeless, transforming lives throughout time and space. The poet's affirmation at this point comes from a recognition of the enigmatic power of beauty:

> Thou wast not born for death, immortal Bird!
>   No hungry generations tread thee down;
> The voice I hear this passing night was heard
>   In ancient days by emperor and clown...

In this dark night of the senses, the poet has received a flash of insight in the bird's song, which he perceives as universal and timeless. He has been baptized in Lethe; his soul has been purged. But despite this imaginative transformation, the human lot still remains hopeless and inconsolable:

> Forlorn! the very word is like a bell
>   To toll me back from thee to my sole self!
> Adieu! the fancy cannot cheat so well
>   As she is fam'd to do, deceiving elf.

And the poet is left to wonder:

> Was it a vision, or a waking dream?
>   Fled is that music:—Do I wake or sleep?

After this authentic experience of the splendor and ambiguity of beauty, the poet is abandoned. What truth, then, does the imagination reveal? Is there any correspondence at all between the beauty discovered by the imagination and life's very real anguish?

The next poem in the sequence, the "Ode on a Grecian Urn," as I have earlier tried to show, is a serious and prolonged attempt to answer that question, proceeding to an examination of the finished work of art itself in its relation to both its origin and destiny. The urn, like Beatrice, is an incarnation. But what is the intention, the final purpose of the work of art? Why does the artist create? For whom is the urn—or the poem—intended? What is its ultimate destination? What difference does it make to the actual living process? The answers to these questions mark the conclusion of the entire lyric quest. All that remains to complete this sequence describing the creative process is, finally, the harvest, the time of emptiness and peace after the actual making of the work of art.

In the last of the odes, the reflective and richly paradoxical "To Autumn," the poet is left as mortal being after the almost superhuman suffering of his creative task. This season "of mists and mellow fruitfulness," conspiring with the sun in blessing the vines with ripeness, has its own bittersweet peace. All effort is over; there is only the completion of a process set in motion, a rhythm of fruition that "swell[s] the gourd, and plump[s] the hazel shells/With a sweet kernel; to set budding more,/And still more, later flowers for the bees...." A hazy reverie lulls the poet into an abdication of responsibility for his own mortality. But the note of sadness intrudes. He remembers the joy/pain that created this finished product: "Where are the songs of Spring? Ay, where are they?/Think not of them, thou hast thy music too...." The "wailful choir" of gnats mourning "among the river sallows" combines with lambs bleating, hedge-crickets singing, the red-bird whistling, "gathering swallows twitter[ing] in the skies." A mellow mood of renunciation and acceptance dominates the poem, testifying to the impersonal wisdom and peace toward which human creativity has been headed.

What Keats has produced in this series of odes is a probing examination of the imagination. In these last poems he uses the lyric for its ultimate purpose: to ask the heart's deepest questions. Each of the odes has been motivated and formed by a desire to confront the underlying reality of human existence. As a unit, their integrity depends not on any kind of structural devices linking them together or even any surmise concerning the artist's conscious purpose. It depends, rather, on their own interior witness, their progressive concern with the correspondence between language and reality, or as Keats thinks of it, beauty and truth.

Rising to and falling away from this key poem of the series, the other odes surround the address to the Grecian urn, which is concerned directly with the Beatrician mystery. Each of the others is an enactment of a moment within the poetic process, the sequence making up a larger entity of which the urn poem is the culmination. All are addressed to some sort of feminine deity; all are meditations, spoken from what Jacques Maritain has called "the single root of the soul's powers" (*Creative Intuition* 48, 75-80); and all are in the poet's own voice (as is any genuine lyric unless specifically indicated otherwise, as in a dramatic monologue). Throughout his brief career, Keats had been struggling with this most difficult challenge for the poet—the authentic voice of the lyric. He knew that, in order to speak for the human heart, the speaker must detach himself from his own personality, so that he might possess negative capability and be in the presence of "Mysteries...without any irritable reaching after fact & reason." The poet who reaches this stage of lyric anonymity faces the prospect of losing touch with his private self, enduring a kind of disorientation, and hence becoming in his own eyes something of a monstrosity. Keats had been readying himself for such an ordeal; and in his sequence of odes he takes the risk of this negative knowledge, undergoing that transhumanization that Dante speaks of. With the shadows of the dark wood, the *Inferno*, and even the *Purgatorio* behind him, it is the terrors of light that confront Dante at this point. For Keats, in contrast, the process begins with an entry into darkness. In the cave of the melancholy goddess, with joy converted into pain, the poet must endure the process of contradiction. Keats's search, like Dante's, is for the meaning of what to him seems the highest human activity: "soul-making," the seizing of positive experience by the imagination. The address to the Grecian urn is thus his *Paradiso*, where after lengthy questioning he is given a glimpse of the ultimate goal toward which earthly life is headed: toward a truth that, in the end, can be perceived only as the beautiful.

Note

1. In *Paradiso* 1, Dante prays to Apollo, god of poetry, to make him capable of writing about heaven:

> Enter my breast, breathe into me as high
>   a strain as that which vanquished Marsyas
>   the time you drew him from his body's sheath.
>
>   (19-21; trans. Musa)

Later in that canto he compares himself to Glaucus, who was transformed into a sea god:

> "Transhumanize"—it cannot be explained
>   *per verba*, so let this example serve
>   until God's grace grants the experience.
>
>   (70-72)

7

"And that is why my Garden lasts":
Emily Dickinson's Herbarium,
Her Garden, and the Poems

Anna Priddy

In spring 2008 Harvard released a facsimile edition of what Judith Farr, in the Preface to *Emily Dickinson's Herbarium*, calls Emily Dickinson's "first book" (15). It is a stunningly beautiful production, the beauty a testament not only to its maker's skill but also to the remarkably preserved state of the flora the herbarium contains, now over 150 years old. The sixty-six oversized pages contain a variety of plants and flowers gathered by Dickinson, pressed and identified by her, and until now preserved in the Harvard Library, judged too fragile for viewing even by the most careful of scholars. Turning the pages in this facsimile edition permits a welcome glimpse into the mind of Emily Dickinson. Further, it provides some sense of the importance of the natural world to the poet, who, according to Richard Sewall, wrote poems that include "some thirty different species, a few appearing a number of times—daisies, roses, dandelions." To these are added "twenty in the letters and about eighteen trees, shrubs, herbs and grasses, and her list is complete" ("Science" 25). As Sewall says, this is "not remarkable, perhaps, but not many comparable lyric poets can equal it" ("Science" 25).

Emily Dickinson's Herbarium also brings certain questions to mind. For instance, is creation, at least in part, an act of seeing and preserving? What is the relationship between the physical and the metaphysical? Between science and faith? Between art and the artifact? How is a poem, like a plant, both organic and cultivated? Other questions arise that no doubt I can hardly hope to answer here, but considering a sample of Dickinson's verses (though only a small number of those related to botany that it would be possible to read) along with the evidence of her herbarium may illuminate something more about her vision. The flowers of Dickinson's poems seem to convey, at the very least, further information about her thoughts on poetry, religion, and immortality, what she called the "flood subject."

Emily Dickinson began assembling the herbarium while an adolescent. Her enthusiasm for the project was conveyed in a letter written when she was fifteen, addressed to her friend Abiah Root. She asks, "Have you made an herbarium yet? I hope you will if you have not, it would be such a treasure to you; most all the girls are making one" (Letter 6).[1] In the same letter she tells Root of her own wanderings, her collecting of specimens, and the news of Edward Hitchcock moving into a new house. Although Dickinson's interest in botany was no doubt awakened by the beauty and abundance of the Amherst countryside, it was furthered, according to Farr, by the teachings of Hitchcock, a professor at Amherst College. She notes:

> ED's botanical education was the fruit of Edward Hitchcock's profound influence. The author of both the Religious Lectures, which taught the truth of the Resurrection, and Catalogue of Plants Growing without Cultivation in the Vicinity of Amherst College was responsible for the curriculum Dickinson followed at Mary Lyon's Seminary, and his essay "The Resurrections of Spring" finds echoes in her mature poems about the seasons. At his funeral, the elegist observed grandly, "We often hear of the language of flowers. There is much of fancy in the details, but the idea is based on a profound truth. There is a language of flowers...and it is the language of God." (Farr, Gardens, 311-12, n. 58, quoting from Sewall, Life, 2:355)

And as the letter to Root implies, and Annie Merrill Ingram's article "Victorian Flower Power: America's Floral Women in the Nineteenth Century" makes explicit, the creating of herbariums was a popular, and even pious, activity, particularly for women in the nineteenth century. Several notable books on botany were written by women who were contemporaries of Dickinson. *Familiar Lectures on Botany* (1848) by Amira Phelps noted that flowers "are designed, not merely to delight by their fragrance, color, and form, but to illustrate the most logical divisions of Science, the deepest principles of Physiology, and the goodness of God" (Ingram 2). Even Mrs. Phelps felt moved to advance this sentiment in poetry, here quoted in Sewall's introduction to *Emily Dickinson's Herbarium*:

> Then how should man rejoicing in his God
> Delight in his perfection shadowed forth
> In every little flower and blade of grass!
> Each opining bud, and care-perfected seed,
> Is as a page where we may read of God.
>
> ("Science" 32)

Ideas similar to Mrs. Phelps's appear in Sarah Josepha Hale's *Flora's Interpreter: or, the American Book of Flowers and Sentiments* (1833). Hale attempts to describe a national language that, curiously, consisted of flowers and poetry. Ingram explains: "Many of the flowers in her book reveal distinctly 'American sentiments,' which are in turn reinforced by copious excerpts from American poets. For, she asserts, [the American] people should express their own feelings in the sentiments and idioms of America" (Ingram 3). *Flora's Interpreter* features a number of poets who are not widely read in the present day, alongside such luminaries as Emerson and Thoreau, both as readily accessible now as they were when Dickinson was reading them. Flowers and plants seem to these authors to hold, almost as a secret or as a passport to another realm, a value far beyond their beauty. To unravel their mystery would require a rare combination of intellect and sensitivity, perhaps to a degree that might be possessed only by a poet.

In his series of essays called *Secondary Worlds,* W. H. Auden refers to this passage from Emerson's "Nature" on the responsibilities of the poet: "Man is an analogist and studies relations in all objects. He is placed in the centre of beings, and a ray of relation passes from every other being to him. And neither can man be understood without these objects, nor these objects without man. All the facts in natural history taken by themselves, have no value, but are barren like a single sex. But marry it to human history, and it is full of life" (Emerson 1:19). Auden comments that "because of this radical correspondence between visible things and human thoughts, in poetry all spiritual facts are represented by natural symbols" (114). It is easy to imagine Dickinson agreeing with this passage. According to Sewall, she, like Blake, saw "Heaven in a wild flower" ("Science" 19). The evidence is in her letters. In Letter 91 she echoes Hitchcock's belief that flowers are "Emblems of the Resurrection": "Did you ever know that a flower, once withered and freshened again, became an immortal flower,—that is, that it rises again? I think resurrections here are sweeter, it may be, than the longer and lasting one—for you expect the one, and only hope for the other." In Lettter 488 to Thomas Wentworth Higginson, she writes: "When Flowers annually died and I was a child, I used to read Dr. Hitchcock's Book on the Flowers of North America. This comforted their Absence—assuring me they lived." That flowers are an emblem of the resurrection is not a thought that originates in America with Dickinson; Jonathan Edwards plainly states in his "Images of Divine Things" that the "spring of the year is the image of the resurrection, which is repeated every year" (95). What is striking about Dickinson's statement is the force of the belief. Edwards sees a great difference between the flora of earth and that of heaven, since one withers and dies and the other is eternal (96). Further, the flowers and plants of this world may appear healthy, as some people appear to be spiritually healthy, when actually what is inside them may be unwell. Or, in lacking the proper spiritual nourishment, they perhaps may never flower (105). But for Dickinson, the garden offers a positive model, one of hope and reassurance.

Reportedly, Dickinson told her Norcross cousins she was "reared in the garden" (Bianchi 1), easy enough to believe even if we restrict ourselves to only the visual evidence. In the only two extant images of her, she is pictured with flowers. In the Otis Bullard portrait of Dickinson as a child, she holds a book and a rose. In the famous daguerreotype she clutches pansy violets. We know that from early childhood her passion for her garden was so intense that her father added a conservatory to their house so that Dickinson could tend to her plants year round (consider what a tremendous gift this would be for a young girl, either today or in the early nineteenth century). And we know that the winter was her least favorite season, in part because it was oftentimes fatal to her plants. She afforded them human characteristics (they were proud or shy, they lived and died), and she associated the people in her life with various flowers (Farr, *Gardens* 49-59). She herself appears in the poems and letters as various flowers, perhaps most famously as "Daisy." In a number of letters and poems addressed to Samuel Bowles, she is the "Daisy" to his "Sun" (Letters 161, 272, 567, 830, 908, and *Poems* #106). So she came to be associated with her flowers in the minds of those who knew her. As Emily Fowler Ford wrote to Mabel Loomis Todd, "I have so many times seen her in the morning at work in her garden where everything throve under her hand, and wandering there at eventide, that she is perpetually associated in my mind with flowers—a flower herself" (Sewall, "Science" 29). Clearly, Dickinson would have been pleased with Ford's observation. She herself wrote to Abiah Root: "I have lately come to the conclusion that I am Eve, alias, Mrs. Adam" (Letter 9). Sewall points out in his essay "Science and the Poet" that Dickinson would have known the lament of Milton's Eve, expelled from Eden:

> Must I thus leave thee, Paradise?
> ...
>   Oh flowers,
> That never will in other climate grow,
> ...
> ...which I bred up with tender hand,
> From the first opening bud, and gave ye names:
> Who now shall rear ye to the sun, or rank
> Your tribes...?
>
>   (11. 269-79)

Dickinson did not want to be far removed from her garden. When she was at school at Mount Holyoke, the state of her plants was among her chief worries. Indeed, following her throughout her life and on into death was the desire to be surrounded by flowers and near her home. Describing Dickinson's funeral, Farr writes:"[F]lowers were of rare importance on that day, May 19, for Dickinson had asked to have her coffin not driven but carried through fields of buttercups to the West cemetery, always in sight of the house. Moreover, Lavinia's placement of heliotrope in her sister's hand and violets and pink cypripedium at her throat had a symbolic significance that Emily would have understood. While some who attended the funeral knew she had been a poet, all knew that Emily Dickinson was a gardener" (*Gardens* 3).

It is clear that her flowers, her garden, were important to Emily Dickinson the gardener. But what was their importance to Emily Dickinson the poet? As Sewall indicates, "From her early years on, it was Emily's custom, certainly encouraged by her studies in school, to send flowers to her friends—often a single flower and often accompanied by a short poem. The Harvard edition of the Poems lists thirty-three such poems, ranging in dates from 1858 to 1884 (the dates are approximate)" ("Science" 27). This one was sent to her cousin Eudocia Flynt in 1862:

> All the letters I can write
> Are not fair as this—
> Syllables of Velvet—
> Sentences of Plush,
> Depths of Ruby, undrained,
> Hid, Lip, for Thee—
> Play it were a Humming Bird—
> And just sipped—me—
>
> (*Poems* #334)

In these eight lines are ideas that run throughout Dickinson's work: the letter as poem and the poem as letter, the flower (organic, god-given though Dickinson-tended) as poem, and Dickinson herself as flower (or poem?). The categories become nearly muddled. Dorothy Huff Oberhaus in *Emily Dickinson's Fascicles* asserts that the "flower" (the word and the idea) functions as a "trope" for the "poem" (180). It seems either the most unusual coincidence or a moment of sheer prescience and understanding that Mabel Loomis Todd was moved to call Dickinson's bound manuscripts 'fascicles,' "a nineteenth-century synonym for bunches of flowers" (Farr, *Gardens* 14). At times, Oberhaus writes, Dickinson "blurs the distinction between both herself and her poems" (180). In poem #1037 the relationship between Dickinson and the flower is all the more explicit, and in this poem can also be found some explanation for her habit of sending a flower in her stead:

> Where I am not afraid to go
> I may confide my Flower—
> Who was not Enemy of Me
> Will gentle be, to Her—
> Nor separate, Herself and Me
> By Distances become—
> A single Bloom we constitute
> Departed, or at Home—

Poem #675 eerily recalls Lavinia Dickinson's discovery, after Emily Dickinson's death, of the poems kept in her dresser drawer:

> Essential Oils—are wrung—
> The Attar from the Rose
> Be not expressed by Suns—alone—
> It is the gift of Screws—
>
> The General Rose—decay—
> But this—in Lady's Drawer
> Make Summer—When the Lady lie
> In Ceaseless Rosemary

But it also brings to mind the herbarium. As the poem's first lines describe the process by which the attar is wrung from the rose, they also describe the process by which the flower is pressed and preserved. An emotion, a moment, or a person may be preserved in a poem, but like the rose that lasts, these must undergo a process of transformation. That is "the gift of Screws" (4). Although the process sounds painful, it is finally a "gift," because it brings immortality. To Dickinson, this state might also be characterized as endless summer.

Dickinson's belief in the immortality of flowers was based on their ability to return. She wrote to Sarah Tuckerman in 1877 that "the immortality of Flowers must enrich our own, and we certainly should resent a Redemption that excluded them" (Letter 528). In a letter to Mrs. George S. Dickerman in 1886, Dickinson asked, "If we love Flowers, are we not 'born again' every Day" (Letter 1037). This belief is illustrated in poem #1519, as well as in many others:

> The Dandelion's pallid Tube
> Astonishes the Grass—
> And Winter instantly becomes
> An infinite Alas—
> The Tube uplifts a signal Bud
> And then a shouting Flower—
> The Proclamation of the Suns
> That sepulture is o'er—

Sophocles' Oedipus says in the garden at Colonus, "[O]nly the gods can never age, the gods can never die. All else in the world mighty Time obliterates, crushes all to nothing" (322). But perhaps, miraculously, time can crush without rendering all to nothing, still leaving something behind. Looking at poem #448, "This was a Poet—It is That," alongside #675, "Essential Oils—are wrung," and meeting the metaphor of "attar" and poetry once again, we are tempted to imagine the poem traveling with a flower. What if a flower is the "this" the first line points to?

> This was a Poet—It is That
> Distills amazing sense
> From ordinary Meaning—
> And Attar so immense
>
> From the familiar species
> That perished by the Door—
> We wonder it was not Ourselves
> Arrested it—before—
>
> Of Pictures, the Discloser—
> The Poet—it is He—
> Entitles Us—by Contrast—
> To ceaseless Poverty—
>
> Of Portion—so unconscious—
> The Robbing—could not harm—
> Himself—to Him—a Fortune—
> Exterior—to Time—
>
> (*Poems* #448)

The poem points to qualities Dickinson ascribed to both flowers and poets. There is the reference to "Attar" (4). Further, there is the point made that this is a "familiar species" (5) that might well have "perished by the Door" (6) had it not been captured, pressed, or robbed. ("Robbed" was the way she often described the act of picking flowers: "robbing" nature, though nature, like the poet, was too rich to mind.) Because the poet and flower have, basically, the ability to convey "amazing sense/From ordinary Meaning" (2-3), "Time" (16) is powerless against them.

But again a process must occur: someone must recognize the "familiar" as being also miraculous. Otherwise death is the result, and time does crush all to nothing. Rarities, like the bulbs Dickinson would sometimes force in the winter, cannot be had without work. As she writes in poem #1058,

> Bloom—is Result—to meet a Flower
> And casually glance
> Would scarcely cause one to suspect
> The minor Circumstance
>
> Assisting in the Bright Affair
> So intricately done
> Then offered as a Butterfly
> To the Meridian—
>
> To pack the Bud—oppose the Worm—
> Obtain its right of Dew—
> Adjust the Heat—elude the Wind—
> Escape the prowling Bee
>
> Great Nature not to disappoint
> Awaiting Her that Day—
> To be a Flower, is profound
> Responsibility—

In his preface to *Emily Dickinson's Herbarium* Sewall discusses the "Bright Affair/So intricately done" ("Science" 30-32) as key to this poem, linking it to science and the knowledge of botany that would have given Dickinson familiarity with the parts of the plant and the process by which it comes to flower. But the poet requires deeper understanding than those of us who appreciate the flower for its beauty alone. Even after learning "corolla, calyx, stamens, filament, anther" ("Science" 30), the mystery remains. The flower is more than the sum of its parts, more than the eye or brain can comprehend.

I am struck, however, by a powerful phrase in the poem that is rather independent of the argument for mystery. I want to consider for a moment what it means to "oppose the Worm" (9), for it gets at another theme in Dickinson's poems: that poetry can be a defense against mortality. If it cannot bring immortality, it can stand in opposition to mortality. It can become another flowering, another type of life.

Auden wrote that one of the chief reasons one becomes a poet is to create secondary worlds, not because of dissatisfaction with this, the primary one, but rather from too much love of it, something Emily Dickinson often confessed to feeling. Auden says that the poet looks at this world and understands that "we are born into it and by death disappear from it without our consent." However, he continues, "the secondary worlds we make, since they are embodied in verbal or visual or auditory objects, come into being because we choose to make them and are not subject to natural death" (43). One creates, at least in part, to outwit death and to show love for the primary world, out of a wish for it to continue. The secondary world of the poet's creation attempts to capture the primary world. For Dickinson, that meant her verse could not achieve immortality were it not first, as she wrote to Higginson, "alive" (Letter 260). Although his reply is lost, we know from her next letter that he did apply some "surgery" and provided his estimation, for which she thanks him, saying, "I could not weigh myself—Myself" (Letter 261). So though she also tells him she is but the "representative" of the verse, here we find Dickinson equating herself with the verse. They are one and the same. But can the poet's immortality be achieved in the absence of the audience? Dickinson's sister Lavinia in 1890 wrote to Mabel Loomis Todd that "the 'poems' would die in the box where they were found" if they were not published (Bingham 18). Are the flowers of the *Herbarium* given new life now that they can be viewed?

Poem #441, "This is my letter to the World," like #448, "This was a Poet," also begins in such a way that the reader is forced to consider what the "letter to the World" actually is. The most obvious answer is that it is the poem, and the "this" refers directly to the poem the reader holds in her hands. Again, let's imagine that the "this" refers to a flower and that the poem, like others, is accompanied by one of Dickinson's emissaries:

> This is my letter to the World
> That never wrote to Me—
> The simple News that Nature told—
> With tender Majesty

> Her Message is committed
> To Hands I cannot see—
> For love of Her—Sweet—countrymen—
> Judge tenderly—of Me

Suddenly this poem begins to resemble #1037, "Here, where the Daisies fit my Head." The poem is here; perhaps the flower did not survive. Some of Dickinson's missives bear the impression of a vanished flower. For the pleasure of it, here is another Dickinson poem that begins with the word *this*:

> This is a Blossom of the Brain—
> A small—italic Seed
> Lodged by Design or Happening
> The Spirit fructified—
>
> Shy as the Wind of his Chambers
> Swift as a Freshet's Tongue
> So of the Flower of the Soul
> Its process is unknown.
>
> When it is found, a few rejoice
> The Wise convey it Home
> Carefully cherishing the spot
> If other Flower become.
>
> When it is lost, that Day shall be
> The Funeral of God,
> Upon his Breast, a closing Soul
> The Flower of our Lord.
>
> (*Poems* #945)

Is it a flower or is it a poem that she speaks of? Is it both or something else entirely? Of course, we cannot know if a flower was being referred to when Dickinson wrote "This is my letter to the World." But it is intriguing to consider how this poem evokes the image of Dickinson pressing two day lilies into the hands of T. W. Higginson at their first meeting.

She later wrote to Higginson: "I was thinking, today—as I noticed, that the 'Supernatural,' was only the Natural, disclosed—Not 'revelation'—'tis—that waits But our unfurnished eyes" (Letter 280). From her studies Dickinson knew the science of flowers, what we would call the natural. In poem #19 she begins to name the parts of the flower:

> A sepal, petal, and a thorn
> Upon a common summer's morn—
> A flask of Dew—A Bee or two—
> A Breeze—a caper in the trees—
> And I'm a Rose!

But it is not only the parts that make the rose. There is also what she characterizes as a "caper," which sounds suspiciously like happenstance or magic or the supernatural, which would require some sort of faith. Dickinson's #185, "'Faith' is a fine invention," complicates the matter by appearing to question the idea of faith.

> 'Faith' is a fine invention
> When Gentlemen can *see*—
> But *Microscopes* are prudent
> In an Emergency.

Does she suggest that science is more reliable than faith? Or does the poem intimate that 'faith' is only for those who can see? Science, represented by the microscope, is for those who lack in belief because they are blind to the evidence all around them. If one can see the evidence plainly, then the need for faith disappears, replaced by simple belief. As she wrote in admonition in one of the Master Letters, "Thomas' faith in Anatomy, was stronger than his faith in faith" (Letter 233).

At times the love for flowers seems to replace all conventional religious practice. It may even be seen by some to border on blasphemy. "The Gentian weaves her fringes" closes with a most unconventional prayer:

> The Gentian weaves her fringes—
> The Maple's loom is red—
> My departing blossoms
> Obviate parade.
> A brief, but patient illness—
> An hour to prepare,

> And one below this morning
> Is where the angels are—
> It was a short procession,
> The Bobolink was there—
> An aged Bee addressed us—
> And then we knelt in prayer—
> We trust that she was willing—
> We ask that we may be.
> Summer—Sister—Seraph!
> Let us go with thee!
>
> In the name of the Bee—
> And of the Butterfly—
> And of the Breeze—Amen!
>
> (*Poems* #18)

Of course, it is a prayer made for a flower, and we are unaccustomed to flowers being mourned so elaborately. Dickinson replaces the Trinity with the bee, butterfly, and breeze, which mirror the "Summer—Sister—Seraph!" (15) just above. And the "Gentian" is the mirror of the poem's speaker, as the flower is again in a later Dickinson poem that seems to speak of her ambitions as a poet:

> God made a little Gentian—
> It tried—to be a Rose—
> And failed—and all the Summer laughed—
> But just before the Snows
>
> There rose a Purple Creature—
> That ravished all the Hill—
> And Summer hid her Forehead—
> And Mockery—was still—
>
> The Frosts were her condition—
> The Tyrian would not come
> Until the North—invoke it—
> Creator—Shall I—bloom?
>
> (*Poems* #442)

This poem directly addresses the Christian God. One of the marvelous aspects of Dickinson, seen in both the poems and the letters, is her sense that God was close enough for direct address. One might even say that he could be found in her garden, as she suggests in "Some keep the Sabbath going to Church":

> Some keep the Sabbath going to Church—
> I keep it, staying at Home—
> With a Bobolink for a Chorister—
> And an Orchard, for a Dome—
>
> Some keep the Sabbath in Surplice—
> I just wear my Wings—
> And instead of tolling the Bell, for Church,
> Our little Sexton—sings.
>
> God preaches, a noted Clergyman—
> And the sermon is never long,
> So instead of getting to Heaven, at last—
> I'm going, all along.
>
> <div align="right">(<i>Poems</i> #324)</div>

Although the poem could be interpreted as an apology for all those Sundays Dickinson didn't attend services, alternately the verse gives an account of one who keeps Sabbath every day. Such a church requires no attendance and no straying from home. It is possible that the poem describes a belief that is lived rather than practiced. Of course, this belief also finds its fullest expression in the garden.

Joanna Yin writes that in Dickinson's poems, as a "locus of both delight and loss, the garden serves as a setting for musing on the sublime and fallen mortal world and imagining the immortal." Both "natural and supernatural mingle in gardens under the hand and gaze of Dickinson's speakers" (122). Judith Farr insists that Dickinson's garden was "in its own way a *hortus conclusus*, a private domain like the conservatory or her unpublished manuscripts." But it was the "actual garden she gazed at in various seasons" that "helped to inspire the garden of the poems" (*Gardens* x). The garden was likely these things and more. It seems to have offered her great hope, evidence that belief was not mistaken, evidence that immortality was possible. Just three months before her death,

Dickinson wrote in a letter words that would seem to apply significantly to her life: "In Childhood I never sowed a Seed unless it was perennial—and that is why my Garden lasts" (Letter 989). Her garden is there still for those who visit the Dickinson Homestead. The words of poem #2, which is actually excerpted from a letter to Austin Dickinson, seem as persuasive today as when Emily Dickinson penned them:

> There is another sky,
> Ever serene and far,
> And there is another sunshine,
> Though it be darkness there;
> Never mind faded forest, Austin,
> Never mind silent field—
> Here is a little forest,
> Whose leaf is ever green;
> Here is a brighter garden,
> Where not a frost has been;
> In its unfading flowers
> I hear the bright bee hum;
> Prithee, my brother,
> Into my garden come!

Looking through *Dickinson's Herbarium* and noting her careful labeling of such a great variety of plants and flowers, I am reminded of Auden's *Secondary Worlds* and his thoughts on naming. Auden writes: "It is our right and duty, as it was Adam's, to give names to all things, and to any thing or creature which arouses our affection we desire to give a proper name. Even in the case of generic names only flowers and animals which we can name are quite real to us. As Thoreau said: 'With a knowledge of the name comes a distincter recognition and knowledge of things'" (107). And so the work of the botanist, or Emily Dickinson as gardener, becomes an essentially religious vocation. Although the job of naming fell to Adam, the flowers were Eve's special care. The job of naming in the fallen world is the poet's. But since the names have already been given in the earthly paradise, the poet has only to recognize and pronounce those names. If the poet can perform this task and make the distinct nature known, the thing that is named lives.

This function makes the role of the poet a religious one. In *Secondary Worlds* Auden quotes the now-too-little-read George MacDonald, who observed: "In every man there is an inner chamber of peculiar life into which God only may enter. There is also a chamber in God himself into which none can enter but the one, the peculiar man—out of which chamber that man has to bring revelation and strength to his brethren. That is that for which he was made—to reveal the secret things of the Father" (115). Of course, such a task is not easily said and is even less easily done. Emily Dickinson's achievement in this respect is daunting. Her revelation is, at this point of reckoning, immortality. It is as if she looked at the physical world and clearly saw and revealed the metaphysical. If creation is an act of seeing and preserving, the first hard job is not preservation but having the vision to see. Perhaps the lyric poet has to possess, first, this ability to see outside oneself, even if, like a narcissus, what one sees is mainly a reflection of oneself. We know that Dickinson saw herself in her flowers.

The image of Dickinson as a recluse, as someone whose experience was tragically circumscribed, will likely persist. But Dickinson traveled far at home, further than most of us are able to. She was able to look outside herself. By looking deeply at the world around her, notably her gardens and her flowers, she was able to see into things largely considered invisible.

One of my teachers remarked that great poetry could occur only where there is a shared mythos. Is the lyric in our time dying because of an absence of faith or, failing that, of a common myth or belief system? Has there been a disappearance of the divine or only a failure to see? Christianity was so much a part of Dickinson's world that in her letters she refers to and quotes from the Bible with complete ease and with the certainty that her correspondents would know the full context of her references. Following the gift of lilies to the mother of a newborn, Dickinson wrote, "Let me commend to Baby's attention the only Commandment I ever obeyed—'Consider the Lilies'" (Letter 904). Here is slightly more of that passage from the Sermon on the Mount:

> Consider the lilies of the field, how they grow, they toil not, neither do they spin: And yet I say unto you, That even Solomon in all his glory was not arrayed like one of these. Wherefore if God so clothe the grass of the field, which to day is, and to morrow is cast into the oven, shall he not much more clothe you, O ye of little faith? (Matt. 6:28-30)

There are a few aspects of these three verses that I imagine were important to Dickinson, both as poet and as gardener: the role of the flower, the emphasis on beauty, and the importance of faith. These last two are necessary for any poet. If the faith is not a religious faith, it must still be a faith in the poem as something that lasts, that is beautiful, and that is true. Dickinson's flowers may have formed her first book, but they are also intricately bound in her later work, just as so many times her flowers and poems and letters were sent together. Perhaps her garden lasts because the flowers provide a vocabulary readers can share even beyond the theological language upon which her poems overtly depend.

Note

1. All of Dickinson's letters quoted herein are from *The Letters of Emily Dickinson* and will be referred to by letter number throughout.

8

Word, Sacrament, and the Divine Lover:
Gerard Manley Hopkins and Emily Dickinson

BERNADETTE WATERMAN WARD

If he could have been persuaded to ask his superior for permission to travel to Amherst, Massachusetts, and take a cup of tea at a visit—and she could have been induced to unlock her door and go down the stairs to meet an English Catholic priest—Gerard Manley Hopkins and Emily Dickinson could have had a memorable visit. He might have felt qualms about taking more than one piece of gingerbread; perhaps they would repair to her garden, where she would quite understand if he crouched down to see the way sunlight reflected off the gravel. With the peculiar intensity of personal vision, each would introduce the other to some delicate grace in bird or leaf or petal, in cloudscape or insects' wings. The Irish servants and Dickinson would enjoy Hopkins' puns, but he might feel too much bite in Dickinson's wit, especially about religion. One critic has mined Catholic dogmas from Dickinson's nature poetry (Power), but our scrupulous Jesuit could hardly be expected to practice the necessary selectivity in texts and latitude of interpretation. Still, English reserve would prevent his actually saying what he wrote to his intimate friend Robert Bridges, a devotee of the "religion of beauty": "[Y]ou told me something of your views about the deity, which were not as they should be" (*Letters to Bridges* 60). Eager to discuss Christianity in earnest, Hopkins would find Dickinson elusive. In her poems, Dickinson's galled irony about God disappears when she envisions Christ as bridegroom, but skittish about such matters with anyone, she would be reticent with

Hopkins. If he knew her reasons, he would approve: when Coventry Patmore showed him a manuscript about mysticism and marriage, Hopkins read it and said, "That's telling secrets," with such an air that Patmore threw the manuscript in the fire (*Further Letters* xxii-xxxix). Dickinson might turn the conversation to poetry, eliciting a torrent of technical detail and decided, Oxford-educated opinion. They would discover deep differences, but if they pressed on to discuss, as Hopkins put it, "Keats and other interesting people" (*Letters to Bridges* 61), they would find, at the lyric crossroads where spirituality and language meet, that they shared a vision of the marriage of the poet's mind to natural beauty in the mode of the high romantics, who took the poetic gift as a participation in divinity.

No such visit ever took place. Critics rarely group Dickinson and Hopkins together, despite some common biographical elements. Both were baptized Christians[1] who wrote with urgency on religious matters while their pervasively religious culture was undergoing rapid secularization. Both achieved fame only after death, having polished their work in private and refused publication during life. Each honed poems to surgical sharpness: the striking rhyme, the exact word, the tension aroused by carefully trimmed meter. Similarly disciplined were the lives they chose. As a Jesuit, Hopkins practiced bodily mortification, personal poverty, and severe obedience; Dickinson stayed at home, fled visitors, and ate alone. Both aroused Freudian speculation on the cost of virginity,[2] because of Hopkins' scruples and Dickinson's agoraphobia, but in fact their poetic visions converge on an erotic, marital spirituality. They were not poets because of their neuroses; intensity of response to the pleasures of sight and sound and even taste, coupled with keen observation of matters of the heart and of the spirit, gave Dickinson and Hopkins wisdom from which to speak lyrically. These two celibate poets connected matrimony to the high romantic ideal of marriage of mind with the physical world to achieve a connection between poetry and spirituality. In order to find the way from their different cultural places to their common encounter with the Word of God and the words of poetry as a kind of mystical marriage, we must go, like the pilgrim Dante, on a long and sometimes dark road with both poets.

Whatever they share, their styles and even arguments could hardly offer a greater contrast. Dickinson is spare and laconic to the point of enigma, as she presents a figure of fleeting natural beauty as a woman:

> How rapid, how momentous
> What exigencies were—
> But nature will be ready
> And have an hour to spare.
>
> To make some trifle fairer
> That was too fair before—
> Enchanting by remaining,
> And by departure more.
>
> (Poems #1762)

As she dwells on the flavor of loss and the beauty of what cannot stay, Dickinson clips and presses a hymn-tune tetrameter into trimeters. Hopkins was also an innovator working against fluent and conventional lyric structures in nineteenth-century English verse, but he is far more brash. Here he too addresses beauty's transience in the person of a woman, but he crowds the meter with lush and sensual diction.

> How to kéep—is there ány any, is there none such, nowhere known
>   some, bow or brooch or braid or brace, láce, latch or catch
>   or key to keep
> Back beauty, keep it, beauty, beauty, beauty...from vanishing away?
>
> (Poems 91)

Despite appearances, none of this is free verse: all Hopkins' meters are carefully counted and weighed. In fact "all English verse almost" strikes his ear as metrically "licentious" (*Letters to Bridges* 45). He is fond of rules, edges, limits—the sonnet is his favorite form. Nevertheless the way he handles limitation in the lyric—by pressing against the boundaries with tremendous, even boisterous, verbal abundance—contrasts deeply to Dickinson's little, pared-down quatrains. The foci of the poets' visions differ as the spare beauty of a stripped branch does from a rain of wind-whirled spring petals. Again, Dickinson makes drama turn on sharp little twists of slant rhyme in terse verses; Hopkins lavishes his readers' ears with a baroque display of assonance, consonance, and full chiming in overgrown long lines. Dickinson's tremendous power seems turned inward, toward not saying too much; Hopkins' power asserts itself in the rush of speech against the barriers of form.

Although the topics may be similar, the arguments of their poems differ deeply enough to discourage comparison. Both poets, for instance, discuss a feeling that God has offered a benefit and betrayed his offer. Dickinson writes:

> Of God we ask one favor,
> That we may be forgiven—
> For what, he is presumed to know—
> The Crime, from us, is hidden—
> Immured the whole of Life
> Within a magic Prison
> We reprimand the Happiness
> That too competes with Heaven.
>
> (*Poems* #1601)

The slant rhymes give an off-balance piquancy to the underlying resentment of God as a sort of trickster, offering us deceptive treats and snaring us into sins he wants to punish. Hopkins, too, complains that God's friendship seems like enmity, but he confronts the Lord straightforwardly, like a barrister:

> Thou art indeed just, Lord, if I contend
> With thee; but, sir, so what I plead is just.
> Why do sinners' ways prosper? and why must
> Disappointment all I endeavour end?
>
>   Wert thou my enemy, O thou my friend,
> How wouldst thou worse, I wonder, than thou dost
> Defeat, thwart me? Oh, the sots and thralls of lust
> Do in spare hours more thrive than I that spend,
> Sir, life upon thy cause.

The boldness seems irreverent. Packed alliteration hammers home a fierce accusation. However, Hopkins supplies in the manuscript the source of the first few lines from the Vulgate: the prophet Jeremiah, complaining about the sufferings of being chosen to speak God's effective word. Hopkins ends the poem with a tender apostrophe, "Mine, o thou lord of life, send my roots rain."

Hopkins seems to charge to the edge of blasphemy, but the edge is fenced by Scripture; Dickinson hesitates in irony and parsimony, as if on a windy cliff with no certain protection. Her Lord is the one who "gave a Loaf to every Bird—/But just a Crumb—to Me—" (*Poems* #791). Even though she has a mere morsel and recognizes its preciousness to her, she cannot consume it: "I dare not eat it—tho' I starve—/My poignant luxury—/To own it—touch it—." No one who can perceive the riot of the senses in the mature poetry of Hopkins can envision his sympathizing with Dickinson's dictum: "Renunciation—is a piercing Virtue" (*Poems* #745). She apparently endorses the will's

> ...Choosing
> Against itself—
> Itself to justify
> Unto itself—

She does speculate that renunciation might serve a higher cause, but even "When larger function—/Make that appear—/Smaller—that Covered Vision—Here—," her heaven is an abstract "larger function." Often, the very existence of Heaven is dubious: "parting is all we know of heaven" (*Poems* #1732). The flippancy and bitterness are perhaps a natural reaction to the conviction that one is not supposed to desire joy; the good and the desirable once riven apart, the intellect tears at the heart.

Although Hopkins too advises abstinence, he verbally caresses the things renounced:

> Come then, your ways and airs and looks, locks, maiden gear, gallantry
>   and gaiety and grace,
> Winning ways, airs innocent, maiden manners, sweet looks, loose locks,
>   long locks, lovelocks, gaygear, going gallant, girlgrace—
> Resign them, sign them, seal them, send them, motion them with breath,
> And with sighs soaring, soaring sighs, deliver
> Them; beauty-in-the-ghost, deliver it, early now, long before death
> Give beauty back, beauty, beauty, beauty, back to God beauty's self and
>   beauty's giver.
> See: not a hair is, not an eyelash, not the least lash lost....
>   (*Poems* 92)

The repetitions, alliterations, and vivid adjectives invite the reader to dwell upon active, physical pleasures awaiting resurrection in Christ. Dickinson feels the attraction of earthly beauty just as intensely, but in poem after poem she dwells on thwarted desire and seems to find abstinence itself delectable. Richard Wilbur hails her "Sumptuous Destitution" as the prototype of the rebellious modern soul defining its own private heaven and enduring the pain of life in an uncaring anonymous universe, "invulnerable" against a "God who does not answer" (130). As a "secular and aesthetic equivalent of mysticism,"[3] her work is admired by critics for being "perfectly agnostic and perfectly religious."[4] Numerous critics see Dickinson's relationship with God as pure desire without any possibility of consummation save through death. Perhaps, then, she can want death, the total subjugation of her wants, as the God who has banished her from his presence must desire. Without seeking peace in a Stoic or Buddhist quenching of desire itself, she seems to take pleasure in the strength of a will that can cherish an active desire while resisting it by sheer fortitude, without any further good as its object: "The focus of my Prayer—/A perfect—paralyzing Bliss—/Contented as Despair" (*Poems* #756). Despair is, of course, the vice that refuses to desire the Good. Dickinson can establish certainty on her "Columnar Self" and be "not far off/From furthest Spirit—God—" (*Poems* #789), but God's "crumb" may be all she can get. Feminist critics propose an economics of controlled female sexuality that mandates death of self as the penalty for having desire, but as we shall see, sexual desire escapes Dickinson's drive to renunciation. Post-structuralism encourages critics to understand Dickinson's willingness to be excluded as a pure exercise of power, claiming deity for the self, as in this poem:

> Art thou the thing I wanted?
> Begone—my Tooth has grown—
> Affront a minor palate
> Thou could'st not goad so long—
>
> I tell thee while I waited—
> The mystery of Food
> Increased till I abjured it
> Subsisting now like God—
>
> (*Poems* #1282)[5]

The feminist Joanne Diehl glorifies these refusals as an ambition to "dissolve the relation between word and world" in an exercise of pure willful negation that "enacts the appropriation of the natural world into the sovereign self" (122-23).

But neither Dickinson's life nor her poetry indicates any obsession with her own power. The human need to be led in our desires can originate the paradoxical passion of desiring to be the one denied.[6] It is possible even to take satisfaction in imitating the contempt one's idol shows toward one. To hate or deny myself makes me similar to Him who hates and denies me and is so powerful.[7] This refusal of real good for the sake of an empty status, a mere idea, is discussed by social observers as "internalized oppression" and is used by novelists as an element in tales of unrequited love (and in many other quarters it is perhaps more common than we like to admit). Dickinson explores this discomfiting territory with unflinching floodlight clarity in poem after poem about hunger, thirst, renunciation, and death. She can feast on desire itself, and on the pleasure of being the one who does not feast, because that is what the superior will desires for her.

Hopkins too understood the phenomenon of desiring even rejection, though it is far less central to his poetic works. In his fragmentary verse play, *St. Winifred's Well*, he explores the deliberate refusal of hope for the sake of self-image in a murderer named Caradoc, who says of the woman who has paid with her life for rebuffing him,

> Yes,
> To hunger and not have, yet | hope on for, to storm and strive and
> Be at every assault fresh foiled, | worse flung, deeper disappointed,
> The turmoil and the torment, | it has, I swear, a sweetness,
> Keeps a kind of joy in it, | a zest, an edge, an ecstasy,
> Next after sweet success. | I am not left even this....
>
> (*Poems* 190-91)

And why is Caradoc left not even this delectable, frustrating effort? He has asserted his will and killed the one person who gave his life a goal. He says, "Henceforth/Caradoc lives alone, loyal to his own soul, laying his own law down." Therefore he must give up hope. "What do? Not yield,/Not hope, not pray; despair; | ay, that: brazen despair out,/Brave all...."

René Girard first analyzed this desire in an erotic context, and that is where we find it in Hopkins. For Hopkins, however, every erotic impulse must be seen in relation to its goal in matrimony and to the mystical meaning of matrimony, the union of the soul with Christ. On the premise that all sexuality harbors a mystical meaning that refers to the marriage of Christ and the Church, he rejoices to crowd his poems with sensual imagery to represent Jesus. Contemplating the Eucharist in "Hurrahing in Harvest," he asks, "And eyes, heart, what looks, what lips yet give you a/Rapturous love's greeting of realer, of rounder replies?" (*Poems* 70). On a less exalted level, he loves the idea of marriage itself, though he cannot marry: "I have a kind of spooniness and delight over married people, especially if they say 'my wife,' 'my husband,' or shew the wedding ring" (*Letters to Bridges* 198). He left a word of warning about sexual expression outside marriage: "Those who contrary to our Lord's command both break themselves and, as St. Paul says, consent to those who break the sacred bond of marriage…fall with eyes open into the terrible judgment of God" (*Letters to Bridges* 39). Even the Terrible Sonnets exude the lover's confidence that he has already encountered the "dearest him who lives, alas, away." Dickinson relishes rebuke and distance from God sometimes; but Hopkins always finds it bitter, and even his bleakest Terrible Sonnets have behind them a hope, as he says, "that my chaff might fly; my grain lie, sheer and clear" ("Carrion Comfort," *Poems* 99). Love may be cold, faith may be shaken, but he never loses hope, the virtue of desire for the true good.

Hope Hopkins knew, of course, not only as an emotion but as a virtue to be discussed in strict intellectual terms. He recognized and resisted his culture's widespread drift toward rejection of theological hope. Both he and Dickinson tasted abandonment by God; both nevertheless approached Jesus with a lover's intensity, but Dickinson shows less confidence in God's good will and even in his reality. Her apprehension of the existence of God, heaven, and other matters of faith varies with her feelings of rebellion or acquiescence, her sympathy with rulebreakers or saints, her impatience or her sense of gratitude. God may be assumed and addressed, or his existence may become debatable. Perhaps God is merely a human invention and just a generalized human intelligence, as she suggests:

> The Brain—is wider than the Sky—
> For—put them side by side—
> The one the other will contain
> With ease—and You—beside—
>
> The Brain is deeper than the sea—
> For—hold them—Blue to Blue—
> The one the other will absorb—
> As Sponges—Buckets—do—
>
> The Brain is just the weight of God—
> For—Heft them—Pound for Pound—
> And they will differ—if they do—
> As Syllable from Sound—
>
> (Poems #632)

More often Dickinson's doubt is expressed less radically. Her God is as incomprehensible as any mystic's, but her self-consciousness in saying so is a bit tart for apophatic theology.

> My period had come for Prayer—
> No other Art—would do—
> My Tactics missed a rudiment—
> Creator—Was it you?
>
> God grows above—so those who pray
> Horizons—must ascend—
> And so I stepped upon the North
> To see this Curious Friend—
> His House was not—no sign had He—
> By Chimney—nor by Door
> Could I infer his Residence—
> Vast Prairies of Air
>
> Unbroken by a Settler—
> Were all that I could see—
> Infinitude—Had'st Thou no Face
> That I might look on Thee?
>
> (Poems #564)

Even in the poem's resolution, when she seems to make contact with the Deity, he is "Silence," and the anxiety to distinguish worship from prayer draws more attention to the use of language than to the matter to be communicated.

> The Silence condescended—
> Creation stopped—for Me—
> But awed beyond my errand—
> I worshipped—did not "pray"—

As an undergraduate, Hopkins also poetically confronts a baffling, perhaps absent God in "Nondum":

> We see the glories of the earth
> But not the hand that wrought them all:
> Night to a myriad worlds gives birth,
> Yet like a lighted empty hall
> Where stands no host at door or hearth
> Vacant creation's lamps appal.
>
> We guess; we clothe Thee, unseen King,
> With attributes we deem are meet;
> Each in his own imagining
> Sets up a shadow in Thy seat....
>
> (*Poems* 32)

But in his mature poetry, whatever Hopkins' sense of abandonment, God's power and existence are as much facts to him as his own bones. Even in his darkest sonnet, "No Worst, There Is None," he calls to Mary, "where is your relief?" and his unusual epithet for her, "mother of us," has an intimacy impossible in addressing an abstraction. He then demands of the Holy Spirit, "Comforter, where, where is your comforting?" (*Poems* 100). Clearly he is not feeling at peace with God, but his moral state does not affect his acknowledgment of God's existence. Even in the bitterness of his alienation from God, he does not consider himself alone in the universe. He hates his pain and attributes it to God. When he claims, "my taste was me;/Bones built in me, flesh filled, blood brimmed the curse," he calls it the result of "God's most deep decree."

Hopkins was exposed to the nineteenth century's corrosive reductionism about Christian doctrines and history, if anything, more than Dickinson. For a generation before Darwin, educated English believers found their confidence in matters of faith rapidly eroding, while America was experiencing intense chiliastic fervor, fertile in new religious movements. Yet Hopkins has a vivid—even if vividly horrible sometimes—apprehension of an unseen world, glimpsed but doubted by Dickinson. Oxford generously equipped Hopkins with logic and scholarly method amid Victorian battles over rational approaches to history and authority in the Church and about the public place of Christian ceremony. The famous unbelievers Benjamin Jowett and Walter Pater served as his tutors. Pater was a lifelong friend despite his oppressing the religious young man with "two hours talking against Xty" (Hopkins, *Journals* 138). Oxford was an epicenter of rising secularity, and Hopkins knew his Higher Criticism and his Darwinism (he was fond of science). He even relished the rhetorical sweep of Hardy's desperate post-Christian novels. Unbelievers did not cow Hopkins' rigorous reasoning; an atmosphere in which the public nature of Christianity was assumed gave him confidence about the possibility of coming to a resolution of religious questions.

As Hopkins approached conversion, the writings of John Henry Newman seem to have helped him to acknowledge that all human knowledge is based on faith in something, even if only in the reliability of the senses. After Hopkins converted, he joined the household of this most famous Roman Catholic convert. A spokesman for Catholics in England, Newman explained to a perplexed public how Catholics can be sinners without being unbelievers. He wrote that, as a Protestant, his faith depended upon his own action and judgment, in short, upon the state of his virtue. Then he described the new religious culture he had adopted:

> Just as in England, the whole community, whatever the moral state of the individuals, knows about railroads and electric telegraphs…so, in a Catholic country, the ideas of heaven and hell, Christ and the evil spirit, saints, angels, souls in purgatory, grace, the Blessed Sacrament, the sacrifice of the Mass, absolution, indulgences, the virtue of relics, of holy images, of holy water, and of other holy things, are of the nature of facts, which all men, good and bad, young and old, rich and poor, take for granted.
> (*Certain Difficulties* 276)

This communal brand of knowledge can coexist with the evangelical call to "come to Christ" individually, but as we have seen in Dickinson, the focus on the individual decision leaves the mind undefended against a felt obligation to make relentless, even destructive, searches for evidence that is unavailable within one person's range of experience. Always a believer in revelation through Christ, Hopkins refused to take upon himself the responsibility for exercising private judgment over particular doctrines. Reasoning that access to Christ, the source of Christian revelation, was available only through tradition, he struggled his way logically into certainty that the Church must have visible and doctrinal unity. Then he looked for the most historically reliable tradition, for historical reliability was a matter he felt qualified to judge objectively. Hopkins was determined to "repress" emotion in order to deal rationally with his crisis of church loyalty (*Journals and Papers* 58); his father even accuses him of cold rationalism in his conversion letters. He determinedly resisted family pressure as he moved from the serious, patristically informed Anglicanism of the Oxford Movement into the Roman Catholic Church, finally entering the Jesuit order.

Despite his rationalism in ecclesiology, Hopkins does not repress all emotion. His faith is at its core white-hot with passion for the Real Presence of Christ in Communion. He wrote, "This belief once got is the life of the soul and when I doubted it I shd. become an atheist the next day" (*Further Letters* 92). Rather than an intellectual or psychological deity, Hopkins' Eucharist delivers a God he can taste. The flavor is that of the "accidentals" of bread and wine, but the theology asserts that the substance consumed physically, to the benefit of the body, is taken up into the Divinity. Considering the Eucharist to be God personally volunteering to live a human life and suffer human pain as a victim of violence about to be consumed—Hopkins' phrase is "in *statu victimali*" (*Letters to Bridges* 149)—he believes that Communion allows him to participate physically in that divine action. He wrote to a friend: "The great aid to belief and object of belief is the doctrine of the Real Presence in the Blessed Sacrament of the Altar. Religion without that is sombre, dangerous, illogical, with that it is—not to speak of its grand consistency and certainty—*loveable*" (*Further Letters* 17). Certainly no Emersonian pantheist writing for periodicals would so boldly connect God to particular physicality. Neither would any Protestant Amherst clergyman say such a Romish thing about Communion.

Dickinson, who made a "sacrament of starvation,"[8] never enthused as Hopkins did about the sacraments of the Church. She clearly had opinions about somber, dangerous, or illogical aspects of religion, but the "Child...fleeing from Sacrament" (*Letters* 2:524-25) certainly found no comfort in Communion. In Calvinist theology, Communion is a symbolic and spiritual event internal to the believer (Calvin 2:346). Dickinson's sensuality, as powerful as that of Hopkins, seems to collide with a prohibition on physical contact with God. Word substitutes for sacrament. Dickinson fantasizes about abstinence from all pleasures but words, which are only symbolic, not actual, goods. The God whom she desires presents only a sign of himself. Dickinson may go to church with a bobolink for a chorister to hear God, "a noted clergyman," but she does not hear him with physical ears or see him with physical eyes.

Even if God was once historically present in the Incarnation, a point on which she is unsure, Dickinson must rely entirely on words for access to him. Language is inherently indirect, however, and it becomes hollow if removed from the communal experience that produces it. An uncertainly grounded making and handling of words—poetry—is the nearest thing she has to a participation in God's action in the world. She parodies the Gospel of John on the Incarnation:

> A Word made Flesh is seldom
> And tremblingly partook
> Nor then perhaps reported
> But have I not mistook
> Each one of us has tasted
> With ecstasies of stealth
> The very food debated
> To our specific strength—
>
> (*Poems* #1651)

Although there exist two rhymes for the unusual word "stealth"—and food is easily associated with either health or wealth—*this* food is debated. As when she feels it incumbent upon her to judge "whether Deity's guiltless" (*Poems* #178), Dickinson is burdened here with indecision: "tremblingly...perhaps...mistook." The slant rhyme calls our attention to the effort, and she points her readers toward poetic labor. She continues:

> A Word that breathes distinctly
> Has not the power to die
> Cohesive as the Spirit
> It may expire if He—
> "Made Flesh and dwelt among us"
> Could condescension be
> Like this consent of Language
> This loved Philology.
>
> (*Poems* #1651)

It was not the *zeitgeist* of the nineteenth century that gave Emily Dickinson a God who could be wanted but never enjoyed. It was something shared by nineteenth-century liberals like Emerson and hard Reformation scriptural literalists like Calvin. She was called upon to construct a private and personal judgment from a book about a God who seemed not always up to her moral standards. Dickinson never mentions the "tender pioneer," Christ, without love, but she is not sure of his relation to the Father: "God broke his contract to his Lamb/To qualify the Wind—" (*Poems* #1439). Her dark, bewildering—perhaps nonexistent—God has little regard for her hungers. Irony and dissonance haunt nearly half of Dickinson's poems that mention God even casually: "Was God so economical?/His Table's spread too high for Us—" (*Poems* #690).

A cacophony of religious discourse exposed Dickinson to social and emotional pressures, but she was without the defense Hopkins had in his carefully reasoned, researched case for a historically authenticated interpretation of Revelation. When Dickinson attended Mount Holyoke for a year during a wave of religious revival, she anguished about declaring herself "Christian" in the full evangelical manner and was among the few "without hope" who failed to commit themselves verbally to Christ. She never provided the public "testimony" necessary to become a full member of her family's Congregational church, which she stopped attending in her early thirties, as she went into almost complete seclusion. Indeed, there were dust-ups about her refusal to attend, and once Edward Dickinson did ask a clergyman to examine Emily in religion. "Entirely sound," the Reverend concluded. He probably did not ask her about original sin or the benevolence of God, about which she wrote scathingly regarding God's treatment of Moses and Ananias:

> So I pull my Stockings off
> Wading in the Water
> For the Disobedience' Sake
> Boy that lived for "or'ter"
>
> Went to Heaven perhaps at Death
> And perhaps he didn't
> Moses wasn't fairly used—
> Ananias wasn't—
>
> (Poems #1201)

Still, twenty-first-century biography has revealed Emily Dickinson's failure to "come to Christ" as rather less defiant than legend would have it. Dickinson's poems evidence "the Calvinist mind turning against itself and its maker—a rebellion that is seldom whole-hearted," as Albert Gelpi reminds us (41). Divine election was not quite a dead issue in her culture, and Dickinson sincerely feared the rejection was God's and not just the elders'.

However, Amherst's Congregational church was already on a comfortable road to broad church liberalism. High-minded social theory was placidly watering down the curriculum of the severely evangelical Amherst College that Dickinson's grandfather had worked hard to establish.[9] Coexisting with the Puritan possibilities of rejection, she found, was a mistier theology that made God a distant motive for bettering the world through sociable ladies' groups that Dickinson had trouble tolerating. She seems no more allergic to dogma than to the cheery charitable sociability eroding her ancestors' tense spiritual introspection. At any rate, Dickinson was not impressed by the spirituality of her parents' fellow parishioners, if we may judge from the occasional poetic observation on them:

> Such Dimity Convictions—
> A Horror so refined
> Of freckled Human Nature—
> Of Deity—ashamed—
>
> It's such a common—Glory—
> A Fisherman's—Degree—

> Redemption—Brittle Lady—
> Be so—ashamed of Thee—
>
> *(Poems* #401)

Nevertheless, it is not clear to Dickinson, as it is to Hopkins, that any of the options on the table should be rejected out of hand. She seems even to have tried a purely emotional "religion of the heart," dripping with Victorian sentimentality, such as was practiced by young ladies of the time:

> Unable are the Loved to die
> For Love is Immortality,
> Nay, it is Deity—
>
> Unable they that love—to die
> For Love reforms Vitality
> Into Divinity.
>
> *(Poems* #809)

There is little refuge in such exercises for Dickinson's keen mind.

With fifteen periodicals coming into her house, she could not miss the intellectual excitement surrounding Emersonian Transcendentalism,[10] whose pantheistic God does, of course, nothing in particular. Here perhaps is the most painful theological crux: it is the particularity of God's detectable intrusion into the world that Dickinson feels as a most keen need—that God chooses, loves her in particular. Yet there *were* voices in American romanticism proposing a divinity intent on particulars: the divinity of the imagination. The romantic exaltation of poets as creators like God naturally attracted her.

> I reckon—when I count it all—
> First—Poets—Then the Sun—
> Then Summer—Then the Heaven of God—
> And then—the List is done—
>
> But, looking back—the First so seems
> To Comprehend the Whole—
> The Others look a needless Show—
> So I write—Poets—All—

> Their Summer—lasts a Solid Year—
> They can afford a Sun
> The East—would deem extravagant—
> And if the Further Heaven—
>
> Be Beautiful as they prepare
> For Those who worship Them—
> It is too difficult a Grace—
> To justify the Dream—
>
> *(Poems #569)*

Hopkins encountered the notion of the divinity of poets most powerfully in the work of the art critic John Ruskin, whose evangelicalism gave his early works an appealing piety. A true romantic in his notion that "there is a reciprocal action between the intensity of moral feeling and the power of imagination" (257), Ruskin sought to serve Christian morals through "imaginative participation from an audience" in art (Helsinger 225). In 1849, Ruskin daringly compared the function of the imagination to the Bible in an allusion to the metaphor of the Word of God as a two-edged sword from Hebrews 4:12-13: "[T]his penetrating possession-taking faculty of Imagination....I insist upon as the highest intellectual power of man....no matter what be the subject submitted to it, substance or spirit; all is alike divided asunder, joint and marrow, whatever utmost truth, life, principle it has, laid bare, and that which has no truth, life, nor principle, dissipated into its original smoke at a touch" (251). However, Ruskin felt a tension between the artist's "bodily, not spiritual, pleasure" (386-89)[11] and the total depravity he had learned to attribute to human endeavors without specifically biblical justification. In the 1850s (his autobiographies date it to different years in that decade), he abandoned Christianity for art but long took refuge in Christian moralism in his publications. Although he announced that he found art and Christianity incompatible, his fascination with sacred art drew him back to Christian practice.

Hopkins was perhaps prepared to take Ruskin in an entirely Christian way through his contact with the romantic theory of Samuel Taylor Coleridge, who had strongly influenced Ruskin. (Hopkins was great friends, as a boy, with grandson Ernest Hartley Coleridge.) Coleridge's discussion of poetic creation divinizes poetic activity as a "repetition in the finite mind of the eternal I AM" (*Biographia* Chap. 13).

God's creation, like the poet's, then, is a loving regard that calls something new into being. The poet calls forth inscapes, to use Hopkins' term, which emerge into full reality in the human moral world and thence in human action. God, of course, creates a reality both social and physical. Another poet Hopkins admired, William Wordsworth, discussed in his preface to *Lyrical Ballads* the nature of the poet's love for and commitment to his poetic creations. Wordsworth describes how the poet inhabits, in spirit, the reality that he seeks to bring forth. This likeness between poet and Creator, this participation of the poet in the world he created, doubtless made Hopkins more amenable to the doctrine of creation taught by the medieval theologian John Duns Scotus, who treats all creation as originating in the "decree of the Incarnation," as Hopkins puts it (Devlin 111). In other words, God, like a romantic poet, voluntarily participates in his world in order to bring it into full reality.

Of the romantics who hold a high view of the poet's role, both Hopkins and Dickinson especially loved John Keats. Perhaps Dickinson never read his letters about the holiness of the imagination, but she could scarcely have missed the deification of imagination in his late poetry, especially the "Ode to Psyche." The speaker seeks to set up a temple to the Mind, the Imagination, and discovers her in vividly sensual intercourse with fleshly desire, Cupid. But the desire is not transient or coarse; the couple is "true," in every sense of the word. The connection between them is holy; the legend has Cupid married to Psyche in defiance of Venus. The reader tests "upon our pulses," in Keats's term, the physical intercourse evoked delicately by the poet to find it true to the senses. The reader is to recognize truth intellectually as well, led by the poet to participate both in making the scene real and in making it meaningful. The poem attracts its readers by the beauty of the loving couple, and like that couple, the reader experiences desire and fulfillment. Thus the poem not only symbolizes but effects the mind's intercourse with beauty. A real tour de force, Keats's poem enacts what it symbolizes. Hopkins also found in marital eros "a sign which enacts what it signifies," indeed, in his theology the very definition of a sacrament. Catholicism's emphasis on the connection of physical actions to spiritual states has a dry objectivity about it that was probably unfamiliar to Dickinson.[12] But Hopkins considered theology to be news about his best friend or friends, and he was entranced by this way that, according to the Church, Christ continues to enter the physical world of believers since the Incarnation. Dickinson would never have articulated the matter in such terms, but it is in the sacramental intersection of the poetic and the erotic, informed by romanticism, that the two poets meet. Hopkins worked out the theology in formal terms, usually scholastic, but with a romantic flavor; Dickinson worked it out, as it were, at ground level, in her poems about marriage.

The most curious thing about Dickinson's religious poetry is that the doubt and the imagery of starvation vanish in her erotic "marriage group" poems. They break her determined fast from hope, and even in frustration they feast on expectation rather than denial. This may have something to do with the fact that marriage is not an internal matter of feeling but a physical state; in matrimony, unlike either Emersonian or evangelical Christianity, feelings are secondary to facts about objective, external actions.[13] Marriage brings with it plenty of internal education in fortitude, forgiveness, and self-gift, but it is unmistakably sacrament—a social status depending on a physical event. Marriage is, in Hopkins' terms, a natural sacrament, a sign that "effects what it symbolizes." It cannot be reduced to its signification, like Calvin's Eucharist; it is not a private act of grace in the soul. Because marriage is irreducibly sexual, it is never purely an internal sentiment.

Dickinson hung a tremendous significance on eros and the power of the relationships that it creates, which in her poems are overwhelmingly marital. The one place where the love is an irreducibly particular physical event is marriage.

> A wife—at daybreak I shall be—
> Sunrise—Hast thou a Flag for me?
> At Midnight, I am but a Maid,
> How short it takes to make a Bride—
> Then—Midnight, I have passed from thee
> Unto the East, and Victory—
>
> Midnight—Good Night! I hear them call,
> The Angels bustle in the Hall—
> Softly my Future climbs the Stair,
> I fumble at my Childhood's prayer
> So soon to be a Child no more—
> Eternity, I'm coming—Sir,
> Savior—I've seen the face—before!
>
> (*Poems* #461)

Despite her uncertainties about God and even indulgence in religious satire bordering on blasphemy, Dickinson appropriates in her poetry, with sensual and earnest intensity, the imagery of the Bride of Christ from the Apocalypse. Her "marriage group" poems have long constituted a puzzle for critics and biographers. Even Dickinson's friend Samuel Bowles apparently responded to some vivid sexual imagery with questions about whether she was announcing a loss of virginity. Dickinson rebuked Bowles for casting "doubt" on her "snow" (Johnson in Dickinson, *Poems* 142-43). She seems to have been utterly confident that he knew her to be chaste, and a bit impatient with his confusion. Critic William Shurr attempted to construct (from two meetings of which there is any evidence) a torrid tale of seduction by her correspondent, the Reverend Charles Wadsworth.[14] Shurr fantasizes their conducting logistically unlikely secret meetings and a hushed-up abortion, despite the exceeding improbability of clerical sex abuse and subsequent abortion acting as inspiration for poetry that eventually centers on mystical marriage to Christ.[15] Letters may indicate that Dickinson made some sort of spiritual commitment to a man. A spiritualized sexual bond, never to be consummated, was not an uncommon Victorian literary trope. Yet Dickinson's erotic urgency in poems such as "Wild Nights! Wild Nights!" jars with the sentimental Victorian "spiritualization" of sexual love. She evokes sexual desire with startling physicality:

> Come slowly—Eden!
> Lips unused to Thee—
> Bashful—sip thy Jessamines—
> As the fainting Bee—
>
> Reaching late his flower,
> Round her chamber hums—
> Counts his nectars—
> Enters—and is lost in Balms.

(Poems #211)

Sometimes a defiant tone emerges, as in her declarations about the union expected after death. Then again, a virgin in her thirties, living rather than imagining a lover's permanent unavailability, may be more likely than, say, a prostitute to understand the forbidden physical eros with spiritual intensity, envisioning sexual union as an Edenic participation and gift of the whole self. Shurr is indeed alert to something powerful and central in Dickinson; it seems impossible to him that the emotional intensity and powerful eroticism of these poems could be purely spiritual and, in Shurr's eyes, therefore imaginary.

However, it is marriage itself, seen as a total break with one's past, that seems imaginary.

> I'm "wife"—I've finished that—
> That other state—
> I'm Czar—I'm "Woman" now—
> It's safer so—
>
> How odd the Girl's life looks
> Behind this soft Eclipse—
> I think that Earth feels so
> To folks in Heaven—now—
>
> This being comfort—then
> That other kind—was pain—
> But why compare?
> I'm "Wife"! Stop there!
>
> (Poems #199)

Judith Farr describes with wonder the phenomenon of the lover in Dickinson's poems being both himself and Christ to the bride: "So symbolic was her imagination, so convinced her sensation for the transcendent, that many Dickinson poems which may be read for one addressee may also be read as intended for God. In calling her lover 'master,' she immediately complicated eros with adoration" (*Passion* x). Dickinson appears to recognize behind the earthly bridegroom, frankly desired, a deeper hunger for another union of which marriage is the instrument of participation as well as the symbol. In Hopkins' theology, the bridegroom enacts the part of Christ sacramentally in the consummation of his marriage. Culturally, Dickinson is unlikely to have imbibed much Catholic theology from her Irish servants; her other contact with Catholicism seems to have been limited to a few novels treating Catholicism with mild disdain (Goluboff 355-85). It seems extraordinary that literary romanticism should have granted her access to this matrimonial understanding of the coinherence of the human and divine, but Dickinson did have some cultural encouragement to see poets as prophets. Her early religious training would scarcely have suggested anything so mystical. Calvin thought that marriage was no more sacred than shoemaking or shaving and that the biblical image of Christ as Bridegroom of the Church was only a figure of speech, a "similitude" (2:647). But the Victorian vestiges of romanticism exalted sentiment, particularly domestic sentiment, as indisputably religious. Odd variations of it sprang up in American religious culture in the Northeast during Dickinson's lifetime. One did not have to be tempted by such religious movements to share in the cultural preoccupation with homefires. Readers were not so upset by the physicality of Dante Gabriel Rossetti's "The Blessed Damozel" as to make a widespread outcry at the idea of lovers retaining their emotional passion for each other in the afterlife. Dickinson admired Elizabeth Barrett Browning, who sought her beloved dead in spiritualism and envisioned the love between spouses as at least continuing in heaven, if not being heaven itself.[16] But in Dickinson and Hopkins, literary and spiritual matrimony join with the romantic reverence for the creating poet to emerge with something deeper than Barrett Browning's idiom of spirituality and more connected to Christian culture than Keats.

There is no need to minimize either the carnal or the spiritual aspects of Dickinson's eroticism or to make it biographical. Clearly some of the marriage poems refer to a lover who can be distinguished (sometimes sharply) from Christ, with the speaker even hoping to pursue the relationship after death.[17] There is also imagery, no less emotionally charged, that connects the speaker's sexuality to mystical marriage with Christ.[18] She does not mistake her erotic longings for piety; neither does she sublimate them out of existence when she considers their spiritual dimensions. But in light of Dickinson's usual treatment of religion, what is most remarkable in the poems in which she reflects at once on eros and religion is that despite the frustration, absence, and delay she depicts, the speaker does not here shy away from fulfillment as a goal. Hope is in her erotic birds and bees; her marriage poems exude hope in the obvious good of physical pleasure. Based more on the Apocalypse than the Song of Songs, Dickinson's poetry pushes aside the usual biblical images of sexual love that were widely understood to represent the marriage of the soul with Christ, as in the poetry of Christina Rossetti.[19] Her language has the electricity of something discovered, not of a conventionally pious image. If Dickinson envisions Christ as bridegroom—and she does (Dressman 39-43, esp. 42)—she cannot take him for an absent deity feeding her words rather than solid realities. Congregationalism recognized only baptism and the Eucharist as sacraments. These rituals could be reduced to matter for discursive understanding. Sex could not. Insofar as she was trained not to consider matrimony sacramental, only that far could she investigate its spiritual meaning without arousing the tensions she evidently felt against the religion of her immediate neighborhood. In her poems about marriage, and nowhere else, Dickinson discovered a mystical presence of the divine in human, earthly goods.

In the poems celebrating both sexuality and the image of Christ as bridegroom, Dickinson finds what Hopkins seems to find everywhere: a connection between confident desire for "rapture" and Christian spirituality. In poems outside the marriage group, she indeed takes a strong interest in Christ as an inspiring, sympathetic, suffering figure (Oberhaus 341-58), but it is only in the marriage group that Christ seems to take on the capacity to extend any real benefits to the admirer who speaks in the poems. Dickinson's unremitting honesty, turned on her own desire, illuminates in it what Hopkins considered sacramental sexuality.

Hopkins too forges his own language for the encounter with God symbolized in marriage and finds the union with Christ not only symbolized but enacted in sexual desire and its marital fulfillment. Hopkins writes only two poems explicitly about marriage: an unfinished epithalamion for his brother Everard and wife Amy, and "At the Wedding March," evidently written on the day he presided at a wedding:

> Gód with honour hang your head,
> Gróom, and grace you, bride, your bed
> With lissome scions, swéet scíons
> Out of hallowed bodies bred.
>
> Eách be other's comfort kind:
> Déep, déeper than divined,
> Divíne chárity, déar chárity
> Fast you ever, fást bínd.
>
> Then let the Márch tréad our ears:
> Í to hím túrn with tears
> Whó to wedlock, hís wónder wedlock
> Déals tríumph and immortal years.

(164)

There is in this poem not only an earthly wedded couple busily producing children but a wedlock with "immortal years." Both are present in the sacrament as Hopkins sees it. He wrote few poems on marriage but many others in which Christ is seen as a lover; in all of these, his understanding of the theology of marriage pervades the text. When in "The Starlight Night" he says, "This piece-bright paling shuts the spouse/Christ home, Christ and his mother and all his hallows" (139-40), he reveals an impulse that inhabits all his nature poetry and translates all sensual joy into religious celebration of the Incarnation which made the world's beauty possible. More often there appears imagery of Christ as lover, as in "Hurrahing in Harvest" and "I Wake and Feel the Fell of Dark, Not Day." But one need not infer his ideas about Christ as Divine Lover merely from his poems. He explained in a letter to his friend Robert Bridges, "I cannot in conscience spend time on poetry, neither have I the inducements and inspirations that make others compose. Feeling, love in particular, is the great moving power and spring of verse and the only person that I am in love with seldom, especially now, stirs my heart sensibly and when he does I cannot always 'make capital' of it, it would be a sacrilege to do so" (*Letters to Bridges* 66). When he writes in "As Kingfishers Catch Fire" of Christ "lovely in limbs and lovely in eyes not his," Hopkins is consciously depicting Christ as a lover. Christ inhabits the sacrament of the Church in relation to the world just as he acts in the bridegroom in a sacramental marriage: the man's actions are his own but are also the actions of God incarnate.

Critics rightly perceive Hopkins as a poet of faith but often lionize Dickinson as a harbinger of modern fragmentation and despair. Few see that a common vision unites the two poets, with roots both in literary romanticism and in Christian revelation. Dickinson had a very conflicted relationship with her church and its official teachings about a severe and arbitrary God; much of her poetry shows her insight into the terrible state of one who desires God's grace but is refused. Hopkins, too, felt bruised in his relationship with God but clung to his Catholicism. Despite their differing attitudes toward their respective churches, both evince throughout their works a strong attraction to the moral beauty of Christ.

Christ on earth suffering for love of his faithful ones—an image that Dickinson also treasures—comes to mean for Hopkins God's faithful and permanent choice to love the particulars of the world into existence. In this way for Hopkins Christ the bridegroom is also Christ the romantic poet. Here, in this divine and worldly eros—the pointed and committed choice of some other for the sake of love and the creation of beauty—the poets have a common vision. The marital aspect of the celebration of spiritual presence in the physical world is the most striking point of convergence between Hopkins and Dickinson; it is the chief common aspect of that insight into physical joy as spiritual in itself that is behind their lyric power. At whatever tension the poet is strung as its instrument, the song of the spirit through the body is the lyric song; in Hopkins and in Dickinson the lyric poet embodies the acute grace of unseen spiritual reality.

Notes

1. Although Alfred Habegger talks of her baptism as a fiction in *My Wars Are Laid away in Books*, Roger Lundin, more focused on her church's practices in his research, matter-of-factly dates Dickinson's baptism to 1831 in *Emily Dickinson and the Art of Belief*.

2. Allen Tate settles this matter with very sane discrimination in "Emily Dickinson" 19.

3. Steve Carter, quoted in Tripp 52.

4. Examples can be found in Brantley. See also Duncan 120 and *passim*, quoted in Brantley 83.

5. Johnson provides two drafts of #1282; I have chosen the one he prints second.

6. The discussion of Dostoevsky's *The Eternal Husband* in Girard (46-48) provides a tight and insightful analysis of this phenomenon.

7. Psychologist Matina Horner quantified the phenomenon in her groundbreaking article "Bright Women: Fail" 62.

8. See the discussion of the pervasiveness of this theme in M. K. Louis, "Emily Dickinson's Sacrament of Starvation" 346-60.

9. Habegger is my main source for Dickinson's life, though details about the religious state of her surroundings come from the work of Lundin.

10. I find persuasive the identification and characterization of Emersonian strains in Dickinson's religious statements as presented by Richard E. Brantley, *Experience and Faith* 131, 134.

11. This chapter is not dated but was not included in early editions of *Modern Painters;* Cook and Wedderburn's, where it appears, is late.

12. Even the technical terms she would have heard from her Irish Catholic servants would have befogged rather than illuminated these conceptions.

13. For a discussion of sacramentality in Dickinson in the romantic rather than scholastic sense of the term, see Connie Doyle, "'Experiment in Green'" 226-41.

14. This is the central argument of William Shurr, *The Marriage of Emily Dickinson*.

15. For a meticulous summary of the international research on psychological sequelae of abortion, on which I base this assessment, see Elizabeth Ring-Cassidy and Ian Gentles, *Women's Health after Abortion*, Chap. 14, esp. 190, 192. A sensitive discussion of the sequelae of sexual abuse by an authority figure, such as a clergyman, can be found in Dan Allender, *The Wounded Heart*.

16. M. K. Louis oddly speaks of Elizabeth Barrett Browning as "idiosyncratic" but more orthodox than Dickinson (348-49). Barrett Browning was less conflicted, perhaps, but that most likely springs from a feebler sense of urgency about clarity in doctrine.

17. As argued by Louis (353), who, however, takes these early poems as representative of the whole oeuvre.

18. Michael Dressman's discussion of a selection of "Marriage Group" poems is compelling on this point in "Empress of Calvary" 39-43.

19. Examples in Christina Rossetti are multitudinous. "A Birth-day" suffices for a sample.

MODERN CRISES OF LYRIC

9

Lyric as Sanctuary:

Yeats, Davidson, Ransom, and Frost

GLENN ARBERY

Under the law of the medieval Church, as Victor Hugo's Quasimodo knew, a fugitive could take shelter in the sanctuary, where the civil law could not reach him. In the contemporary world, one cannot cry "Sanctuary!" with any such confidence that temporal justice might be suspended by a higher mercy inhering in a holy place. The boundaries between kinds of law steadily erode, either toward the imposition of theocracy or toward purely secular judgment in the West, where the prerogatives of the highest law have been generally ceded to economics. Ironically, the economy of postmodernity thrives on tropes of escape from its own conditions, as though everyone were a fugitive, and sanctuary is the elsewhere of an iPod.

How does lyric poetry, with its archetypal images of the garden, distinguish itself from the other alternatives so profitably offered when the world is too much with us? "Back out of all this now too much for us," writes Robert Frost at the beginning of "Directive," as though the impulse of the lyric imagination were a withdrawal from the distracted world into poetic space. It makes no difference to the poem whether such space is purely imaginary, like the cave in the air behind a man's body "that nobody is going to touch" in James Wright's "The Jewel," or empirically real, like the pond at Lady Gregory's Coole Park, where "nine and fifty swans" once floated in life and now forever float serenely in Yeats's poem. In "To Autumn," Keats imagines a half-reaped furrow where the reaper lies "sound asleep,/Drows'd with the fume of poppies, while [his] hook/Spares the next swath and all its twinéd flowers." It hardly matters whether in all the history of harvesting such a nest of dreaming ever really occurred.

Poetry has always invented such spaces, if not human space itself. To say so, of course, goes against the dominant abstraction of space: the kind of extension, theoretically measurable in a mathematical grid of three dimensions, which locates all material existence indifferently. The specific differences of poetic spaces attracted Gaston Bachelard, who spends an entire book (*The Poetics of Space*) cataloguing the nature of huts, nests, attics, cellars, and clearings, and Martin Heidegger questions the understanding of extension that has reigned since Descartes, specifically in thinking about poetry. In a memorable passage of "Building Dwelling Thinking," Heidegger calls before his audience "the old bridge in Heidelberg." To think of the bridge, he argues, one does not summon up some attenuated memory trace. "Rather, it belongs to our thinking of that bridge that in itself thinking gets through, persists through, the distance to that location." Despite the physical space of separation, thinking encounters the bridge itself, not a simulacrum. "From right here," he writes, "we may even be much nearer to that bridge and to what it makes room for than someone who uses it daily as an indifferent river crossing" (*Poetry* 154).

Like the bridge, poetic images have a standing, not as representations in the Platonic sense, as imitations of things, which are themselves mere instantiations of ideas that have their real being elsewhere, but as the very presence of the things themselves, stripped of conceptual overlays by thinking toward them. In his essay "Language," Heidegger writes that the place of poetic arrival "is a presence sheltered in absence." To be sheltered means to be spared, and sparing takes place "when we leave something beforehand in its own nature, when we return it specifically to its being, when we 'free' it in the real sense of the word into a preserve of peace" (*Poetry* 197). What is this sheltering absence if not language itself, where things can leave the fray of immediate use and come most intensely into their own natures?

Yet modern lyric poets have to recognize in advance the broader culture's indifference to their poetry. Poetry seems "merely aesthetic" in our age, which means that it has been relegated (even before it is written) to the sphere of specialized appreciation—and not as lucrative a sphere as painting or sculpture. What is a poem in the economy of art collection?

A poetic image has no salience in the technological world either, because images stream endlessly on television or the internet. No one disallows poetry, but it has none of the standing it once did, no trace of its former sacred authority. In the postmodern world, the poet does not write from some precinct miraculously sheltered from technological and economic globalization. A MacArthur grant, a distinguished chair, or an old farmhouse in New Hampshire will not change the fact. Technology understands everything, again in Heidegger's terms, as standing reserve, even one's own "poetic" experience.

But Heidegger can be such a purist about what a poem should do that his expectations become almost angelic. Things become so essentially *thingy* that they begin to shed their existential specificity and become pure Platonic loomings: densely gerundive jugs, bridges, and huts, each intently being-at-work. Exactly how absent does the "novelized" world, as Mikhail Bakhtin describes it, have to be? How much do histories, particular people and places, and cultural differences need to be shaken off? Or, to put it perhaps more accurately, how Greek or German must they become for things to thing and worlds to world so that poetic sparing can take place?

Granted that it is easy to satirize the pose of purity, criticism since Heidegger has swung so much toward an emphasis on cultural poetics that poems begin to seem mere epiphenomena of material circumstances, like consciousness itself: always determined, never free. Given such historicist trends, finding the nature of the poetic universal seems more necessary than ever, even though the best lyric poetry always fixes one foot in the circumstances of a particular time and locale, amid the flux of a given language. What I will be asking is why the work of the lyric poet is not only to shelter things, in Heidegger's complex restorative sense, but also to do so by sparing places—New England, the American South, Ireland—with their distinctive historical character but without nostalgia.

The poets who spare particular historical places do so in part because these have afforded poetic knowledge a standing at odds with the contemporary world. In the early 1850s, Matthew Arnold was already looking for poetic sanctuary at the Carthusian monastery in the Grande Chartreuse, where nothing had changed since the Middle Ages. The same monastery recently became the subject of a German documentary called *Into Great Silence*, which reverently observes these monks and dwells without comment on the details of monastic life: water dripping slowly from the rim of a metal washbowl, the hands of an old monk measuring cloth for an alb and slowly cutting it with scissors, bell-ringing, meals, prayerful repetitions. Watching the film and its acts of attention, however, one could make the same objection that Heidegger made of the Rhine. The contemplative life has become "an object on call for inspection by a tour group ordered there by the vacation industry" ("Question" 16). Monastic silence itself, even its meditative recovery of things, can become standing reserve to be recorded and watched rather than experienced.

Part of the difficulty of entering the poetic space of the lyric comes with discerning one's reasons for being there. To what extent, for example, has poetry itself become standing reserve for the essays that are written about it, including this one? The poets I want to explore here come out of circumstances different from Arnold's, at least. They are not visitors on tour, shopping for authenticity, but inhabitants of continuous local cultures that still exist at the time of their writing, though they are already being lost. Frost lived in New England all his life. Ransom left the South for Ohio but not until he was middle-aged, and Yeats never essentially left Ireland, despite his sojourns elsewhere. On the one hand, their poetry comes out of what is already there, and in that sense, these poets cannot be described (as perhaps Ezra Pound can) in the terms that Brabantio used for the mercenary Othello: "an extravagant and wheeling stranger/Of here and everywhere." On the other hand, they cannot pretend to be untouched by modernity, nor can those who read them. They spare what they hold dear by pickling it in irony.

I

Yeats surely understands what Heidegger means by "a presence sheltered in absence." His Ireland is too densely poetic even to describe. Not only its mythological backgrounds but also its long political history as the "other" of England, always looked down on, always excluded, and yet incorporated as a poetic resource (particularly in the twentieth century), make it incomparably rich in the imagination. The greatness of Yeats and James Joyce, not to mention such figures as Patrick Kavanagh, Sean O'Casey, John Synge, and George Bernard Shaw, virtually established twentieth-century literature in English in a way directly comparable to the explosion of postcolonial literatures from India, Nigeria, and elsewhere today. A simple poem like "The Lake Isle of Innisfree" invokes the whole difference of Ireland from England, not only because it holds up rural Ireland as preferable to the very heart of the British Empire in London, but also because it establishes Ireland as the true homeland of the sympathetic reader, thus enacting a kind of colonialism in reverse.

In neither of his frequently anthologized poems "The Lake Isle of Innisfree" and "Sailing to Byzantium" is there any narration of the journey itself. Each dwells only on the arrival, though "Sailing to Byzantium" spends its first two stanzas gazing astern, as it were, and justifying the departure, not only from "that country," but from a heart "sick with desire/And fastened to a dying animal," that is, from nature itself. "I will arise and go now" begins "Lake Isle," as though no explanation were necessary almost a century after Wordsworth's "The World Is Too Much with Us." Modern London has become more complex and inhuman than it was when William Blake wandered through each "chartered street," and Yeats has no peace as he once did in County Sligo. Instead of dwelling on his circumstances, he sheds this logical preparation and begins as though nothing at all preceded the poem but the first indrawn breath of his existence:

> I will arise and go now, and go to Innisfree,
> And a small cabin build there, of clay and wattles made,
> Nine bean-rows will I have there, a hive for the honey-bee,
>   And live alone in the bee-loud glade.

What kind of dwelling is this? Richard Finneran notes in the *Collected Poems* that, properly speaking, Innisfree is "Inis Fraoigh ('Heather Island'), a small island in Lough Gill, County Sligo" (479). The name *Innisfree*, adapted from the Gaelic, has a romantic sound, and its ending with the syllable "free" gives it more resonance in English than its actual meaning, which, as we have seen, signifies heather. Yeats can play the Gaelic off the English, in other words, in constructing his Irish retreat—a game with its private satisfactions.

Richard Ellmann, who thinks the poem was written during a time in London (about 1890) when Yeats loved all "indeterminate things," writes that the poet longed for Innisfree "because an island was neither mainland nor water but something of both, and because the return to Sligo, though he knew it to be impossible, would be a return to that prepubertal state when his consciousness had not yet been split in two" (84). The poem departs, in other words, both from an implied London with its "pavements grey" and from the conflicts of his own psyche. It arrives in the secular poetic monasticism of the hermit with his "nine bean-rows" and his bees. Psychologically, going to the lake isle in Lough Gill in County Sligo represents an imaginative *nostos* for a young poet alienated by his surroundings and his own emotions.

Most of the poem longs for future peace, a peace already present at Innisfree: "And I shall have some peace there, for peace comes dropping slow,/Dropping from the veils of the morning to where the cricket sings." The lines strike us now as mannered, deliberately "poetic." Other conventions, such as inversions of noun and adjective ("pavements grey") feel Miltonic, and the diction, words like "isle" and "glade," which no one but real estate developers could use now with a straight face, point to ways in which the language of the poem fails to stay new, unlike the diction of "Lapis Lazuli" or "The Second Coming."

Among Yeats's poems, this is decidedly immature writing, however often anthologized it may be, but it is not possible to dismiss it on that account. One can see clearly how its imaginative movement toward a sheltered place anticipates "Sailing to Byzantium" and recovers the lyric movement of masterpieces like Keats's "Ode to a Nightingale." In the latter, Keats imagines the nightingale singing on its hidden branch somewhere in the dark and enters its space without having to negotiate distances: "I cannot see what flowers are at my feet/Or what soft incense hangs upon the boughs." He inhabits not so much the bird per se as the pure sensorium of place: absence of light, presence of incense, the balancing grip on the branch, the guessed-at sweets (white hawthorne, pastoral eglantine, coming roses), the sound of murmuring flies. In this "embalmed darkness," sheltered and secured as though by death itself, song has its full liberty, for only here can the bird be "pouring forth [its] soul abroad/in such an ecstasy."[1] In thinking about what makes the unrestrained song possible, Keats conflates the annihilation of his own personality, either in the being of the bird or in death, with the liberation of pure language. He is rapt by the bird's song into this shelter, attainable only in this way, only as absence, never as a place to which he can physically cross. Similarly, with Yeats's lake isle, actual intrusion upon the geographical island would dispel rather than realize the place conjured as a "bee-loud glade."

The question is not what these spaces are for the poets, however, but what they are as a "preserve of peace" in Heidegger's sense, entered and inhabited by those distant from the poet's own psychological concerns. It may be important biographically, for example, that fear of tuberculosis oppressed Keats after the death of his brother Tom or that Yeats had an ambivalent longing for the insular life of Ireland in general and Sligo in particular. But to the extent that the language does its proper work, the poem brings about an impersonal sparing. In "Lake Isle," the details retain their romantic phrasing (the mists on the lake are "the veils of the morning," and instead of the prosaic "ground," we have "where the cricket sings"), but what remains important in the poem is that this poetically secured place allows or grants peace, in sharp contrast to "the roadway" or the "pavements grey." By its very nature, the roadway always leads somewhere else, toward ends so common as to be established in stone pavements. Innisfree urges nothing, certainly not activity in common with others. It invites silence and stillness with a primal rhythm ("lake water lapping with low sounds by the shore") that arrests the speaker and brings him to a stand in the middle of the city and its business. The clause "I will arise and go now" implies that he has been divided, idle, distracted, slothful. It is as though nothing has been truly purposive until now, until this sudden decision frees him: "I will arise and go now, and go to Innisfree." The common roadway will not guide his going.

Ellmann's interpretation of the lake isle as psychologically liminal or prepubertal, "neither mainland nor water, but something of both," misses what the island is *as an image*, less about in-betweenness than refuge, sanctuary. Emphatically bounded, like a walled city or a nest, an island intensifies the difference between dry land and water. In effect, the island always has something emergent about it, a recovery of solid consciousness, like the moment of waking. Out of London, back in the Gaelic homeland, the lake isle offers restorative solitude, even as an image. "Nine bean-rows," "a hive for the honey-bee"—these evoke the geometrical exactness of the comb's hexagons and the parallel lines of the rows. At the same time, they provide a musical and nourishing space of honey and climbing beanstalks, disciplined but also self-exceeding. "There" exists only in the absence of the literal County Sligo and its distracting irrelevance; "there" is concentrated in the linguistic nest of the poem only, and there alone can one be free.

Arguing too seriously for such a poetic presence, though, would require an embarrassing bardic affectation difficult to sustain in the novelized world. As tropes to be manipulated, "getting away" and "going off the grid" became commodities long ago, completely subsumed by technology. Advertisements for SUVs present the most inaccessible reserves as attainable by their bounding vehicles, which pose against the landscape like exotic fauna. Airlines deploy images of islands far more remote than Innisfree as catalysts of desire for the booming getaway industry. What frees up the traveler's money is the skillful deployment of the trope or meme of the spared place, ironically reduced to pure instrumentality. Innisfree easily becomes a cliché, as the older Yeats recognized.

Yet essentially the same impulse toward escape informs "Sailing to Byzantium," written over thirty years later. How does the complex symbol of Byzantium differ from the island as a place? The contrast springs from the fundamental similarity of what both the lake isle and Byzantium offer: refuge or sanctuary. Byzantium replaces solitude with the life of the "holy city," nature with artifice, *nostos* with transformation, bean-rows and hives with "the gold mosaic of a wall." Although the place he calls Byzantium retains a geographical and historical grounding, the coordinates of Istanbul and Hagia Sophia reveal even less than Innisfree's. For Yeats, it is now self-evident that sanctuary has to be constructed: it is "the artifice of eternity," sharply bounded from "whatever is begotten, born, and dies." Like Innisfree, Byzantium exists only as a place to be reached by means of poetic concentration, but with the crucial addition of "unageing intellect," whose difficulty of access separates the speaker from the many (who would otherwise go on Yeats tours with their Michelin guides). The holy city retains the emphatic difference of an island, but this time the strong boundary exists between "singing masters" and "sensual music." Whatever unreflectively comes into being and passes away without mindfulness—that is, nature itself—cannot enter: "And therefore I have sailed the seas and come/To the holy city of Byzantium."

To secure the poetic place of refuge, in other words, the speaker must leave nature altogether, which means either to venture out of poetry into the imageless or to fashion a poetry that points beyond itself to pure forms, as Dante does in the *Paradiso*. The difficulty of understanding the later Yeats might lie in reconciling "such a form as Grecian goldsmiths make/Of hammered gold and gold enamelling" with the heart he seems not to have escaped in "The Circus Animals' Desertion." His heart is "sick with desire/And fastened to a dying animal" in "Sailing to Byzantium," and he wants that heart consumed away in the holy fire, but it proves impossible to escape in the still-later poem, impossible to reach transcendence. The "deep heart's core" invoked in "Lake Isle" becomes as base and inescapably urban as a nightmare corner of Dickens' London: "the foul rag-and-bone shop of the heart."

There is no refuge. More accurately, there is no refuge except within the poem. The lake isle is really a place that exists or "presences" only in language, yet that presence can easily be dispelled by thinking of the poetic space as a commercial trope. What difference is there between a poem that tries to create sanctuary poetically and one that questions the desire for sanctuary while at the same time paradoxically offering it? Can the poem offer refuge at the same time that it explicitly denies the possibility, like someone in a tyranny posing as a supporter of the regime in order to help refugees escape from it?

2

The difference between the early imagination of Yeats and his last visions might also be reflected in the temperamental difference between Donald Davidson in his poem "Sanctuary" and John Crowe Ransom in "Old Mansion" or "Prelude to an Evening." Davidson and Ransom came to maturity in the South several generations after the Civil War and Reconstruction. Henry Grady had already made his inroads in proposing the New South, and most of the region was given over, on the one hand, to those who would make it like the industrial North and, on the other hand, to a tribe of demagogues to whom William Faulkner would later give their enduring name: Snopes. Ransom, Davidson, Allen Tate, and Robert Penn Warren, who first met at Vanderbilt University in Nashville, made a concerted effort not only to counter the usual opinion of the South but also to further its traditions, purified of its Walter Scott romanticism and its almost exclusive interest in political rhetoric. Because the South had largely avoided the Puritan strains of Protestantism and because its agrarian way of life had made it possible to retain some continuity with the life of Europe, the South was continuous, they thought, with the older feudal order of Christendom interrupted by Puritanism and modernity. Yet they were very aware, as T. S. Eliot also was, of what any emphasis on tradition looked like in the world of Henry Ford. As Louise Cowan has shown in her book *The Fugitive Group*, they especially despised the literature of Southern romanticism, pronouncing with mock solemnity in their Foreword to *The Fugitive Group* that "a literary phase known rather euphemistically as Southern Literature has expired" (48). They promoted a thorny, difficult, highly ironic way of writing that did not lend itself easily to sentiment, though Donald Davidson worried that "the impregnable or guarded style...reaches only the literary elite of poets, critics, professors of English, and the students who are electing certain courses and have to submit to it" ("Poetry" 8).

Of these poets, Donald Davidson allowed himself to be the most unguarded, as it were, in poems that make the most direct appeal to the emotions of loyalty and patriotism in the root sense. "Lee in the Mountains," a poem about the general after the war when he served as a college president, speaks of the fire still present in Lee's soldiers, if only he will say the word to awaken it: "this lost forsaken valor/And the fierce faith undying/And the love quenchless." Similarly, in "Randall, My Son," a father's plea for his son not to abandon his inheritance, Davidson ends the poem with lines unfashionably bare of irony:

> Take, what I leave, your own land unforgotten;
> Hear, what I hear, in a far chase new begun
> An old horn's husky music, Randall, my son.

But his poem "Sanctuary" most directly offers a poetic space meant to shelter those who find it from the encroachments of the modern world. The poem seems to be spoken in the voice of a Southern Civil War–era father who remembers older threatening figures (Tryon, Tarleton) as well as men like Sam Houston, but who makes no mention of later men. His warning concerns what might happen if the Union troops invade their land, and the poem (like Robert Frost's "Directive") is a set of instructions, beginning with the condition they both dread and expect: "if ever defeat is black/Upon your eyelids, go to the wilderness/In the dread last of trouble...."

The advice is ironic for two reasons, despite the unguarded style: first, Lee did resort to the Wilderness in Virginia for his last battles against Grant (Grant's overwhelming numbers defeated him nonetheless); and second, the sanctuary to which the father urges the sons to resort,

Lyric as Sanctuary: Yeats, Davidson, Ransom, and Frost

Chilhowee, now lies deep underwater as a result of the Tennessee Valley Authority's dam, though it is unclear whether this is an irony that Davidson intended when he wrote the poem or one that modernization in the South later provided for him. In any case, the father describes it as a place where "Sweet springs of mountain water.../Run always," sacred even "before the Cherokee/Came to our eastern mountains." With its Mosaic tone of Exodus, the poem warns the sons against looking back until they have achieved this sanctuary, at which point they may regard "*His* dust and flame." Then they can decide whether to carry on a guerrilla warfare against the foe.

> Or else, forgetting ruin, you may lie
> On sweet grass by a mountain stream, to watch
> The last wild eagle soar or the last raven
> Cherish his brood within their rocky nest,
> Or see, when mountain shadows first grow long,
> The last enchanted white deer come to drink.

For Davidson, the "rocky nest" of Chilhowee shelters and spares its inhabitants because the sacred things are precisely those that make it worthwhile to fight. They give men something worth passing on to their sons, sons who *may* indulge in "poetic" pleasures but in doing so will guarantee the extinction of their way of life: these will be "the *last* wild eagle," "the *last* raven," "the *last* enchanted white deer." Implied is a judgment against modern poetry itself, to the extent that it cooperates with the dust and flame of the destroyer. In its aesthetic withdrawal, poetry becomes inaccessible to most men and removes poetic power from the emotions that give men a reason for meaningful action. The very beauty of these last lines masks the consolation of despair.

Ransom, on the contrary, embodies the "guarded style" as much as Allen Tate. The classic example of Ransom's dry understatement comes in his poem "Bells for John Whiteside's Daughter," in which the death of a little girl is described in a gently chiding tone, and the sight of her dead body leads to the ironies of the last quatrain:

> But now go the bells, and we are ready,
> In one house we are sternly stopped
> To say we are vexed at her brown study,
> Lying so primly propped.

"Vexed": the word a formal grandparent might use about the antics of an unruly child. In his very character as a poet, Ransom will never speak with the spirited openness Davidson always uses but will rather comment, from a dry, distanced, "old" observational stance, as though he had never been a participant in the life of passion at all, or at least not in recent centuries. There is something oddly detached and self-deprecating, for example, about the way that the "tired historian" in his poem "Old Mansion" approaches the experience of the Southern space par excellence: the big house, the manor. He hopes to go inside since it has already fallen into decay and "Will not forever be thus, O man, exhibited,/And one had best hurry to enter it if one can."

The mistress of the house, however, turns him away without the "dole of a look," which means that "no annalist went in to the lords or the peons." Unlike Edwin Arlington Robinson's "Miniver Cheevy," this historian is less a "child of scorn" than a would-be cavalier, a little foolish, as the last stanza demonstrates:

> But on retreating I saw myself in the token,
> How loving from my dying weed the feather curled
> On the languid air; and I went with courage shaken
> To dip, alas, into some unseemlier world.

Unseemly as the world might be, the fact is that his very attempt to penetrate the inmost heart of the Southern past, the one lauded in moonlight-and-magnolias fiction, turns out to be mere futility. He can get no closer to the lived experience of the antebellum South than Allen Tate's speaker outside the cemetery can approach the experience of those soldiers "hurried beyond decision" in "Ode to the Confederate Dead."

In other words, what the poet provides is neither a substitute experience nor a way of reaching back to some lost South in the way that Heidegger would have thinking prevail across distance to the old bridge in Heidelberg. Ransom differs radically from Davidson in making no attempt to render a poetic space of sanctuary. Instead of finding the image inhabitable, the reader encounters a large sign, hastily tacked up (perhaps by the "warped concierge" alarmed at the intrusion), that says "No Trespassing." This is not to say, either, that anything is being defended or that the old mansion remains in any sense "richly inhabited,/Its porches and bowers suiting the children of men." Rather, it turns away visitors

Lyric as Sanctuary: Yeats, Davidson, Ransom, and Frost   211

because there is nothing there now and no way back to what was, especially for tourists of history. What remains is the trace of its unlikely evanescence, even though "Stability was the character of its rectangle."

Ransom is at his strongest as a poet when he is performing as an ironist at the furthest remove from what Davidson does. Somehow, though, both of them are essentially Southern, and it may be that Ransom holds the same essential pieties. But instead of trying to attach the passions to them explicitly, he brings before the reader the situation in which the pieties ought to thrive and introduces the irony that modifies, or even ruins, them. For example, his poem "Prelude to an Evening," which he revised (to my mind disastrously) late in his life, imagines the father coming home from work (or from war, it hardly matters) and being expected "To sit tonight with the warm children/Naming the pretty kings of France." The speaker sees "images of the invaded mind" somehow getting loose from him and beginning to affect the wife's psyche. Suppose that she can no longer awaken from her nightmares but that even in the house, in her peignoir (an ironic allusion to Wallace Stevens' cheerfully pagan "Sunday Morning"), she can "Feel poising round the sunny room//Invisible evil, deprived, and bold." If the husband infects the household with his own visions, he will doom her to a life of fear in which she will "be listening for the low wind,/The warning sibilance of pines."

It is striking, in other words, to see Ransom so exactingly dismantle the dream of domestic happiness and refuse any image of safe dwelling to the reader. But immediately following "Prelude to an Evening" in his *Selected Poems* is an odd, often overlooked poem called "What Ducks Require" that seems to address the issue directly, since it concerns the literal nesting instinct. In the duck world, it seems, "Male and female/Make a slight nest to arise/Where they overtake the spring." They do not build their nests anywhere solid or safe in the usual sense, but they pick a spot that suits their double nature as both aquatic and aerial:

> The half-householders for estate
> Beam their floor with ribs of grass,
> Disdain your mortises and slate
> And Lar who invalided lies,
> The marsh quakes dangerous, the port
> Where wet and dry precisely start.

One gets the sense that this is as far as Ransom is willing to go toward providing the reader's Eden, and it is a long way from the lake isle of Innisfree. Cold, unappealing, "Where wet and dry precisely start," it speaks to something nomadic and permanently in-between, and it leaves open the question of whether the traditional household with its Lar (one naturally thinks of Aeneas) can still exist.

Perhaps for Ransom, however, the analogy works most powerfully in casting modern man into a certain ambiguous light. He dwells nowhere, yet neither does he have the cosmic, instinctual scope of the bird in William Cullen Bryant's early American poem "To A Waterfowl." Bryant's speaker recognizes that the duck seeks "the plashy brink/Of weedy lake, or marge of river wide," but adds his meditations upon "a Power whose care/Teaches thy way along that pathless coast." Somehow, "the blue chasm of no wharves" that ends Ransom's poem does not afford the same consolation. Ransom often defends the South in his poems (especially in "Antique Harvesters"), but he never provides in the poem itself an image of inviolable sanctuary like Davidson's Chilhowee, even as a place to recover one's strength and remember what the whole battle is for. Yet the paradox may be that Ransom hides and protects the South precisely in his refusal to let the poem be a featured stop for tourists of the imagination.

3

Robert Frost's New England has much more in common with the South of Ransom, in this respect, than it does with the Ireland of Yeats. Unlike Robert Lowell, who delves at length into the historical, especially Puritan, background of the New England psyche, Frost for the most part limits his observations to the present, including opinionated forays into contemporary politics. Most memorably, his poems explore the ethos of rural New England and especially the sometimes uncanny, often tragic domestic lives that take place in the isolated farms. Longer poems such as "Home Burial," "A Servant to Servants," and "The Fear" come to mind. Others, of course, are much more lyrical, less like vignettes out of Aeschylus. Something in the New England tone or mood persists behind all of them, even the lighter ones, and it is difficult to conceive of them as having been written elsewhere. Is it simply the author's name, so intimately associated with the region, that evokes the association, or is there truly some spirit of place that informs these poems, a "sound of sense" unmistakably Frost's? One senses not only a distinctive voice but an underlying stoicism left over from centuries of religious dread interrupted at times by transcendental exaltation.

Frost has a poem, rarely anthologized, called "The Exposed Nest" that might be taken to stand at almost the exact opposite extreme from Yeats's "Lake Isle." "You were forever finding some new play," the poem begins. The speaker sees this "you," probably his young wife (now grown older) to whom the poem is addressed, "on hands and knees/In the meadow, busy with the new-cut hay,/Trying, I thought, to set it up on end."[2] The speaker's willingness to "help pretend/To make it root again and grow afresh" on a day when the grass had just been cut suggests someone with an unusual propensity for pretending things himself (like the speaker in "Birches").

> But 'twas no make-believe with you today,
> Nor was the grass itself your real concern,
> Though I found your hand full of wilted fern,
> Steel-bright June-grass, and blackening heads of clover.
> 'Twas a nest full of young birds on the ground
> The cutter-bar had just gone champing over
> (Miraculously without tasting flesh)
> And left defenseless to the heat and light.

The poem moves from the speaker's expectation of more "play" over into real danger, and the poem's tone darkens accordingly. The woman realizes the danger that the young birds are in, exposed as they are to predators from the air, and she tries to arrange the ferns and grasses so that they won't be seen. The poignancy of the situation lies in the complex play of ignorance, expectation, pity, and knowledge that it evokes:

> The way the nest-full every time we stirred
> Stood up to us as to a mother-bird
> Whose coming home has been too long deferred,
> Made me ask would the mother-bird return
> And care for them in such a change of scene
> And might our meddling make her more afraid.

Having started, though, they have to do the best they can "Though harm should come of it." They build the screen the woman has begun and give this shade back to the birds, "All this to prove we cared."

What is most telling about "The Exposed Nest" is the way it ends, as though this incident were being remembered now for a reason, with an implicit, unstated analogy in mind. The speaker makes a point of the fact that their compassion did not extend past that one deed.

> Why is there then
> No more to tell? We turned to other things.
> I haven't any memory—have you?—
> Of ever coming to the place again
> To see if the birds lived the first night through,
> And so at last to learn to use their wings.

The poem as a whole might almost be the husband's belated response to the distraught, accusatory wife in "Home Burial," who cannot tolerate the fact that her husband responds with such grave-digging efficiency to the death of their son. "From the time when one is sick to death" she says, "One is alone, and he dies more alone." She reproaches, not only her husband, but people in general for leaving behind the dying "And making the best of their way back to life/And living people, and things they understand."

Read in the light of other Frost poems ("Death of a Hired Hand," "The Fear") in which the husband and wife divide fundamental attitudes of realism and emotion between them, "The Exposed Nest" serves as a reminder, strangely like Ransom's in "Prelude to an Evening," that ultimately no shelter protects us. The fate of these small birds, which look to those protecting them as if they were the mother, is too painful to contemplate because they are dying from the moment the cutter blade exposes them. The violation is irreversible. To cover a nest so open to predators, as the speaker knows, might expose it instead to abandonment, and in any case, the impulse (gathering the grasses, ferns, and clover to hide the small birds) reveals the nature of mortal nakedness and the vulnerability of human shelter all too clearly. Yet it must be covered for conscience to be satisfied.

Frost famously calls poetry "a momentary stay against confusion," and it may be that the poetic space least susceptible to commercial use or technological reduction is the one that inheres in the nature of poems themselves. This nature emerges most clearly when poems like the ones we have been examining acknowledge loss in the foreground and shelter the quality of their meanings well beyond what can be explicitly translated in an academic discussion. If they offer sanctuary, it is not an easily purchased one. As constructs, not simply of meters, rhymes, metaphors, or other officially analyzable constituents, poetic spaces arise from the exact suggestions of tone in the bristle of consonants or subtle turns on some expectation set up by a tradition in the history of reading, yet they are not merely linguistic phenomena. "Poetry intends to recover the denser and more refractory original world which we know loosely through our perceptions and memories," writes John Crowe Ransom. "By this supposition it is a kind of knowledge which is radically or ontologically distinct" ("Wanted" 148). Each true poetic place bears within it a particular *habitus*[3] of dwelling, a way of being peculiar to its historical locus, and each has the remarkable power to evoke it long after the reality to which it might refer in actual life has disappeared. Perhaps the concession to disappearance, as Frost puts it in "Directive," hides the nature of the sanctuary, "so the wrong ones can't find it."

NOTES

1. In his essay "The Thing," Heidegger writes: "Death is the shrine of Nothing, that is, of that which in every respect is never something that merely exists, but which nevertheless presences, even as the mystery of Being in itself. As the shrine of Nothing, death harbors within itself the presencing of Being. As the shrine of Nothing, death is the shelter of Being" (*Poetry* 176).

2. There is a certain maternal impulse in the child's play, but the action being described has no gender. The speaker could almost as easily be a mother reminiscing with her son or daughter, now grown older, about something that happened when the child was more susceptible to naïve sentiment.

3. *Habitus*, the Latin translation of Greek *hexis*, Jacques Maritain defines in the plural as "intrinsic super-elevations of living spontaneity, vital developments which render the soul better in a given order and which fill it with an active sap" (*Art* 11).

10

Wallace Stevens' Scrawny Cry

SEEMEE ALI

Wallace Stevens' poetry asks and answers a single, austere question, again and again: is lyric poetry dead? His sobering, realistic answer is: yes. His intoxicating, visionary answer is: no.

To make sense of this apparent incongruity, it helps first to realize that, for the post-romantic Stevens, lyric is not simply an expression of feeling, spontaneous or otherwise. Rather, the lyric is the manifestation of an elusive spiritual force. In "The Noble Rider and the Sound of Words" he compares the lyric to the physical phenomenon of an ocean wave: "a wave is a force and not the water of which it is composed" (*Necessary Angel* 35). Just as there is an interior and natural reality that *is* the wave (that is, its force) and an equally natural external reality that manifests this force (the water), so is there an interior reality, an equally natural force, that propels both Stevens' poems and his hopes, ambivalent as they are, for the future of lyric poetry.

The propelling force that drives lyric poetry is nobility. Nobility is to language what energy is to the wave. Nobility constitutes "our spiritual height and depth," Stevens declares (*Necessary Angel* 33-34). He writes: "[Nobility] is not an artifice that the mind has added to human nature. The mind has added nothing to human nature. It is a violence from within that protects us from a violence without. It is the imagination, pressing back against the pressure of reality. It seems, in the last analysis, to have something to do with our self preservation; and that, no doubt, is why the expression of it, the sound of its words, helps us to live our lives" (36). The idea is bold, especially when one remembers that nobility is itself an archaic virtue, of uncertain value in the present day. Nonetheless, Stevens maintains that even in modernity, human nobility is an animating force—and, when necessary, a kind of violence—that is necessary for our self-preservation.

Stevens' writings, both prose and poetry, thus presuppose a fundamental conception of the soul. He insists, it seems, that we all know and feel in our depths a wholeness that unites our single souls with the rest of creation. Each of us therefore intuits, deeply if dimly, an aboriginal sense of oneness in Being. Our nobility consists in recognizing this oneness even when all the evidence of the phenomenal world points to disintegration and decay.

In Stevens' poems, the intuition of a radical unity of Being can be overwhelming. It cannot be denied, even in the face of the most insistent and skeptical questioning. His lyrics bring to consciousness an impossible, yet nonetheless overpowering, desire for a return to the absolute, metaphysical unity in which all distinctions dissolve. Divisions disappear between objects and their beholders, between modes of time (past, present, and future), between lovers and their beloveds. And in the constant yearning after this unity, the poems are riven by an undercurrent of pain (a nostalgia for a unity that in reality can never be recovered) and buoyed by the delight of recognition (in apprehending this unity imaginatively, even if fleetingly).

Stevens' deep conviction in the absolute unity of Being is hardly modern and, indeed, hardly unique to him. Belief in the oneness of things is a recurring constant in the Western literary and philosophical tradition. In ancient Greece the pre-Socratic philosopher Parmenides posited a unity that is the true path. In the monotheistic religions, an all-encompassing oneness is the particular attribute of divinity, in which we all mysteriously participate. In modernity, the nineteenth-century poet Samuel Taylor Coleridge proposed that this unity remains always available to the "primary imagination," the creative activity that he described as "the repetition in the finite mind of the eternal act of creation in the infinite I AM" (313). It is hardly accidental, one might venture, that the reports of Parmenides (whose extant writing consists of a fantastic epic poem involving a pilgrim's journey to meet a goddess), of the prophets of the great monotheistic religions, and of Coleridge (the author of "Kubla Khan" and *The Rime of the Ancient Mariner*) eschew realism. Rather, all of these writings from Parmenides to Stevens form what might be termed a visionary tradition: in other words, a tradition of seeing things not simply *as they are* to any profane observer but from a prophetic perspective, which is to say, *as they really are* in the soul's deepest reaches.

Far from expressing the agnosticism of his times, then, Stevens' lyrics aim to make perfectly transparent a vision of reality that perceives human beings as one with birds ("A man and a woman and a blackbird/Are one," *Collected Poems* 93), one with musical instruments ("The blue guitar/And I are one," 171), one with books ("The reader became the book," 358), one with the deepest mystery of divinity ("God and the imagination are one," 524). Ultimately, for Stevens, the "real" (that is to say, merely phenomenal) world serves him only as an analogy for the radical vision of unity his poetry yearns for and claims as truth. He proposes, "The corporeal world exists as the common denominator of the incorporeal worlds of its inhabitants" (*Necessary Angel* 118). Thus, the familiar objects of the real world, as they are commonly apprehended, become for him an alphabet for the language of a far more enigmatic other world (of which anyone who can imagine it is a citizen). By means of such a cosmic-scale analogy, Stevens declares his aim to compose "a fundamental poetry even older than the ancient world" (*Necessary Angel* 145).

An early poem, "The Comedian as the Letter C" (1923), provides some insight into Stevens' sense of his poetic task:

> Here was the veritable ding an sich, at last,
> Crispin confronting it, a vocable thing,
> But with a speech belched out of hoary darks
> Noway resembling his....
>
> (*Collected Poems* 29)

The speech belched from the hoary darks is a mark of the poet's confrontation with the *ding an sich*, the thing itself. Although Stevens is often accused of a kind of dandyism or escapism in his poetry, it is this pure vision, the unadorned truth of things, that his lyrics are after. Indeed, rather than escaping reality, Stevens' poems intend to drive their readers more deeply toward and into it. When the confrontation with the thing itself is finally attained (the lyrics insist this can happen), Stevens' readers discover with Crispin that the world, apprehended in its absolute purity, is no longer exactly familiar. The *ding an sich* will always be alien to us. Its fantastic strangeness requires a correspondingly fantastic and strange language in which to report it. This is the language of Stevens' lyrics.

Stevens' confrontation with what he calls elsewhere "the plain sense of things" is, then, a confrontation with a supra-reality that is beyond ordinary perception but always tantalizingly *there*. This quest for an absolute clarity of perception is the key to Stevens' lyric vision and the clue, too, to what he means when he speaks of nobility as a "force."

In a poem published toward the end of his life, "Long and Sluggish Lines" (1954), Stevens again insists upon the poet's privileged access to the secret of the hoary darks. To his reader, he declares, "You were not born yet when the trees were crystal/Nor are you now, in this wakefulness inside a sleep" (*Collected Poems* 522). These lines illustrate perfectly something that Stevens claims in the "Noble Rider" lecture: "A poet's words are of things that do not exist without the words" (*Necessary Angel* 32). Here, he does not mean simply that poets create fictions that cannot be seen or comprehended without the language that forms them. Rather, he means that the words of poets depict apparent impossibilities. For his own poetry, he invents an abstract "visionary language." (Stevens uses this phrase in a letter comparing the sculptor Jean Arp unfavorably with Constantin Brancusi: "His forms will never constitute a 'visionary language.' Unlike the things of Brancusi they never intimidate one with their possibilities" [*Letters* 629 S].) The visionary mode is perhaps more readily associated with poets of a bygone era than with the modernists of the twentieth century; Stevens' lyrics are closer in mood to William Blake, for example, than to any of his contemporaries (e.g., Robert Frost, T. S. Eliot, Ezra Pound, William Carlos Williams). For Stevens, the visionary mode—the commitment to revealing "things that do not exist without the words"—enables poets to invoke in their writings a dimension of Being that language not only does not ordinarily name but more often serves actively to veil.

The conundrum of the poet's visionary task is Stevens' particular subject in "The Man with the Blue Guitar" (1937). The poem's title invokes Pablo Picasso's many painted and sculpted guitars, all of which purposefully blur the line between representation and abstraction:

> They said, "You have a blue guitar,
> You do not play things as they are."
> The man replied, "Things as they are
> Are changed upon the blue guitar."

(*Collected Poems* 165)

Things "Are changed upon the blue guitar" because the guitar—the twentieth century's lyre—here serves as the symbol of a poet's genius. Its music is emphatically *not* made to show "things as they are." Instead, it plays the music of disjunction, testifying to the distance between ordinary existence and some larger, more vivid possibility, rendering the world in its full glory, in its purest essence. As the poem elaborates, the disarming music of the guitar is called into being by "an absence in reality" that the artist refuses to ignore. Since absence, too, is a dimension of reality, awareness of it paradoxically enlarges a sense of the real and thus necessarily changes the nature of "things as they are." The poem continues:

> Poetry is the subject of the poem,
> From this the poem issues and
>
> To this returns. Between the two,
> Between issue and return, there is
>
> An absence in reality,
> Things as they are. Or so we say.
>
> (*Collected Poems* 176)

In other words, in the void that exists between the creation ("issue") of the poem and its signification ("return"), the line between representation and abstraction becomes blurred of necessity. Again, merely the awareness of this absence by itself can change the nature, if not the look, of "things" in general. As the poem goes on, the speaker proposes that this place of absence indeed exists *for* the poem, "which acquires//Its true appearances there" (i.e., in this absence). Dwelling in this absence, the poem draws into itself the visionary language of the "sun's green,/Cloud's red, earth feeling, sky that thinks." These colorful and feeling words necessarily distort the look and texture of "things as they are" to accommodate the void that the visonary poet, perhaps uniquely, intuits in reality.

Stevens acknowledges, though, that the poet's power is not the only one that alters "things as they are." The movements of time and history impose their own, more dire changes. These modifications mean that poetry, in its own turn, becomes a "thing" upon which change is imposed. The poet's careful report from the void is therefore always in danger of being itself effaced by blinding epochal shifts.

To illustrate, let us turn away from "The Man with the Blue Guitar" for a moment and return to the "Noble Rider" lecture. There, Stevens points to a passage from Plato's *Phaedrus* that he identifies as "pure poetry" (*Necessary Angel* 3). The passage presents Socrates' famous image of a charioteer and two horses, intended to serve as a metaphor for the soul. The modern reader's experience of this metaphor, Stevens observes, is instructive of a problem inherent in all poetic achievement. He counts himself among those who respond to Socrates' metaphor first with joyful recognition. Yet this joy, for him and other sensitive readers like him, is inevitably transient, for "[t]hen suddenly we remember, it may be, that the soul no longer exists...." In the course of the modern reader's self-correction, Plato's poetry inevitably becomes "antiquated and rustic" (4), and the sudden, instinctive recognition of a truth is quietly discredited.

As he accounts for this erosion of feeling particular to modernity, Stevens writes: "In trying to find out what it is that stands between Plato's figure [of the soul as a noble charioteer] and ourselves, we have to accept the idea that, however legendary it appears to be, it has had its vicissitudes. The history of a figure of speech or the history of an idea, such as the idea of nobility, cannot be different from the history of anything else" (5). So the noble and uplifting image from Plato's *Phaedrus*, precisely because of what Stevens sees as its undeniable beauty, here becomes a surrogate for all poetry. No matter how gorgeous or perfect its composition, Stevens shows the capacity of the image for communicating across the ages to be dishearteningly feeble. Inevitably, a shift in sensibility, itself a consequence of a historical or cultural turn, will serve to render the poem's essential components (e.g., figures of speech, ideas of human greatness) alien to new readers.

Returning to "The Man with the Blue Guitar," then, we see Stevens proposing that in the modern era the artist's work is first and foremost a salvaging of ideas, visions, states of being, and even emotions, all of which, though intrinsically noble, are no longer valued. Having invoked Picasso's painting, he now relies on a phrase from Picasso's writing to elaborate his idea:

> Is this picture of Picasso's, this "hoard
> Of destructions," a picture of ourselves,
> Now, an image of our society?
> Do I sit, deformed, a naked egg,

> Catching at Good-bye, harvest moon,
> Without seeing the harvest or the moon?
>
> Things as they are have been destroyed.
> Have I? Am I a man that is dead
>
> At a table on which the food is cold?
> Is my thought a memory, not alive?
>
> Is the spot on the floor, there, wine or blood
> And whichever it may be, is it mine?
>
> (*Collected Poems* 173)

In these lines, the quotation "hoard/Of destructions" is a translation of one of Picasso's "dicta" for art, *une somme de destructions*. Alongside other maxims, it appeared in a special issue of the journal *Cahiers d'Art* devoted entirely to the epoch-making painter. Stevens apparently read the issue with interest (McLeod 364-65). Certainly the phrase resonates in Stevens' imagination, for he quotes it again in a later prose piece: "Does not the saying of Picasso that a picture is a horde [*sic*] of destructions also say that a poem is a horde of destructions?" (*Necessary Angel* 161). Here, it is worth remembering that both the English word *hoard* and the French *somme* signify a kind of repository, where things of value are *saved* or, more simply in the French, added together. (Stevens' odd later spelling, *horde*, again refers to a living entity, even if it refers precisely neither to a *hoard* nor a *somme*.) This paradox in Picasso's dictum is crucial to understanding Stevens' meaning, for the locution "hoard of destructions" concerns the redemption of what has been destroyed.

In the same essay in which he quotes Picasso, Stevens links the painter's curious phrase ("hoard of destructions") with Simone Weil's term *decreation*: "Simone Weil in *La Pesanteur et la grâce* has a chapter on what she calls decreation. She says that decreation is making pass from the created to the uncreated, but that destruction is making pass from the created to nothingness. Modern reality is a reality of decreation, in which our revelations are not the revelations of belief, but the precious portents of our own powers" (174-75).[1] Decreation, in other words, is an intellectual discipline. It signifies a movement away from a mode of thinking solely concerned with material reality and, instead, toward a recognition of the spiritual essence underlying material things. Like Picasso's "hoard," the word *decreation* here is a paradox. In coining it, Weil offers a redemptive alternative to the destruction that, for its most sensitive observers, marks modern life. What Weil perceives so astutely in the passage cited by Stevens is the quest for the elusive, unvarnished reality of the *ding an sich* on which the modern philosopher, as much as the modern poet, so earnestly embarks. What the poet and the philosopher both seek, in Weil's understanding, is the impossible vision of the reality of things as they are, *before* human consciousness supplies its overlay.

Decreation is therefore not so much a way of naming an actuality, nor is it alone a "goal" of philosophic or poetic investigation. Rather, the concept of decreation opens for otherwise jaded moderns a possibility—"a precious portent"—of an unclouded prelapsarian vision. Thus, Weil's great insight, wholly embraced by Stevens, is that modernity, with all its skepticism, can nonetheless offer its own rich philosophical and visionary possibility (and not simply the dead end of nihilism). For Stevens, Weil's intuition of a "pass from the created to the uncreated" provides a method by which an artist or thinker can transcend the fixed everydayness of ordinary perception and, instead, move toward a transcendent, luminous vision.

In a letter probably written some time before the reference to Weil in his paper on poetry and painting, Stevens observed to his friend Hi Simons:

> When a poet makes his imagination the imagination of other people, he does so by making them see the world through his eyes. Most modern activity is the undoing of that very job. The world has been painted; most modern activity is getting rid of the paint to get at the world itself. Powerful integrations of the imagination are difficult to get away from....This power is one of the poet's chief powers. (*Letters* 402)

The power Stevens describes here appears, unsurprisingly, to be similar to, if not the same as, Weil's decreation ("making pass from the created to the uncreated") or Picasso's image of art as a "hoard of destructions."

Together, then, Picasso, Weil, and Stevens understand their decidedly modern work first and foremost as an unveiling of the shining glory, the numinous dimensions of Being that, in modern times, are too often callously disavowed. What they reveal in their work thus cannot be beautiful by any recognizable standard of beauty. Instead, the language of "the hoard of destructions" (Picasso), the "uncreated" (Weil), and "force" (Stevens) gestures implicitly toward an imagined point of origins, a modern vision of what the ancient Greeks symbolized in their sacred sculpture of the *omphalos* in Delphi. From a different vantage point, this language also recalls the Christian allegory of the return to purity, as expressed in the religious vision of apocalypse. In each instance, Attic, Christian, or modern, the aim is the same: to tear away, with force, all profane illusions in the hope of seeing the full glory of the world as it *really is*: to discover the *ding an sich*. In each case, the subsequent visions—the *omphalos*; the apocalypse narratives; the distorted figures of Picasso's canvases; the "uncreation" of Weil's thought; and the odd, elliptical language of Stevens—all offer an intentional, fantastic counterbalance to things as they merely *seem*.

In "The Man with the Blue Guitar," Stevens pauses to inquire about what happens after the art-induced apocalypse that Weil and Picasso describe so acutely ("Things as they are have been destroyed./Have I?"). Where and how, Stevens wonders, does the decreative impulse of the modern artist end? In this poem, the wistfulness of popular-song lyrics, "Good-bye, harvest moon" (*Letters* 783), becomes irrelevant, even meaningless, when it appears that neither the harvest nor the moon can be seen by the speaker, for all his catching at them. (Indeed, both the romantic moon and the agrarian harvest have already become fodder for the "hoard of destructions" mentioned earlier.) Further, Stevens asks, what happens to the soul in the artist's quest to unmask the emptiness of old pieties—"Am I a man that is dead//At a table on which the food is cold?" The "food" on the table is a reference to art and poetry, as the previous lines about the harvest and the moon already suggest. More bracing, the cold food represents the entirety of the cultural past.

History, after all, creates its own apocalypses that the artist must also document. In the poem, the religious faith that once buoyed past generations is now cold comfort. Indeed, it eludes the modern speaker of the poem. The act of "Catching at Good-bye," after all, is a vain aspiration to hold onto what *Good-bye* traditionally means: God be with you. The speaker, under the influence of Picasso's painting, is now forced to ask himself, "Is the spot on the floor, there, wine or blood/And whichever it may be, is it mine?" A "decreated" life may not indeed be worth living, Stevens suggests, for as his speaker confronts the stain of his own wine/blood, pondering starkly what Weil has called "the precious portents of our own powers," he must wonder too whether the "hoard of destructions" ultimately signifies his own demise.

The larger question Stevens poses here, and throughout his oeuvre, is whether modernity itself creates a kind of death that grimly changes "things as they are" to things that, essentially, are not. His anxiety about "an absence in reality" is customarily read as a typical modern lament with a typically modern solution. (Lament: the gods have fled. Solution: poetry, and only poetry, can summon them back again.) Both Matthew Arnold's and Martin Heidegger's poetic theories lend strength to such an interpretation, not only of Stevens' lyrics, but of modern poetry in general.

But this conventional reading is misguided. Long before the advent of modernity, the tradition of lyric poetry has always presupposed the awareness of an unbearable gulf between humanity and divinity (and thereby, also, between humanity and nature). These absences have been expressed in a coherent language of symbols—a "visionary language," to remember Stevens' phrase—that, in turn, connects otherwise far-flung generations of poets. The poet's lyre, translated by Stevens into a fiction-making blue guitar, is one such rich symbol.

A similar symbol is to be found in the bird poem. A bird, its cry, or its wings alone appear in an astonishing number of Stevens' major and minor poems. In addition to his most famous composition in the genre, "Thirteen Ways of Looking at a Blackbird," one may recall, for example, "Sunday Morning," which opens with a seemingly casual reference to "the green freedom of a cockatoo/Upon a rug" (*Collected Poems* 66). Some lines later, the contemplative speaker muses:

> ..."I am content when wakened birds,
> Before they fly, test the reality
> Of misty fields, by their sweet questionings;
> But when the birds are gone, and their warm fields
> Return no more, where, then, is paradise?"
>
> (68)

Here, the sweetness of the birds' song is itself a "test" of reality. Their song is the world's native music, adding to mundane earthly existence a harmony that seems supernatural. In the speaker's vision, the mistiness of fields at dawn signifies an ontological haziness that birdsong penetrates. Without the singing birds, however, the universe becomes bleak, and cherished pieties disintegrate. At the conclusion of "Sunday Morning," these meditations end almost as they began, as the loneliness of the metaphysical crisis culminates with an image of Dionysian celebration and then, once more, a reiteration of the freedom that is peculiar to birds. In the poem's final lines, Stevens envisions what seems to be an enviable "isolation" that whole flocks of birds enjoy in flight:

> And, in the isolation of the sky,
> At evening, casual flocks of pigeons make
> Ambiguous undulations as they sink,
> Downward to darkness, on extended wings.
>
> (*Collected Poems* 70)

When the pigeons fly into the night sky, they take the day's existential queries with them, unresolved. Reciprocally, their extended wings are now part of the imagination, lending their ambiguous capacity to move freely in a heavenly ether that earlier in the poem felt "dividing and indifferent."

The bird poem is widely understood to form a poetic class of its own, but it is too humble a thing to merit a formal name in the august catalogue of poetic types (aubade, ballad, ode, pastoral, villanelle, and so on). Perhaps the iconography of the bird is too deeply infused in *all* the forms of Western lyrics to be isolated and categorized apart from any one of them.[2] For Stevens, who otherwise rejected traditional lyric forms *per se*, the bird poem offers a virtually inexhaustible point of imaginative departure: in his corpus, one finds, not a single, obligatory poem invoking the symbolic bird, but dozens upon dozens of them.

Beginning with Stevens' first published volume, *Harmonium* (1932), and continuing through his two volumes of posthumously published poems, *Opus Posthumous* (1957) and *The Palm at the End of the Mind* (1971), birds consistently appear as the iconic reminder of everything that poetry can, or should, signify to its devotees. (For the encyclopedically minded or ornithologically intrigued reader, a brief survey of titles may give an idea of Stevens' enthusiasm: "Bantams in Pine Woods," "Gray Stones and Gray Pigeons," "Of Bright and Blue Birds in the Gala Sun," "Dry Birds Are Fluttering in Blue Leaves" [Part IV of "The Pure Good of Theory"], "The Bird with the Coppery, Keen Claws," "Wild Ducks, People, and Distances," "The Dove in the Belly," "The Owl in the Sarcophagus," "Looking Across the Fields and Watching the

Birds Fly.") Further, the absence of birds from a landscape is matter for comment in Stevens' poetry, as may be seen in another much-anthologized Stevens work, "The Anecdote of the Jar." What is distinct about the jar is that "It did not give of bird or bush,/Like nothing else in Tennessee."

Nor do Stevens' birds limit themselves to appearances in poetry. They nest in the rhetoric of his prose as well. In "The Figure of the Youth as Virile Poet," an essay that testifies to the exalted feeling of freedom poets achieve in the course of their creative work, readers come upon this observation: "In this state of elevation, [poets] feel perfectly adapted to the idea that moves, and *l'oiseau qui chante*" (*Necessary Angel* 51). In his own apparent fixation with birds and their mysteries, Stevens thus establishes in his writing a complicated, if not esoteric, commentary on the Western lyric tradition and its future.

One of the most prominent clusters of images in the iconography of the lyric bird traces its origins to the Greek myth of Procne and Philomela. In this violent story, the virgin Philomela is raped by the husband of her sister, Procne. The husband cuts out Philomela's tongue to ensure her silence. In their pity for her plight, the gods transform Philomela into a nightingale, whose cry of lament pierces the heart of her hearers and thus communicates what is otherwise unspeakable. In recalling this myth structurally (if not overtly), the bird poem provokes a recollection of painful violation and ineffable loss. The myth's tale of miraculous transformation, celebrated in the bird poem's exaltations of song and flight, simultaneously offers the hope of a singular and miraculous transcendence.

It is in his dialogue with this lyric tradition, with its venerable roots in Greek mythology, that Stevens' questions about the vitality of lyric poetry reach their ambivalent conclusions. One of his relatively early bird poems poses this question and offers a tentative answer. The poem is "Autumn Refrain," which appeared in *Ideas of Order* (1936), the second published volume of Stevens' poetry:

> The skreak and skritter of evening gone
> And grackles gone and sorrows of the sun,
> The sorrows of sun, too, gone...the moon and moon,
> The yellow moon of words about the nightingale
> In measureless measures, not a bird for me
> But the name of a bird and the name of a nameless air

> I have never—shall never hear. And yet beneath
> The stillness of everything gone, and being still,
> Being and sitting still, something resides,
> Some skreaking and skrittering residuum,
> And grates these evasions of the nightingale
> Though I have never—shall never hear that bird.
> And the stillness is in the key, all of it is,
> The stillness is all in the key of that desolate sound.
>
> (*Collected Poems* 160)

This is, typically for Stevens, a poem concerned with absence: "The skreak and skritter of evening gone." To adopt Weil's language once more, at its outset, the poem has already made pass from the created (the nightingale's song) to the uncreated (the yearning for the nightingale's song). No bird song accompanies the speaker's meditation in what is nonetheless, very clearly, a poem about bird song.

As it progresses, the language of the poem offers a litany of negation (*gone, gone, gone, not...for me, never, never, gone, never, never*). It is simply impossible, the speaker of "Autumn Refrain" proposes convincingly, that a bird of such romantic or noble pedigree as the nightingale will ever be heard in a landscape abandoned even by the ignoble and cacophonous grackles.

Nevertheless, though all the conventional elements of poetic happiness are absent, something of the nightingale's music remains: "Some skreaking and skrittering residuum." Since no bird remains on the scene, however, this residuum can hardly refer to the remaining notes of a song. (It may be worth noting that the poem's form is itself a "residuum": the sonnet, fourteen lines of carefully rhymed iambic pentameter, is evoked but not achieved in these fourteen lines of irregular scansion and rhyme.) Rather, the "residuum" Stevens here invokes is the ancestral presence of the lyric nightingale, a bird most famously summoned in modern times by John Keats. But in "Autumn Refrain," the iconic nightingale of traditional lyric poetry is elusive, if not completely vanished.[3] Stevens' narrator, enmeshed in his own skepticism, has, willingly or not, forgone what Weil might describe as the revelations of belief, even if only a belief in poetry's soothing powers (the nightingale's "measureless measures"). It seems, at first, impossible for Stevens' speaker to imagine the nightingale's song, which for him is not even a song but only the promise of one: "the name of a nameless air/I have never—shall never hear." The break in thought is again evidence of the paradoxical *reality* of the imagined bird. The dash here invites an amendment, as it mimics the point of recognition when the speaker suddenly remembers that the bird he longs to hear—because he thinks it real—sings (or "sings") only in a poem. One thinks of Eliot's Prufrock and the mermaids who sing "each to each." But Prufrock notes gloomily, "I do not think that they will sing to me" ("Love Song" 8). Here, it would seem that even Prufrock's capacity to eavesdrop upon a beautiful song affords more pleasure than Stevens' desolate terrain, in which no songs at all are audible and in which the very idea of a mermaid is too romantic, too glamorous to mention.

Modernity, as Stevens perceives it, is not an occasion for the poet's self-loathing (Prufrock) or willful escape into artifice (e.g., Yeats's "Sailing to Byzantium") but a moment when facing up to one's creative potency, *as well as* the blankness it confronts, is the only genuinely poetic response. As Stevens will write in a much later poem, "The Plain Sense of Things" (1954), "the absence of the imagination had/Itself to be imagined" (*Collected Poems* 503). Indeed, the lyric action of "Autumn Refrain" appears to take place precisely after facing such an imaginative dearth. It seems likely that in conjuring his own fugitive grackles Stevens is offering a counterpoint to Yeats's mechanical bird:

> ...such a form as Grecian goldsmiths make
> Of hammered gold and gold enamelling
> To keep a drowsy Emperor awake;
> Or set upon a golden bough to sing
> To lords and ladies of Byzantium
> Of what is past, or passing, or to come.
>
> (*Collected Poems* 194)

Here, Yeats's aging narrator finds no comfort in "that sensual music" that nature offers and that Keats, among others, celebrates. Instead, to use Weil's formula of decreation, Yeats "makes pass" from the created Keatsian nightingale to the as-yet-uncreated reserves that linger in his imagination. The old man finds redemption by sailing imaginatively toward "the artifice of eternity." There, his poem asserts, one may declare one's independence of "any natural thing."

For Stevens, though, the birds that populate the lyric world must be *real* birds, not golden machines. He seems to reason that if the birds in poems aren't living, neither can the poems be. Stevens' fictive birds therefore fly in directions both bleaker and more hopeful than Yeats's Byzantine song would allow. For if bird song has traditionally offered a symbol of the aspirations of lyric poetry, "Autumn Refrain" declares that such an easy relation between symbol and reality has long been exhausted. In the present moment, the adequate apprehension of birdsong—and what it might signify to the human spirit—necessarily involves a full, elegiac awareness of its absence, or, to return once again to Weil's language, its uncreation in poetry. The voice of Stevens' poem moves, then, from the "measureless measures" of the archetypal lyric bird to a blank space of possibility as it "grates these evasions of the nightingale."

And yet "evasions of the nightingale" is a mischievous phrase. Its double genitive serves to deepen the mystery of the absence that the poem reports. The shy nightingale may, of its own nature, be elusive. But if "Autumn Refrain" is indeed a poem of decreation, it is necessarily the poet, too, who himself evades the bird—in its symbolic capacity—in his effort "to get at the world itself," as Stevens wrote in the letter to Simons quoted above (*Letters* 402). Harold Bloom reads "Autumn Refrain" as an instance of his theory of poetic influence and calls the poem "a debate between the grackles and Keats" (91). What actually motivates the poem, however, is not so much Stevens' anxiety over Keats's influence upon him as it is his anxiety over Keats's *lack* of influence upon the larger world. Thus, the decreative impulse of "Autumn Refrain" targets the sentimental fiction of the lyric poet's—rather than the lyric bird's—immortality. For of course Stevens knows, like any number of American poets before him, that nightingales, birds of storied and distinctly European pedigree, do not and will not sing for him. He knows too that Yeats is right to emphasize their belonging to "dying generations." Not least, Stevens knows that the modern experience of the old kind of poetry—poetry that genuinely aspires to birdsong—is necessarily different from that of our forebears because, for all its sensuous beauty, the beauty of lyric poetry punningly "grates." It reminds us too acutely of a kind of greatness of soul in which we have lost faith.

Thus it is the modern exhaustion with poetry, as lamented in "Sailing to Byzantium" and figured in its mechanical bird, that is reiterated and ultimately defied in "Refrain." For Stevens holds that modernity *makes* grackles of nightingales, reducing their poignant music to vexatious "skreaking and skrittering." The harsh onomatopoeia of these seemingly nonsensical words[4]—imitations of the grackle's call—nonetheless reminds the poet of the fabled nightingale's ineradicable presence in his imagination.

Indeed, the speaker realizes with some surprise that the nightingale's poignant music lingers in even his most rudimentary awareness of the landscape around him.

"Autumn Refrain" thus becomes hopeful in its final lines, as it depicts a poet imaginatively stripping the terrain down to its bare minimum, in his own aesthetic act of decreation, to discover an indestructible metaphysical presence still stubbornly lingering. The poet's yearning to hear the nightingale, and his awareness of the impossibility of his desire, uncovers for him instead the unpainted reality, the radical yearning for the lost unity with all of Being, of which the nightingale was once, for a passing moment, the symbol. Still, the poet's laborious attempt to achieve the "uncreated" vision of the world ends, ineluctably, in recalling a creation: "the words about the nightingale" that hang in the air as matter-of-factly as the yellow moon.

Stevens' unshakeable faith in the luminous metaphysical reality that unites lyric poetry with the everyday things of the world is the consistent feature of his writing. He claims, "There is, in fact, a world of poetry indistinguishable from the world in which we live," and adds, "what makes the poet the potent figure that he is, or was, or ought to be, is that he creates the world to which we turn incessantly and without knowing it and that he gives to life the supreme fictions without which we are unable to conceive of it" (*Necessary Angel* 31). (It can become difficult, after recognizing this article of faith, to trace anything that might be called development in Stevens' work.) As we learn in the early poem "Autumn Refrain," the lyric nightingale is the exemplar *par excellence* of these "supreme fictions": an unreal bird whose unheard and unimaginable song is nonetheless intuited in the air of an actual autumn. Poetry lurks in things.

The undeniable reality—the supreme fiction—of the un-bird's un-song inheres in what Stevens calls the "stillness" of Being. This word, *stillness*, is the crux of "Refrain." It denotes a condition of stasis ("sitting still"), certainly, but it also refers to something more: being still. Or, more emphatically, *Being...still* (existing, now, as ever). The irreducible reality of the nightingale, even as a symbol, has its own redemptive being, quite apart from the sensual music of the actual bird it evokes. Keats's "words about the nightingale" act upon us, therefore, in a different way from the aural phenomenon of song. Even a vague memory of these words awakens in the speaker of "Autumn Refrain" a fundamental optimism about the unending generosity of Being. For Stevens insists that the lyric nightingale sings *still*, in moments of the most profound imaginative and cultural impoverishment.

Stevens' homage to Keats, evident throughout "Autumn Refrain," is capped by the poem's title, a reference to the final ode in Keats's great sequence. The last stanza of Keats's "To Autumn" begins with the unspoken but overwhelming concern of Stevens' lyric: "Where are the songs of spring? Ay, where are they?" Keats's reassuring answer—"Think not of them, thou hast thy music too"—is, in Stevens' lyric, pitched to a different key: "stillness is in the key, all of it is,/The stillness is all in the key of that desolate sound." The pun on *key* in these lines suggests the ambivalence of Stevens' own lyric recognition. The lyric's music is perforce desolate, since it emerges from an impossible desire. But the articulation of this desire itself provides a key to the bountiful still-ness and the ever-presence of Being.

Stevens' ambivalent hope for poetry emerges, then, from the deceptive stillness and evasions of the lyric imagination. "Autumn Refrain" depicts the imaginative turn that precedes what Stevens sees as a rebirth of poetry from the spirit, if not the sound, of birdsong. As he wrote to Hi Simons, "Those arts which are so often regarded as exhausted are only in their inception" (*Letters* 350). Later, his poem "St. Armorer's Church from the Outside" (1954) celebrates "That which is always beginning because it is part/Of that which is always beginning, over and over" (*Collected Poems* 529). Here, the sense of "beginning" is thoroughly consonant with the poet's ambivalent discovery of desolation in "Refrain." Poetry itself is the subject of both these poems; the spiritual desolation of "Refrain" is the key that opens the door to the lonely point of lyric origins, that place where the nightingale's song may be felt but cannot be sung. "Autumn Refrain" is thus not solely a lamentation of the desolate state of the modern writer. Rather, it embodies in a modernist tone a constant refrain that recurs from era to era as the essential condition of lyric poetry: the fundamental encounter with poverty and desolation.

Of course, it is possible that as a twentieth-century poet, Stevens sees the lyric's roots in this desolate and impoverished spiritual state more clearly perhaps than the poets who came before him. In the same 1951 lecture at the Museum of Modern Art in which Stevens cited Picasso's "horde of destructions" and Simone Weil's "decreation," he observed, "Poet and painter alike live in a world that is experiencing essential poverty in spite of fortune" (*Necessary Angel* 171). The language and feeling of poverty pervade Stevens' corpus, as numerous critics have noticed.[5] Too, "Autumn Refrain" offers its own bleak testimony to the modern poet's lack of resources. Other poems in this rich vein include "The Ordinary Women" ("Then from their poverty, they rose.../They flung monotony behind,/Turned from their want..."); "The Idiom of the Hero" ("I am the poorest of all./I know that I cannot be mended"); "Extracts from Addresses to the Academy of Fine Ideas" ("in poverty,/In the exactest poverty"); "In a Bad Time" ("He has his poverty and nothing more./His poverty becomes his heart's strong core"); "To an Old Philosopher in Rome" ("It is poverty's speech that seeks us out the most"). Diligent readers will find that the list goes on.[6]

Harold Bloom persuasively traces the roots of Stevens' thematic poverty through Emily Dickinson and Walt Whitman to Ralph Waldo Emerson's essay "Experience," in which he says that the word *poverty* signifies "imaginative need" (Bloom, *Wallace Stevens* 9). But Bloom does not take the genealogy of poverty to its deepest origins. Indeed, Stevens' most august poetic ancestor is Diotima, Socrates' interlocutor in Plato's *Symposium*. It is her account of the birth of Eros that is most crucial to apprehending Stevens' large lyric vision. Here is the story, as Diotima tells it:

> On the day Aphrodite was born the gods were feasting, among them Contrivance (*Poros*), the son of Invention (*Metis*); and, after dinner, seeing that a party was in progress, Poverty (*Penia*) came to beg and stood at the door. Now Contrivance was drunk with nectar—wine, I may say, had not yet been discovered—and went out into the garden of Zeus, and was overcome by sleep. So Poverty, thinking to alleviate her wretched condition by bearing a child to Contrivance, lay with him and conceived Love (*Eros*). Since Love was begotten on Aphrodite's birthday, and since he has also an innate passion for the beautiful, and so for the beauty of Aphrodite herself, he became her follower and servant. Again, having Contrivance for his father and Poverty for his mother, he bears the following character. He is always poor, and, far from being sensitive and beautiful, as most people imagine, he is hard and weather-beaten, shoeless and homeless, always sleeping out for want of a bed, on the ground, on doorsteps, and in the street. So far he takes after his mother and lives in want. But, being also his father's son, he schemes to get for himself whatever is beautiful and

good; he is bold and forward and strenuous, always devising tricks like a cunning huntsman; he yearns after knowledge and is full of resource and is a lover of wisdom all his life, a skilful magician, an alchemist, a true sophist. He is neither mortal nor immortal; but on one and the same day he will love and flourish (when things go well with him), and also meet his death; and then come to life again through the vigour that he inherits from his father. What he wins he always loses, and is neither rich nor poor, neither wise nor ignorant.
(*Symposium* 81-82)[7]

In Stevens' mythopoeic revision of Diotima's tale, Poverty, which couples with aesthetic and intellectual Contrivance (or Resourcefulness, as *poros* is often translated), is the generative mother of poetry. This means that poetry, in turn, is itself a form of *eros*. Its father, *Poros*, is in Stevens' rewriting of this story, the imagination itself. As an expression of *eros*, poetry, too, as Stevens sees it, is "neither mortal nor immortal; but on one and the same day he will love and flourish (when things go well with him), and also meet his death; and then come to life again through the vigour that he inherits from his father." In Stevens' parable, therefore, it is only through the vigor of the imagination that Keats's silent nightingale can be heard to sing or Plato's winged horses can be seen in the skies. Without this vigor, the nightingale's song is extinguished, and Plato's charioteer droops in mid-flight.

In Stevens' poetry, the love affair between poverty and the imagination is enacted most vividly in these lines from "Final Soliloquy of the Interior Paramour" (1954):

> Within a single thing, a single shawl
> Wrapped tightly round us, since we are poor, a warmth,
> A light, a power, the miraculous influence.
>
> Here, now, we forget each other and ourselves.
> We feel the obscurity of an order, a whole,
> A knowledge, that which arranged the rendezvous.
>
> Within its vital boundary, in the mind.
> We say God and the imagination are one....
>
> (*Collected Poems* 524)

Reading the verse in light of Diotima's instruction, we instantly recognize thought (or imagination, "the miraculous influence") as the "paramour" of poverty. "Since we are poor," it wraps us warmly, like a shawl and like a lover. In this enfolding, "we forget each other and ourselves"; the diversity of Being becomes the aboriginal unity in which God and the human imagination are one in the "vital boundary" of the mind. The mind is thus a boundary in the sense of a *limen*, a living threshold, where one is neither one thing entirely nor the other, but both—God and the imagination—at once.

The union of poverty, in Stevens' Platonic sense of the word, and the imagination also yields a clarity of feeling. An earlier poem, "Credences of Summer" (1947) offers an example of one of Stevens' many exuberant love poems to the universe. The poem shouts its joy:

> Let's see the very thing and nothing else.
> Let's see it with the hottest fire of sight.
> Burn everything not part of it to ash.
>
> Trace the gold sun about the whitened sky
> Without evasion by a single metaphor.
> Look at it in its essential barrenness
> And say this, this is the centre that I seek.
>
> *(Collected Poems* 373)

A reader may notice the prominence of the word *evasion*, an echo of the "evasion" of "Autumn Refrain." In both instances, the word is linked to the devices of poetry. In the earlier poem, it is the romantic companionship of a particular symbol (the nightingale) that proves evasive. In the later "Credences," evasion is the property of all metaphor. In "An Ordinary Evening in New Haven" (1950), Stevens returns to this theme of the "intricate evasions of as,/In things seen and unseen, created from nothingness" (*Collected Poems* 486).

Stevens' locutions here about the evasiveness of poetry are familiar reprises of the ancient quarrel between poetry and philosophy. Plato characterizes all literary representation as being perforce at a remove from absolute truth because of its status as an "imitation of an imitation" (*Republic* Book X). The twentieth-century philosopher Donald Davidson framed the problem more stridently: the metaphor's outrageous assertions of ontological identity, he says, are "patently false"

("Metaphors" 42). The problem philosophers confront with metaphor is that it always moves its reader's attention from a thing being contemplated to yet another thing. Metaphor thus demands an imaginative diversion from the essence of the first thing, even as it strives to reveal this essence. This multiplication of thing upon thing is a distraction, a kind of worldly wealth that a philosophic poet, as Stevens is, longs to eschew in his quest for the *ding an sich* but cannot. In "Autumn Refrain," as we have seen, for all his trying, he cannot imagine the world forlorn of Keats's symbolic nightingale. But in his aesthetic commitment to the purity of "decreation," he longs to rid himself of all such *richesse* in order to get closer "to the very thing and nothing else." He writes in a late poem, "Prologues to What Is Possible" (1954):

> The metaphor stirred his fear. The object with which he was compared
> Was beyond his recognizing. By this he knew that likeness of
>   him extended
> Only a little way, and not beyond, unless between himself
> And things beyond resemblance there was this and that
>   intended to be recognized,
> The this and that in the enclosures of hypotheses
> On which men speculated in summer when they were half asleep.
>   (*Collected Poems* 516)

What evades metaphor, not only in "Credences of Summer" and "An Ordinary Evening in New Haven," but in all of its manifestations, Stevens says here, is Being itself. The poet simply cannot trust his own metaphors. His awareness of their imprecision only deepens the sense of impoverishment that drives him to a place "between himself/And things beyond resemblance." This place, between the appearances of things and the reality of things, may also be imagined as an "absence in reality," or a "hoard of destructions." Stevens' dilemma is that this imagined place, where the poetic soul dwells, can only be described in figures of speech—figures that amount to ideas about the thing but are never the thing itself.

    Or so it would seem to an imagination without vigor, an imagination that sees the world as atomized and disintegrated. But Stevens' ultimate vision, I maintain, is one of absolute unity: in it, nothing separates Being from Becoming; likewise, nothing separates words from what it is they express. This integration appears full-fledged in at least one of his last poems. The final section of *The Collected Poems*, entitled

"The Rock," contains twenty-five late works composed by Stevens for inclusion in the volume to be published in celebration of his seventy-fifth birthday (*Letters* 829). The selection is highly self-conscious, particularly in the title poem of this section (which opens with the autobiographical subtitle "Seventy Years Later") and in smaller pieces such as "The Planet on the Table." Among other poems in "The Rock" are meditations on death (e.g., "Madame La Fleurie," "To an Old Philosopher in Rome"). These are predictable choices, perhaps, given the circumstances of the publication. The final lyric in a compendium of final lyrics, however, is entirely unpredictable, except that it is, of necessity, a bird poem. Its title, "Not Ideas about the Thing but the Thing Itself," sums up the singular aim of Stevens' poetics.

> At the earliest ending of winter,
> In March, a scrawny cry from outside
> Seemed like a sound in his mind.
>
> He knew that he heard it,
> A bird's cry, at daylight or before,
> In the early March wind.
>
> The sun was rising at six,
> No longer a battered panache above snow...
> It would have been outside.
>
> It was not from the vast ventriloquism
> Of sleep's faded papier-mâché...
> The sun was coming from outside.
>
> That scrawny cry—it was
> A chorister whose c preceded the choir.
> It was part of the colossal sun,
>
> Surrounded by its choral rings,
> Still far away. It was like
> A new knowledge of reality.

(*Collected Poems* 534)

The "new knowledge" this poem invites is the union of the internal world of thought and dreams with the external world of snow and sun. We have seen already that the bird is the symbol of the internal world in Stevens' poems and generally in the lyric tradition. The sun in this poem is, or has been, a *panache*. The word means a tuft or plume of feathers (OED), which in turn means that the sun is a species of bird itself. It is difficult to evade the metaphor: the sun that lights the world and which augurs the rebirth of spring is a bird of fire, a phoenix. The word "like" in the penultimate line softens the indicative mood and makes the metaphor tentative. This qualification is a necessary gambit for a poet with an affection for the plain sense of things because, of course, no one actually *knows* that the marriage of external and internal reality has been, or ever can be, achieved. But one intuits it with a kind of certainty, in the way one intuits the change of seasons or the coming of dawn in the dream state between sleep and wakefulness, an intuition that marks the fluidity of the phenomenal world (birds, sun, snow). The intuited, and longed for, unity of phenomena and consciousness, however, is still far distant. Nonetheless, the bird's cry is not only felt but *heard* and recognized as the first reconfiguration in an ever-expanding metamorphosis. The sun is colossal and growing. The "scrawny cry" celebrates a miraculous consummation, but it is still anticipatory, having "preceded its choir." This final poem of Stevens' self-selected corpus[8] closes, then, with an implicit invitation to other choristers, a new generation of poets, to raise their voices and join the singing.

The lyric is not a dead art, Stevens proclaims. It is a fire-bird, born and reborn, over and over again.

Notes

1. See Pearce, "Toward Decreation," on the importance of this concept for Stevens' poetics.
2. See Doggett, "Romanticism's Singing Bird."
3. See Egan, "Allusions to Keats."
4. *Skreaking* and *skrittering* are not, by any means, nonsense words. More than onomatopoeia, they are richly suggestive of the oral and written dimensions of poetry. The OED defines *skreak* as a dialectical and ancient form

of *shriek*. It also offers the word *skrit* as a variant of *scrite*, which means "a writing, a written document." If we license our imaginations to play with language as a poet does, the "skrittering" in Stevens' "Refrain" may begin to feel like a way of summoning the written words of Keats's famous odes. Likewise "skreaking" evokes the grackles/nightingales whose cry, the piercing lyric cry of yearning, lingers in the air. As Stevens writes later in "An Ordinary Evening in New Haven," "The poem is the cry of its occasion/Part of the res itself and not about it" *Collected Poems* 473).

5. Helen Vendler, for example, says, "It is not a Keatsian ripeness that Stevens claims for his poems....It is something far more destitute—the poverty of words; and yet something resolute and permanent" (*Wallace Stevens* 38).

6. See the on-line concordance to Stevens' poetry: http://www.wallacestevens.com/concordance/WSdb.cgi.

7. The italicized Greek names in parentheses are my own addition.

8. Stevens continued to write poetry after the publication of his *Collected Poems* until his death shortly thereafter. These later poems are published in *Opus Posthumous* and *The Palm at the End of the Mind*, having been gathered and arranged by Stevens' daughter after his death.

11

Pound and Eliot:
Tradition and the Co-opetitive Talent

ROBERT SCOTT DUPREE

1

Lyric poetry in the twentieth century was unprecedented in its range, innovation, and number of practitioners, yet such profusion was attended by a paradox. Although the era was surely one of the most fertile in the history of literature, it was characterized by a shrinking readership for whom the lyric had less and less appeal. This outcome was partly the fault of the poets themselves. In their attempts to rid the current lyric of effusiveness and emotional superficiality, they challenged readers to rise to a remarkably high level rather than conform to traditional expectations. Readers in the preceding century, in fact, had actually preferred verse narrative to prose. Despite the concurrent proliferation of prose fiction in the Victorian period, Elizabeth Barrett Browning's widely read *Aurora Leigh* was a popular success, not because it was a narrative, but because it was in verse. Yet this preference for rhyme and meter was soon to change. A careful attention to the *mot juste* in prose fiction and in essays began to challenge the aesthetic prestige once accorded to verse. Ezra Pound, thinking of the painstaking craft of Flaubert, subsequently pronounced that good poetry had to be at least as well written as good prose, implying that the highest standards for writing were no longer set by rhyme and meter. In order to maintain the prestige of the lyric as a source of serious knowledge about human nature and reality, the pioneers of modernism had to destroy the easy popularity enjoyed by Victorian verse. In so doing they also had to present a united front, and it is this unity of purpose that contributes to the uniqueness of the early modernist movement.

That the English-speaking literary world came to be dominated to a considerable extent by two expatriate Americans is key to understanding the nature of the modernist program. As Americans, they had to prove from the start their worthiness in the world of English letters and to demonstrate their prowess every step of the way. Unlike their British contemporaries, they had to show that they were not provincials and were more learned, more thoroughly acquainted with contemporary continental European currents, and better literary craftsmen than the London establishment writers.[1] Like their romantic counterparts a century earlier, Ezra Pound and T. S. Eliot sought to challenge and unseat their immediate predecessors. Furthermore, they sought to redefine and even reinvent the canon of English literature by bringing to it a fresh perspective, less narrowly "English" than before, all the while appearing more sophisticated (or at least more knowing) than those in charge of contemporary literary taste by making common cause with the most radical elements among recent European, especially French, writers. Eliot eventually emerged as the "literary dictator of the English-speaking world," and Pound prevailed as its leading impresario. In the years that they reshaped contemporary letters in a *coup de goût* by rewriting literary history, they replaced Milton with Donne, Virgil with Propertius and Gavin Douglas. Eventually, they overcame the old order and became the leading voices of a new literary regime. They accomplished their coup through the hard work of educating themselves, obliging their readers to follow suit.

However, though Harold Bloom's version of the modernist challenge in his *Anxiety of Influence,* inspired by Freud's Oedipus complex, has gained wide acceptance, it does not seem quite apt when applied to Pound and Eliot. They clearly acknowledged debts to literary ancestors such as Browning and Whitman, even if they regarded the latter as an especially "pig-headed father." The chief impetus behind the modernist movement was less a Freudian rivalry than an amazing degree of co-operation. If there was a conflict internal to early modernism, it resided not so much in family relations as in the ambiguities of fellowship. Like Shakespeare and Jonson, Donne and Jonson, or Wordsworth and Coleridge, they were both mutual admirers and rivals. When we extend the history of the enterprise beyond Eliot and Pound, this paradox appears everywhere. Modernist writers inspired and supported colleagues even as they tried to outdo one another. Coming from widely differing social or regional backgrounds, political convictions, religious beliefs, or even intellectual principles, they were nevertheless conscious of being part of a common endeavor.[2]

Observers of the business world have been intrigued in the last decade or so with what has come to be called "co-opetition," a portmanteau word combining "co-operation" and "competition" whose etymological awkwardness not even Lewis Carroll's Humpty Dumpty would have tolerated.[3] Communications, commerce, and sports are domains in which competition and cooperation are bound together in an essential relationship, and in this respect they are remarkably similar to the arts. Although there have been many studies of occurrences of such co-opetition in the visual arts and in music,[4] the process has not received sufficient attention as a literary phenomenon. An examination of the dynamics of the early modernist lyric reveals its importance as an organizing principle of literary "marketing" and avant-garde promotion as its main practitioners cultivated a new and ultimately receptive audience for their wares.

Pound and Eliot began as independent and very dissimilar poets, but despite strikingly different personalities, they found common ground at their very first meeting. Both were academics who had been vacillating between careers as scholar-professors and as independent men of letters. Both had done virtually all the work for the Ph.D. and failed to complete it. Both were Americans born in the Midwest who had traveled to Europe and studied a number of languages even before settling there more or less permanently. Both had written some impressive and original poetry before World War I. Pound's first impressions of Eliot were recorded in a letter from London, dated 30 September 1914, to Harriet Monroe, herself an important node in his own already-extensive web of contacts and fellow conspirators:

> I was jolly well right about Eliot. He has sent in the best poem I have yet had or seen from an American. Pray God it be not a single and unique success....He is the only American I know of who has made what I can call adequate preparation for writing. He has actually trained himself and modernized himself *on his own*. The rest of the *promising young* have done one or the other but never both (most of the swine have done

neither). It is such a comfort to meet a man and not have to tell him to wash his face, wipe his feet, and remember the date (1914) on the calendar. (*Selected Letters* 40)

After reviewing and editing *The Waste Land*, Pound wrote Eliot from Paris, in his guise as literary "midwife," on 24 December 1921: "Complimenti, you bitch. I am wracked by the seven jealousies, and cogitating an excuse for always exuding my deformative secretions in my own stuff, and never getting an outline. I go into nacre and objets d'art. Some day, I shall lose my temper, blaspheme Flaubert, lie like a - - - - and say 'Art should embellish the umbelicus.'" He concluded, "It is after all a grrrreat littttttterary period" (169-70).

Pound's complimentary and complementary envy marked the high point in his and Eliot's co-opetition, though it continued to be operative throughout their careers. They criticized each other in print but never abandoned their friendly relationship. Eliot later returned the favor as an editor at Faber by publishing Pound's works and even assembling a volume of his criticism, and after the war he was influential in Pound's receiving the Bollingen Prize and in gaining his release from St. Elizabeth's Hospital.

The early prose writings of Pound and Eliot contain the most telling evidence of the way this poetic revolution was successfully executed through co-opetition. The most important element in their influence was a shared way of thinking about the literary past in relation to the present, one perhaps possible only to Americans, who had to recover their literary tradition through "great labor" and who were not born to "the historical sense," as Eliot suggests. Their particular view is first encapsulated in Pound's 1910 preface to his *Spirit of Romance*: "All ages are contemporaneous....This is especially true of literature, where the real time is independent of the apparent, and where many dead men are our grandchildren's contemporaries, while many of our contemporaries have been already gathered into Abraham's bosom, or some more fitting receptacle" (6). Pound's oblique comment sets the program: that much of the poetry of the present is stillborn and deserving of eternal confinement in limbo, while that of the future has already been written. Eliot echoed this idea in his famous 1919 essay "Tradition and the Individual Talent":

No poet, no artist of any art, has his complete meaning alone. His significance, his appreciation is the appreciation of his relation to the dead poets and artists. You cannot value him alone; you must set him, for contrast and comparison, among the dead....The existing monuments form an ideal order among themselves, which is modified by the introduction of the new (the really new) work of art among them....Whoever has approved this idea of order, of the form of European, of English literature, will not find it preposterous that the past should be altered by the present as much as the present is directed by the past. And the poet who is aware of this will be aware of great difficulties and responsibilities. (Selected Prose 38-39)

This influential passage was further elaborated in December 1920 in a subsequent article: "It is part of the business of the critic to preserve tradition—where a good tradition exists. It is part of his business to see literature steadily and to see it whole; and this is eminently to see it not as consecrated by time, but to see it beyond time; to see the best work of our time and the best work of twenty-five hundred years ago with the same eyes" (*Sacred Wood* xv-xvi). As Pound had put it a decade earlier, theirs was a call for a literary scholarship that would "weigh Theocritus and Yeats with one balance" (*Spirit* 6).

At first glance, this linking of an ancient Greek with a modern Irish poet appears casual, even arbitrary, yet it reveals a second aspect of early modernism in its complex mix of rivalry and collaboration. Theocritus the Sicilian courtier created a poetry depicting a rustic "half savage country, out of date" ("Hugh Selwyn Mauberley" l. 6), and Yeats spent his early career recovering the ancient Irish past from the rural countryside. Both Pound and Yeats were intent on reinventing poetry for their time, but they had to go about it in different ways. Ironically, Pound's America—"no country for old men"—failed by and large to exploit its "newness" poetically, despite the "barbaric yawp" of Whitman. Pound envisaged an artistic renaissance that would take place in his homeland; however, this was to be a recovery not of a mere two-centuries-old past (too callow to be of use) but of the European background from which America derived yet which it pretended to reject. Too resolutely provincial, the United States needed a greater sense of the global nature of the imagination. It was, paradoxically, still savage in its past and outdated in its self-consciousness. Yeats's complicated relationship with his English and Irish past was a viable model for dealing with the European and American tension felt by Pound and Eliot. For Longfellow and even for Mark Twain, everything had been *English* literature. Whitman offered an alternative, a distinctively *American* voice and style opposed to the traditional qualities of English literature, but he was gross and deliberately unrefined, presenting himself as the anticraftsman, the free spirit, the voice independent of influences from elsewhere, past or present. "Tradition" necessarily has to be a site of co-operation for all writers, but the modern world demanded originality and individuality along with a rejection of the past, even as it failed to break free of the past entirely. Thus, conscious of the literary past and aware of a need for reinterpreting rather than rejecting it, the two Americans abroad strove to awaken an awareness of the problem among not only their compatriots but also their English contemporaries. Eliot and Pound insisted on seeing all poets, whatever their era, not just as rivals but also as collaborators in the creation of a "simultaneous order." Thus their competitive collaboration was hardly confined to their personal relationship; rather, it was massive and broadly cultural, in its way as ambitious as any had been since the Renaissance.

In 1909 Pound wrote in the essay "What I Feel About Walt Whitman" that from the perspective of one dwelling in Europe, he was for the first time able to consider Whitman "the only one of the conventionally recognized 'American Poets' who is worth reading":

> He is America. His crudity is an exceeding great stench, but it is America. He is the hollow place in the rock that echoes with his time. He does "chant the crucial stage" and he is the "voice triumphant." He is disgusting. He is an exceedingly nauseating pill, but he accomplishes his mission.
>
> Entirely free from the renaissance humanist ideal of the complete man or from the Greek idealism, he is content to be what he is, and he is his time and his people. He is a genius because he has vision of what he is and of his function. He knows that he is a beginning and not a classically finished work.
>
> ...Mentally I am a Walt Whitman who has learned to wear a collar and a dress shirt (although at times inimical to both). (*Selected Prose* 145-46)

This sartorial tension presents the young Pound as one willing to participate in European culture but not to be entirely subsumed by it. He recognized a similar spirit in Eliot, whom he was later to call "Old Possum."

It was the vital relationship between these two men—working together and at the same time competing—that secured the success of the new approach to lyric poetry they sought to achieve. Both knew that America represented a new way of seeing yet recognized that it could be implemented only by exile and cunning (as that other great Irish writer, James Joyce, put it). But while for Yeats and Joyce, distance and indirection allowed them to recover and reinvent Ireland, they did so as rivals. Pound and Eliot achieved their common goal as co-conspirators and competed only in collusion, with, for example, Eliot's notion of a simultaneous order formed by the works of all great poets fulfilling Pound's hint at this idea in his earlier collocation of Theocritus and Yeats.

What does Eliot's "ideal order" of masterpieces represent? It would seem to be the totality of human self-understanding as transmitted by means of the verbal imagination. The masterpieces persist because poems compete among themselves for readers long after they are written, and certain ones of them (or their creators) become "branded." Eliot's "tradition" consists not of everything ever written but only of the poems that continue in our collective awareness. What the new, really new, work does is change our perception of the "branding." It alters, however slightly, the value we assign to this persistent body of works whose worth is acknowledged by the general consensus of the audience.

What of the other talents? Some of them compete by offering alternative ways of revising the tradition, since each new work not only claims to add to the body of insights that is the tradition but also revalues it as a whole and pinpoints aspects of it needing revision, however slight. Poets compete with each other not simply in the way that two different brands of coffee compete in the marketplace. Rather, each offers a different flavor of insight. Sometimes these flavors are supplementary or complementary; at other times they conflict with one another. A poet is like a company with many products or brands. Those that become household names are valued for their consistency of quality and value. Their utility resides in the way that they alter the tradition. The individual talents can work together, in complementary fashion, to move the tradition in one direction or another of change. In this concerted effort, usually styled a "literary movement," writers who typically compete in altering the tradition agree to alter it in a broad or radical way and nudge or bully the audience into accepting the new configuration. In his essay "Ulysses, Order and Myth," Eliot claimed that such a phenomenon had occurred as the result of the publication of Joyce's breakthrough novel (*Selected Prose* 175-78). Pound's persistent presentation of the lyric poet as hero—in fact, given his various personae, as a "man of many turns"—was a complementary effort.

What has been left out of the picture, however, is the channel of transmission, which is seldom a direct one from talent to audience. One must also take into account the role of the publisher and the reviewer, to say nothing of the kind of unofficial impresario that Pound himself represented. The impresario is the helmsman of the movement, its facilitator. As critic, he fills the role that in the usual business environment is exercised by advertising and marketing. But he can also play a less visible role by persuading publishers to take risks in bringing out the works of new talents. Pound, of course, was vigorous in assuming both roles, as did Eliot later, in his capacity as a member of the publishing establishment. Their credentials were their poetry, but first they had to work their way into the system and gain the confidence of the audience by creating a market for their verbal goods. Pound won his way by taking on the London literary establishment, by storming its bastions and undermining it from within and without. He gained the confidence of his audience early and then put it to the test. Once he was in, he wielded considerable power; but he had to sacrifice his own work as a consequence, since while he created a space for new talents, he also generated new competitors. Eventually, he gave up on London and left England for the continent, where he could play the role of American advisor to Europe, a role to which he had always aspired.

Pound was a student of European literature who exiled himself deliberately from his native land in order to learn more about poetry than any man alive, arriving first in Italy (epicenter of the Renaissance) and then in London (epicenter of recent English letters). Nevertheless, he never stopped being an American. To have done so would have been to admit defeat, to have become what he was later to describe as a possibility for himself in "Hugh Selwyn Mauberley" (1919):

> For three years, out of key with his time,
> He strove to resuscitate the dead art
> Of poetry; to maintain "the sublime"

> In the old sense. Wrong from the start—
>
> No, hardly, but seeing he had been born
> In a half savage country, out of date;
> Bent resolutely on wringing lilies from the acorn...
> ...
> Unaffected by "the march of events,"
> He passed from men's memory in *l'an trentiesme*
> *De son eage;* the case presents
> No adjunct to the Muses' diadem.
>
> (*Personae* 187)

To give up his distinctively American character would have meant foregoing his role as leader for his generation to achieve a new kind of lyric poetry, and indeed he expresses this very fear in the 1921 letter to Eliot quoted above. It was the example of Eliot's long poem that spurred him on to continue the *Cantos*, his own competitive effort to create the great modern long poem.

Pound's early letters, essays, and poems are full of references to his "half savage country," but they are not indications of rejection. On the contrary, he saw great potential for the arts in the future of America. He set the tone in his four-part 1913 essay *Patria Mia*, in which he envisioned an American renaissance that would vie fully with its Italian counterpart.[5] Taking on the voice of a prophet (specifically Ezekiel), he proclaimed in "From Chebar" (1913, but not published until 1976), "Before you were, America!/I did not begin with you,/I do not end with you, America" (*Collected Early Poems* 269). Although diffuse, its alternations of bravado and complaint enumerate rather well the program that Pound had adopted just before his encounter with Eliot. What is clear from these early statements from 1909 to just before the onset of the war is that his was a two-pronged approach. America was to be refined by renewing contact with its European past, and Europe was to be revitalized by America's energy and the sap that would bring its literary deadwood back to life. America had taken a great deal from Europe, but it was in a position to give as well. In other words, both cultures were to be brought together in a relationship amounting to a fruitful play of common features and distinctive differences.

The young American poet was at a distinct disadvantage, however, if he ventured to compete with his European contemporaries. He was a backwoodsman, a provincial, a cultural hick; and Whitman's example was hardly the one to invoke in order to make a favorable impression. Here the academic background of both Pound and Eliot was notably useful. They needed not only to demonstrate their knowledge of the European past but to vie with Europeans, even surpass them, in their knowledge of it. They did so by extending the range of what an educated person, American or European, ought to know. Pound and Eliot brought economics and philosophy into the purview of the lyric. They looked into past poetry for instances of intellectual sophistication instead of expressions of the Whitmanesque egotistical sublime. For the most part, they avoided transatlantic exotica and the American Indian in favor of the non-European or the neglected aspects of classical antiquity. Even then they sought to naturalize what they introduced from Chinese or Asian Indian culture. Pound's translations, despite their frequent use of archaic language, are anything but scholarly. They make the past sound contemporary, even when the idiom is not. Hardly the strange land of Marco Polo, his Cathay is a place where the wife's lament is just as poignant and direct as its cousins in medieval French or Old English. His Propertius is an Englishman who turns his back on the glories of the British Empire.

In short, Pound and Eliot outdid European poetry at its own game. They deposed the old mentors and chose new ones: Confucius, Li Po, Buddha, Dante, Arnaut Daniel, Baudelaire, Laforgue, Mallarmé, Donne, Landor. They offered reassessments of canonical poets, emphasizing neglected aspects of their themes and styles. They packed their poems with allusions, often to texts or poets considered too obscure or learned to be appropriate for a lyric mood. Finally, they introduced free verse and mixed diction, violated the stylistic proprieties that had dominated nineteenth-century verse, and substituted for the moral and didactic a concern for the integrity of art and the vitality of the present. If their poetry taught anything, the lesson was aesthetic in nature. They had in common with all their predecessors a conviction that poetry is principally a conveyor of emotions, but they warned that emotions are not the equivalent of concepts, abstracts, or behavioral formulae and that pious thoughts, secular or sacred, do not make poetry poetic. They campaigned against verbosity and padding. Imagism, a clever publicity ploy concocted by Pound, encouraged economy of statement and precision of description. But concision and concrete imagery were not the main goal of their campaign. They wished to eliminate all kinds of provincialism, whether American or European, and bring into the lyric some of the strategies being pursued by their painter and sculptor friends.

2

Pound and Eliot may have agreed on many important matters, but their lyric voices were strikingly different. Pound's is characterized by vigor, indignation, and love of the beautiful; Eliot's, in contrast, is uncertain of itself, skeptical, and world-weary. Pound's early lyrics, from those published as *A Lume Spento* in 1908 (which he later denigrated as "creampuffs" because of their neo-Rossettian language) to *Canzoni* in 1911, are exactly what he later said they were: attempts to adopt different masks as a means of exploring various lyric attitudes and themes. They seem decidedly unmodern now, but at the time they were thought to represent a fresh new voice, at once attractive and innovative. Throughout them one is aware of a Browningesque poetic psychology of the individual. The speakers are usually ancient, medieval, or Renaissance figures, often poets, and through them Pound parades a long succession of attempts to survey the history of the lyric voice, on the one hand, and to give them contemporary or perhaps timeless relevance on the other. But somewhere toward the end of the 1911 volume a more critical tone creeps in with "Song in the Manner of Housman" (later revised as "Mr. Housman's Message") and, just before it, a poem entitled "L'Art," which was not reprinted until recently.

> When brightest colours seem but dull in hue
> And noblest arts are shown mechanical,
> When study serves but to heap clue on clue
> That no great line hath been or ever shall,
> But hath a savour like some second stew
> Of many pot-lots with a smack of all.
> 'Twas one man's field, another's hops the brew,
> 'Twas vagrant accident not fate's fore-call.
>
> Horace, that thing of thine is overhauled,
> And "Wood notes wild" weaves a concocted sonnet.
> Here aery Shelley on the text hath called,
> And here, Great Scott, the Murex, Keats comes on it.

> And all the lot howl, "Sweet Simplicity!"
> 'Tis Art to hide our theft exquisitely.
>
> (*Collected Early Poems* 163)

It is not a poem that ranks among his finest, to be sure, but along with the critique of Housman, it does offer an insight into Pound's campaign against what he regarded as the practice of the most esteemed romantic poets at the time ("Great Scott" is an exclamation but might also be a glance at Sir Walter Scott). Shelley is "aery," but Keats is a murex, the sea-snail from which royal purple dye was derived in antiquity. "Wood notes wild" combines Shakespeare, the poet praised for his native simplicity in "L'Allegro," with Milton, the poem's author, whose influence on the language of poetry Pound considered baleful in its promotion of convolution. "The perfection of art is to conceal art"—a *bon mot* of Quintilian (but not Horace, if that is indeed what is meant by the "thing being overhauled")—has turned into the concealment of poetic theft. Pound manages to suggest that the criteria of simplicity, untutored genius, and originality (the hallmarks of nineteenth-century criticism) are only dishonest denials of the second-hand nature of its most praised productions. Ironically, the poem is itself in the form of a sonnet. The allusive poetry of Pound and Eliot, on the contrary, seeks not to conceal but to display its sources.

The critique of Housman, an older contemporary, is of a different kind. Here it is the all-too-facile, general gloom of the author of *A Shropshire Lad* that is his target. Since Pound had little patience for this variety of universal pessimism ("Therefore let us act as if we were/dead already" [*Collected Early Poems* 163]), one wonders how he could be impressed with Eliot's early lyrics. The difference, doubtless, is that Eliot describes or dramatizes but never moralizes or preaches, that he implies the need for some solution to the desperate isolation and futility that have come to dominate his consciousness, not a hopeless resignation. By the time Pound assembled *Ripostes* (1912), he had reached his maturity as a lyric poet. The volume includes some of his best-known shorter poems, among others, "Portrait d'une Femme," "The Seafarer," and "The Return," though there are still a number of pieces that continue to affect the language and subject matter of Renaissance poetry. One of the poems cut from the volume, "Redondillas, or Something of That Sort," is an anticipation of "From Chebar." It reads:

> I sing the gaudy to-day and cosmopolite civilization
> Of my hatred of crudities, of my weariness of banalities,
> I sing of the ways that I love, of Beauty and delicate savours.
> ...
> I would sing the American people,
>   God send them some civilization;
> I would sing of the nations of Europe,
>   God grant them some method of cleansing
> The fetid extent of their evils.
>   I would sing of my love "To-morrow,"
> But Yeats has written an essay,
>   Why should I stop to repeat it?
> ...
> We are the heirs of the past,
>   it is asinine not to admit it.
> ...
> I am that terrible thing,
>   the product of American culture,
> Or rather that product improved
>   by considerable care and attention.
> I am really quite modern, you know,
>   despite my affecting the ancients.
> ...
>   I'm not specifically local,
> I'm more or less Europe itself,
>   More or less Strauss and De Bussy.
>   (*Collected Early Poems* 215-22)

With the exception of a handful of Englishmen such as Ford Madox Ford and Wyndham Lewis, Pound found his British contemporaries to be more provincial than he, the midwestern American. It was the academic American turned independent man of letters, then, who was more open to the new currents from the continent, to the neglected riches of the past, and to the wisdom and beauty of the Far East. Pound finally gave up "affecting the ancients" in his next volume, *Lustra* (1916), the title of which he glossed by quoting from the Latin dictionary of Charlton Lewis:[6] "an offering for the sins of the whole people." Predominantly satirical in tone, *Lustra* marks a definite turn away from his earlier manner of occasional preciosity and archaism. Now he sees clearly that he must expiate for his own sins as well as those of the reading public and the literary establishment. In "Salutation the Second" he mocks the very audience who had welcomed the verse in which he learned to tune his instrument:

> You were praised, my books,
> because I had just come from the country;
> I was twenty years behind the times
>   so you found an audience ready.
> I do not disown you,
>   do not you disown your progeny.
>
> Here they stand without quaint devices,
> Here they are with nothing archaic about them.
> Observe the irritation in general:
>
> "Is this," they say, "the nonsense
>   that we expect of poets?"
> "Where is the Picturesque?"
>   "Where is the vertigo of emotion?"
> "No! His first work was the best."
>   "Poor Dear! he has lost his illusions."
>
> (Personae 85)

Lustra bears the imprint of three years of continuous collaboration and experimentation. At the time of *Canzoni* and *Ripostes*, Pound had devised Imagism and begun the move toward concision and economy, "direct treatment of the thing," that was to have a major impact on modernist poetry. He had published the ground-breaking translations of Chinese poetry in *Cathay* (1915) and continued to organize a network of friends and fellow writers, from Yeats to Wyndham Lewis, who were to be his principal collaborators during the following years. Yeats gave the lie to any anxiety of influence on Pound's part when he said years later of his younger friend: "[Pound's] art is the opposite of mine, whose criticism commends what I most condemn, a man with whom I should quarrel more than with anyone else if we were not united by affection" (*A Vision* 3). Indeed, the two men influenced one another, and Pound's admiration for Yeats as an important poet never seems to have flagged. He and

Wyndham Lewis picked up on Cubism and Futurism and created a short-lived movement Pound named "Vorticism." At the same time, he was engaged in promoting any number of emerging writers' and artists' work, including Eliot's, which was finally published in 1917 as *Prufrock and Other Observations*.

Pound's hopes for an American renaissance, as well as for a renewal of European art, could be summed up at this point in a poem from his 1916 volume entitled "The Rest," addressed to the "helpless few in my country," the "remnant enslaved":

> Artists broken against her,
> A-stray, lost in the villages,
> Mistrusted, spoken-against,
>
> Lovers of beauty, starved,
> Thwarted with systems,
> Helpless against the control;
>
> You who can not wear yourselves out
> By persisting to successes,
> You who can only speak,
> Who can not steel yourselves into reiteration;
>
> You of the finer sense,
> Broken against false knowledge,
> You who can know at first hand,
> Hated, shut in, mistrusted:
>
> Take thought:
> I have weathered the storm,
> I have beaten out my exile.
>
> (*Personae* 92-93)

This poem, like the whole of *Lustra*, was Pound's triumphant demonstration of his achievement in letters. He had taken American poetry to the next step after Whitman, had brought it, and not merely his own poetry, to maturity. Not only had he proved that American poets could survive in the greater realm of international letters; he had shown that they could eventually prevail.

3

Eliot's way of modifying the tradition could hardly have been more different from Pound's. It was certainly subtler and more intellectually cautious. It was not for nothing that Pound called Eliot "Old Possum" and claimed that he became powerful in British literary circles by pretending to be a corpse (that is, as dead as those contemporaries already gathered into Abraham's bosom). Pound's comments to Harriet Monroe in praise of Eliot had to do with the younger man's being an American who could vie with Europeans, with Englishmen especially, and on their own terms. An examination of his poetry up to the period of intense collaboration with Pound toward the end of World War I (a conspiratorial effort that culminated in *The Waste Land*) shows why Eliot's transformation of the literary scene could merge so seamlessly with Pound's.

What survives of Eliot's youthful productions, from his teens through his undergraduate years, reveals a remarkable ability to "do the police in different voices," like his friend and colleague-to-be Pound. He could write in the manner of Ben Jonson or the Metaphysical poets or in the official orotundities of the commencement ode without missing a beat. But when he sought a literary mentor to guide him in making use of this conspicuous talent, he could find none in the English-speaking world that might help him refashion the tradition, and so he was at a loss until he discovered the poetry of late nineteenth-century France. Applying his gift of mimicry at first to imitations of the manner of Jules Laforgue, he soon found his own voice and developed a posture unique in the English-speaking world. Reinforced by extensive reading not only in literature but in philosophy and contemporary psychology and anthropology, he emerged as a sophisticated young man who could hold his own with the brightest of his European counterparts and, in many instances, best them. After all, how many could claim to be conversant not only with Greek, Latin, French, German, and Italian but also with Sanskrit and Pali? His vacillation between becoming a man of letters and pursuing an academic career in philosophy was tipped toward the former by his mother, who had encouraged his literary gifts from an early period, and by the field itself, for it was there that he felt most at home.

The publication of Eliot's early verse under the title of *Inventions of the March Hare* in 1996 provided a fascinating peek into Eliot's lesser-known, mostly unpublished poetry written between 1905 and the eve of *The Waste Land*. What is especially remarkable is its tendency to parallel

Pound's verse, even when it seems to travel a different path. Before meeting his "frenemy," Eliot had not been particularly impressed with Pound's published work, nor was there much that he could draw on in what he knew of Yeats's poetry (he was not to change his mind about the virtues of Yeats until much later) nor, indeed, from any other contemporary English-language poet whose work he knew.[7] Consequently, he sought alternatives among the French (Baudelaire, Rimbaud, Laforgue, Corbière, Mallarmé), in the European past (Dante), or in English poets before the nineteenth century whose writings had not yet become canonical. He also drew on non-literary sources: recent philosophy, psychology, ethnography, and other contemporary thought that had been opened up for him by his undergraduate and graduate studies at Harvard but that were not usually considered proper poetic material. Exceptions such as the early work of Browning or the so-called French symbolists were ignored by the reading public at large and by professional critics as well. It was the strikingly similar notions of the nature of "tradition" that Eliot and Pound had in common that must explain their parallel development and ultimate convergence. They not only shared but exchanged their various enthusiasms with each other.

One might argue, as a result, that the co-opetition of the modernists involved not so much the rivalries and promotions among individual members of the movement as the movement itself with the past. By seeking to redefine "tradition," a word very much out of favor by 1919, Eliot and Pound were aiming to show that the competition was among differing versions of the past. They had to create an alternative past, one that was favorable soil for the growth of the new poetry. It was this other "tradition" that gave the impression among so many early twentieth-century readers that Eliot's and Pound's was a highly intellectual poetry. But neither of them ever claimed that the nature of lyric poetry was other than to objectify emotions; "go in fear of abstractions," Pound would counsel, and Eliot stated that the only way a poet could present ideas was as emotion. In some ways this contention is the least radical part of their program. Emotions had to be conveyed with economy and precision through an "objective correlative," but they were not to be downgraded as peripheral. The centrality of emotion as the fact and stuff of lyric poetry was what they shared with all past poets, romantic or classical. Where they diverged from the recent past was in the means of achieving an embodiment in language.

According to Christopher Ricks's chronology of the poems in the *March Hare* notebook and scattered publications, by the time Eliot was twenty-six he had written about fifty-four poems of which we have some record. While some allowance must be made for poems or drafts that have not survived, it is startling to note the suddenness of the transition between his very conventional earliest verse and that of 1909. Apart from an imitation of Ben Jonson composed as a class assignment when he was sixteen, they reveal a young man quite adept at adopting the voices of public oratory (official in "At Graduation 1907" or comic-satirical in "Ballade of the Fox Dinner"). Even so, there is already something a bit sly about them all, as though they were simply lying in wait for a moment to become emancipated from the expectations of their audiences. That moment is well known; it occurred in 1908 when he read Arthur Symons' *The Symbolist Movement* and subsequently ordered the poems of Laforgue from a Paris bookseller. Eliot spoke of it as a "personal enlightenment": "I felt for the first time in contact with a tradition, for the first time, that I had, so to speak, some backing by the dead, and at the same time that I had something to say that might be new and relevant" (*Varieties* 287).

Four poems written after he turned twenty-one give a sense of this contact: "First Caprice in North Cambridge," followed by a "Second Caprice," then "Opera," a poem about his experience of Wagner's *Tristan und Isolde*, and "Humoresque (After J. Laforgue)." The musical terms in all four are a clue to a new emphasis: where his previous lyrics had carried the designation "Song," he is now following the lead of the symbolists—"De la musique avant toute chose," as Verlaine puts it—by replacing the traditional, but by now tired, allusion to musical origins of the lyric with the fresher metaphor of contemporary musical forms. The "First Caprice," dating from November 1909, is already closer to Pound's ideals of directness, contemporaneous diction, and sharp observation than anything in his volumes before *Ripostes,* almost all of which continued to be dominated by the deliberately archaic language and the syntactical inversions deemed necessary by the poets of the Nineties. Little wonder that Pound was so gratified by the younger man's sheaf of poems. Eliot had anticipated the whole program of imagism in this one poem but even added a touch of his own irony:

> A street-piano, garrulous and frail;
> The yellow evening flung against the panes

> Of dirty windows: and the distant strains
> Of children's voices, ended in a wail.
>
> Bottles and broken glass,
> Trampled mud and grass;
> A heap of broken barrows;
> And a crowd of tattered sparrows
> Delve in the gutter with sordid patience.
>
> Oh, these minor considerations! . . . . .
>
> (*March Hare* 13)

The "street-piano" is perhaps the lower-class counterpart of the fashionable pianos "des quartiers aisés" of which Laforgue speaks, yet the language of the poem strikes one as imagism filtered through *The City of Dreadful Night*. However, in place of the easy sensationalism, vagueness, and verbosity of James Thomson is a novelist's economy and attention to precise detail. Readers of Eliot's later "Preludes" (another title with a musical metaphor) and "The Love Song of J. Alfred Prufrock" (an ironic return to the "song" title) will spot several familiar phrases that emerge from the crucible of Eliot's new linguistic experiments.

The "Second Caprice" is clearly influenced by a Baudelairean poetic in its description of "the debris of a city":

> Far from our definitions
> And our aesthetic laws
> Let us pause
> With these fields that hold and rack the brain
> (What: again?)
> With an unexpected charm....
>
> (*March Hare* 15)

The "unexpected charm" of debris suggests a fascination not only with the aesthetic possibilities of the ugly, already thoroughly studied by the French poets, but with the delight in breaking down the barriers of abstractions and the "laws" of a moribund tradition that is as "vacant" as the lots that so charm the poet.

The need for a new art is adumbrated indirectly in another poem from the last months of 1909. In "Opera," Eliot describes an experience of the most avant-garde and most romantic of all nineteenth-century composers through the medium of his most passionate music drama, *Tristan und Isolde*. Years later, Eliot spoke to Igor Stravinsky about his reaction to this performance, but where the Russian composer (no fan of Wagner) gathered that it had been a very passionate experience, the poem gives a quite different impression.

> Tristan and Isolde
> And the fatalistic horns
> The passionate violins
> And ominous clarinet;
> And love torturing itself
> To emotion for all there is in it,
> Writhing in and out
> Contorted in paroxysms,
> Flinging itself at the last
> Limits of self-expression.

The language and the free verse are surprisingly flat. The emotional triggers associated with the orchestral instruments suggest manipulation and unbridled, unmanageable self-expression rather than genuine objective correlatives. The irony is signaled in the claims of Wagner and his followers to a totality of aesthetic experience in a *Gesamtkunstwerk* that is the highest art. Accordingly, Eliot compares the opera to the poetic genre that Aristotle thought superior to all others, tragedy, and he was surely aware that the first efforts at "dramma per musica" in the late sixteenth century were an attempt at retrieving the cathartic power of Greek theater. Unfortunately, the Schopenhauerian backdrop shared by Wagner, Nietzsche, and, not incidentally, Laforgue prevails over all attempts to arrive at such heights of emotional experience:

> We have the tragic? oh no!
> Life departs with a feeble smile
> Into the indifferent.
> These emotional experiences
> Do not hold good at all,
> And I feel like the ghost of youth
> At the undertakers' ball.
>
> (*March Hare* 17)

The intrusion of a final rhyme into a free-verse poem ties up the Whitmanesque freedom from traditional forms with a neat, ironic knot. The music has failed as an objective correlative of the excessive emotions it tries to induce. A decade later, Eliot wrote of a similar failure in *Hamlet*, though the infamous essay in which Shakespeare's art of emotional embodiment is found wanting is really directed more at the romantic Hamlet of the nineteenth century than at his Elizabethan source.

"Humoresque," published in the *Harvard Advocate* in January 1910 (*March Hare* 325), is a more overt tribute to the French poet whom Eliot found the most useful as a model in this early phase. The point of this imitation is precisely the lack of genuine emotion in contemporary society, which he reduces to a series of role-playing marionettes who are essentially dead beings that only appear to be alive. At the end of 1909, Eliot had already anticipated his masterpieces to come a decade later. Little wonder that Pound was impressed. Eliot, his junior by three years, had already anticipated some of the older man's boldest moves.

At the time of their meeting, then, the two poets were poised to offer two alternative poetic visions to the twentieth century. Eliot's was the voice of the skeptic in search of the Absolute, a journey that was to end in *Four Quartets*. Pound, who refused to yield either to pessimism or to an unmediated transcendence, saw the task of the poet as the heroic recovery of beauty and craftsmanship in the lyric for an understanding of the past, versatility and ingenuity in the present, and a concern for the future. It is no surprise that he chose Odysseus as the figure to introduce his *Cantos*. The theme of his poetry is *nostos*, or homecoming, the return to one's proper place or office in society. One must first enter into the land of the dead to learn about the future. As Odysseus learns from Tiresias, however, "time present and time past are both perhaps contained in time future," to quote lines from his friend Eliot. The *Cantos* is no less than a long, rambling distention of the motifs of the early poetry, an attempt to expand the lyric assertion of the essential need for real poetry into a more substantial and comprehensive statement. Pound wants to become not Virgil or even Homer but Dante. His will be the example that can point others to poetic salvation from the limitations and backwardness of American origins, the dark wood of provinciality that can be overcome only by taking in the whole scope of the imaginative past.

The price of this ambition is a certain alienation and the accusation of megalomania. Poets may wish to become cultural heroes, but readers are not often inclined to such aspirations. As modernist poets made increasing demands on their audiences, they discovered emerging changes in the relationship of the poet to his public. As the product became less appealing to the public at large, demand began to flag. The rules of the poetic game underwent some major transformations, so that by the end of the 1930s and with the onset of a second world war, the market for verse changed radically. Pound became at once defiant and tragic in his *Pisan Cantos*, and though he continued doggedly to work on his long poem including history, he knew that in the end he could not "make it cohere." Eliot, having achieved the moment of seeing our end in our beginnings, fell more or less silent as a poet, having reached the end of all his spiritual journeying. But the story does not end at mid-century because the meaning of lyric poetry for modern society had been transformed for good.

Eliot's and Pound's convergence in 1914 was a crucial moment for modernist literature, a convergence of methods and goals that led to mutual reinforcement and ultimate domination after the war years. They were rivals with the same agenda, in disagreement about certain details, as Eliot presents them in "Eeldrop and Appleplex," where he describes himself as a skeptic with a mystical bent and his friend as a materialist with a skeptical bent. Where Pound disagreed most profoundly with Eliot, though, had nothing to do with the younger man's religious tendencies but was rather about Eliot's skepticism and frequent brushes with pessimism about the future of society and culture.

Their disagreement surfaces much later in *The Pisan Cantos*, where their co-opetition is handily summed up in a few lines in Canto LXXIV, the very first in its section. After lamenting the collapse of the Italian political regime he had supported, Pound replies: "yet say this to the Possum: a bang, not a whimper,/with a bang not with a whimper,/To build the city of Dioce whose terraces are the colour of stars" (*Cantos* 439). Dioce, one notes, comes from Herodotus, a suitably earthly historical reference that Pound opposes to the vague but hopeless desert land of Eliot's "The Hollow Men." However, this rebuke masks the fact that Eliot was now Pound's editor at Faber and Faber and responsible for publishing these very words. Eliot had chosen to believe in Augustine's City of God. Pound persisted in believing in a paradise on earth or at least a harmonious and well-ordered City of Man, such as the Greek historian describes as once existing in ancient Persia.

Two cantos later in LXXVI, Pound alludes once more to their

relationship: "Le Paradis n'est pas artificiel/States of mind are inexplicable to us" (*Cantos* 474). In his complex allusion to Baudelaire and perhaps Marx, Pound seems to recognize that the paradise of most religions is a kind of opiate that steers believers away from achieving some kind of order in the here and now. In this sense he rejects Eliot's Augustinian vision and Buddhist ambition to escape suffering. Nevertheless, both he and Eliot recognized that emotional as well as mystical experiences are beyond analysis but not beyond poetry, which, along with music and the drama, is the medium through which they are best conveyed to others. Eliot had publicly criticized the depiction of an Inferno for usurers in Cantos XIV-XVI by saying that Pound's hell was for other people. At the beginning of Canto XLVI, Pound offers a rejoinder immediately after his famous "usura" canto (XLV):

> And if you will say that this tale teaches...
>   a lesson, or that the Reverend Eliot
> has found a more natural language...you who think
>   you will
>   get through   hell   in   a   hurry....
>
>   (231)

But in Canto LXXVI, four lines after his original reference to Baudelaire's treatise on hashish, Pound repeats his allusion to that work with a somewhat conciliatory tone:

> Le paradis n'est pas artificiel,
>   l'enfer non plus.
>
>   (474)

Having lived through his own hell in the detainment camp at Pisa, he was now prepared to deliver a less "literary" version of the reality of damnation. His own, somewhat abstract, intellectualized version of evil had given way to personal tragedy, and though Pound came close to being judged executable for treason, Eliot was among those who came to his assistance, despite their public disagreements during the war.

    The attendant irony characterizing two of the most influential poets of the twentieth century is that their poetry was deeply immersed in concrete political positions that, for most readers in their century, were separable from their lyric visions. A secularist with an individualistic and mystical bent who once said that he would become a Catholic if he could choose his own saints and theologians, Pound was a materialist idealist (but not a leftist) who believed in the imagination's transformative power that could lead, if not to an earthly paradise, at least to a reasonable and livable City of Man. Eliot, his collaborator, publisher, lifelong friend, a philosophical skeptic, put his stock not in this world but in the City of God, a lyric place that was also revealed to us only through the poetic imagination. Put another way, one was an incipient Confucianist, the other an incipient Buddhist. One was attracted by China, the other by India.

Can poetry save us? What role does it play in revealing these "states of mind"? Is paradise an inexplicable state of mind or a definite physical place? In the "Notes for CXI," Pound contrasts the would-be builders of empire with a Dantesque vision suggested by his kindly editor-friend A. R. Orage:

> A nice quiet paradise,
>   Orage held the basic was pity
>   *compassione,*
>   Amor
>
>   (*Cantos* 797)

Or are Theocritus's Sicilian shepherds and Yeats's Irish peasants the emblem of a city like Dioce, where earthly architecture reflects heavenly order? Although Pound constantly reveals a mystical streak in his writings, he also evidences his Enlightenment roots. Ultimately, his notion of the poet is vatic, like that of Whitman, his "pig-headed father." Even while admitting defeat in his final fragmentary cantos, he continues to believe that his role is to prophesy and change the world with his vision:

> I have brought the great ball of crystal;
>   who can lift it?
> Can you enter the great acorn of light?
>   But the beauty is not the madness
> Tho' my errors and wrecks lie about me.
> And I am not a demigod,
> I cannot make it cohere.
> If love be not in the house there is nothing.
>   ...

>   the verb is "see," not "walk on"
>   i.e. it coheres all right
>   even if my notes do not cohere.
>   Many errors,
>   a little rightness,
>   to excuse his hell
>   and my paradiso.
>   (CXVI, *Cantos* 809-11)

And he concludes in the "Notes for CXVII et seq." by recognizing his personal tragedy:

>   That I lost my center
>   fighting the world.
>   The dreams clash
>   and are shattered—
>   and that I tried to make a paradiso
>   terrestre.
>   (*Cantos* 816)

He follows these lines with "I have tried to write Paradise" and asks for forgiveness for all he has made. His acknowledged failure contrasts sharply with Eliot's assertion, at the conclusion of *Four Quartets*, that "the fire and the rose are one," though readers may feel that Pound's own self-revelation of personal error is ultimately the more convincing of the two.

Pound's last work evinces a struggle with human limitations that is quite different from Eliot's, but in the end we must take both their dilemmas as evidence not so much of their personal trials as of the problem of creating a meaningful lyric vision in an age that no longer recognizes its value. Both tried to reassert the need for a poetry that could address larger issues than the individual's self-understanding and move beyond the limitations of their romantic heritage. In their attempt to extend the lyric mode, though, they lost touch with the very community that it has traditionally served. The conflict between a view that sees the lyric as revelatory of individual feelings and one that would see it as speaking for the family of man could not be readily resolved without falling back on oversimplified language and shopworn imagery. Yet the very demands a truly new poetry made on its readers tended to suggest that the game was not worth the candle.

These two views have continued into this century, but they are no longer driven by the prestige of the bard or poetic sage. In destroying poetry as therapy for the middle classes and as easy panacea for personal and social ailments, Pound and Eliot had, necessarily, to diminish its overstated claims to power. The separation of poetry from grand abstractions and feel-good messages was necessary and salutary, but it came at a price. With the emergence of new media, the word began to become not flesh but sound-bite. More poets are writing now, perhaps, than ever before; but it may be a long time before the lyric paradise hovers before us in the traditional verbal medium we think of as poetry. Eliot and Pound's Polish-Italian-French contemporary Guillaume Apollinaire, another celebrated modernist, predicted more than he realized when he proclaimed ecstatically in his poem *Zone* (1913):

> Tu lis les prospectus les catalogues les affiches qui chantent tout haut
> Voilà la poésie ce matin et pour la prose il y a les journaux
>
> You read flyers catalogues posters that sing out loud
> There's your poetry this morning and for prose you've got newspapers.
>
> (39; my translation)

The garden persists in our imaginations, but it has taken on a note of urgency rather than one of solitude or escape. The prophesied threat of ecological disaster looms too imminently in our imaginations for us to take an artificial paradise seriously, given the prospects of an artificial hell. Yeats's "supreme theme of art and song" has its rival in "mutually assured destruction." Like the natural environment, the poetic environment has also suffered an imbalance; and we can no longer expect, with the much-admired lyricists of an earlier period, to annihilate "all that's made/To a green thought in a green shade." Yet it was Pound and Eliot who did, in the end, foresee these consequences. It was they who first began to rethink the lyric in terms of a crisis of being, caused by our lingering too long "in the chambers of the sea," as Prufrock warns us, ignoring the human voices of *amor* and *compassione* that are the subject of every "Love Song" and lured to destruction by the sirens of a specious trust in what we have made rather than in what our poetic imagination has allowed us to see.

Notes

1. When Eliot and Pound got to Europe, with the idea of educating themselves in the great tradition, they found European letters to be in bad shape as well and immediately dived into the small but soon-to-be-powerful stream that was international modernism. Interestingly, the arrival of Eliot and Pound in England is considered a landmark in English literary history by the British, whereas the two Americans thought that they were escaping provincialism at home, only to find even more of it in the UK (with the exception of Yeats, Joyce, Hulme, and Ford).

2. They could speak of themselves collectively, for example, as "We Moderns," the title of a catalogue published in 1940 by the Gotham Book Mart in New York to celebrate and promote the publications of two decades of the literary vanguard.

3. There is some dispute about who originally coined the term. Claimants include Raymond Noorda, former head of Novell, and Darrell Waltrip, the race-car driver and racing commentator, but it has been a prominent topic of discussion since the mid-1990s, when Adam Brandenburger and Barry Nalebuff published *Co-opetition*. The authors combine networking with game theory as they rethink the way that business operates in a domain where suppliers, customers, and competitors are all interlinked. Recently, a more demotic version, "frenemies," has cropped up. This variant of friendly enmity describes the actors rather than their generalized, collective activities.

4. Two outstanding examples are those of Picasso and Braque in their co-operative yet competitive invention of Cubism; Braque described them as being like two mountain climbers, tethered together while each was vying to reach the peak. But Picasso and Matisse had an even longer relationship as friendly competitors. See, among many other studies, William Rubin, *Picasso and Braque*; Françoise Gilot, *Matisse and Picasso*; Yve-Alain Bois, *Matisse and Picasso*; Anne Baldassari et al., *Matisse Picasso*; Jack Flam, *Matisse and Picasso*. Igor Stravinsky, likewise, had a similar, if less direct relationship with Arnold Schoenberg. In fact, there were a number of versatile figures, such as Jean Cocteau, who were at once rivals and collaborators in different arts at the same time. The modernist movement, like the European Renaissance and the Enlightenment, consisted of a community of thinkers, artist, poets, musicians, and others who were united in a shared cause, even as they disagreed about the means to attain their common goal.

5. However, the manuscript was misplaced soon after being received by the publisher and not recovered until thirty-seven years later.

6. Known among classicists today as "Lewis and Short."

7. Later, concerning both, Eliot remarked, "I was introduced to *Personae* and *Exultations* in 1910, while still an undergraduate at Harvard. The poems did not then excite me, any more than did the poetry of Yeats" ("On a Recent Piece" 91-92).

12

The Symbolic Imagination:
Allen Tate's Search for Analogy

LARRY ALLUMS

In *The Spirit of Romance* (1910), Ezra Pound wrote that Dante's *Divine Comedy* is "in a sense lyric, the tremendous lyric of the subjective Dante," even though, to be sure, "the soundest classification of the poem is Dante's own" (Hawkins and Jacoff 3). If giving voice to the moment of highest insight or most complete union is the consistent objective of the lyric poet, certainly Pound is correct: the vast poem of one hundred cantos that progresses from the grotesque images of hell to the sacred verse of paradise offers an enduring pattern of the poet's desire to discover the possibility of ultimate blessedness in this life. If Dante's craft falls short of his vision at the end, still he extends the poetic imagination to what is arguably its limit. In this respect his achievement remains unparalleled in Western poetry; the *Commedia* merits the adjective designated not by him but by later admirers: *Divina*.

Dante's self-acknowledged "failure" in the Empyrean is at the root of all lyric attempts, differing in degree but not in kind from others: in proximity to the Divine Essence, his poetry remains grounded in, and must be expressed in terms of, the things of this world. Peering intently into the Triune Light, with all the created order behind and beneath him, what he sees and records at the last is the human image ("*la nostra effige*," *Paradiso* 33.131), the mystery of which at once escapes his understanding and moves him powerfully toward the Love that the image both reveals and conceals. The highest insight comes to Dante as an image presented from the world of sense for its symbolic and analogical potential. The Beatific Vision is the consequence of Dante's symbolic imagination, and it works—it operates and is successful—because of the nature of analogy, which is universally discernible and through which even in the most transcendent realm imaginable, poetry avoids abstraction.

From its first appearance in the early fourteenth century to the present, *The Divine Comedy* has served as a paradigm of the lyric poet's quest for oneness with the Beloved, God, Beauty, or Truth, but no other poet, ancient or modern, has more assiduously sought to understand and claim the symbolic potential of Dante's high poetic vision than has Allen Tate, the poet and critic whose entire career in letters may be measured in terms of his progressive embracing of the Dantean imagination. Born in 1899, Tate was a key figure in the group of Southern American poets centered at Vanderbilt University in the early 1920s who called themselves the Fugitives. Beginning then, Tate embarked on a search for poetic meaning in a world that seemed to offer little, and by the time he completed his major poetry and prose in the early 1950s, he had achieved lasting insights into both the obstacles to and possibilities of the lyric mode of knowledge in the modern age.

In the aftermath of World War I, it is no surprise to find a serious struggle for authenticity of voice and vision occurring among the Fugitive poets. America's late engagement in the Great War had the strange effect of drawing Southern artists out of their post-Civil War isolation and revealing a much larger world inviting their response. As Tate put it in "The New Provincialism," an essay published in 1945, "With the war of 1914-1918, the South reentered the world—but gave a backward glance as it stepped over the border: that backward glance gave us the Southern renascence, a literature conscious of the past in the present" (*Essays* 545). The poets who gathered in Nashville proved to be a major factor in that renascence, and for almost four years, from April 1922 to December 1925, *The Fugitive* stood as one of the most distinguished and influential "little magazines" in the United States.[1] Four of the Fugitives in particular, John Crowe Ransom, Donald Davidson, Tate, and Robert Penn Warren, represented the group's highest aspirations and worked through with greatest tenacity and gravity the artistic problems confronting the poets of the post-war world.[2] All four were "sons of the South" and thus had at their disposal a venerable tradition on which to draw. That the tradition had suffered the defeat of the Civil War was no obstacle; on the contrary, the Old South's vanquishment provided them a particularly advantageous, if exposed, perspective from which they could regard the Southern past in all its ambiguity and measure their prospects for the future. In the Foreword of the first number of *The Fugitive*, the group registered the "demise" of "a literary phase known rather euphemistically as Southern Literature," announced its own birth, and declared its credo: "THE FUGITIVE flees from nothing faster than from the high-caste Brahmins of the Old South" (*Fugitive* 1).

Behind this buoyant tone of unanimity, a protracted struggle was taking place particularly among Ransom, Davidson, and Tate, a literary debate among friends who cared deeply for one another but just as deeply about being truthful to the demands of poetry in their age. Could traditional poetry still speak to the culture or at least to the individual? How high could the contemporary poet aspire in his quest for insight? Could he hope for transcendence, or was irony his only possible stance? Could there somehow be a combining of traditional values—Faulkner's "verities"—with the modernist attitudes and strategies to which contemporary artists seemed inevitably committed? In both published documents and private correspondence, Ransom, Davidson, and Tate, who unlike almost all the other Fugitives had given themselves early to a life of letters, worked out their beliefs and convictions about poetry and its role in culture. As Louise Cowan writes in *The Fugitive Group*, "the exchange of energy between these three men was enormous, setting up an interior movement within the group, the direction of which was unnoticed by some of its members, resented by some, and immensely exciting to others" (39-40).

Ransom quickly discovered the signature style and tone by which he became known and that he never relinquished: a distancing wit and irony couched within precisely wrought traditional forms and the strategic use of archaic words and phrases. The body of Ransom's lyric work reveals both a deep love of the South and a willingness to look truthfully at its apparently inevitable fate in the modern world, where industry and commerce moved quickly into the vacuum once filled by traditional values and ancient certainties. Ransom both was and was not a traditionalist, was and was not a modernist. At his best he achieved an equilibrium between modern and traditional, never leaving the "world's body" but never fully descending into the conflict between modernism and traditionalism that Davidson and Tate enacted during the Fugitive years. In addition to his gifts as a poet, Ransom also possessed a strong disposition toward aesthetics and philosophy. His literary criticism and cultural commentary are marked by the same traits of irony and wit that infused his poetry; at the same time they attain levels of metaphysical insight rare among poets of stature, more so than the prose writings of such poet-critics as Pound, Eliot, and Stevens.

By contrast, Davidson clung tenaciously to a traditionalist stance, even when provoked by Tate to experiment with the modernist practices of certain contemporary poets. Relishing a lifelong friendship, he and Tate had the most spirited exchanges about poetry within the Fugitive group during its existence, each man pushing the other to the limits of his capacity. Tate praised Davidson most effusively when the latter ventured out of his area of comfort and into the thinner air of modernist techniques. Davidson, however, was gravitating all that time toward the kind of poetry he was apparently born to write: a studied consideration, in effect a celebration, though often obliquely, of tradition in traditional forms, of the people, artifacts, and historical turning points of his native South. If Davidson's voice was lyric in its early stages, recasting the material of ballad and folktale into the idioms of the Deep South, there was at the same time an epic strain at work in his imagination that began to emerge early with such poems as "Lee in the Mountains" (in the 1927 volume *The Tall Men*), continued in the two-volume work entitled *The Tennessee* (1946 and 1948), and culminated in the poetry collected in the 1961 volume *The Long Street*.

For Tate, the conflict between traditionalism and modernism was not so quickly or clearly resolved as for either Ransom or Davidson. The youngest of the Fugitives at the time he was invited to join and something of an upstart by nature, he began his career in letters by challenging the group with the poetry of the French symbolists, introducing them to T. S. Eliot, and presenting Hart Crane and others as examples of where they should direct their attention. His youthful interest in modernism was ardent, and behind it lay an intense desire to discover a source of spiritual meaning in the post-war West. Deeply devoted to his quest, he was willing to step beyond youthful allegiances, and by the late 1920s, he had become an active spokesman on behalf of his native South as a traditional society. In 1927 he published the poem for which he is probably best known, "Ode to the Confederate Dead," not a conventional celebration of the Southern fallen but certainly a reverent reflection on the "furious murmur of their chivalry." By the mid-1930s, he was looking backward toward Virgil's Rome to find cultural archetypes and patterns that might cohere, or at least displace, the "fragments" of Western culture serving only, as Eliot had written in *The Waste Land*, to shore a refuge "against my ruins."

Tate's profound encounter with Dante around 1950 was the culmination of his entire career, the trajectory of which shows in retrospect a definite path: his earlier explorations of modernism, the Old South, and Rome together constitute a continuous progression toward the explicitly Dantean stance that he assumed in his final poetry. The goal of this last phase turned out to be ambitious indeed: to appropriate Dante's gift of analogy and, in Pound's phrase, to "make it new" for his own age. Dante's capacity for seeing his world analogically, which to Tate's contemporaries appeared an artifact of a lost time, finally presented itself to him as a real possibility through which he could find coherent meaning in—and thus could reclaim and redeem—his own experience of the modern world. In 1951, he wrote two essays that acknowledged his literary kinship to Dante and revealed a perception of the Dantean method far surpassing that of any of his contemporaries, including Pound and Eliot. More specifically, "The Angelic Imagination" and "The Symbolic Imagination" indicate that Tate had come to a fresh understanding of Dante, had rediscovered him much as Dante rediscovered Virgil and incorporated that rediscovery into the *Comedy*.

The tremendous impact of this late encounter (Tate was fifty and had already published the bulk of his writing) becomes clear in contrast with how he used Dante in working out his earlier poetic and critical stance. More than twenty years before the two essays of 1951, Tate had been aware of the great medieval poet and his coherent universe, noting like Eliot its remoteness from the disorder of the modern age. After a time, though, he began to use his knowledge of Dante's poetry to examine what he considered flaws in the work of his contemporaries. In "Hart Crane," a composite essay from papers written in 1932 and 1937, he describes his friend as "one of those men whom every age seems to select as the spokesmen of its spiritual life" (*Essays* 319). Then he judges the modern age by judging *The Bridge*, Crane's attempt at an American epic, to be a failure:

> The impulse in *The Bridge* is religious, but the soundness of an impulse is no warrant that it will create a sound art form. The form depends on too many factors beyond the control of the

poet. The age is scientific and pseudo-scientific, and our philosophy is Dewey's instrumentalism. And it is possibly this circumstance that has driven the religious attitude into a corner where it lacks the right instruments for its defense and growth, and where it is in a vast muddle about just what these instruments are. Perhaps this disunity of the intellect is responsible for Crane's unphilosophic belief that the poet, unaided and isolated from the people, can create a myth. (Essays 317)

In Tate's estimation, Crane tried to overcome the disunity of his age by attempting to impose upon the external world a pattern that was not authentic, perhaps not even really there, and what resulted was his "betrayal" by the natural order: "The persistent, and persistently defeated, pursuit of a natural absolute places Crane at the center of his age" (*Essays* 319). Crane's failure becomes more obvious, Tate says, when one compares *The Bridge* with a poem such as *The Divine Comedy*, which issued from a mind submissive to the natural order and possessed of a harmony between intellectual conception and concrete presentation. He concludes: "Crane could only assert a quality of will against the world, and at each successive failure of the will he turned upon himself. In the failure of understanding—and understanding, for Dante, was a way of love—the romantic modern poet of the age of science attempts to impose his will upon experience and to possess the world" (*Essays* 321).

Tate's brief but insightful use of Dante in his critique of *The Bridge* could be considered an early gesture of desire to understand the source of Dante's sacramental attitude toward the created order. Beyond understanding it, could a poet writing in a very non-sacramental age somehow appropriate that attitude for his own verse? Very early in his career Tate had accepted Eliot's "dissociation of sensibility" as the condition of modernity and reflected it often in the poetry of his Fugitive years as a spiritual loss or incompleteness that modern man intuits without comprehending. The following poem from 1925, "Ignis Fatuus," is a representative example:

> In the twilight of my audacity
> I saw you flee the world, the burnt highways
> Of summer gave up their light: I

> Followed you with the uncommon span
> Of fear-supported and disbursèd eyes.
>
> Towards the dark that harries the tracks
> Of dawn I pursued you only. I fell
> Companionless. The seething stacks
> Of cornstalks, the rat-pillaged meadow
> Censured the lunar interior of the night.
>
> High in what hills, by what illuminations
> Are you intelligible? Your fierce latinity
> Beyond the nubian bulwark of the sea
> Sustains the immaculate sight.
>
> To the green tissue of the subterranean
> Worm I have come back, two-handed from
> The chase, and empty. I have pondered it
> Carefully, and asked: Where is the light
> When the pigeon moults his ease
> Or exile utters the creed of memory?
>
> <div align="right">(<i>Poems</i> 153)</div>

The title's "false fire" or "fool's fire," like the "will o' the wisp" of folklore, may be for the pursuing poet an ideal past or the expansive poetry of a former age, neither of which appears available to his world. The year before publishing this poem, Tate wrote to Davidson, "I don't think literature can be merely a medium of individual satisfaction; I believe that truly honorable men work for the fine abstraction called Literature, as a contribution to another abstraction called Civilization" (Fain and Young 101-2). In the "audacity" of his youthful commitment to those abstractions, what he discovered was a continual threat of darkness, a threat of a poetry either unilluminated by any certainty outside itself or deceived by an inaccessible light. The quest is lonely, "companionless," and for one whose sight is not "immaculate," whose vision is obscure in a faithless age, a poetic ideal that beckons with its "fierce latinity" seems scarcely "intelligible." Having failed in his pursuit of the light, he returns "two-handed from the chase, and empty" to a world that now appears abandoned to darkness. The question at the end situates the narrator: he is both a sickly bird that cannot fly and an exile who must be content to "utter" only the memory of his vision. It is a cruel circumstance for the young poet who has responded in earnest to the lyric imperative not only to imagine but to find language adequate for the highest, most complete insight of which perception is capable yet to fail of the insight.

The concluding question of "Ignis Fatuus"—"Where is the light?"—was to become the theme of Tate's poetry, and considering the movement and scope of his overall achievement, one may easily connect the "light" that has fled the world in this early poem to the source of Dante's inspiration in the *Comedy*. At every turn Tate looked for it, and his sense of lostness in the modern world, like Dante's in the dark wood of the *Inferno*, was genuine and profound. What drew him to the Italian master in the first place was that in his own lostness, Dante nevertheless had the assurance, through analogy, of the light's existence. For Tate in his early years, there was no such assurance built into the structures of his age. But it *was* there in Dante's achievement, in a poem whose progress is ever upward toward lyric completeness.

After his formative period with the Fugitives, images from the *Comedy* began increasingly to appear in Tate's poetry as it matured, notably in his most difficult poems, such as "Winter Mask" (1943) and "Seasons of the Soul" (1944). It became clear in the best work of Tate's middle period that he was nourishing within his imagination the Dantean idea of a universe rendered intelligible through the reflection of spiritual light—a light that clearly existed on Dante's anagogical level of meaning and that was still accessible even in the murky atmosphere of modernity. By 1951, when Tate wrote "The Angelic Imagination" and "The Symbolic Imagination," the Dantean order and intelligibility had become a deep-seated conviction that he was able at last to incorporate into his own poetic scheme. The latter essay is perhaps the most remarkable tribute by a twentieth-century poet to Dante's poetic method, and it is at the same time the most penetrating attempt by anyone up to Tate's time to gain access to the domain of Dante's analogical imagination. In fact, what Tate suggests in "The Symbolic Imagination" is astounding: that the modern poet, even given his "disunity of the intellect" (his phrase from the essay on Hart Crane), may discover, cultivate, and practice his craft from a sacramental perspective.

Before Tate could fully articulate his understanding of the Dantean method, he had first to identify its opposite pole, in something of the same way that the lost pilgrim of the *Comedy* had to confront Satan before he could arrive at the Beatific Vision. Tate made this identification in "The Angelic Imagination," which has its roots in Jacques Maritain's formulation of "anthropocentric angelism" as manifesting the Cartesian heritage of the modern age. "Man the center of an intelligible universe which he has created in his own image," Maritain wrote, "himself loses his centre of gravity and his own consistence, for his consistence is to be the image of God. He is in the middle of a desert" (*Dream* 171-72). Tate parallels the Cartesian exaltation of reason in the realm of science and logic to the exaltation of the imagination in the realm of poetry, and to him Edgar Allan Poe, who abdicated the world of the human for the world of disembodied spirits, represents most dramatically the poet possessed of the "angelic fallacy." In opposing the excesses of the "demi-religion of scientism," Poe unconsciously exalted the "poetic intellect" to a position of like autonomy and attempted to "put himself not in the presence of God, but in the seat of God." But the poet cannot function alone in a spiritual vacuum, Tate argues, apart from the total human complex of feeling, intellect, and will. He cannot know God "as essence"; rather, he can know him only "as analogy":

> Analogy to what? Plainly analogy to the natural world; for there is nothing in the intellect that has not previously reached it through the senses. Had Dante arrived at the vision of God by way of sense? We must answer yes, because Dante's Triune Circle is light, which the finite intelligence can see only in what has already been seen by means of it....The reach of our imaginative enlargement is perhaps no longer than the ladder of analogy, at the top of which we may see all, if we still wish to see anything, that we have brought up with us from the bottom, where lies the sensible world. (*Essays* 422)

The "angelic imagination," we might say, takes the direct route toward the object of its desire, rather than reaching it by way of the "ladder of analogy," and in the process short-circuits the possibility of attaining the lyric unity: "Poe as God sits silent in darkness" (*Essays* 422). For Tate, Poe represents the extreme of the disillusioned poets of modernity who look to escape the spiritual barrenness of their age by overleaping the debased condition of the human in order to reach God but who plunge instead into satanic regions where there is no light at all.

In "The Angelic Imagination" Tate puts his commentary on Dante's method to use as a counter to Poe's angelic zeal—a zeal that seems to represent a way out of the modernist dilemma (to believe or not to believe in the light) but, in Tate's view, is actually a capitulation to the powers of darkness. If Tate's analysis is disposed to abstraction—is he, for instance, describing the mystical or the poetic experience, or is he implying that they are the same?—he nonetheless makes clear in "The Symbolic Imagination" what this insight into the Dantean imagination means to the actual task of poetry in any age.

Tate grounds his formulation of the symbolic imagination in Canto 30 of the *Purgatorio*, the famous passage in which Dante gazes on Beatrice again long after her death. He is smitten by her divine radiance at the top of the mountain, but that spiritual effulgence is not all. He is also possessed again by the net of his former natural desire: Beatrice's smile "simultaneously revives his human love (Eros) and directs his will to the anticipation of the Beatific Vision (Agape): both equally, by means of the action indicated by the blinding effect of both; he is blinded by the net and by the light, not alternately but at one instant" (*Essays* 427). What strikes Tate so powerfully is the unifying capacity of the imagination that he has discovered in Dante: "To bring together various meanings at a single moment of action is to exercise what I shall speak of here as the symbolic imagination; but the line of *action* must be unmistakable, we must never be in doubt about what is happening; for at a given stage of his progress the hero does one simple thing, and one only. The symbolic imagination conducts an action through analogy, of the human to the divine, of the natural to the supernatural, of the low to the high, of time to eternity" (*Essays* 427).

To the medieval scholar, Tate's analysis will most likely seem a simple recasting of the "doctrine of the four senses" that was the common property of Dante's age. But indirectly that is Tate's point: the four senses, or levels of interpretation, are a scholarly distinction that became intellectualized and apparently lost to the practice of the modern poet. But not lost irrevocably or by divine decree. Here Tate writes with the urgency of a poet discovering his way into his craft, into the possibility of writing, not a "dissociated" poetry, or in fragments of a lost spiritual realm, but a poetry from the domain of *analogia entis*, the "analogy of being" that is the natural desire of every lyric poet, ancient or modern. In fact, it is not only the poet who still, even today, has access to this realm. "Analogical symbolism" may provide the "Illuminative Way" for the theologian or the "Unitive Way" for the mystic. For the symbolic poet, whose task is to "return to the order of temporal sequence—to action," however, it is the "Poetic Way":

> It is at any rate the way of the poet, who has got to do his work with the body of this world, whatever that body may look like to him, in his time and place—the whirling atoms, the body of a beautiful woman, or a deformed body, or the body of Christ, or even the body of this death. If the poet is able to put into this moving body, or to find in it, a coherent chain of analogies, he will inform an intuitive act with symbolism; his will be in one degree or another the symbolic imagination. (*Essays* 428)

As he continues, Tate presses the point that the modern poet has access to the symbolic imagination in spite of Cartesian dualism or science's reductionist view of nature. First, he sets forth the lineage: "The symbolic imagination takes rise from a definite limitation of human rationality which was recognized in the West until the seventeenth century; in this view the intellect cannot have direct knowledge of essences" (*Essays* 428). By contrast, according to Tate's earlier formulation, the "angelic imagination" reflects the West's capitulation to the scientific attitude that the human race enjoys a "quasi-divine independence" and thus has no "commitment to the physical world." The loss is ours, Tate says, and is natural, moral, and spiritual, since "it is through feeling alone that we witness the glory of our servitude to the natural world, to St. Thomas' accidents, or, if you will, to Locke's secondary qualities." Feeling "is our tie with the world of sense," the limitations of which the angelic mind despises and believes it can circumvent (429).

"This is the simple secret of Dante," Tate says, "but it is a secret which is not necessarily available to the Christian poet today" because the "abstraction of the modern mind has obscured [Christian poets'] way into the natural order." Dante's secret is as profound as it is simple, and the example of his poetry breaks over Tate like a revelation: the natural order that was for Dante an infinite series of apertures into the spiritual order of the universe is intact even for Tate and his contemporaries, whether or not they formally profess a faith. As long as creation lasts, nature will offer "to the symbolic poet clearly denotable objects in depth and in the round, which yield the analogies to the higher syntheses." The problem with the modern poet is that he "*unnecessarily* rejects the higher synthesis, or tosses it in a vacuum of abstraction" (*Essays* 429-30, emphasis added). For Tate, breaking the code of analogy is the secret to overcoming the "abstraction of the modern mind."

An obvious but crucial distinction for Tate here is between being Christian and being spiritual. After all, Dante himself has the imperial eagle in the sphere of Jupiter declare that "many cry Christ, Christ, who, at the Judgment, shall be far less near to Him than he who knows not Christ" (*Paradiso* 19.106-8). It was about this time in his career, however, that Tate became a Roman Catholic, a decision that had been some twenty years in the making. His contribution to the 1930 Agrarian manifesto *I'll Take My Stand* was "Remarks on the Southern Religion," and in the years immediately following, his poetry began to reflect the religious dimension of his spiritual crisis. In "The Cross," written in 1930, Tate depicts Christ's sacrifice as presenting to human beings the ultimate choice—"The last alternative they face/Of life, without the life to save"— and he ends "The Last Days of Alice" (1931) with a strange and troubled prayer, a modern poet's version of Donne's "Batter my Heart": "O God of our flesh, return us to Your wrath,/Let us be evil could we enter in/Your grace, and falter on the stony path!" In a 1929 letter to Davidson, Tate presaged this transition into a permanent, explicitly spiritual mode: "We are all at present doomed to live a harrowing life, and it may or may not be more harrowing than the lives of all men everywhere who have tried to find some ultimate discipline of the soul. It was just as hard to attain to salvation in the 13th century as it is now (perhaps harder), although the results of the quest in literature were grander and more coherent....I am more and more heading toward Catholicism. We have reached a condition of the spirit where no further compromise is possible" (Fain and Young 223). After more than two decades on the quest, Tate speaks in "The Symbolic Imagination" as though he is no longer at one with those modern poets whom he admired and emulated as a Fugitive. As a critic at any rate, he indeed left them upon his discovery of Dante as the true poet to be emulated. His conclusion in "The Symbolic Imagination" indicates the extent to which Dante permeated his creative efforts. Dante's "failure" at the end of the *Comedy* is in fact the measure of his success as a poet. His imagination took him as far as possible and, because he understood his limits as both a pilgrim and a poet, no further: "The high order of the poetic insight that the final insight must elude us, is dramatic in the sense that its fullest image is an action in the shapes of this world: it does not reject, it includes; it sees not only with but through the natural world, to what may lie beyond it. Its humility is witnessed by its modesty. It never begins at the top; it carries the bottom along with it, however high it may climb" (*Essays* 446).

Tate wrote "The Symbolic Imagination" when he was at the height of his critical power. In terms of poetry, his achievement in the Dantean mode is as clear, though its quantity is significantly more limited. He wrote only three poems of major significance after acknowledging *The Divine Comedy* as the enduring example in the West of the "Poetic Way." Originally he intended to write a long work of nine parts, all in *terza rima*, but some time later he altered his plans and announced that six poems would comprise the project. Finally the sequence included these three: "The Maimed Man," "The Swimmers," and "The Buried Lake." None has received more than scant critical attention, but taken together they give an indication of how completely Dante had captured Tate's imagination and the extent to which he was prepared to go to ascertain the availability of Dante's sacramental sense of analogy for the modern lyric poet. Inexplicably, Tate's creative power seems to have entered a permanent decline at this very time: *Allen Tate: Collected Poems 1919-1976*, published some two years before his death in 1979, contains only two poems written after his Dantean sequence. Both of them are slight and uncharacteristically private for Tate, addressed in failing health to his wife and their two young sons. He continued to write criticism and commentary, but with "The Buried Lake" in 1953, his career in poetry was effectively at an end.

The period of the early 1950s, however, clearly marked a culmination that began on a personal note with his entry into the Roman Catholic Church in 1950 and ended in 1952-1953 with the three poems that emanated from his Dantean perspective, showing rather clearly that this last phase in his career was at once experimental and conclusive. His early tutelage among the Fugitives had fixed in him an already strong disposition against nostalgia and sentiment, and his subsequent poetry and criticism had forged an understanding that the poetic language and techniques of his contemporaries were inevitable strategies in confronting a world largely devoid of communally held certainties. Indirection and ambiguity were the givens of his age as surely as planes and correspondences were of Dante's, and he could not change that. As a pilgrim, Tate now had the Church; as a poet, he was largely on his own except for the strength of his own faith in the existence of anagogical truth and the authority he was able to find in other poets. The decisive difference in this final stage of Tate's career was that here at the end, rather than the middle, of his own journey, he had discovered the poet who could be his leader, master, and teacher, as Dante designates Virgil in the *Inferno* (2.140).

Tate's Dantean sequence, his own lyric triptych, emerges from a mature conviction, nascent in poems such as "Ignis Fatuus," that light has not fled the world but is still accessible, though not in the way it was to Dante. The three poems also reveal a reach of ambition singular in Tate's poetry; the questioning, uncertain, or tentative undertone of much of his best earlier verse, such as "Ode to the Confederate Dead," "The Cross," and "Aeneas at Washington," is replaced by a quiet confidence that is also submissive to an expectation of insight. It is, in short, a poetry of faith that whatever the light is about to reveal will be desirable and significant, even transformative. According to his usual practice, Tate sent the three poems in draft form to Donald Davidson, who was impressed indeed. Of the first in the sequence Davidson had this to say: "I have read & re-read 'The Maimed Man' various times and can find very little in it to criticize. You are moving at the level of Vergil and Dante, vision and verse-instrument truly both one, and completely yours and you, all indistinguishably. So it is not possible, as in our salad days, to venture with rude hand among your lines. The laurel you invoke is on your brows, and what can I do but salute you, and await the fulfillment of the great journey you have begun?" (Fain and Young 356). The "laurel you invoke" mentioned by Davidson refers to the opening lines of "The Maimed Man." Here are several tercets from the beginning:

> Didactic Laurel, loose your reasoning leaf
>   Into my trembling hand; assert your blade
>   Against the Morning Star, enlightening Thief
>
> Of that first Mother who returned the Maid.
>   Beguiling myrtle, shake no more my ear
>   With your green leaf: because I am afraid
>
> Of him who says I have no need to fear,
>   Return, Laurel! Dying sense has cast
>   Shadow on shadow of a metal tear

Around my rim of being. Teach me to fast
 And pray, that I may know the motes that tease
 Skittering sunbeams are dead shells at last.

Then, timeless Muse, reverse my time; unfreeze
 All that I was in your congenial heat;
 Tune me in recollection to appease

The hour when, as I sauntered down our street,
 I saw a young man there, headless, whose hand
 Hung limp; it dangled at his hidden feet

I could not see how, in the fading band
 Of low light; nor did I feel alarm
 But felt, under my eyelids, grains of sand.

Worth noting at the outset is Tate's precise use of *terza rima*, sustained throughout the rest of this poem, "The Swimmers," and "The Buried Lake." As Davidson wrote to Tate in the same letter quoted above, "you are doing the all-but-impossible thing in English verse—making *terza rima* work at the sublime level" (Fain and Young 356-57). Davidson went on to make some minor critical suggestions, mostly about diction, but more significant was his judgment that Tate had clearly arrived at a new plateau in his poetry in terms of both vision and craft:

> It would never do for me to niggle at small cruxes in a work of large scope. Augustus was right (though whether for the right reasons who can know?) in setting aside Vergil's wish that the *Aeneid* ms. be destroyed. It could never have been as "polished" as one of the Eclogues, even if Vergil had lived another decade! I am implying something that I hardly know how to describe, about the necessities of the "large" poem. But your venture already begins to illustrate what I am talking about, and it shows how far you now are beyond the point when, in Fugitive days, you temporarily accepted John Ransom's argument (though it wasn't only his) for the "minor" poem....But here you are, writing the "major" poem. Go ahead—and please let me see more! (Fain and Young 358)

Tate's lengthy invocation in "The Maimed Man" sets the tone for the entire three-poem sequence: his desire is that the presences presiding over the creative act be in harmony and at their highest potency so that he can reclaim, or better yet redeem, what has already been given to him but has not before now been understood. For the task, "Didactic Laurel" must be ascendant, since in this new Dantean mode, Apollo's "reasoning leaf" rather than Aphrodite's "beguiling myrtle" will teach him the humility and faith he needs for his work of reclamation. His request of the "timeless Muse" to "reverse [his] time; unfreeze/All that [he] was in [her] congenial heat" indicates that this new way of seeing, or analogically seeing through, will allow—rather insist upon—his returning to key incidents in his past and seeing them anew, now in the light of their significance as crossroads or turning points. Although afraid and unsure, he is at last spiritually and poetically equipped to do this, so he asks his Muse to "tune [him] in recollection to appease/The hour" when he first encountered the grotesque figure of the maimed man. Robert Dupree has noted that the invocation consists of "complex symbols [that] unite pagan and Christian figures in an original but coherent fashion" (211).[3] Into this mixture Tate also introduces the jarring textures common in modernist verse, including his own: within the traditional device of the invocation, his fear of spiritual death is rendered not in conventional images but as "a metal tear/Around my rim of being." His request is not to write the Great Poem but to learn how "to fast/And pray"; his tone is humble and even contrite, as though the poet is a suppliant approaching a great task for which he needs strength and blessing first.

"The Maimed Man" seems in fact to be a preparation, an almost tentative stepping into this new region of poetic possibility. Tate's elaborately layered invocation appears to be modeled on the one in the opening canto of the *Paradiso*, when Dante calls on both peaks of Parnassus, the one inhabited by the Muses (also invoked in the *Inferno* and the *Purgatorio*), the other by Apollo himself, to assist him in writing this highest, most purely lyric part of what he will later designate the "sacred poem" (*Paradiso* 25.1). Dante's purpose in invoking all the poetic powers at the threshold of his ascent with Beatrice into the heavens is similar in kind to Tate's, but the difference is that Tate's invocation unexpectedly results in his fresh encounter with the past in an infernal region. This first poem in Tate's sequence begins in Hell, the poet's customary habitation up to this point. He has been comfortable here, has "sauntered" the streets until the moment of his confrontation with the maimed man, a version of himself that has been there all along. His most difficult task is at hand, and thus it is here that a new beginning is most urgently required, a situating of the past once and for all that will allow a transcendent movement into the future. For what Dante is about to embark upon in *Paradiso*, he has to invent a word, *trasumanar*, "passing beyond humanity" (1.70), and describing the experience will occupy the entire third canticle of his majestic poem. Tate's invocation, while more modest in its expectation, is just as necessary and potentially transformative for his own poetic task: to negotiate a Hell of which he has been unsuspecting because he has been too much in it and of it. In fact, the entire thrust of this first poem in the sequence seems to be to discover the right disposition toward the mutilated figure whom the poet feels he must "appease" and who turns out to be his double, headless because he has lacked "the good of intellect" (*Inferno* 3.18) and rooted in the present, immobile, with "Blue grass instead of feet," because he has had no sense of direction.

When the poet resumes the invocation later, he asks, "let me touch the hem/Of him who spread his triptych like a fan." This explicit reference to Dante as his precursor and guide more or less announces Tate's exit from the surreal regions of hell and his entrance into the natural order that was the workshop of Dante's symbolic imagination, "the busy, lurked, discrete/Mandible world sharp as a broken tooth." This world of apparent fragments is where meaning has resided all along. At the conclusion of "The Maimed Man," Tate presents a futher invocation:

> Now take him, Virgin Muse, up the deeper stream:
>   As a lost bee returning to the hive,
>   Cell after honeyed cell of sounding dream–
>
> Swimmer of noonday, lean for the perfect dive
>   To the dead Mother's face, whose subtile down
>   You had not seen take amber light alive.

The final part of his invocation is now to the "Virgin Muse," Mary, "that first Mother who returned the Maid," as the poem's second tercet describes her, to take "him," no longer an isolated "I," "up the deeper stream:/As a lost bee returning to the hive,/Cell after honeyed cell of sounding dream." Is this deeper stream Eunoe, the restorer of redemptive memories, and does the hive prefigure Dante's celestial rose? With these intimations of the higher reaches of Dante's poem, "The Maimed Man" ends with a striking image of the "Swimmer of noonday" leaning for "the perfect dive" into a new, unexplored realm, a precise transitional image into the next poem of the sequence, "The Swimmers."

"The Swimmers" is probably the most representational poem Tate ever wrote, and its situation between two poems much more characteristic of Tate's elliptical style, "The Maimed Man" and "The Buried Lake," can be no accident. This middle poem is fully located in a purgatorial realm much like Dante's: events happen in real time, and objects are presented in the round. In fact, the poem is Tate's recollection of an incident from his childhood, the aftermath of a lynching he and four friends witnessed in a Kentucky town in 1911. The poem depicts the before and after of the event. He sees the posse of vigilantes pass, with the condemned man at their front, his face "worn as limestone on an ancient sill," and he sees them return, but this time without their "leader": "eleven same/Jesus-Christers unmembered and unmade,/Whose Corpse had died again in dirty shame."

The boy's friends run away, only he remains, and only he goes into the water, a fearful escape. His immersion turns out to be a moment of terrible baptism, though, for when he breaks the surface coming up from his dive, the dead black man is there, visible to his eyes, and he feels an inscrutable urge to follow the "limber corpse" as the sheriff and a stranger "dragged it towards our town." At the conclusion of the poem, the young narrator bears witness to the momentousness of the event, not in moral outrage at its injustice, but in solemn wonderment in the presence of this death, which for some mysterious reason seems "given" for him alone to experience. Why, some four decades after the lynching, does it come back to the poet in his maturity, at the height, in fact, of his creative capacity? This is the way the world appears, Tate seems to be saying, to the sacramental imagination, in the presence of which not only the natural order but one's past experience within that order is recast as a vast field of analogy between lower levels of literal experience and higher levels of spiritual meaning. As a boy witnessing a lynching, he was merely terrified by the event. Now, so much later, after his deep encounter with Dante, Tate sees this incident from his childhood—and potentially every other incident in his past—in a new light or, more accurately, in the light of analogy for the first time. He couldn't have written this poem before his Dantean insight. Now he can, and suddenly the event is weighted with meaning that connects its historical dimension with spiritual significance.

The hanged man takes on the aspect of Christ's sacrifice, the posse, Christ's accusers and killers, yet the lynching, as damnable as it is, bears meaning, not only for the boy, but for his community: "Alone in the public clearing/This private thing was owned by all the town,/Though never claimed by us within my hearing." Tate intends the image to speak analogically, that is, in its own voice, needing no qualifying didactic comment. What in the mature narrator allows him to know that there needs to be no public expiation of the town's guilt is not made explicit. He simply understands that they all acknowledge the injustice, that they all "own" it and are somehow changed by it. Similar to Joe Christmas's murder and mutilation at the end of Faulkner's *Light in August*, this lynching has been buried beneath consciousness in the boy—we might say, in an Augustinian metaphor, preserved in the lake of his heart—until he is spiritually mature enough to summon it from the "swimming-hole" of his youth and give it its analogical due. In the language of "The Symbolic Imagination," the corpse is at once "the body of Christ" and "the body of this death," Tate having found in it "a coherent chain of analogies" that simultaneously reveals both literal and anagogical meanings (*Essays* 428).

Like the first two poems in Tate's sequence, "The Buried Lake" is also a poem of reclamation. It begins by moving backward into the poet's past and inward into the most interior reaches of his mind. In style and tone, "The Buried Lake" closely resembles "The Maimed Man" and in many respects seems an extension of the earlier poem. It, too, begins with an invocation: "Lady of light, I would admit a dream/To you, if you would take it in your hand." Toward the end of the poem Tate identifies the "Lady of light" as Saint Lucy, whose province is vision or enlightenment and who, at the request of Mary, informs Beatrice in *The Divine Comedy* of the lostness of Dante the pilgrim. The poet's request of Lucy here is to accept the telling of his dream, dreamt at her command, as a rite of passage for his deliverance from it. "The Way and the way back are long and rough," he writes, and the blessing of Lucy upon his telling will be proof that he has negotiated his journey in terms that reveal its truth for those to whom he will report it. Here Tate desires as intense and intimate a submission to poetry as the one Dante relates to Bonagiunta da Lucca on Mount Purgatory when he describes the "sweet new style": "I am one who, when Love inspires me, takes note, and goes setting it forth after the fashion which he dictates within me" (24.52-57).

Tate dramatizes that submission toward the end of his poem, and it is like the trembling of Dante's mountain when a soul is released to move upward to the heavens:

> In the tart undersea of slipping night
> The dream whispered, while sight within me, caved,
>
> Deprived, poured stinging dark on cold delight,
> And multitudinous whined invisible bees;
> All grace being lost, and its considering rite,
>
> Till come to midmost May I bent my knees,
> Santa Lucia! at noon—the prudent shore,
> The lake flashing green fins through amber trees—
>
> And knew I had not read your eye before
> You played it in the flowing scale of glance;
> I had not thought that I could read the score,
>
> And yet how vexed, bitter, and hard the trance
> Of light—how I resented Lucy's play!

The humility represented by the bent knees is the vehicle through which the natural world is given to the poet as though for the first time. This glimpse of a new world that will yield meaning by way of light reflected from above, received indirectly, in "the flowing scale of glance," is a sobering prospect. Once he sees that meaning exists and is accessible through analogy, the momentousness of the poetic work increases exponentially. Meaning is everywhere, in everything, in every action past and present, in every event. So the poet rebels at the overwhelming revelation and perceives the vision of light as "vexed, bitter, and hard," leading to a resentment of "Lucy's play!" He considers that it might perhaps be better to "stay dead, better not try the lance." Yet he knows he has been blessed with this vision and accepts it as his privilege and obligation. Once he does so, he understands at once that he will never be spiritually impoverished again, though he will doubtless suffer during times "when the eye is lean." What he knows with certainty, however, is that "nature could not more refine/What it had given in a looking-glass and held there." What he has been given to know, and the means by which he can know it, is sufficient, for he has seen it "part/The palpable air," the air that is both above and below Lucy, whom he addresses as "light Lucy." With a triple repetition of light—"light Lucy," "light of heart," and "Light choir"—and the speaking of the Dove, his dream is done and the darkness fled. His insight overwhelms him as Dante's did him: "I knew that I had known enduring love."

Tate claims much for himself in these final lines of his major poetry, but the claim is grounded in his career-long search for Lucy's light and the means by which to glimpse it. Lucy's mode of vision, with the eye that sees not merely the surface of things but into and through things, is a divine gift imparted to the poet submissive to it. It is in fact the gift of analogy, and the vehicle of its expression is the symbolic imagination. Through Dante's great poem Tate discovered not only that his world is not empty of light but that there is a supervening abundance of it from above, from the invisible realm that the lyric poet is always striving to glimpse. It is there for the seeing if the poet possesses the analogical eye.

In the scope of twentieth-century poetry and criticism, Tate's appropriation of the Dantean imagination is unsurpassed, and its neglect today is lamentable. "The Symbolic Imagination" has disappeared from all major anthologies and is rarely if ever mentioned by Dantists. In a 2001 collection of poets' commentaries called *The Poets' Dante*, for instance, Tate is omitted completely, whereas those included range from predictable figures such as Pound and Eliot to currently practicing poets such as Robert Pinsky and Edward Hirsch. In "Allen Tate and the Garment of Dante," Louise Cowan maintains that Tate not only was allowed to touch "the hem/Of him who spread his triptych like a fan," as he asked of his muse in "The Maimed Man," but at last actually to put on Dante's garment "to hide the nakedness of the modern" (382). In this regard, Cowan says, Tate's achievement "is unique in modern poetry" (377) in the degree to which it reflects Dante's habitual way of perceiving invisible truths through the visible realm of the natural world. However late Tate was in finally coming to his Dantean perspective, his arrival reflected a triumph of the lyric poet's perennial desire to achieve the spiritual through the physical.

NOTES

1. Louise Cowan's thorough and insightful study, *The Fugitive Group*, remains the definitive history of the Fugitive poets, having received their imprimatur upon both its original composition as a dissertation at Vanderbilt University and later its publication as a book by LSU Press. In his introduction to Peter Smith's 1967 publication in a single volume of all numbers of *The Fugitive*, Donald Davidson wrote that *The Fugitive Group* "stands as the one authoritative and reliable history of the magazine and the group up to the year 1928" (iv).

2. Ransom, Davidson, and Tate were the principal spokesmen of the group, though Warren went on to become the most famous of the Fugitives. He was considerably younger, joined the group after the magazine was launched, and didn't figure as prominently in shaping the Fugitive "voice" as the three older poets did. (Ransom was born in 1888, Davidson in 1893, Tate in 1899, and Warren in 1905.)

3. Dupree's *Allen Tate and the Augustinian Imagination* (1983) contains the most detailed and perceptive reading of the three-poem sequence I am treating here. My debt to his close and careful reading will be obvious to anyone familiar with his masterful volume on Tate's poetry.

13

The Harlem Renaissance:
Identity and Poetic Redress

CLAUDIA ALLUMS

In 1903, at the same time that noted African American historian and sociologist W. E. B. Du Bois was collecting data and drafting his important "Talented Tenth" essay, he was also composing what is considered to be his most direct response to the ideas he had resisted in Booker T. Washington's 1895 "Atlanta Exposition Address." Du Bois had been chafing under Washington's urging both races, "Cast down your bucket where you are" (595), and suggesting that a posture of temporary accommodation and a focus on vocational skills would enable African Americans to build a base of economic stability that would *eventually* secure their place in social and political realms. In his "Talented Tenth" essay, Du Bois argued for a more rapid program of civil rights led by an elite cadre of liberally educated African Americans. This debate between Washington's "bottom up" theory and Du Bois's "top down" theory divided the conversation about race at this time, an issue that seemed destined to be deliberated in both political and social arenas of influence.

While his "Talented Tenth" essay speaks, not surprisingly, from a sociologist's perspective, Du Bois's other volume published that same year—*The Souls of Black Folk*, a volume as significant for its form as for its meaning—takes up the issue in a very different vein. He speaks from the authority of his scientific discipline when he presents the problem in the "Forethought," where he writes: "Herein lie buried many things which if read with patience may show the strange meaning of being black here at the dawning of the Twentieth Century. This meaning is not without interest to you, Gentle Reader; for the problem of the Twentieth Century is the problem of the color line." But a few sentences later, when he forecasts the method of his inquiry, the terrain he outlines seems an unusual choice for a sociologist: "I have sought here to sketch in vague, uncertain outline, the spiritual world in which ten thousand thousand Americans live and strive" (3). This book, then, is not like his "Talented Tenth" essay, nor is it like the other essays in the volume in which that essay was first published. *The Negro Problem: A Series of Articles by Representative Negroes of Today* (1903) was a distinguished effort by the leading African American intellectuals of the time who focused on the race issue—the issue *du jour*—with essays that explored both the present and the future status of African Americans in politics, law, and the social order. *The Souls of Black Folk*, to the contrary, is a spiritual exploration in which Du Bois sets his tone with lyrics from the spirituals that in his last chapter he claims to be "the most beautiful expression of experience this side the seas" (180).

Each essay in *The Souls of Black Folk* is introduced with lines of lyric poetry followed by a staff of musical notes from a traditional black spiritual. At the opening of "The Sorrow Songs," his last chapter, Du Bois offers a justification for his choice of topic and his tone: "They that walked in darkness sang songs in the olden days—Sorrow Songs—for they were weary at heart. And so before each thought that I have written in this book I have set a phrase, a haunting echo of these weird old songs in which the soul of the black slave spoke to men" (180). A description later in this same chapter is an obvious declaration of poetic atonement. The songs, Du Bois says, "tell in word and music of trouble and exile, of strife and hiding; they grope toward some unseen power and sigh for rest in the End" (185). In what must have been intended as a rebuke to the narrowness implied in Washington's thrifty, practical worker, Du Bois offers up a vast soul, a lyric lament of an oppressed people. While Washington bestows dignity on the toil of the hands, Du Bois seeks, through poetry, to reclaim for his race the value of simply being and, as William Faulkner was later to say, enduring.

What Du Bois is employing is what Seamus Heaney would identify as the "redress of poetry" (*Redress* 1). In fact, Heaney's claim that poetry is the means of "tilting the scales of reality toward some transcendent equilibrium" (*Redress* 3) echoes Du Bois's insistence, in *The Souls of Black Folk*, that through "all the sorrow of the Sorrow Songs there breathes a hope—a faith in the ultimate justice of things" (188). In poetry, redress eschews revenge. It arrives rather at what we might call its justice through a balancing of the scales—by a transmutation of painful and unjust circumstances so that where before was ugliness, now by a strange alchemy are beauty and form. It is nothing new, of course, for a people to see poetry as their means to rectify, even in some sense to avenge, social and political wrongs. Beginning in the last part of the nineteenth century, the Irish literary renaissance was such a movement. In America in the 1920s and 1930s, the literature and literary theory of the Southern Renascence changed the course of letters in the twentieth century. But it, too, was a "redress of poetry," in part against such critics as H. L. Mencken, who claimed in his 1920 essay "The Sahara of the Bozart" that the culture and intellect of the South were the most barren and provincial in this intellectually barren and provincial country. Arising at this same time was the Harlem Renaissance, a flourishing of arts and culture from circumstances of defeat and marginalization that seemed to belie, like the Southern Renascence, the likelihood of its occurrence. These artistic surges all attest to the authority of the poetic voice. But considering the history of gospel and spiritual songs, with their elaborately coded and deeply meaningful lyrics, one sees that the exercise of lyric redress has always been an important resource within the African American tradition. Taken in this light, the more formal body of black lyrics produced during the Harlem Renaissance seems a natural extension of the gospel tradition. Although, like any similar resurgence, such a movement was an extraordinary occurrence, it may actually have been a logical conclusion to a longstanding tradition of an African American poetic sense of rectification for wrongs suffered. Its story needs to be included in any account attempting to examine the relation of lyric poetry to its communal origins.

But in spite of the blues and gospel traditions, poetry seemed an unlikely means of vindication for African Americans in the early years of the twentieth century. The "Negro problem," as it was called by intellectuals from all races, was taken up in the new social sciences and hotly debated in political arenas. In spite of Du Bois's soulful claims in 1903, perhaps the idea of poetic redress was too closely associated to slavery for the African Americans at that time, who seemed to be defining themselves apart from their painful past, lyric redress included. Certainly, beginning with the introduction of the Jim Crow laws in 1876, political and social agendas may have seemed to suggest the most necessary avenues for action. Consequently, Washington founded the National Negro Business

League in 1901 and, in collaboration with other prominent black leaders, the National Association for the Advancement of Colored People in 1909 and the National Urban League the following year. In addition to these organizations, the "Back-to-Africa" movement of the 1910s, directed in America by Jamaican Marcus Garvey and his American chapter of the Universal Negro Improvement Association, provided African Americans with an outlet for political and social aspirations. In 1915, the increasing violence of the Ku Klux Klan prompted the "Great Black Migration" from the South to northern industrialized cities, with large numbers of African Americans settling in Harlem. A general postwar unrest in 1919 prompted an eruption of racially motivated attacks across the country, creating a violent social and political ferment that extended far beyond the southern cities (D. Lewis, Introduction xxii). It was no surprise, then, that from a year before the 1905 death of the widely read African American poet Paul Laurence Dunbar until 1922, when Jamaican-born poet Claude McKay brought out *Harlem Shadows*, no significant volumes of lyric poetry were published by American people of African descent (D. Lewis, Introduction xv).

In the midst of this political and social turmoil or, we might say, *because of* it, protest began again in poetic language within the African American community, and New York became the logical setting for this passionate verbal response. The combination of the rapidly expanding African American population in Harlem and the "fusion" of what David Levering Lewis calls the "two bohemias—Harlem and Greenwich Village" (Preface xvii) provided an environment for creative expression in drama that opened the way. In 1917, the "public announcement of the rediscovered Negro" (D. Lewis, Introduction xviii) occurred when the production of three one-act plays about African Americans by white playwright Ridgeley Torrence was spectacularly received by white audiences at the Old Garden Street Theater. These plays were significant in representing a new style of drama, "where the casts were black and the parts were dignified" (D. Lewis, Introduction xviii). Other similarly spirited plays followed with a new wave of African American composers and playwrights.

In the wake of this new mode of expression, the lyric began to appear as protest when, a few years later, as an angry response to the race violence of 1919, Claude McKay wrote the pivotal poem "If We Must Die," voicing the anguish of what Heaney calls the "potential that is denied or constantly threatened by circumstances" (*Redress* 4). Widely quoted, the poem came to serve as an anthem of dignity and self-respect for African Americans:

> If we must die, let it not be like hogs
> Hunted and penned in an inglorious spot,
> While round us bark the mad and hungry dogs,
> Making their mock at our accursed lot.
> If we must die, O let us nobly die,
> So that our precious blood may not be shed
> In vain; then even the monsters we defy
> Shall be constrained to honor us though dead!
> O kinsmen! we must meet the common foe!
> Though far outnumbered let us show us brave,
> And for their thousand blows deal one deathblow!
> What though before us lies the open grave?
> Like men we'll face the murderous, cowardly pack,
> Pressed to the wall, dying, but fighting back!
> (Gates and McKay 1007)

Echoing Du Bois's claims for the capacity of his liberally educated "Talented Tenth," Henry Louis Gates suggests that McKay's classical education enabled him to write poems such as this, that so effectively bridged seemingly irreconcilable attitudes and gave him his capacity for redress. McKay thus combined an "explosive condemnation of bigotry and oppression" (Gates and McKay 1003) with his favorite poetic style, the sonnet, and was able to accommodate the sensibilities of both.

McKay's powerful lyric, like Torrence's drama a few years earlier, served as another "watershed" in the African American community, expressing a sense of being excluded, not only from political society, but from the lyric realm itself, that "happy garden state" in which men and women come to know themselves truly through poetry. In response, there were dramatic productions that portrayed the dignity and intelligence of the race and poems following McKay's that articulated the heroic emotions of an oppressed people. African Americans were finally being presented as human beings, as men and women, and as a people, in a new and positive light.

Detractors unaware of the authority of the poetic voice sometimes criticize African American leaders of that day for their seemingly naïve turn to the arts instead of politics as the means for defining African

American culture. Whether or not these early leaders fully understood the *nature* of poetic redress, however, they certainly understood its *impact*. The men David Levering Lewis calls the "deans" of the Harlem Renaissance saw, at this significant moment, "a unique opportunity to tap into the American mainstream" (Introduction xx), and during the height of the movement (from around 1919 to 1935), art and poetry became the "official" means by which a burgeoning African American culture would present and define itself to the nation and the world. With it, the Harlem Renaissance—stylish, smart, sophisticated yet naïve, like its medium, the lyric—was born. Lewis identifies three stages of the movement. The first, from 1917 to 1923, began with Torrence's plays and ended with the publication of Jean Toomer's "unique prose poem *Cane*." It was a period when white "Bohemians and Revolutionaries," as Lewis identifies them, showed a particular and unprecedented interest in the "life of black people." In the next stage, from early 1924 to 1926, the African American establishment put its efforts behind the movement and actively recruited African American writers and artists to participate in the movement of rectification. Considering the poetic sensibilities of these "Talented Tenth" leaders, men like Du Bois and James Weldon Johnson, however, their "enthusiastic, and programmatic embrace of arts and letters" may not have been quite as "abrupt" as Lewis claims (Introduction xx). The last stage of the Harlem Renaissance extended from 1926 to 1935, when, according to Lewis, it "was increasingly dominated by African American artists themselves" (Introduction xv-xvi).

In the second stage of the movement, the association between "politics" and art was no longer covert. Alain Locke makes clear the political-poetic connection between the struggle of the African Americans and other "nascent movements of folk-expression and self-determination" that he saw as playing an important part in the world at the time, as he says in his Foreword to the 1925 volume *The New Negro* (xxvii). In his signature essay in the volume, "The New Negro," he claims Harlem as "the home of the Negro's 'Zionism'" (14). Perhaps more strikingly he asserts, "Without pretense to their political significance, Harlem has the same rôle to play for the New Negro as Dublin has had for the New Ireland or Prague for the New Czechoslovakia" (7). These claims on Locke's part prompt Lewis to point, disapprovingly, at what he calls an "ideology of cultural nationalism at the heart of the Renaissance" (Introduction xxvi), but clearly Locke is not emphasizing a mere political construct but rather evoking the nature of a people's creative voice out of which a "political" identity can emerge.

In the preface to an earlier anthology entitled *The Book of American Negro Poetry*, published in 1922, James Weldon Johnson had also connected the movement in African American arts and letters with the Irish when he declared, "What the colored poet in the United States needs to do is something like what Synge did for the Irish; he needs to find a form that will express the racial spirit by symbols from within rather than by symbols from without, such as the mere mutilation of English spelling and pronunciation" (902). Johnson might have read the early Yeats, but he had surely heard of, if he had not actually seen, J. M. Synge's production of *The Playboy of the Western World* when it premiered in New York in 1911. In *The Harlem and Irish Renaissances* (1998), Tracy Mishkin explains the controversy that Synge inspired as involving his "irreverence and biting social commentary," asserting that "his dialect and characters were literary inventions in a country hungry for and expecting realistic representations of speech and person" (17). Mishkin convincingly outlines the connection, both political and poetic, between the Irish and the African American struggles for freedom and identity.

Synge's one-page preface to his play is really a defense of folk language and of the spirit of "fancy" lent to their creative expression by a people still connected to their folk tradition. He speaks of his debt "to the folk imagination of these fine people," the "country people of Ireland." He concludes, "In Ireland we have a popular imagination that is fiery and magnificent, and tender; so that those of us who wish to write start with a chance that is not given to writers in places where the springtime of the local life has been forgotten, and the harvest is a memory only, and the straw has been turned into bricks." He is describing a lyrical voice unspoiled by civilization, what Lewis alludes to, in another context, as the fundamental potential of the marginalized African American culture in the early twentieth century. The African American, he says, "was a perfect symbol of cultural innocence and regeneration" because of having been "excluded" from the American "factory, campus, office, and corporation," which had by this time become "dehumanizing, stultifying, or predatory" (Introduction xviii). Lewis intends this statement to underline the irony of the country's cultural need for the very people it had oppressed. But Locke and others in the movement saw this cultural innocence as a strength for the African American people, what Locke called the "very heart of the folk-spirit" that provided the "essential forces" of the "folk interpretation [that] is truly vital and representative," only "in terms of the internal world of the Negro mind and spirit" (Foreword xxv).

Thus, though the Harlem Renaissance represents a general flourishing of the arts, it is largely known for its literary achievement. This recognition may be due to the dominating influence of the leading "Talented Tenth" and of its white patrons, who, as intellectuals and philanthropists, were interested in laying a formal foundation of African American letters on which to build a cultural identity. And in their attempt to focus on an intellectual and poetic tradition, they actually neglected the distinctly African American forms of music that were developing at the same time. Public opinion finally made it impossible for the "deans" to ignore jazz, ragtime, and blues, forms that ultimately had an inestimable effect on American poetry (D. Lewis, Introduction xv). But some of the most influential African American leaders undeniably understood the potential for redress in the *poetic* voice. In the first paragraphs of his preface to *The Book of American Negro Poetry*, James Weldon Johnson begins with an acknowledgment of the power of *poiesis*:

> A people may become great through many means, but there is only one measure by which its greatness is recognized and acknowledged. The final measure of the greatness of all peoples is the amount and standard of the literature and art they have produced. The world does not know that a people is great until that people produces great literature and art. No people that has produced great literature and art has ever been looked upon by the world as distinctly inferior.

The cultural attitude toward African Americans, Johnson maintains, was somewhat disparaging; but, as he claims, "nothing will do more to change that mental attitude and raise his status than a demonstration of intellectual parity by the Negro through the production of literature and art" (Gates and McKay 883). Johnson's anthology is a collection of African American poetry up to the time of his volume, he says, not because the works are equal in excellence, but rather, as he states near the end of his preface, because their voices, like the voices of other peoples, are needed and have been unheard (Gates and McKay 905).

Published three years after *Harlem Shadows,* McKay's 1922 volume of poetry, Locke's *The New Negro* represented for many the creative talent and burgeoning potential of American Blacks. Not only did it offer to a curious public evidence of the reality of African American creativity in arts and letters, but it also was taken by many and actually proclaimed itself to be a volume of redress, a herald of a new order. Locke's foreword begins: "This volume aims to document the New Negro culturally and socially—to register the transformations of the inner and outer life of the Negro in America that have so significantly taken place in the last years" (xxv). His last paragraph reveals a conviction about the significance of the movement and the importance of a record of its creativity: "Negro life," he asserts, "is not only establishing new contacts and founding new centers, it is finding a new soul. There is a fresh spiritual and cultural focusing. We have, as the heralding sign, an unusual outburst of creative expression. There is a renewed race-spirit that consciously and proudly sets itself apart. Justifiably then, we speak of the offerings of this book embodying these ripening forces as culled from the first fruits of the Negro Renaissance" (xxvii).

A professor of philosophy at Howard University, Locke had studied modern literature, and if his contributions to the volume represent his true sensibilities, as they seem to, he understood the authority of the poetic imagination. Although not himself a poet, his perspective is imaginative, as evidenced in the beginning of the foreword by phrases such as "finding a new soul," "ripening forces," and "first fruits." And his essay entitled "The New Negro," instead of resorting to statistics as proof of his social and political claims about the age, as one might expect, uses lyric poems to make his important points. When he speaks of the "promise and warrant of a new leadership," he connects his comments to the "life-attitudes and self-expression of the Young Negro, in his poetry, his art, his education, and his new outlook," by citing Langston Hughes's poem "Youth":

> We have tomorrow
> Bright before us
> Like a flame.
>
> Yesterday, a night-gone thing
> A sun-down name.

> And dawn today
> Broad arch above the road we came.
> We march!
>
> (5)

To express what he calls the "variations of mood" among the "thinking Negro," Locke quotes poems by Claude McKay and James Weldon Johnson (12-13). In the second part of *The New Negro*, Locke solicited what literary critic Arnold Rampersad calls essays of "social studies of a particular kind." In prose that "fastidiously eschews statistics in favor of artful, reflective, anecdotal essays" (Locke xvii), sociology is poeticized, made similar in tone and form to the imaginative use of poetry in Du Bois's *The Souls of Black Folk*. Among those essays are "The Gift of the Black Tropics," in which the Caribbean immigrant activist W. A. Domingo concludes his essay with the last two lines of McKay's "If We Must Die" (Locke 349), giving the lyric voice the last say, the last vindication in his argument. Locke injects lyrics throughout the volume to set the tone for a section or, as he had done in the first essay, to punctuate a point. He goes so far as to use Countée Cullen's poem "Heritage" as an entire "essay" in the section entitled "The Negro Digs Up His Past" (Locke 250-53). In a nostalgia exposing the conflict of identity that Derek Walcott picks up in his lyric "A Far Cry from Africa" in 1962, Cullen's narrator begins "Heritage" with a question, "What is Africa to me[?]," and answers with Edenic description:

> Copper sun, a scarlet sea,
> Jungle star and jungle track,
> Strong bronzed men and regal black
> Women from whose loins I sprang
> When the birds of Eden sang?
> *One three centuries removed*
> *From the scenes his fathers loved*
> *Spicy grove and banyan tree,*
> *What is Africa to me?*
>
> (Locke 250)

Somewhat overestimated by one critic as the "Black *Waste Land*," Cullen's poem is nevertheless an exercise of lyrical redress in which the narrator wrestles with being caught between two worlds of faith defined by race. He even ends the poem with an acknowledgment of his awareness of redress as a state of mind: "Lord, forgive me if my need/Sometimes shapes a human creed" (Locke 253). Given that the rest of the volume is largely made up of art, lyric poems, short stories, music, and excerpts from novels and dramas, all intended to "let the Negro speak for himself," as Locke has said (xxv), the voice of the volume when taken as a whole is distinctly a voice of *redress* and, in Locke's mind, fundamentally poetic.

Rampersad suggests that the volume underrepresents the full range of African American culture of the day (as if any one volume could adequately undertake this task in any age), but he begins his own remarks in his introduction with the admission that *The New Negro* is still considered by scholars and critics as the "definitive text" of the Harlem Renaissance, the "Bible" of the movement. Further, he concedes, "Most of the participants in the movement probably held the book in similar regard" (Locke ix). And in spite of his scornful branding of *The New Negro* itself as the "Talented Tenth in liaison with its Mainstream analogues" and his insistence that the "course of American letters was unchanged by the offerings in *The New Negro*" (Locke xxvii), he *also* makes this concession: "Yet it seemed to work, for although the objective conditions confronting most African Americans in Harlem and elsewhere were deteriorating, optimism remained high. Harlem recoiled from Garveyism and socialism to applaud Phi Beta Kappa poets, university-trained painters, concertizing musicians, and novel-writing officers of civil rights organizations" (Locke xxviii). As a cultural declaration, the volume "worked," to use Lewis's term, because in spite of the uneven quality of its contributions, its commitment to *poiesis* provided the creative landscape out of which the race sought to find its voice and inner being.

It seems reasonable, then, to think of the lyrics that Locke selected for the "Poetry" section of *The New Negro* in the same light in which we are asked to view the entire volume, as "first fruits of the Negro Renaissance," and to see it as a conscious effort of reparation for the African American people at that critical point in their history. Locke's choice of poetry is as interesting for the poems that he excluded as it is for the ones he selected. While he includes in the volume drama and prose written in dialect, in the poetry section no lyric is written in dialect. Until the death of Dunbar in 1906, dialect lyric and prose had formed the base of the African American poetic tradition. However, dialect was too closely associated with the historical language of the slave for the interests of the "Talented Tenth," who saw it as working against their desires to elevate the intellectual reach of the race beyond its oppressed, if familiar, past. In his introduction to *The Book of American Negro Poetry*, Johnson had articulated this tension between "Negro dialect" and his desire for the future of African American letters. He first describes an "artistic niche" for which "dialect" is the "exact instrument" for "voicing this phase of life," the "happy-go-lucky, singing, shuffling, banjo-picking being." However, he explains, "there are phases of Negro life in the United States which cannot be treated in the dialect either adequately or artistically" (Gates and McKay 901-2). Johnson goes on to speak of his hopes for the day when the "colored poet in the United States may sit down to write in dialect without feeling that his first line will put the general reader in a frame of mind" (Gates and McKay 902) of the "two full stops" of dialect writing, "humor and pathos" (Gates and McKay 901). But when he describes dialect here as "the mere mutilation of English spelling and pronunciation," he reveals the "Tenth's" bias that spurred some in the next generation of Harlem Renaissance writers in the 1920s, such as Zora Neale Hurston, to rebel and recover dialect for its own beauty of prose style. However, even younger poets disdained the use of dialect, like McKay, who had achieved fame in his homeland Jamaica by publishing books of dialect poetry in 1912 when he was barely twenty-three but wrote no more poetry in dialect once he came to the United States.

As a result of this sensitivity to dialect, all the poems in *The New Negro* are stately and at times artificial. Johnson's poem in the volume, "The Creation," is patterned after African American folk sermons, but the language and tone are reserved and dignified. Compared to Dunbar's earlier preacher in "An Ante-Bellum Sermon," Johnson's preacher comes from a different world. The former seeks justice for the injustices of the world in a "hellfire and brimstone" conclusion:

> But when Moses wif his powah
>   Comes an' sets us chillun free,
> We will praise de gracious Mastah
>   Dat has gin us liberty;
> An' we'll shout ouah halleluyahs,
>   On dat mighty reck'nin' day,

> When we'se reco'nised ez citiz' —
> Huh uh! Chillun, let us pray!
>
> (Gates and McKay 914)

Johnson's preacher offers a different kind of rectification, a story in verse, a stately reflection about the creation of the world. The closest that Johnson's preacher comes to dialect or to anything distinctly African American is near the end of the penultimate stanza, when he says,

> This Great God,
> Like a mammy bending over her baby,
> Kneeled down in the dust
> Toiling over a lump of clay
> Till He shaped it in His own image....
>
> (Locke 141)

Another interesting artistic exclusion from the "Poetry" section of *The New Negro* is Langston Hughes's innovative poem "The Weary Blues," published in 1923, in which he attempted to create a distinctly African American lyric by fusing it with jazz rhythms. Instead, among other poems by Hughes, Locke chose "The Negro Speaks of Rivers," which was the young poet's first published work and one that had the added benefit of having been dedicated to Du Bois. To maintain the particular tone of vindication that he was seeking in the volume, Locke also avoided the scorching voice of invective. This restriction meant that he had to select carefully from among Claude McKay's works. He actually changed the title of McKay's "The White House" to a less offensive "White Houses" without McKay's permission, which seriously damaged his longtime relationship with the young poet (Locke xxii). Although he did not select McKay's "America," in which the speaker expresses (for McKay) a rather uncharacteristic ambivalence for the country, Locke also did not include McKay's militant sonnet "If We Must Die" in the volume. By avoiding these uniquely African American styles and extreme voices, Locke side-stepped the polemics that they invite, achieving, one might say, a broader voice of race pride mingled only with an understandable discontent. While the poems in *The New Negro* do not express extremes, they must have expressed a voice that Locke believed could lay a foundation for a people whose suffering and joy had been ignored and whose imagination and intellect had been denied.

What Locke's entire volume *does* represent, according to Rampersad, is all the major voices, both young and old, of the Harlem Renaissance writing at that time (Locke xiii). In the "Poetry" section, Locke included poems by women: Georgia Douglas Johnson, Angelina Grimké, and Anne Spencer, the established African American women poets of the day. Among these choices, Grimké's "The Black Finger" is the most interesting and refined as an instance of redress:

> I have just seen a most beautiful thing
>   Slim and still,
>   Against a gold, gold sky,
>   A straight black cypress,
>   Sensitive,
>   Exquisite,
>   A black finger
> Pointing upwards.
> Why, beautiful still finger, are you black?
> And why are you pointing upwards?
>
>   (Locke 148)

None of the poems in the "Poetry" section are dated, so Locke was not attempting to represent them in historical order or as a linear progression of thought. Like the material presented in the other sections of the volume, the poems are offered without introductions or explanations, so a critical bias is avoided and the ideas and images are called upon to speak for themselves.

In spite of the restrained tone of the lyrics in the "Poetry" section of *The New Negro*, injustice is one of its primary topics. Of the thirty-three poems presented, more than half are about the racial tension in which the African American lived, from the burdens of the enslaved past to the bigotry of the present. In its less potent forms, injustice is presented in poems of gentle lament, such as Cullen's "Fruit of the Flower," Toomer's "Song of the Son," and Hughes's "I, Too," along with McKay's "The Tropics in New York" and Hughes's "Our Land," which are both written in the tradition of exile songs. In "Our Land," the speaker's refrain "We should" expresses the longing of a people denied place and dignity:

> We should have a land of sun,
> Of gorgeous sun,
> And a land of fragrant water
> Where the twilight is a soft bandanna handkerchief
> Of rose and gold,
> And not this land
> Where life is cold.
>
> ...
>
> Ah, we should have a land of joy,
> Of love and joy and wine and song,
> And not this land where joy is wrong.
>
> (Locke 144)

The speaker is longing for Africa, his native land, with the same tone as the singer in the first verses of Psalm 137. The speakers in both lyrics, Hughes's and the Hebrew singer's, long for the garden state, a place of peace and identity:

> By the rivers of Babylon, there we sat down, yea, we wept, when
> we remembered Zion....
> For there they that carried us away captive required of us a song...
> saying, Sing us one of the songs of Zion.
> How shall we sing the LORD's song in a strange land?

Along with these tender laments in this section, a few poems, though still constrained, reflect more rigorous attitudes of castigation for injustice. The narrator in Cullen's "Tableau" speaks with a detached coldness about the skeptical reaction from both races toward an interracial friendship, but his "Harlem Wine" is a revolt against those who would constrain the "thick rebellious streams/That hurtle flesh and bone past fear/Down alleyways of dreams" (Locke 130). As one might expect, McKay's are the most defiant lyrics here. His "Baptism" and "The White House" (or "White Houses") attack both races for their apathy and lethargy in the racial fight. In "Baptism," which is clearly directed at his less socially active African American brothers, the narrator taunts: "Into the furnace let me go alone;/Stay you without in terror of the heat." In the closing lines, he speaks triumphantly: "I will come out, back to your world of tears,/A stronger soul within a finer frame" (Locke 133). In "The White House," the narrator's venom is turned toward the white political order that keeps him enslaved.

Among the themes in this "Poetry" section of the volume, the other primary focus is the physical body, the body of the African American that had been commodified and abused throughout the history of enslavement. Countée Cullen's "To a Brown Girl" and "To a Brown Boy" are a bold way to begin this section because of the physical lustiness conveyed in their *carpe diem* tone. Not only was Locke apparently not afraid to associate members of his race with passions of which they had been excessively accused during their enslaved history, but he also allows Cullen's poems to celebrate the particular sensuality and energy of "brown" youth. With a Herrick-like wit, "To a Brown Girl" reads:

> What if his glance is bold and free,
>   His mouth the lash of whips?
> So should the eyes of lovers be,
>   And so a lover's lips.
>
> What if no puritanic strain
>   Confines him to the nice?
> He will not pass this way again
>   Nor hunger for you twice.
>
> Since in the end consort together
>   Magdalen and Mary,
> Youth is the time for careless weather;
>   Later, lass, be wary.
>
> (Locke 129)

"To a Brown Boy," the poem Cullen dedicated to Langston Hughes, is the masculine perspective on the situation presented in the "Girl" poem and intensifies the action of physical desire. The poems introduce a more sophisticated tension beyond the body, however, with allusions to the "puritanic strain" and "Magdalen and Mary" in the first poem, and in the second, the claim is made that brown "lips know better how to kiss/Than how to raise white hymns" (Locke 129). These images and the sensual energy remain playful in both poems, primarily because of their focus on a "girl" and a "boy," so that the youth to which Locke had dedicated the volume are cast here in a passionate and vibrant light. The freedom and pleasure of the "brown" and "black" bodies are celebrated in a number of the poems in this section, from these first two to the last three: Cullen's "She of the Dancing Feet Sings" is joined by Langston Hughes's "Walkers with the sun and morning" in his lyric "Poem" (Locke 142), as well as by Hughes's sometimes frenetic speaker in "Dream Variation" who longs "To fling [his] arms wide/In some place of the sun,/To whirl and to dance/Till the bright day is done" (Locke 143). Of the physical actions illustrated in the poems, many are represented with tenderness, as in Hughes's "Song," when the narrator implores the "child of night" to "Bare [her] bosom to the sun" (Locke 143). Others convey respect, as in Jean Toomer's "Georgia Dusk," where the "men, with vestiges of pomp,/Race memories of king and caravan/.../Go singing through the footpaths of the swamp" (Locke 136), and in Anne Spencer's "Lady, Lady," whose hands are praised for enduring their interminable service, washing clothes in a "sudsy tub" (Locke 148). Like Hughes's "The Negro Speaks of Rivers," poems such as McKay's "Like a Strong Tree" associate the body with archetypal images of strength and stability:

> Like a strong tree that in the virgin earth
> Sends far its roots through rock and loam and clay,
> And proudly thrives in rain or time of dearth,
> ...
> So would I live in rich imperial growth,
> Touching the surface and the depth of things,
> Instinctively responsive unto both,
> Tasting the sweets of being and the stings,
> Sensing the subtle spell of changing forms,
> Like a strong tree against a thousand storms.
>
> (Locke 134)

Locke also includes in this section more intellectual themes in poems about death, worship, and nature. As a whole, however, the focus of the redress of the poems here is on "brown" and "black" bodies dancing, laughing, lusting, mourning, loving, singing, working, dying. In this lyric expression, "brown" and "black" African American bodies are restored to a community and to the humanity that, for centuries, they had been tragically denied. The poem that Locke chose to conclude the "Poetry" section of his volume is particularly interesting in that the bodies represented in Lewis Alexander's "Enchantment" are not just "black"; they are native Africans dancing to enchanted drums. In the "Medicine Dance" section of the poem, there is "A body smiling with black beauty/Leaping into the air." It is "A black body—dancing with beauty/Clothed in African moonlight,/Smiling more beauty into its body" (Locke 149-50). In the end, the "black body clothed in moonlight/Raises up its head," confident of its power and right. As a result, the poem concludes, "Terror reigns like a new crowned king" (150). So Locke ends his lyrical vindication here with a complicated image of the "black" body that is not domesticated by the Western world. This body is strong and mysterious, powerful and fleet, proud and strange. *This* "black beauty" is not nor has it ever been enslaved, and so with "face dancing in delight," it inspires something other than servile defeat.

In spite of the protests of its politically active detractors, the imaginative, poetic voices of both *The New Negro* and the Harlem Renaissance had an immediate as well as a lasting impact, continuing to show how a rather minor lyric voice can have a major influence in culture. As in other traditions, the next generations of African American poets such as Robert Hayden, Jay Wright, Yusef Komunyakaa, Rita Dove, and Lucille Clifton speak not only with their own graceful, strong voices but rise, as T. S. Eliot in his "Tradition and the Individual Talent" would have it, off the shoulders of those who came before. The lyrics of the Harlem Renaissance and particularly those from *The New Negro*, its defining "poetic" document, were a noble effort of redress, especially for African Americans, who were seeking a voice, seeking a *people* out of a tragic history of injustice and suffering.

14

Awake at the Top of the Mast:
Elizabeth Bishop's "The Unbeliever" and Lyric Identity

Mary Di Lucia

Was there ever a time when becoming a poet could be a conscious professional choice rather than a gift of the Muses? More than at any other time in the history of poetry, the contemporary American lyric poet holds this unusual position; professional self-fashioning by poets can seem at times even more important than the very soul of their work. At the outset of her career in the mid-twentieth century, several decades before the establishment of the first creative writing M.F.A. programs, Elizabeth Bishop was part of what shaped this sociocultural phenomenon: she was among the young college graduates who wanted to be poets and who believed they had the talent and the connections to call down the laurels, if not the Muses. Bishop understood deeply what becoming a poet would require in pragmatic terms; she finessed the publication history, the prizes, the patrons, the cultivation of a readership. But were these the most pressing of her concerns? How deeply would she also reckon with the tradition that lay both before her and, existentially speaking, beneath her?

Part of Bishop's unique role in shaping the identity of the lyric poet is her almost spiritual understanding of the power of tradition as her "school" and her willingness to lay the foundations of a conversation between her muse and tradition so early in her life as a poet. Her early notebooks reveal her reverence for the mysticism of her "profession," while at the same time she remained remarkably unflustered by the increasingly pragmatic demands of American poetry. Her poem "The Unbeliever" emerges at this moment, and it addresses the questions every lyric poet must ask as she accustoms herself to her perch between the earth and the sky. First of all, and notable in Bishop's case, the earth above which the speaker and the poet perch in this poem is covered by the ocean. As she gazes outwards over this vista, questions arise. What will this poet's song be about—will it be the whales? Will it be the stars? Will it be the song of what the poet fears she will see by falling to the bottom of that ocean which covers the visible world? And who can survive that fall unchanged? Is it merely an occupational hazard that every poet falls to the bottom of the ocean when her job is to sing out whales, and her comfort is to sing out stars?

Or is that the job itself—to fall to the bottom of the ocean, and to come to the surface, and to sing what one has seen? To lose one's self wherein one has fallen and not to be distracted by that loss but only possessed by what one has seen?

Part of what Bishop did, in the writing of "The Unbeliever," was respond to the tradition she had steeped herself in with the kind of song only she could sing. What else could any true lyric poet do? But tradition is never that simple: not only was Bishop reading Herbert and Crashaw, but she was also reading Stevens—and Melville, another lyric soul, who almost a century earlier negotiated his own identity as a lyric novelist. Did Melville write the novel in which Bishop saw herself appearing? As I reflect on Bishop's early relationship to her muse and to her tradition, I begin to understand it that way—to imagine that lyric poets fashion themselves from figures of literature. That is, in their performance of the encounter between the literal and the figurative, they bring literature to life in a way that demands both imagination and suffering, as Bishop became first Pip, then Crusoe.

Perhaps the space of the lyric poet in this century and the one just passed is the space of Pip: the poet cannot escape by partaking of a modest encounter with tradition and with the demands of publication; he must almost drown himself in these dry pragmatic matters. Yet in so losing his identity to such earthly concerns, and in thus losing all he sought in desiring to make poems in the first place, he still somehow, even miraculously, gains the identity of the lyric poet. The ocean of demands becomes the soul of the world; his voice is its voice, no longer his. It has baptized him. The lyric tradition, here in the world of the unbeliever, still manages to emerge as a sacred tradition.

The Unbeliever

He sleeps on the top of a mast. — Bunyan

He sleeps on the top of a mast
with his eyes fast closed.
The sails fall away below him
like the sheets of his bed,
leaving out in the air of the night the sleeper's head.

Asleep he was transported there,
asleep he curled
in a gilded ball on the mast's top,
or climbed inside
a gilded bird, or blindly seated himself astride.

"I am founded on marble pillars,"
said a cloud. "I never move.
See the pillars there in the sea?"
Secure in introspection
he peers at the watery pillars of his reflection.

A gull had wings under his
and remarked that the air
was "like marble." He said: "Up here
I tower through the sky
for the marble wings on my tower-top fly."

But he sleeps on the top of his mast
with his eyes closed tight.
The gull inquired into his dream,
which was, "I must not fall.
The spangled sea below wants me to fall.
It is hard as diamonds; it wants to destroy us all."

When Elizabeth Bishop's poem "The Unbeliever" (*Complete Poems* 22) appeared in the *Partisan Review* in July of 1938, the young poet was already a believer—in herself, in her powers as a poet, and in the notion that with the proper discipline of reading, attention to life, mentoring and travel, she could and would indeed produce poems. She was also an unbeliever, for in making this intention to the universe, Bishop also knew that inherent within it was failure, the fear that all this belief would result in nothing, no poems, no perseverance, no art, nothing for others to read. At the age of twenty-seven, she had already graduated Vassar, struck up her legendary mentoring relationship with Marianne Moore, begun her study of the clavichord and her travels across the ocean, and more or less commenced upon her own self-defined sense of what a poet's life should look like, or what she would need to do in order to become a serious poet, as if such a thing were ordinary and possible. In addition to these pursuits, Bishop, who had lost both her parents, had also drunk deeply of the well of despair and the well of homelessness, two defining conditions not accidentally paired here in the metaphorical language of drinking. These three personal motifs also informed her development as a poet and as a human being even this early in her life.

Although a poet engages in part in an unconscious and intuitive process, communing with both the universe and the existing lineage of poets in each act of creation, there are no accidents in poetry. The influences not only of the literary atmosphere but also of the physical landscape, personal relationships, and the poet's individual experience, of course, all shape a poetry and a poem. The poet's primary tool is the ear, not just in terms of prosody and sound, but also as an "organ" of absorption through which reverberate the sounds of the universe—an ambitious, modernist harp strung across a river between two cities full of workers, in the case of Hart Crane; Whitman's thrush in the swamp, despite Eliot's desire to escape its song; flashes of Keats's urn incarnate amidst Stevens' carnations—and also the works of other poets, their imagery, sounds, rhyme, turns of phrase, melodies, tune, as if the poet's ear were also a kind of transcendental radio, trying to tune in to the news of the universe. Arguably, as a poet matures into her own poetry, these influences become transformed through more complex functions of the poetic process; the works, ideas, sounds, and images of others appear less evidently in the poet's works, the influences resembling icebergs rather than volcanoes, their considerable substance sinking deep and invisibly below the surface of a poem. Yet all poets partake of the same universe. The same families and themes of images appear uncannily across poems over time, as if not only poems conversed with other poems, incessantly, but also the poets who wrote those poems always spoke with one another about the same things, or poets noticed the same things about their environments: the other song makers (the birds); the sublime in nature and culture (oceans, skyscrapers); the homely (lilacs, woodpiles, swamps). Scholars have used the language of the "eye" to describe Bishop's art, her remarkable gifts of observation, her visual precision,[1] but her early poem "The Unbeliever" does not inhabit this same visual world; rather, this poem resonates with the "ear" of the young poet and what that ear listened to in the echo-chamber of its early apprenticeship to poetry.

Critical Overview

Bishop's poem "The Unbeliever" provides a rare and clear opportunity to explore her influences, partly in its use of an epigraph and partly because it is written by a strong poet at an early stage of her development. For the purposes of this essay, I will limit my exploration of these influences to passages from John Bunyan's *Pilgrim's Progress*,[2] the Book of Proverbs from the Bible, and Melville's *Moby-Dick*, as well as a few secondary and biographical motifs. This analysis reveals patterns that were true not only for Bishop but also for poems negotiating the differential zone between literal and figurative language, with the resulting destabilizations of rhetoric.

The critical conversation about "The Unbeliever" begins as far back as Marianne Moore's initial review of Bishop's first collection, *North & South*, where the poem appeared. Moore's review praised the musical qualities of Bishop's poems, an effect achieved by avoiding the closure of rhyme in place of "alliteration or the reiterated words to suggest the reaching after meaning" (Kalstone 100-101). By "meaning" Moore probably understood the "meaning" of religious belief, the "meaning" of spirituality. Some critics have discarded "The Unbeliever" as an exercise of youth, "a weird experiment" in Anne Stevenson's words (77), and certainly there has been much written elsewhere about Bishop's early readings of Herbert, Donne, Hopkins, and other poets who addressed questions of religion and spirituality.

In her discussion of the material, Bonnie Costello, the eminent critic of Bishop, places "The Unbeliever" in relation to another poem of the same period, Bishop's "Imaginary Iceberg," and pairs both poems with Melville's heavily alliterative "The Berg" as the precursor text that haunts the memory of both. She speaks for many critics when she reads all three poems as comments on the sublime as well as upon the nature of human spiritual belief. After all, the title of the poem is "The Unbeliever," the epigraph quotes a spiritual allegorical text (*Pilgrim's Progress*), and the general stanzaic structure and some of the language seem to be borrowed from the Metaphysical tradition, all of which indicate a primarily religious allegorical interpretation of the poem. If, as Costello implies, the poem is chiefly of allegorical interest, then the mast-sitting primary figure of Bishop's poem is an "atheist" in the style of Melville, for this figure shuts his eyes to the "treacherous magnetism of the void" above which he, the Unbeliever, dwells (Costello 94). According to Costello's analysis, the Unbeliever "aspires to no transcendent principle" but instead "sleeps" atop the mast, with no support; his mode of transport is without foundation or belief. But his belief in the world behind his eyes and the fantasy of what perils may await him in the natural world create in themselves a sort of replacement belief (95). The poem's third and fourth stanzas offer two contrasting figures, both of whom, in contrast to the stance of the Unbeliever, are elevated by transports they but pretend to understand: first, the "cloud," who represents a "subjective absolute" which he believes keeps him aloft but which he is always checking and unsure of as he "peers" at his own "watery" reflection; and second, a seagull, who in Costello's reading represents those who find self-deluded stability in a "transcendent principle," in this case the very air that enables his flight and is misunderstood by him to be marble (96).

Costello further justifies this "spiritual" reading of the poem by juxtaposing it with a pertinent entry from Bishop's notebook, dated 1934, as well as by pointing out that Bishop's lifelong interest in the Metaphysical poets was not aesthetic but spiritual. She quotes Bishop's letter to the Herbert scholar Joseph Summers, in which she remarks, "how really concerned Herbert was with all these insoluble and endless and nagging problems of man's relationship to God," adding, "It is 'real.'—It was real and it has kept on being and it always will be, and Herbert just happened to be a person who managed to put a great deal of it into magnificent poetry" (Costello 97, 252 n. 5). Here, Bishop's voice, long after having written "The Unbeliever," is poignant in its frank desire to understand the spirituality of "a person"(97). This is the voice of a mature poet and woman, indeed, not to be mistaken for the approach of a scholar of Metaphysical poetry (Bishop never considered herself, even later in life, a scholar or particularly well read).³

Contemporaneous with the genesis and composition of "The Unbeliever," which occurred during her travels from Key West to Cape Cod and Europe, and during a period of intensive self-schooling as a poet, Bishop articulated questions to herself about the relationship between spirituality and metaphor. Seeking an archive of figures available to her, the best she found was "God's book," or "nature," as she writes: "If we could only get through our own 'figurativeness'...God is for in [*sic*], image within image, metaphor of metaphor—Even from day to day I think the levels I take my own figures on change, back & forth. So far I have only used four or five. (People less one sense—deaf, blind, etc.—how does it affect this general metaphor life we all make use of?)" (qtd. in Costello 98).⁴ This meditation invites an analysis of "The Unbeliever" as a poem that addresses not only spirituality in its content but also the *religio* or ordering of Bishop's rhetorical and figurative language, the spiritual poetics of a young lyric poet. A believer or an "Unbeliever" in figurative language as the vehicle to truth in poetry—or in poetry as the vehicle to divine truth?

Harold Bloom formulates a much more literary interpretation of "The Unbeliever," finding in the poem a statement not simply of spiritual beliefs or questions but of more forthright poetic identity in relation to the romantic poets and the sublime. Bishop's letters and journals bear witness to the fact that she was an avid reader of the poetry of her contemporaries, not only the Metaphysical and romantic poets; for example, she refers famously to knowing Stevens' *Harmonium* "by heart" in college (qtd. in Millier 83). In light of this, Bloom interprets the three figures of the poem, the Unbeliever, cloud, and seagull, quite literally as precursor poets:

> Think of the personae in Bishop's poem as exemplifying three rhetorical stances, and so as being three kinds of poet, or even three poets...the cloud is Wordsworth or Stevens. The gull is Shelley or Hart Crane. The unbeliever is Dickinson or Bishop....The cloud, powerful in introspection, regards not the sea but his own subjectivity. The gull, more visionary still, beholds neither sea nor air but his own aspiration. The unbeliever observes nothing, but the sea is truly observed in his dream. (Foreword x)

In Costello's comment upon this seminal passage from Bloom, the Unbeliever does not experience the egotistical sublime, in which he might ascend to or become absorbed in a "transcendental ideal," but uses a "negative sublime" whereby he wards off these pitfalls. Yet all of this negativity need not be expended; for upon closer, realistic examinations, the Unbeliever too is "laboring under illusions of perspective" (Costello 96-97). The ocean is merely water, if only the Unbeliever would open his eyes and look closely; as long as the Unbeliever's eyes remain closed, the ocean is a figure of hallucinated peril.

Bloom's reading raises two questions. First, is the sublime a crucial topos for Bishop's poetry? And second, isn't the person of the Unbeliever distinct from the speaker of the poem, and thus from Bishop?[5] As regards the sublime, while she reacted strongly against the confessional poets and against her contemporaries' self-revelation in poems,[6] the world of the sublime was not necessarily the alternative preoccupation for Bishop as poet. The world of the strictly "figurative" was also under interrogation, as the passage quoted from her notebooks in 1934 attests. What to make of a poem, then, so indebted to the imagery of the sublime and the figures of allegory? Despite Bloom's observation, Wordsworth and Shelley, or even Crane, Stevens, and Dickinson,[7] cannot have been the only "spheres" of influence upon her at this phase of her formation. Perhaps the evaluation of this poem as indicative most strongly of Bishop's transition, her process of decision between one form of rhetoric and another, and as gesturing toward her own distinct poetic rhetoric and register is the most useful interpretation. Starting with Bloom's suggestions, and with the readings of other critics, represented by Costello, close in mind, I want to examine what happens when this poem is interpreted in close proximity to its governing—for better or for worse—forebears.

An Original Analysis of "The Unbeliever":

The Epigraph

Elizabeth Bishop's Unbeliever sleeps on the top of the mast, not just once, but twice, in the epigraph, attributed to Bunyan, and in the first line of the poem:

The Unbeliever

He sleeps on the top of a mast. —Bunyan

He sleeps on the top of a mast...

The repetition of this line, "He sleeps on the top of a mast," first by Bunyan, who quotes the Book of Proverbs 23:34, and then as Bishop's own verse, the first line of her poem articulated in the words of her unnamed speaker, places this poem really at the mast-head of who she is and how she defines herself as a poet. What indeed is the function of an epigraph? Although not part of the poem *per se* (or is it?), the epigraph is read as the part of the poem between the title and the body of the poem, so it makes an aural impression, an echo, as well as a visual impression, a repetition, on the page. Whatever the strict semantics, the doubling at the start of the poem endows this phrase with an emphatic weight. Indeed, it is as if the phrase itself were at the top of a mast that is the poem itself. To hold a position at the top of the mast gives a potentially almighty perspective: the entire sweep of the ship, the ocean, the horizon; the entire sweep of one's life and experiences, one's poems and talents and what one is capable of as a poet. What clarity to have this perspective, and what abject failure to inhabit this position and to keep one's eyes closed, to sleep. Or is it failure? Perhaps a dwelling within, the meditation of an unacknowledged view, is a sacrifice of the literal view for an interior perspective more exalted? Should we read this poem—more specifically, the epigraphic statement "He sleeps at the top of the mast," which is already privileged in its literal placement, first quoted from her strong precursors then echoed or mimicked in her own early voice—as the mast-head, the colophon, the self-authorization of Bishop's work? If so, then the poem will show us what is at stake and will indicate whether the epigraph is in fact a principle of a poetics.

In considering the identity and importance of the speaker as separate from the poet and from "the Unbeliever," it is important to note here at the beginning that this initial phrase and quotation are in the third-person masculine, a firm statement about the relationship between the poet and the speaker, or, rather, about the difference between them.

The speaker of the poem is in a position external to the Unbeliever and so can comment on the Unbeliever's position without being inside of it, though most readers, Bloom included, assume that Bishop herself is the Unbeliever.[8] Not the Unbeliever but the speaker, instead, is Bishop, a speaker who can also be identified as the "believer." The "believer" is "inside" the Unbeliever, both quite literally as another word enclosed and also as a "Believer," a persona who can accompany the Unbeliever to the precipice of self-knowledge, or the fear of self-knowledge, and at the same time narrate it, or even "publish" it, from the outside, for the reader. It is important not to confuse the speaker and the persona of "the Unbeliever" and at the same time not to detach one too far from the other, so that the "believer" and the "Unbeliever" are distinct yet also united, both opposites of one another and yet complements. The inside/outside function of the speaker in relation to the drama of the poem mirrors the inside/outside function of the epigraph in relation to the body of the poem; even the inside/outside function of "believer" to "Unbeliever," or speaker to poet, constructs the chain of meanings and significations generated by this poem. In light of this discussion of the relationship between the inside and the outside, the epigraph also invites the reader to consider outside texts before even reading the poem proper. It is particularly significant here because "The Unbeliever" is an early effort, just at the outside of—or just inside—what may or may not become a succession of poems by one Elizabeth Bishop; and as stated above, at the early phase of the poet's career, the poems reckon themselves in relation to the external "outside" tradition that they aspire to become part of, as "insiders." As she progressed in her poetry, Bishop did not use epigraphs; yes, she translated poems and wrote about other poets, most notably Pound, but her poems do not openly gesture to an outside referent the way "The Unbeliever" does. At this important moment then, even before the reading of the body of the poem, the important gesture is toward "outside" texts, the precursors.

The Epigraph: Bunyan, Proverbs, and Melville

Bishop's quotation from *Pilgrim's Progress* reflects her fascination with the Metaphysical poets and with works on spirituality and allegory from the seventeenth century, all of which imbue this poem. The full title of Bunyan's allegory already places it closer to the scenario of "The Unbeliever," for it is, like the experience of the Unbeliever, about the events of a dream: *The Pilgrim's Progress from This World to That Which Is to Come Delivered Under the Similitude of a Dream Wherein Is Discovered the Manner of His Setting Out, His Dangerous Journey, and Safe Arrival at the Desired Country.* Even the engraved frontispiece from the earliest editions of Bunyan's work, the so-called Sleeping Portrait, emphasizes the dominant imagery of sleep and dreaming. The Sleeping Portrait shows the speaker of Bunyan's work who witnesses the journey of the Christian, all of which occurs in the sleeper's own head, behind eyelids represented as firmly shut with head tilted in sleep, while the body remains fully clothed and upright as if awake, in a dream occurring not at night but within the context of the waking world. For the poet whose work was preoccupied with a sense of literal travel—from the maps and sea-crossings of her early life to the exploration of foreign lands and the search for stable residence in the later life—it is appropriate that the narrator of *Pilgrim's Progress*, too, is traveling, and traveling in Sleep, in the imagination, where Bishop the poet, too, traveled.

The speaker in *Pilgrim's Progress*, like the speaker in "The Unbeliever," is distinct from the character whose drama he narrates (just as Christian is distinct from the Sleeper who narrates his actions, and so on—the chain of fine distinctions between poetic speakers and narrated characters, while interesting, is not useful here). Thus, Bunyan's speaker is free to observe the actions of the external figure, Christian. And if Christian is anything amidst the transitions of his journey, then as a "believer" in Christianity, he also functions as the opposite of Bishop's "Unbeliever" (and yet somehow re-inscribes the "believer" poet who is Bishop's disembodied speaker). Bunyan writes:

> I saw then in my Dream that [Christian] went on thus, even until he came at a bottom, where he saw, a little out of the way, three Men fast asleep, with Fetters upon their heels. The name of the one was Simple, another Sloth and the third Presumption.
>
> Christian then seeing them lye in this case went to them if peradventure he might awake them. And cried "You are *like them that sleep on the top of the Mast*, for the dead Sea is under you, a Gulf that hath no bottom: Awake therefore and come away; be willing also and I will help you off with your Irons." He also told them, "If he that goeth about like a roaring Lion comes by, you will certainly become a prey to his teeth." (38, emphasis added)

To summarize: a "sleeping" narrator witnesses a "pilgrim" traveler named Christian, a "believer" in Christianity, who encounters three men, unable to move because of the iron fetters at their heels, and though all three within this dream are fast asleep, they are also able to speak. Similarly, the unnamed speaker of Bishop's poem witnesses three figures, the central one of whom (the Unbeliever) talks in his sleep. In order to wake his sleepers, Christian employs a verse from the Bible (the book of believers). The sounds of the words themselves should wake the sleepers; the content of the words ("You are like them that sleep...") seems to describe their exact condition, sleep, but can only describe what their condition is "like," for they are not literally atop a mast, and the bottomless "Gulf" beneath them is figurative, not literal. In Bishop's poem, the three figures are aloft, and the central figure is not just "like" the figure asleep at the top of the mast; Bishop's figure *is* at the top of the mast. Her poem has literalized Bunyan's passage. From a figure of speech, a comparison, Bishop has created a "real" landscape. (How much of this falls under the influence of Bishop's mentor, Moore: "imaginary gardens with real toads"!) Unlike Christian the speaker, however, Bishop's speaker has no "person" with which to awaken the "Unbeliever," perhaps significant in that there is then no poet's voice, an undermining of the performative desire of the speech, the wake-up call which the poem aspires to be. Is it easier to wake a man of Sloth, Simple, or Presumption, all three material vices, or to wake figures that represent precursor poets or embody a relationship to the sublime, entities animated only by a poet's inner eye and imagination? Or, at last, to awaken readers to the emergence of a new poet's published voice?

With the quotation of Bunyan, Bishop also quotes the gesture of quotation itself. Bunyan's speaker-within-a-speaker quotes God's book, not "nature" as the repository for all potential figurative language, as discussed above in Bishop's notebook, but the literal book of the Bible. In this twenty-third chapter of Proverbs, one of the Wisdom books, an unnamed speaker (this is not one of the chapters attributed to Solomon) provides a list of exhortations to his pupil, in a tradition linked to the instruction books of Egyptian sages,[9] a detail that will later be significant in the discussion of Melville's influence on this text. Again, however, the extended quotation from Proverbs tells more than it shows in Bunyan's use of it, and it is more telling in Melville's use and Bishop's selection of this embedded quotation. The one who "sleeps" on the top of the mast exists in the originary quotation, too, as a figure of comparison, used only because he is "like" another figure, in this proverb, like the ones who "tarry long at the wine":

29	Who hath woe?
	Who hath sorrow?
	Who hath contentions?
	Who hath babbling?
	Who hath wounds without cause?
	Who hath redness of eyes?
30	They that tarry long at the wine;
	they that go to seek mixed wine.
31	Look not thou upon the wine when it is red,
	when it giveth his color in the cup,
	when it moveth itself aright.
32	At the last it biteth like a serpent,
	and stingeth like an adder.
33	Thine eyes shall behold strange women,
	and thine heart shall utter perverse things.
34	Yea, thou shalt be as he that lieth down in the midst of the sea,
	or as he that lieth upon the top of a mast.
35	They have stricken me, shalt thou say, and I was not sick;
	they have beaten me, and I felt it not:
	when shall I awake?
	I will seek it yet again.
	(Proverbs 23: 29-35, emphasis added)[10]

According to the literal sense of this verse, the "Proverbial" mast-sitter is not concerned with sitting on the mast at all but about drinking too much, falling into "drink," which produces an effect similar to falling quite literally into the figurative drink, the ocean, from the great, sickening height of the mast. But a poet, or a Christian dreamer, must concern herself with ex-stasis—how to remain static on this perch up above, atop the mast, and far above the literalism of one's spiritual conveyance, yet also how to attain a state of ecstasy, where the singing of poetry, the awakening of the other sleepers from whatever holds them in fetters, may do its work. The language of Proverbs understands that this is the responsibility of the "believer," that it is not simply a behavioral admonishment to avoid drinking, but that the larger effect of drinking "perverts" the normal function of the senses and, by extension, the function of the person in the community. The body cannot "feel" appropriately, the "eyes" lose their accuracy, and worst of all for a believer or a poet, the "heart shall utter perverse things." By drink or by comparison to drink, the result is a figure of ab-use, the ab-use of the voice; speech or poetry cannot occur, even when the entire meaning or continued use and existence of this passage depends on the rhetorical misprision of the figurative for the literal.

To re-narrate this chain of phenomena chronologically, the image of the mast-sitter first appears in Proverbs, where it functions as the figurative half of a rhetorical comparison, the literal half of which is the person who drinks, who has abused alcohol. The result of drinking is seasickness, or the feeling that one either sits upon the mast of a ship or is the mast of the ship, moving from side to side. This statement is uttered by a rhetorical "sage" to his rhetorical student as an admonishment against drinking, one of the results of which is violence and another of which is perversity of utterances. Bunyan takes this quotation and embeds it in the speech of his speaker, the "dreamer," who tells his dream, which is a dream about a third figure, a pilgrim named Christian who encounters three sleepers and uses the quoted words from Proverbs in order both to describe, in figurative language, the sleepers he finds to themselves and to awaken them, literally by crying out, "You are like them that sleep on the top of the Mast" (Bunyan 38). There is no mention of drink in Bunyan's passage. Since this is an allegory, the sleep may indeed be drunkenness, but it is more likely the less literal sleep of sin and vice, the sleep that keeps them from self-awareness, the result of healthful functioning of the senses.

In his quotation of the words from Proverbs in *Pilgrim's Progress*, Bunyan does not mention the abuse of drink as the speaker of Proverbs does. The stupor and sleepiness of his three personae are not linked at all with alcohol; this nuance is missing, absent, invisible. The reader might assume that Bunyan, in his use of the quotation, is quoting some maritime poet's literal passage about the imagery of the sea, its sublime and potentially destructive power, so Christian can employ its vivid, poetic power in order to awaken the three Sleepers. The next image in Christian's speech, after all, is the comparison between a similar danger resulting from staying asleep and a "roaring lion." But perhaps not so differently from one of Bishop's last poems, "The End of March," where we know the figure by its absence, we have here the footprints of the lion without the lion, so to speak (also a Stevensian topos, for example his later poem "Not Ideas about the Thing but the Thing Itself" [Stevens, *Collected Poems* 534], another poem set in the month of March). The absent or elided figure in Bunyan's passage, the maker of the sleep, is not a lion; it is simply the "drink," which is central to the meaning of the passage in its original context in the Book of Proverbs.

In terms of the rhetorical mechanics, Bunyan uses what was originally the figurative part of a rhetorical comparison to invoke a literal image. A transformation occurs, or rather a pattern of transforming a unit of language, "He sleeps on the top of a mast," from a figurative statement to a context in which it is a literal statement. The elided connotations, however, do not easily detach themselves from a unit of poetic language, even when quoted in an abbreviated manner or ruptured from their original rhetorical context. For example, in the passage from *Pilgrim's Progress*, after Christian exhorts them, the three sleepers continue sleeping while Christian continues on his journey. However, these sleepers appear in the Second Part with this comment: "They were asleep when Christian went by and now you go by—they are hanged"—hanged, with the result that their hanging generates not a "perverse" utterance but a song, a song that celebrates their value as a sign:

> Now then, you 3, hang there and be a Sign
> To all that shall against the truth combine:
> And let him that comes after, fear this end,
> If unto Pilgrims he is not a friend.
> And thou my Soul of all such men beware,
> That unto Holiness Opposers are.
>
> (Bunyan 213)

The forceful iambic pentameter of these heroic couplets marks them as anything but a "perverse" utterance; indeed, by their avoiding drink, staying awake and away from the top of the mast, and befriending the pilgrim, the result is a song. Granted, this song does not perform the act of waking but instead describes the effect of sleeping too much—no doubt with the hoped-for effect that it will rouse the "believing" reader. By "hanging," though, the three sleepers are assuredly saved from ever falling.

Yet this song is already shown to be a result of a misreading—there is no mast-sitter *per se* in the Proverbs passage, only a mast and a seasick drunk, according to the Hebrew. Bunyan uses this quotation, and indeed he makes concrete the figures who sit on top of the masts but in the plural: "*them* that sleep on the top of the mast" (emphasis added). Bishop, to return to the first line of the poem, transposes the line from Proverbs into the singular, even when attributing it to Bunyan. This changes everything at the same time as it remains in keeping with the chain of changes brought about by misreading, or misprision, already inchoate in this poem. The quoted quotation alludes to tradition (the subverted plural pronoun) and performs creativity (the replacement with the singular pronoun); the entire poem literalizes the drama of the figurative events of the precursor texts by offering a literal scene of a mast-sitter (which also invites interpretation as an extended figurative drama, i.e., an allegory). The exchanges between figurative and literal rhetoric could re-inscribe themselves here infinitely and maddeningly.

In Bishop's misquotation of the line, too, she transforms it from the meter of Bunyan's speech, with its strong but arrhythmic stresses, to a poet's line, as Moore stated, a "tentative" lyric:

U   ′ / U U ′ / U U   ′
He sleeps/at the top/of the mast

Here an iamb in the first foot doubles its weak stress, so that it becomes an anapest in the next foot and then, in the sequence of repetition, repeats that anapest for the final foot of the trimeter line. But even this line of iamb and anapests is not repeated consistently in the next line of the poem. And in the fifth stanza of the poem, the same words appear again, in the same position as the first line of the stanza, except a slight "misquoting" changes the meter entirely, so the line is no longer a unit of broken echo and repetition but rather a unified line of anapestic trimeter:

U U   ′ / U U ′ / U U   ′
But he sleeps/at the top/of his mast.

So the misquotation or variation in the repetition of the first line by the addition of the literal word *but* at the start of the line adds stability and uniformity to the meter of the line but also literalizes the instability: the literal word of instability, of reservations, "but" itself.[11] The movement here is from performed instability (performed by the irregular rhythm) to literal instability, reflected in the language but no longer performed in the now regularized rhythm.

Does Bishop purposely misquote Bunyan, who is misquoting the KJV, which has misconstrued the Hebrew? Unknowable. What is significant here from the point of view of a biographical or psychoanalytic reading of this poem is that her entire life Bishop struggled with alcoholism, the significant memory of "the drink" denied her by her mother.[12] She struggled to hide it both in her life and from her writing, a cover-up she achieved with amazing finesse and at great cost. This personal history renders more poignant the questions from Proverbs "Who hath sorrow? Who hath woe?"[13] At the time of the composition of "The Unbeliever," Bishop was beginning to understand the problematic role alcohol would play in her life, understanding it well enough to begin to try to hide it. Thus, by its incompleteness, its act of elision, the quotation and what it avoids in address are telling, rhetorically as well as biographically; more significant, uncanny convergences of meaning avouch the strength of the passage from Proverbs and of the intuition of the poet who chose it and labored under its influence. Part of the richness of this evidence attests to Bishop's strength as a poet, her language and its resonances functioning on many, many levels—levels that she could not have calculated or consciously controlled but only performed in the highest register of her "singing," even as she was blind-sided by the implications of the quotation! Even when Bishop "misquotes" herself in the fifth stanza of the poem, the effect is significant: a subtle change in the meaning and a participation in the tradition of getting the tradition wrong.

Amidst the tension between the rhetorical misreading of the uses of the literal and figurative between Bunyan and Proverbs, Bishop enters and re-establishes the literal aspects of the mast-sleepers, but she does this with the influence of a third, strong precursor text, Melville's. This final layer of allusions nuances the Bunyan quotation and, with the image of the mast-sitter, brings it closer to her native shores: Melville's *Moby-Dick,* in particular Chapter 35, "The Mast-Head" (146-52). Critics have mentioned, in passing, the importance of this chapter and Chapter 93, "The Castaway," to understanding Bishop's poem,[14] but one could add the quotation-filled "Extracts" at the beginning of *Moby-Dick* and the Bunyanesque figure of Father Mapple. The homologies in subject matter and in visible and invisible themes in Melville's book and "The

Unbeliever" tell quite a tale. Without once mentioning the Bible, let alone the passage about masts from Proverbs, Melville's chapter no less provides a commentary on the subverted passage from Proverbs and thus an analogue to Bishop's poem. Melville's passage begins by linking the "business of standing mast-heads" to arcane knowledge, specifically Egyptian knowledge, much as the scholarship on Proverbs mentions that the form of the "instruction" narrative, too, had its origins in an Egyptian genre. What genre of knowledge? Not the knowledge of other tongues, that of "the Babel builders" who preceded the Egyptians. Rather, here the mast's first function was to provide an opportunity of knowledge for the astronomers who "mount to the apex and sing out for new stars." Embedded in the literal figure of the astronmer is the metaphor for what the Unbeliever does, or should be doing, at the top of his mast, surveying the horizon before him, looking up, and "singing" about what he discovers there. This is the function of the poet or, in the language of Bunyan, the virtuous one who creates "utterances" which are not perverse. In this case, the most virtuous and fitting utterances for Bishop's Unbeliever are poems.

Significantly, after the astronomer, the next ancestor according to Melville's genealogy of mast-sitter is the "Stylite," or ascetic Christian saint, who inhabits the equivalent of the mast-head on land, "a lofty stone pillar" where he lives and dies. The image of the pillar, and by extension the tower, is part of the dominant imagery of Bishop's poem. Yet while, according to Melville, the Stylite sits atop his pillar in order to make himself closer to God, the sublime object of his devotion, and to isolate himself from worldly temptations and distractions, both Bishop's "cloud" and "seagull" see themselves as supported by external agents of elevation. These agents are, in the cloud's case, pillars, and in the seagull's case, marble wings and a "tower-top." The cloud and the seagull, however, are not virtuous "believers" in their posture: they are both utterly ignorant about what really keeps them aloft, though they pretend to have knowledge. The cloud, at the same time he pronounces his self-security—"I am founded"—nervously "peers" at his own reflection, betraying his uncertainty. The seagull is so misguided as to think the very air the opposite of its airy self, "like marble." Figures of self-justification and misguided belief in transcendence, the seagull and the cloud could never be Stylites. The Stylite knows that his pillar is only man-made, yet it is man-made for an exalted intention, to attain and honor the divine. In his appropriate use of an appropriate thing, then, the Stylite is a "believer":

a pillar is just a pillar, a means. What about the conditions of isolation and observation-at-a-remove inherent to being on top of a pillar, mast-head, or column?[15]

Melville's next meditation upon the literal function of the mast-sitter, "the one proper mast-head, that of the whale-ship at the sea" (148), holds direct relevance to Bishop's poem for several reasons. Like the Unbeliever, the mast-sitter is one of "three."[16] He occupies a position where the rolling waves and the view induce a "sublime uneventfulness" punctuated by sips at the "case-bottle" (148). Still, the mast-head is a poor substitute for a house: "it is much to be deplored that the place to which you devote so considerable a portion to the whole term of your natural life, should be so sadly destitute of anything approaching to a cosy inhabitiveness, or pertains to a bed, a hammock, a hearse, a sentry box, a pulpit, a coach, or any of those other small and snug contrivances in which men temporarily isolate themselves" (149). Or a page? A stanza? These details—the contemplation of the sublime, induced by isolation and alcohol, in lieu of a home of one's own—hold uncanny resonance for Bishop's spiritual and temporal condition at the time she wrote this poem, where her only "house" or consistent habitation was her own self, her own body, much as the mast-sitter's best approximation of his house was his own "watch-coat."[17] As Melville's passage continues, it warns against the hire of dreamy, over-meditative mast-sitters and other types akin to "Childe Harold" himself, who "not infrequently perches [himself] upon the mast-head of some luckless disappointed whale-ship" (Melville 151). And why luckless? Because the self-absorbed mast-sitter, immersed in his own questions of belief and "unconscious reverie," has lost his identity, inasmuch as it literally requires him to "sing out" on the appearance of whales. Here Melville's passage itself slips from third to second person. No longer a chatty Ishmael describing a mast-sitter, the speaker here addresses himself. As the literal condition of the distracted ephebe-as-mast-sitter becomes more and more figurative, more and more "enchanted" by the spiritual figments of sublime reverie, what pervades is a use of rhetoric similar to that witnessed in Proverbs and in *Pilgrim's Progress*: the performative nature of the utterance is to AWAKEN the speaker lulled by the prose itself! Or even, by extension, the reader! Here are the key sentences where this switch occurs, complex in their syntax and poetic in their speech, again, where prose itself almost becomes prosody:

...lulled into such an opium-like listlessness of vacant, unconscious reverie is this absent-minded youth by the blending cadence of waves with thoughts, that at last he loses his identity; takes the mystic ocean at his feet for the visible image of that deep, blue bottomless soul, pervading mankind and nature; and every strange, half-seen, gliding, beautiful thing that eludes him; every dimly-discovered, uprising fin of some indiscernible form, seems to him the embodiment of those elusive thoughts that only people the soul by continually flitting through it. In this enchanted mood, *thy* spirit ebbs away to whence it came; becomes diffused through time and space.... (Melville 152; emphasis added to indicate switch in person)

As with the Unbeliever, with Melville's mast-head sitters in general, with the sleepers in Bunyan's bottomland, and with those stupefied with drink in Proverbs, the "you" addressed in this speech must also awaken before it "ebbs away." Is the awakening literal or from unbelief to belief? From languor to action? From one state to another, as caused by a destabilizing utterance? Bishop's Unbeliever responds, in his dream-state, to the external interlocutor (the seagull), in order to express horror at the negation anticipated in opening his eyes: "it wants to destroy us all." To awaken is to view the sea, to know, real or sublime, the horror of what it is. The "you" addressed here by Melville's speaker does not want to awaken and face that which seems inevitable as long as it remains hypothetical, the violent fall to waking: "But while this sleep, this dream is on ye, move your foot or hand an inch; slip your hold at all; and your identity comes back in horror. Over Descartian vortices you hover. And, perhaps at mid-day, in the fairest weather, with one half-throttled shriek you drop through the transparent air into the summer sea, no more to rise for ever" (152). Perhaps worse than the literal fall into the sea, the destruction lurking in the ocean, is the fear of the destruction of the self by the self, the fear of self-knowledge, and the uncertainty over whether its effects will be violent or salvific.

The voice of the self addressing the self here guards against, however, the future possibility of a violent awakening, at a time governed by a "mid-day" demon: self-wounding, self-rousing, self-transcendence, by the act of facing the ego. The result here of Melville's passage, Bishop's poem, the poet's "utterance" which describes a fear of self-knowledge yet in so doing nonetheless performs it, is a piece of published work. A real thing, not a perhaps, is produced. What is a mast-head, after all, but the sign of authorship on the title-page of any publication, even the sign of a published voice? And not a perverse utterance, but an utterance put to correct and healthy use, a voice even in its self-criticism and fear of being voiced that wants to be heard.

Concluding Observations

At the last stanza of "The Unbeliever," the lines uttered by the Unbeliever himself, Bishop uses a tripled rhyme to link the final three staggered lines. The variation in line-length from dimeter to hexameter throughout the poem creates an instability of meter; here, the metrical instability combined with the hyper-emphasized rhyme creates a pattern that continues to echo Coleridge's *Rime of the Ancient Mariner*, as well as Crashaw's "The Weeper" and Tennyson's six-line fragment "The Eagle." The first stanza of Crashaw's "The Weeper" uses the same /-all/ rhyme that Bishop uses in the final three lines of "The Unbeliever":

> But we are deceived *all*
> Stars they are indeed too true
> For they but seem to *fall*
> As Heaven's other spangles do:
> It is not for our earth and us,
> To Shine in things so precious.
>
> (33, emphasis added)

To speak of the precious, when there is so much talk of the sublime: Bishop's stanza shares the imagery of falling from a great height hypothetically just as Crashaw's stars only "seem" to fall. She borrows Crashaw's word for meteors which really do fall, "spangles," and transforms it into an adjective modifying the sea, where, presumably, those spangles drown when they fall. Most important here, the stars do not fall, nor does the mast-sitter, nor does the Unbeliever. "Spangled" also appears in the description of the sea in Melville's "Castaway" chapter, where a minor but oracular character does fall into the ocean and emerges permanently altered in his mind and for the worse. The literal action of falling into the sea conjures a family of themes and figures different, however, from the hypothetical posture, the seeming or fearing to fall but not falling, that plays between Crashaw's and Bishop's stanzas.[18] Bishop's final stanza reads:

> But he sleeps on the top of his mast
> With his eyes closed tight.
> The gull inquired into his dream,
> Which was, "I must not *fall*.
> The spangled sea below wants me to *fall*.
> It is hard as diamonds; it wants to destroy us *all*.
>
> (emphasis added)

Almost the same syllable, rhymed, is used, /-alls/, as Tennyson's eagle watches from atop his own equivalent of a mast-head, motif of the sublime, a mountain wall:

> The wrinkled sea beneath him *crawls*;
> He watches from his mountain *walls*
> And like a thunderbolt, he *falls*.
>
> (713, emphasis added)

The eagle, agent of the sublime, falls because he is in perfect control of his action and pursues his will, his appetites. There is no doubt here that the eagle's fall will precede the eagle's rise to his heights; this is not a position of torment or angst. Even if the figure of the Unbeliever is a parody of this sublime self-knowledge, control, and willingness to fall with the security that the self, poetically or spiritually, will rise again, as in "The Eagle," at this juncture it is important to place the entire poem back in the realm of the rhetorical, at least to understand Bishop's larger poetics. Let the Unbeliever fall, or remain a sleep-talker, mumbling perverse utterances to the deluded gull: his words are in quotation. Instead, it is the speaker who overhears this quoted conversation—the entire poem, in fact—and who is not the same as the Unbeliever. The speaker observes the three figures and has narrated the figurative tableau with literal mastery; the speaker has also presumably "spoken" the title and had some rhetorical commerce with the epigraph. Is the speaker the poet? Unknown—but the speaker is not the Unbeliever.

At the conclusion, we are also left with the question of how the epigraph relates to the poem, the title, and the poet. The epigraph is what invokes the imagery of the "mast-head" itself and invites the performance of both the literal and figurative exchanges that occur between the poem and its precursor texts and imagery. The gap between literal and figurative opens up a seemingly infinite series of bifurcations—between sublime and precious, biographical and universal, believer and unbeliever, tradition and future—all leading to a question. Of all these bifurcations, which one has the most important material at stake? That would be the split between the speaker and the Unbeliever. The speaker is closer to the poet than the Unbeliever is, though she may not be the poet herself, exactly. Is the speaker a believer? Does this utterance, published under a mast-head, rouse the speaker from her reverie and lead her more closely to a unified self and away from the slough of despond that describes the allegorical complexities and contradictions of this poem and the attempt to understand it?

Indications would be to the positive: in the collection of poems where Bishop published this early work, *North & South*, she also published the poem that follows this, a poem where she has sung out clearly, spotted "the whale," woke up, offered her utterance to the world, from the top of her mast, eyes open, with precious and sublime observation intact: a poem about—what else?—not a whale, strictly speaking, but more modestly and more wieldy in the newly minted language of her poetics: "The Fish."

Notes

1. Her watercolors and drawings, exhibited posthumously, attest to her quite literal cultivation of the "painter's eye." The exhibit was published as *Exchanging Hats*.

2. The first Clarendon Press edition, released in 1928, may well have been available to Bishop in her early reading. That particular edition included not only several versions of the frontispiece but also an engraving of the "Sleeping Portrait," which informed my analysis.

3. Discussion of this occurs in the critical biography of Bishop by Brett Candlish Millier, according to whom, even in the last year of her life, when she won the Guggenheim fellowship, she set for herself a schedule of "serious" reading (540), including St. Augustine and Samuel Johnson, and also considered herself distinct from her "academic friends" (374), those who had begun teaching

university long before she had had to and were thus academically better prepared than she.

4. See also Costello 252 n. 6.

5. She criticized herself for being preoccupied with the "precious"; for example, in this letter to Anne Stevenson, 8 Jan. 1964: "I have written so far what I feel is a 'precious' kind of poetry, although I am very much opposed to the precious" (qtd. in Millier 352). However, the question remains whether the sublime is the remedy for her ambivalence about the precious in her own work.

6. Attitudes toward confessional poetry, particularly in the work of her close friend Robert Lowell, are discussed and quoted in Millier (462): "In general I deplore 'the confessional,'" she wrote to Lowell in a letter of 21 Mar. 1973. See also Millier 485, 489-90.

7. Robert Dale Parker pairs this poem with one by Dickinson with which he finds a similarity, "A Pit—but Heaven over it—," a poem he notes was "not published until 1945" (34).

8. That the Unbeliever is also a male figure, a "He," would make this elision of Bishop with her own figure fitting, however, since one of her hallmarks is to cloak her own gender and person under the opposite gender, the ambivalent male. The disguise of gender here is in keeping with Bishop's antipathy for the confessional. For a discussion about "gender-crossing," see, for example, Joanne Diehl 17-45. Diehl quotes Bishop herself on this topic: "Women's experiences are much more limited but that does not really matter—there is Emily Dickinson, as one always says. You just have to make do with what you have after all" (19).

9. In particular, "The Instruction of Amen-em-ope," which dates from at least 1,000 B.C., as quoted in the article introducing the book of Proverbs (R. B. Y. Scott 769).

10. For the sake of comparison, the Revised Standard Version for Proverbs 23:29-35 reads:

> [29]Who has woe? Who has sorrow? Who has strife? Who has complaining? Who has wounds without cause? Who has redness of the eyes? [30]Those who tarry long over wine, those who go to try mixed wine. [31]Do not look at wine when it is red, when it sparkles in the cup and goes down smoothly. [32]At the last it bites like a serpent, and stings like an adder. [33]Your eyes will see strange things, and your mind utter perverse things. [34]*You will be like one who lies down in the midst of the sea,* [n. 34, *"who is prostrated (with seasickness) far at sea"*] *like one who lies on the top of a mast* [n. 34 continued, *"or perhaps rolls drunkenly (from side to side) like the top of the mast"*]. [35]"They struck me," you will say, "but

I was not hurt; they beat me but I did not feel it. When shall I awake? I will seek another drink." (Emphases added)

11. She also uses *his* as if to intensify the literalness of the character's person and gender in this third iteration: he is a representative figure but also a real figure, poised to serve both literal and figurative functions, depending on what the poem is to perform.

12. For a scholarly discussion of this, see the analysis of notes for an unpublished poem, "A Drunkard," as well as other unfinished literary accounts, ending on page 6 with the following quotation from Bishop: "Since that day, that reprimand...I have suffered from abnormal thirst" (qtd. in Millier 4-6).

13. At the age of twenty-five, was she to know that someday she would break arms and shoulders, repeatedly, or hit her head and wake up with wounds from her excesses of alcohol? No; however, she had already embarked upon her first seasick voyages, drinking sidecars and martinis each night, as she easily crossed the ocean and lived on both sides of it with her college friends Margaret Miller, Louise Crane, and Frani Blough on her first forays into Europe. As she mentions in a letter from Paris to Frani (Blough) Muser, 20 Oct. 1935, now in the Vassar College Library, she and Louise bought a shaker and mixed and drank "an excellent side-car before our excellent dinner every night" (qtd. in Millier 93; see also 554 n. 7). This growing awareness of an attachment to the consumption of alcohol begins only one year after the death of Bishop's mother in a mental institution in 1934. Significantly close to the time she probably wrote "The Unbeliever," in a letter dated 3 June 1938, again to Muser and also in the Vassar College Library, writing why she so enjoys life in Key West, Bishop explains that "drunkenness is an excuse as correct as any other" for not fulfilling responsibilities (qtd. in Millier 140; see also 556 n. 8).

14. Robert Dale Parker mentions Chapter 35 of *Moby-Dick* in conjunction with his lengthy discussion of this poem, but his concerns are not rhetorical, only interpretive (33). C. K. Doreski relates a line of the poem to Melville's Chapter 93, "The Castaway" (6). See also n. 18 below.

15. Another precursor text to Bishop's poem is Baudelaire's "La Vie antérieure" (1855), a description of a life before the waking of birth, whose imagery of the sublime—sea-swells, pillars, rock—and of the languid epiphanies possible there also echoes that of Melville's chapter. Bishop at this time was freshly familiar with Baudelaire's work, after two extended stays in France, reading nineteenth- and twentieth-century French poetry.

16. "The three mast-heads are kept manned from sunrise to sunset" (Melville 148).

17. Melville: "In cold weather, you may carry your house aloft with you, in the shape of a watch-coat; but properly speaking, the thickest watch-coat is no more of a house than the unclad body" (149). On the importance of the motif of make-shift houses in Bishop, see Bromwich 77-94.

18. Doreski comments on *spangled*: "This seems a deliberate recollection of Melville's 'spangled sea, calm and cool' in 'The Castaway' chapter of *Moby-Dick*" (6). The "pure-watered diamond drop" and "evil-blazing diamond" described in Melville's "Castaway" chapter also resonate with the language of the diamond in the simile of the final line of Bishop's poem.

15

The Heart's Metronome:
Dennis Scott and Jamaican Lyric

BAINARD COWAN

Lyric roots a people's authentic relation to home, to land, and to language. Perhaps Robert Frost best captured, in the opening and closing lines of "The Gift Outright," the special conditions that make it difficult for poets in the United States to achieve genuine lyric: "The land was ours before we were the land's." Even when "we gave ourselves outright" in "many deeds of war," the land to which our American forebears gave themselves was—and has remained, he suggests—"still unstoried, artless, unenhanced,/Such as she was, such as she would become."

What Frost's poem leaves unstated was made explicit a century or so before him by Alexis de Tocqueville. A bourgeois democracy, he feared, would have difficulty seeing anything in a genuinely noble light, let alone a divine one: that is, in viewing anything in itself as part of a living cosmos rather than as primarily intersubjective, the product of other equal minds and desires. For Tocqueville "equality...dries up most of the old sources of poetry"; democratic nations "willingly dream of what will be, and in this direction their imagination has no limits; here it stretches and enlarges itself beyond measure" (2.1.17). Such a condition makes for scarce pickings in lyric and tragedy, fostering instead, if anything, a natural inclination for epic and comedy, though even the yearning for epic is, for that same intersubjective reason, often a chimerical one, disappearing when a temporary enthusiasm of the people evaporates. For Tocqueville, America has little sense of or interest in the beautiful. Hence what lyricism its writers achieve, he maintains, tends to occur while they are denying the sublimity of lyric by uttering it in a homespun voice or framing it in a prosaic performance like a novel.

A different set of conditions has prevailed in Jamaica, where English is spoken by the descendants of slaves and a bourgeois prosperity has never taken hold. The largest of the English-speaking Caribbean islands, Jamaica is also the third-largest English-speaking country in the Americas. Ninety per cent of its almost three million inhabitants are of African origin. Not only despite but in part *because* of the sufferings endured by its overwhelmingly black population and their ancestors, Jamaica is in a much more fortunate situation to produce poetry. It well may be, as Laurence Breiner has termed it, "the most self-conscious and culturally the most advanced of West Indian nations" (62). Without a prominent middle class, Jamaicans have had to look at power from the outside. British rule from 1655 until 1962 shaped any available education unapologetically for an elite, but geography and race kept the educated close to the culture and concerns of the common people.

There may well be such a thing as a poverty of spirit that is blessed, as the Beatitude has it; and if so, such blessing may pass over those who enjoy prestigious means of self-expression in order to engender a creative richesse of language in those who have little. The *logopoeia* of West Indian English is well known to Americans, especially through reggae music, though it is too often viewed solely as a consumer item. More soberly considered, however, this fluency is constant testimony to a people's relation to their idiom, a grasping of its cadences rather than a thoughtless adoption of its peculiarities. The many puns of Rastafarianism, aimed at reversing the disempowering empty meaning of abstract words—*head-decay-shun* for education, *downpression* for op-pression, *ovastan* for understand—are an especially intense example of a concreteness of imagination and a wit applied to language. Rastafarian belief and rhetoric have served as a kind of collective *imaginaire* for Jamaicans. And as its themes appear in poetry, it is strong testimony to the communion between what used to be called folk culture and the high culture of poetry.[1]

However, Jamaican English also leaves a pronounced impression of elegant diction, a combination of the high-culture imprint of British English and the characteristic Caribbean lilt. Where the United States is so predetermined by middle class attitudes that aristocratic accents are instinctively shunned, West Indian poets have been able to take T. S. Eliot more as a facilitator of poetic cadence than as a forbidding and austere presence. His poetry and, even more, his voice recordings were highly influential for an entire generation of West Indian poets (Brathwaite 30-31).[2] With his street scenes and argot, intermixing of languages, and alternating free verse and rhyme, the early Eliot was particularly a figure of liberation for young poets held to stricter standards by British-influenced education. Far more than Eliot, though, the most widespread influence in West Indian poetry has been the King James Bible, its sonorities spanning the social strata of the islands. Through the KJV the dual influence of Protestant Christianity and a robust seventeenth-century English diction remains strong. For serious poets a constantly available tap into the language of Shakespeare's day, the KJV is also the Bible used by Rastafarians.

Since the early twentieth century in Jamaica, moving in step with the twin desires for political independence and greater education, a vigorous subculture has produced coteries of writing. Notable poetic activity goes back to the beginning of the twentieth century, as Claude McKay's 1912 *Songs of Jamaica* and *Constab Ballads* attest, since they were his first published volumes, antedating his departure for New York and the rising artistic movement in Harlem. Edna Manley, a sculptor and the wife of one Jamaican prime minister and the mother of another, supported the 1943 founding of Jamaica's first entirely literary periodical, *Focus*. In a public letter to Dennis Scott, Manley recalls the growth of Jamaican poetry, "the slender line coming down from what we call our early days, a time when our poets leaned too heavily on the English tradition, but nevertheless produced poetry with a love of nature and the felt and seen thing." She goes on to write of the political revolution, "the explosion of 1938 when 'universal suffrage' and 'self-government' were the magic words that set Jamaica afire, and to be a poet, one had to be a Jamaican first." This political conflagration kindled a poetic revolution as well: "we were always reading to each other in those days" (*Uncle Time* xiii).

Mervyn Morris, who was at the epicenter of perhaps the most distinguished coterie, maintains that writing in Jamaica took off from about 1952 (*Making* 1). The University of the West Indies (UWI), founded in Kingston in 1948, became a center for the formation of West Indian consciousness, not just for Jamaica but for the entire Caribbean and its English-speaking populations. The regional university became a point where groups of writers could assemble, propelling poetry to distinctive new achievements. It also legitimized a connection between the region's intellectuals and popular cultural forms, vitalizing serious poetry with a contemporary source of language, imagery, and attitude. Beginning with the dialect performance poetry of Louise Bennett in the 1940s, a powerful body of poems grew that was meant not only for silent reading but for oral performance.

The group intensity necessary to ignite a regional poetry would have been impossible to achieve on the smaller islands of the English-speaking Caribbean, so UWI and Jamaica became an attractor for the entire region. The two most famous West Indian poets, Derek Walcott of St. Lucia and Edward Kamau Brathwaite of Barbados, emerged from their studies and poetic formation at UWI to become major figures on the world poetic scene. Their presence gives evidence of the prominence of West Indian poetry, indicating through their contrast the two poles of European influence and Afro-native centrism.[3] Although each is accomplished in a range of poetic forms, both tend to devote themselves to grander statements than the lyric. It has been said, not without insight, that both poets tend toward epic, and it may be true that a people must be capable of epic in order to be capable of lyric.[4] Certainly the epic strain can be often enough detected in the annals of West Indian literature. A. J. Seymour, the founder of the literary journal *Kyk-Over-Al* in Guyana, wrote in its opening issue: "*Kyk-Over-Al* we hope will be an instrument to help forge a Guianese people, to make them conscious of their intellectual and spiritual possibilities....the accident of forced immigration into the Caribbean has isolated us to the impact of a dying civilization so that we can pass on some flaming torch higher up the line" (7; qtd. in Breiner 78). This note of a great historical and social wrong bearing fruit in a higher vision, or in a sensibility tempered with hotter fires, sounds throughout the impressive body of West Indian poetry.

Walcott and Brathwaite bear a deserved fame in our time, but I would like to suggest that their development as poets draws on the indispensable resource of those gatherings at UWI. Furthermore, the heart of those gatherings was a lyric expression to which poets of varying stature recurred, producing many outstanding poems centering on the sense of place, the life of the islands, and romantic love. For the exploration of lyric in contemporary verse, one group, and in particular one of its members, deserves special attention. Dennis Scott worked together in the sixties and seventies with friends and fellow poets Mervyn Morris, Edward Baugh, Wayne Brown, Anthony McNeill, Rex Nettleford, Lorna Goodison, and others, all of whom read each other's poetry and exchanged criticism and encouragement. Morris, who has reflected in verse and prose on the atmosphere in the group, distinguishes Jamaican from English poetry in the poem "Literary Evening, Jamaica."[5] Many such poems by these authors shed light on the general relation of place to the concerns of lyric. Seamus Heaney, writing more generally about region and poetry, articulates well some of the characteristics of West Indian lyric, namely "a language imbued with the climate and love and history of the place" ("Place" 41) accomplishing "a marriage between the geographical country and the country of the mind" ("Sense" 132).[6] Morris's "The Pond" could be compared to Heaney's poem "Death of a Naturalist" in its situation. A boy is drawn to explore a pool that the grown-ups of the village have warned him away from, for "in its depths, old people said,/swam galliwasps and nameless horrors." Finally, able to resist no more, "he found himself/there at the fabled edge." Then the sun comes out, the pool's darkness is banished, and "shimmering in guilt,/he saw his own face peering from the pool" (qtd. in Chamberlin 103). It is a simple poem about a rite of passage, about crossing the boundary into self-knowledge, but also about what the self's own mysteries give to the spirit of place.

As Baugh has said of members of the group, "Each...has both feet firmly planted on his native soil, but each is open, consciously and critically so, to the stimuli which any wind may happen to blow in off the ocean" (qtd. in Hanna). Baugh's "Getting There," which begins, "It not easy to reach where she live./I mean, is best you have a four-wheel drive," is a delightful evocation of the very qualities just named by Morris and Heaney, even evoking explicitly the perennial New World figure of the Tenth Muse. A more haunting performance is Baugh's "Sometimes in the Middle of the Story," which tells of a recurring moment when "something/move outside the house, like/it could be the wind, but is not the wind...." The old people say it is Toussaint passing by on his horse Bel-Argent, but it also sounds like "the sleep-sigh of a drowned African," an added overtone that leads to an imagined synthesis of the two, that Toussaint was coming back "from secret rendezvous, from councils of war/with those who never completed the journey."[7] This founding legend demonstrates that defeat and oppression, which form no part of legends of the U.S. founding fathers, can be the natural seed ground of a lyric sensed by a whole people.

Of the Jamaican poets it is Dennis Scott who has accomplished most in recovering the playful and meditative voice of lyric in an unlyrical, over-analytic age. Scott's life, ended by cancer at fifty-one, saw him reach distinction and recognition as a poet, playwright, actor, dancer, critic, editor, and teacher. He was chairman of the directing program at the Yale School of Drama when he died. Leaping over high-low cultural barriers with alacrity, he had a recurring role on TV's *Bill Cosby Show*. One of his students, now a poet himself, recalling Scott as a teacher of drama and literature at Jamaica College, has spoken of his mentoring on the love of country and of place and, in particular, on the writing of poetry: "cut all the unnecessary words, so that each word sparkle[s] with its associative meanings" (Philp, "Happy Birthday").[8] *Uncle Time*, Scott's first book of poems, winner of the Commonwealth Poetry Prize for 1972 and an International Poetry Forum Award, is worth prolonged attention for its following of his own advice. In it he is able to combine the concerns of poetic self-making, natural to a young poet, with memory, the love of place, history, suffering, and violence, all without losing the reflective tone that is his keynote.

Perhaps one could say that Scott points the way possible for a genuine spirit of lyric in our time. It is too easy to confuse lyric with the expression of self-involvement in a United States dominated by the discourses of Harold Bloom and Oprah. Easy, also, to say (in some variant of Theodor Adorno's dictum about art after Auschwitz) that the horrors of our time have rendered lyric impossible. Could it not be that such horrors make the true lyric spirit all the more urgent? I am proposing Scott not as a major poet but as a lyricist who does what a genuine poet does and what few in our time do: he makes us see our world more gracefully and more generously.

The opening poem of this collection, "Bird of Passage," is at first look scarcely an auspicious beginning, but it is a threshold poem *about* beginning to sing. It attests to the difficulty of the creative process:[9]

> The poet sweats too.
> There is a beak at the back of his throat—
> the poem is difficult,
> his tongue bleeds.

The metaphors that proliferate here accentuate Scott's aspiring lyric voice, an entity betwixt and between. "Visionary" is about that perennially recurring figure of the winged man, like the "very old man with enormous wings" in Gabriel García Márquez's eponymous story and, even more closely, like the winged man in Robert Hayden's poem

"Angle of Ascent." Scott's poem begins, "One great wing marks his shoulder." This is not only a description of Icarus but a reimagining of Sophocles' Philoctetes, the gift coexisting with the curse, the wound with the bow. This is a "brave/limping bird" with

> the stubborn,
> heavy pounding of that
> one wing wonderful. Not quite
> can earth recall him....

The wounded man "making/such fierce way/to a hoped-for home" is a recurrent feature of some of the best writing of that America where dreams so often go unrealized. The impressive thing is not so much the content of the vision as the will of the flyer against the onslaught of the elements that join in the conspiracy against him.

The opposition to the young poet's self-realization may be indirect as well. "Sentry" is an interesting poem about the need to be on guard, even in one's dreams, against the imagined reapers who threaten death to that self that is the care of the poet: "old men with fingers like scissors,/snip, snip. Harvesting heads." In "Fisherman" he imagines himself fishing for the self and slitting it open as a fisherman does a fish. The perils of this early passage are written about with the resources of a more mature poet. Although this is a theme to which, as such, he does not return in later poems, what emerges clearly here is that the project of self-making does not imply schism for Scott. He is not caught in the familiar Joycean dialectic confronting Stephen Dedalus of *Portrait of the Artist*, determined to "fly by those nets," but rather is brought closer to his past, his people, and his land.

The poems in Scott's first book are short, and though they bear a heightened diction, showing still the Eliot-Pound high modernist spell (almost reminiscent of John Crowe Ransom's poetry in their poise and understatement), they nonetheless have their own integrity and project an unmistakable voice and mind that is clearly Scott's. Several of the poems are in dialect but without the air of special performances. Rather, they are slipped into naturally with the same lyric stance—admiration—that characterizes his other poems. "Grampa" is a commemorative poem at his grandfather's death. In it he marvels over the old man in words that evoke an awe over his now-lost qualities:

> laughing? It running from him
> like a flood, that old molasses
> man. Lord, how I never see?
> I never know a man could sweet so, cool
> as rain....

"Uncle Time," the title poem, evokes in dialect the personified spirit of sudden aging and alienation: "When 'im play in de street/wid yu woman—watch 'im! By tomorrow/she dry as cane-fire.../an' when 'im teach yu son, long after/yu walk wid stranger...."[10]

Many of the poems in this early volume emphasize the poet's inner relation to his native land. "Exile" and "Homecoming," placed in sequence, are two such pieces. The first emphasizes inevitable change: "Suddenly, mouth is dumb; eyes/hurt; surprised, it is we/who have changed....To travel/is to return/to strangers." The second sings a poignant love song to the island. With the wind "making countries/in the air," the poet sees faraway lands in the clouds, as he used to do as a child. But he is drawn down to the streets and to the wind coursing through them:

>   it tears
> the thin topographies of dream, it blows me
> as by old, familiar maps,
> to this affectionate shore, green
> and crumpling hills,
> like paper in the Admiral's fist.

The Admiral is William Penn, father of the founder of Pennsylvania, who first took the island from the Spanish and thereby set it on course toward its distinctive rejuvenation of English. Scott discerns a thread running through history as it runs through personal experience: the old dichotomy of spirit and soul, the yearning for freedom and self-realization ranged against the need to be connected to a community with a common focus worthy of love and admiration.

>   It is time to plant
> feet in our earth. The heart's metronome
> insists on this arc of islands
> as home.

What is place in poetry, really, but a communal anchor for memory? Several of these poems search through personal memory, finding in it that tie to the island's and the heart's metronome. Even the fear of memory's absence marks them, as when in "Cotyledon" he registers the increasing effect of a friend's absence: "I am forgetting//how carefully this growing/imitates death." "Nightflight" consists of two night vignettes, one of hunting fireflies some past evening and one of bats coming tonight: "Squealed, shook the wet splashing/air down through trees/and came to the feast." In a kind of process of seeding his dreams, the poet hears out of the silence the rain on the roof "chanting/a childhood rhyme [he] cannot/exorcise," and "the bright fruit" (that attracted the bats?) falls into his sleep "like fireflies." The innocent pastime is darkened by the predation he has witnessed, but a reverse action has happened too as both images have become bright patterns to negate the darkness.

The tempering by hotter fires that I referred to earlier as a special West Indian trait—the violence suffered in order to produce, which is hinted at in the image of the bats' attack in the poem just quoted or in the poet's speaking of slitting his self open like a fish for the fry—is so pervasive in these poems that it affects Scott's notion of poetic inspiration itself. "At that frail and absent evening house" is a poem of encounter with the kind of dream spirit that seems to be his muse, whom he sometimes portrays as surrounded by danger or darkness:

> The long day
> has cut trenches in her voice.
> That is why the garden is breaking.
> There are sharp blue lines around her mouth.

The implication is notably different from the classical Muses, who inspire while remaining characteristically untouched. This muse seems to bear permanent marks of long endurance of hardship. The poem ends with the poet going where his desire calls him: "The crystal stems make a forest of thorns./Raked, I go carefully/in." Such scarring is the price he has to pay to follow where this spirit leads.

Combining and culminating the meditations on memory and place in *Uncle Time* is "Pages from a Journal, 1834," a beautiful and surprising act of what Coleridge would have called the primary imagination, that inner granting of life and personhood to someone or something quite different from oneself. The journal evokes an English colonist and the moments of memory that tie him to the island. Set in the year slavery was formally abolished in the British Empire, his leave-taking is probably meant as a slavemaster's farewell. This fact simply makes it more remarkable that Scott brings out moments of tenderness amidst an unmistakable arrogance of character:

>The island floats behind
>me not leaving...
>   spiders breed
>their scuttling memories in
>the green stems
>below, the Captain tells me;
>and below, I am glad to be gone—
>   yet
>
>the hills are woodcut wild,
>inked at my heart
>and hard to erase;
>...
>the carved black dancers—
>I have printed myself
>their wooden glances
>with an iron pride
>more savage than theirs.
>I have signed them.
>...
>   The spiders
>Throw their silk across the hold,
>The turning fruit prepare
>A tropic gold.

Scott shows elsewhere in this first volume that ability to rest in the contemplation of a complex other. "Resurrections," beautiful in its spareness, is a meditation on a poor Jamaican woman who sweeps floors and has lost her husband and all her sons:

>There's nothing delicate
>
>about this tree they chopped.

The Heart's Metronome: Dennis Scott and Jamaican Lyric

> The blunted bole has healed
> a makeshift gray. Each day
> the rain applies its poultices
> of dust. Patient, it seems,
> it seems—

Drawn into this portrait, one may not notice that the poet has forbidden himself the cheaper satisfaction of impressing the reader with how he feels about its subject. If the endurance of suffering is an authentic cause of beauty, it has to be presented and not editorialized or sentimentalized.

"The Suddentree" sums up in few words the intuitions of *Uncle Time* about time, death, grief, the poetic process, and the rebirth of beauty. Here it is in its entirety:

> The suddentree has begun to bloom, killing
> whatever passes.
> Whipping birds out of the air.
> A sad horse chokes on its own mane.
> That man is covered with flowers, and he won't ever wake.
>
> Only you remain
> casual under its shadow, untouched,
> closing your skin to its sharp, fragrant leaves,
> forbidding the nourishment of grief to that terrible root.
>
> I have seen you lift from its hollow combs of honey.

One sees here the kind of range Scott wants to make his own, though he does not quite make the elements harmonize as well as he will do later: the higher poetic diction of the modernists, as in the opening lines; colloquial simplicity, as in the last line of the first stanza; and literary allusion, found in the closing line, which owes something to Pound's "Ballad of the Goodly Fere" but improves it in a context rich in poetic images—the honeycomb in the Book of Daniel and the beehive in the ox carcass in Virgil's *Georgics*. Both W. E. B. Du Bois and Toni Morrison have written poignant laments for young black people of bright promise who fade early or plummet to catastrophe. That eventuality is personified in this poem in the "suddentree." Is the "you" he addresses his beloved or the lyric muse? The latter interpretation amounts to a second personification, but if it is not misleading to do so, one might consider this apostrophe to the muse as an affirmation that through inspiration the lyric image in its beauty can be "lifted" out of experiences of destruction and suffering. Moreover, such an interpretation attests that this process works quite apart from grief, that it is in a sense a crucial sheltering of the lost beloved from grief.

In recent years this kind of assertion has been attacked vehemently, with the imputation that "redeeming" massive suffering and loss through art that does anything other than return us to the immediacy of the loss is traitorous to those who suffered. Beginning as a warranted stricture against the cheapening of such redemption, this censoriousness ends in claiming that only a fixation on the abyss can be authentic. But a "comb" of beauty or good, serene from grief, coming out of crushing destruction, it seems self-evidently, would be a victory against such destruction, a tribute to the lived experience in itself of the sufferer. We had better hope that such victory is possible; and if by "we" is meant American readers, then how much more readers in the Caribbean, where that suddenness much more regularly cuts life short. The double action of "The Suddentree," with its lamentation and elevation, characterizes Scott's stance as he reflects on Jamaican history with the vulnerability of an open heart and the scant protection of poetic language.

"Epitaph," perhaps Scott's most frequently anthologized and one of his most impressive short poems, dwells on the image of a hanged slave to turn it into an occasion for meditation. Morris observes that the poem "seems to suggest that anger is an easier, less appropriate response than reverent regret." The opening oxymoron is hard to forget:

> They hanged him on a clement morning, swung
> between the falling sunlight and the women's
> breathing, like a black apostrophe to pain.

The whole poem, thirteen lines long, is about the still moment in the interstice, the space of the apostrophe that interrupts the word, the moment of violence, of death. The remarkable thing here, however, is the atmosphere of silent wonder and meditation cast over the action in the poem:

> All morning while the children hushed
> their hopscotch joy and the cane kept growing
> he hung there sweet and low.

>   At least that's how
>   they tell it. It was long ago
>   and what can we recall of a dead slave or two
>   except that when we punctuate our island tale
>   they swing like sighs across the brutal
>   sentences, and anger pauses
>   till they pass away.

In memory the hanged men have become moments that give pause to the brutality of history. In that pause is the defining characteristic of Jamaican lyric.[11]

Edna Manley's open letter to Scott observes that he shares with other Jamaican poets "a special kind of tolerance" in which "there is protest, strong protest, but not bitterness." She compliments him as having "the gift of engaging in discussions with himself," a "dynamic self-development" that is less a wrestling than a "dialogue" with the angel (*Uncle Time* xiii). Toward the end of *Uncle Time* there appear several poems expressing in somewhat ritualized, formal ways a coming black uprising. "Endgame," for instance, using the language of chess, closes laconically: "A bishop watches patiently. How/she will scream!//Black to move." Before Scott, Herman Melville had explored the lyric of war by slowing down, ritualizing, and formalizing the terrible confrontations of the Civil War, but a retrospective reflection is easier than a prospective one. In the four "Black Mass" poems that follow "Endgame," the unholy rite depicted is a human sacrifice, treated with solemnity.[12] The strange combination of extreme violence and a quiet, meditative performance of it is Scott's signature throughout this sequence. The closing poem in the quartet, "Black Mass: Recessional," reflects calmly on the blood rite: "it is time to praise/whatever after such killing will make us kind."

"No sufferer," the final poem in *Uncle Time*, is an evocation of the Rastafarian spirit by someone who, as the poem's title announces, is not one of them but finds common ground enough and, through the connotations of words, a common culture. The title employs the Jamaican connotation of "sufferer" as someone who is black and poor. Continuing from the title (therefore implying that the speaker is not one of the poor), it begins, "but in/the sweating gutter of my bone/Zion seems far/also," and proceeds to its final five lines that mix the special vocabulary of Rasta with Scott's high poetic diction:[13]

> : in the dread time of my living
> while whatever may be human chains me
> away from the surfeit of light, Mabrak
> and the safe land of my longing,
> acknowledge I.

From the start of Scott's poetry the homeland has been loaded too richly with memory to form a simple nostalgic image. Now through Rastafarian typology it becomes merged with the Promised Land, and the homesickness is tinged with a righteous rage that now, in the last line, etches the outline of his selfhood.

Scott's second book of poems, *Dreadwalk* (1982), attempts to come to grips with the violence over race and political movements that characterized the Americas and especially Jamaica in the 1970s. Here he sets aside much of the grace, beauty, and calm of his earlier poems in searching for a new intensity; in some places Frederico García Lorca and Pablo Neruda seem to be influences. The people and animals of the first volume who were cut open sacrificially are now more prominent. Breiner states succinctly the danger to lyric in such a time—it is in the poets themselves: "At the height of the 1970s the attack on 'Europe' becomes in some hands an attack on 'poetry' itself as an alien conception" (136). This conscious and intentional deculturalizing movement, felt certainly all over the world in the 1960s and 1970s, elicited Scott's defense of poetry in "More Poem":

> "No more poem!" he raged, eye red;
> "A solitary voice is wrong,
> Jericho shall fall, shall fall
> at the People's song!"...
>
> No. See the flesh? It is cave, it is
> stone. Seals every I away from light.
> Alone. Man must chant as Man can
> gainst night.

"For Scott," writes Breiner, "poetry is not a luxury, is not the exclusive property of either the elite or the subaltern. It is a human imperative" (138).

Scott's third volume, *Strategies* (1989), indicates his growth and deepening as he blends the sharper consciousness of history present in *Dreadwalk* with the concerns of *Uncle Time*. "Crossing" may be the best of these, a poem about the Middle Passage, though it takes considerable time dwelling with the poem to discern clearly that this familiar subject is indeed the scene depicted. Much more elusive than Hayden's famous "Middle Passage," Scott's poem musters its language in a palpable struggle with the mystery of *how* destiny, a collective destiny for spirit and a rooting for the soul, can come out of such a wrenching event. The breakers against the ship "left like whispers/turning quiet, thin/voices hitched against the tar-caulked timbers." Only the attitude of evocativeness, without content, is suggested. The sound grows more distinct—at least in description—and "drown[s]...the ship's creaking litany of loss" in what now seems describable as a drumbeat:

>something hatched in old fires
>something behind us
>something that we knew
>like hands on a drumhead...
>the noise of Its coming
>washed every wound
>Its flight repeating
>great hoarse hymns of longing, and Sanctify. And
>followed.

By the end of this passage the faint, ill-defined, unknown, and merely rhythmic thing has become an "It" with a holy and cleansing power. "It" reappears in the midst of their activities from moment to moment; finally it "testif[ies]": "*I am memory. Here. Follow*/crying against death we heard It/testify...." That the lyric spirit can come out of pain is an affirmation one can make thoughtlessly, superficially, but perhaps no poet in recent years has struggled with it so earnestly and yet arrived at a sense of lyric that is not a commodity or an anodyne but a power, a mystery, an It.

While love poetry is the staple of lyric, few of Scott's early poems are love poems, though he embraces the topic later. An exception in *Uncle Time* is "The Reunion," a short poem that examines two lovers reuniting, in which the only trait hinting that this could develop into a powerful theme is the remarkable attentiveness of his language.

Strategies contains an important announcement of a new level of Scott's attention to this theme: one of his finest and most anthologized poems, "Marrysong":[14]

> He never learned her, quite. Year after year
> that territory, without seasons, shifted
> under his eye. An hour he could be lost
> in the walled anger of her quarried hurt
> on turning, see cool water laughing where
> the day before there were stones in her voice.
> He charted. She made wilderness again.
> Roads disappeared. The map was never true.
> Wind brought him rain sometimes, tasting of sea—
> and suddenly she would change the shape of shores
> faultlessly calm. All, all was each day new:
> the shadows of her love shortened or grew
> like trees seen from an unexpected hill,
> new country at each jaunty helpless journey.
> So he accepted that geography, constantly strange.
> Wondered. Stayed home increasingly to find
> His way among the landscapes of her mind.

This is a remarkable poem not least in that one can read it as being about a man and a woman or about a man and Jamaica. Many of his poems are built on extended similes that go so far as sometimes to become reverse similes, leaving the ostensible tenor of the figure as only a kind of spiderweb-like framework. Here, both are equal: love, marriage, homeland, and the poet's endless exploration of the muse are fused in this important poem. It portrays knowing not as command but as intimacy. Whether about his beloved or about his beloved land, "Marrysong" gets at an aspect of being that is often associated with the feminine but manifests the beauty of all living being: changefulness, unpredictability. Its inexhaustible freshness is indicated through the images of water, "cool water laughing," whose currents "change the shape of shores/faultlessly calm." Consequently, "All, all was each day new." The stance of the lyric poet toward this ever-fresh source is given by the man, who is typically male enough to start out wanting to control, to reduce the territory to a map; but as he learns, "the map was never true." Always with a patient appreciation, he decides to go ahead and devote himself to learning her "geography," her "landscapes," both formed by the tracing out of lines. What U.S. poet could write anything like this?

It is now over twenty years since *Strategies*, the last volume of poems Scott assembled before his death. For this and for a happier reason, now is a particularly auspicious moment to review his work and his stature: his friend and mentor Mervyn Morris has brought out a posthumous collection of his poems after *Strategies*, selected and edited according to his estimate of Scott's own intentions, and titled, with appropriately pregnant understatement, *After-Image* (2008). Thanks to Morris's efforts, one is able to ascertain that in the scarcely more than two years remaining to him after the publication of *Strategies*, Scott produced a resilient and serene sheaf of poems, all conscious of his impending death, not yielding to it but using the pressure of that ultimate event to develop his craft and vision further.

In *After-Image* Scott's economy with words reaches a new level, paired with his dancer's sense of rhythm and a mood of calm, openness, and reflection that is suffused throughout the eighty-four poems in this volume. One notable poem is simply titled "Open" and sets the scene at the center of many of these poems: his room. Momentarily blocked in his writing, the poet opens his window, prompted by rain outside, "hoping/this itch and dry of images will change," and sees a world alive, "fluent lizards/writing their sentences of joy." He is transformed subtly and is "suddenly guest": a change of role that can refer to his decentering from himself as he witnesses the exuberance of nature but also to his foreignness in Connecticut, "learning still the phonemes/of a bird's trill," and finally, implicitly, to his awareness of his limited tenure on earth.

Scott's stock-taking of his combined cultural heritage continues to be instructive. "Third World Blues" assesses this betweenness directly as he designates himself sole citizen of his own "Third World," which draws on Africa and Europe alike:

> Something of darkness here, of jazz-horn heat,
> but something too of minuet...
>   ...And not all the blues, the concrete
> jungles of this Third World, mine, can defeat
> that pale and civil music when it comes.

> So I make my own new way; I entreat
> no tribal blessing or honour. I build—
> lonely a little—my house. It is filled
> with ghosts, with their summoning air, I greet
> them all....

The Western tradition serves him as a ready resource. Two poems are biblical evocations of lyric moments, one of making and one of grieving. "Day Six" turns out to be about the creation of Adam, and it resembles the early poem "Bird of Passage" on the difficulty of making a poem. "A Sound of Birds" meditates on the cockcrow of the gospels and Peter's betrayal. Classical material is less prominent, but one poem, "Helen," drawing tacitly on Homer's tender look at her returned home in *The Odyssey*, sketches her in a reflective mood. That the Greeks, the Bible, and the English lyric are constant bearings in his work is a point made in a seemingly playful shorthand in "Nibblesong":

> Sometimes
> a sheet slips from the table.
> Catch it and read; it says
> Call no man blessed
> till. Where are the songs of.
> What shall it profit a man. All
> incomplete.

The tragedians, Keats, and the evangelists. Are the lines meant to await new endings in a Caribbean spirit? But each "mouse-nibbled" line originally ended saying something about finality, about death or dying ("Where are the songs of [spring?]" is answered proleptically in the poem's first words, "Spring poems are over"). In that mortal context the lost line endings become inevitable, irremediable.

The image of the union of lovers has its strongest presence in these late poems. Reminiscent of Donne, Scott puns significantly on his spouse's name: "Joy" becomes a kind of shorthand indicator of her trace at the point most indicative of his lyric approach: "Adam-bright response to joy" in "The Sunday Loving," for instance, which figures lovemaking as religious service. (There are also bawdier explorations; in general sex brings out more of wit than of ritual here.) "Tracksong" and "Cross

Country," though they are lesser poems, explore the situation of Donne's "Valediction" poems, separation from one's beloved on a necessary journey. Several other poems record his absence from and the joy of his return to Joy. In "Beast" he writes, "I keep/a certain hunger//muzzled....I take it on journeys/to and from/your face." The perfect openness of "Manuscript" is a brief but complete triumph, recalling the implication of endless wonder evoked in "Marrysong":

> That year
> arranged you
> on a clean page of my life
> like a new poem. I read you, line by line
> I learned your rhythms, calm and sure,
> observing how your warm hand rhymed with mine.
> No one had written on me so before.
> I treasure that strange poem more and more.

Some of these poems risk moments of declaring, however briefly, the ultimate attainment of the lyric state. "The Sunday Loving" ends:

> I celebrate no fall, no
> descent from grace,
> the achievement of no cross.
> Here I regain what is in us of loss,
> Found in your face.

And "Tracksong" has a lyric retort to Frost: "In a little while/there will be promises to keep, but now/journey is its own end."

Yet love and lovemaking achieve this order and peace for Scott now only in view of an imminent end. As one rereads these final poems, one senses in most of them the pressure of death; and as arranged by Morris they build increasingly toward facing it openly. At first they are hopeful according to a comforting scheme: in "After-Image" he is confident that his poems will survive his demise, figuring his body as a machine and the poems as plants flowering. "Seedsong" uses a more complicated analogy. He sees a bird eat the seeds of plants in the cemetery, and then the bird's unexpected return the next day is depicted in the poem's short last lines that begin comically and end with a significant wonder:

> It shits on my neat
> green
> garden.
>
> I do not know
> what will grow.

In a somewhat longer poem, "A Comfort of Crows," it is the graceful pattern the soaring crows form as they gather above anything dead that offers "a mercy," "a new and difficult solace," and the poem ends with this reflection:

> there is no dead place nor dying so terrible
> but weaves above it surely, breaking
> the fragile air with beauty of its coming,
> a comfort of crows.

Often, however, death is a waiting presence, as in "Minos," in which he knows he must go to the center of the labyrinth and the king of the poem's title is waiting "with kind hands." The last nineteen poems, taken as a whole, are almost unbearable in their combination of poise and grace in facing what is ultimately unimaginable. Although new analogies for his situation emerge, notably dance exercises, still a sense of running out of creative responses runs beneath them. "Icon" and "Diary of a Counter-Revolutionary," like "Minos," focus on mysterious presences that seem to be waiting for him or seeking him out. Some few poems make simple assertions against the victory of death, like the clever "Game" and "Poem against Magic: For Mella," which recalls the 1929 assassination of a Cuban revolutionary and ends by addressing him: "Share what is yours/and grow stronger/...mas fuerte/que el Presidente/Muerte." Two pieces especially face dying without evasions: "On the Edge" ("there is a certain satisfaction from/questions articulated/like bone under the appetites") and "Goodbyesong" ("We always knew the quick, splendid affections/of this carnival would fade/...tent and field exchanged/for the applause of other, darker places"). Scott practices no Art of Holy Dying, but in "Butterfly Dream" he examines himself dancing ("They say it's a long time...before/there's only dust; I want to look my best") and then asleep, "listening to the traffic/of my dreams." And in the last poem, "The Editor," he takes his last comfort from the analogy of writing, imagining "that One/who will justify all/at the margin"—the final editor of one's rough draft of living:

> ...that blue hand that
> could be here, now,
> shaping the end of my line
> to his

Even though, taken alone, many of these closing poems might not seem to be about dying at all, together they provide evidence that the approach of an early death afforded Scott the occasion to muster his powers and look on this supreme lyric enemy with serenity, gravity, and honesty. No trace of special pleading mars his work. Nor does any question of identity trouble its depths. For, though he accepted graciously the existential gifts that graced the lives of two of the greatest English lyric poets—a cherished marriage (Donne) and a slow death from disease (Keats)—Scott was not a British poet. He thoroughly inhabited his "third" world, blending the modern West, the older Western tradition, and the beauty and suffering of the West Indies. But he was essentially free from the domination of any influence. Death itself, of whose growing pressure he was keenly aware, could not crush before the end the sense of lyric wonder that gave rise to his poems.

NOTES

1. See Chamberlin's discussion (55).

2. In this short book Brathwaite goes much more thoroughly and incisively into all that I am merely hinting at here about West Indian idiom and cadence.

3. Forty years ago, interviewing Derek Walcott, Dennis Scott challenged him by reporting that "Eddy Brathwaite...once said that you were a humanist poet as distinct from a folk poet." Walcott disagreed (Scott, "Walcott," 77-82).

4. See especially Walcott's *Omeros* and his Nobel Prize lecture, *The Antilles: Fragments of Epic Memory*, and Brathwaite's *The Arrivants: A New World Trilogy* and his two-volume creative essay *MR*.

5. See Breiner's discussion of "Literary Evening" (138-39).

6. See Chamberlin's discussion (155).

7. See Chamberlin's discussion (37-38).

8. Philp's encomium continues: "More than anything, however, Dennis taught me that Jamaica was a place to be loved and that there are many faces to love....Dennis taught us Joyce, Shakespeare, Frost and DH Lawrence, and when we finished the official curriculum in four months, Dennis invited some of his friends (Rex Nettleford, Lorna Goodison, and Christopher Gonzalez) to come to Jamaica College or we visited their homes to learn about their work" ("Happy Birthday").

9. Morris in his Introduction and Hanna have good discussions of "Bird of Passage."

10. "Uncle Time," notes Hanna, "was the first attempt at writing serious poetry in the creole in Jamaican literature, preceded only by Louise Bennett's foundational comedic offerings."

11. Philp's very good discussion of "Epitaph" quotes as an analogue to Scott's implied attitude Derek Walcott's comment: "I feel no shame in having endured the colonial experience....It was cruel, but it created our literature" ("Meanings" 50).

12. According to Morris these were written while Scott was in Athens, Georgia, in the early seventies, at the height of black-white conflict.

13. Mervyn Morris' Introduction explains some of the locutions.

14. Also anthologized in the *Heinemann Book of Caribbean Poetry.*

A MANIFESTO:

THE CURRENT SCENE

16

Lyric and the Self

FREDERICK TURNER

The distinguishing mark of lyric as against any other kind of poetry is the intense presence of the self of the poet. That self is dominant both in the content and in the form of a lyric poem. Even when a lyric poem does not directly describe or express the emotions of the poet, its point of view is distinctively subjective, and the world it describes is marinated with the poet's feelings and intentions.

Perhaps one could say the same of all poetry, indeed all writing and speech. But the fact that lyric exists as a form in which subjectivity is both expected and required points to an interesting possibility. It is that *other* forms do achieve, or at least pretend to achieve, a certain objectivity or disinterestedness, an impersonality that demands an entirely different sort of trust on the part of the reader from that we accord to lyric—a trust that appeals to our own experience of the world as opposed to that we have in the honesty of the writer to his own impressions. Even to pretend to objectivity is to concede the possibility of its existence, hypocrisy being the tribute vice pays to virtue. The lyric, then, plays an odd quiet role beside its more obvious ones: of setting, by its own exception from it, a benchmark for the objective kinds of veridicality. Although the lyric's subjectivity is the figure that stands out against an objective ground, that figure is also the ground of a kind of objectivity that today is called deeply into question by discourse analysts of all kinds, feminist, queer, postcolonial, new historicist, neo-Marxist, and the rest. If, as Wordsworth put it, lyric poetry is "the spontaneous overflow of powerful feelings," such a claim posits the existence of its opposite, the premeditated shapings of balanced reason. And the very presence of the former is a sort of guarantee of the integrity of the latter.

The subjectivity of the lyric constrains the content it can comfortably cover. It is not at its best, for instance, in dealing with scientific discoveries (unless they have medical consequences for the poet) or distant or past political events (again, unless they have personal relevance). I have noticed, translating Goethe, that much of his finest poetry is ignored not only by translators but even by editors because its subject is scientific, such as the metamorphosis of the plants or the science of light, and its gaze is directed, with utmost care and disinterestedness, upon the being of the non-human other. The reader's expectation of lyricism is dashed, and in an age when lyricism is all that is demanded of poetry, the attention flags. Herman Melville's fine collection of poems on the Civil War, *Battle Pieces*, has also been ignored in comparison with Whitman's because its collective, public, and historical voice was so much at odds with the expectations aroused by its lyric-like form.

Lyric poetry is not good at other people's feelings either, unless those others are emotionally connected to the poet. The authorial impartiality required for true drama, the disappearance of the author from the work as Flaubert envisioned him, "aloof, indifferent, paring his fingernails," is antithetical to the lyric voice. Perhaps the love lyric, of which all other lyric poetry is almost a minor branch, is successful partly because it can to some extent break out of the poet's self-concern and into the dramatic life of the beloved while never abandoning the expected tone of personal passion.

Lyric poetry tends to be in the present tense, the domain of unique personal identity. This is the case even when its subject is, as it often is, the poet's past; the past tense of the poem's ostensible subject is bracketed by the implied present tense of its real subject, the feelings aroused now by the poet's memories. Wordsworth's definition is again excellent: "it takes its origin from emotion recollected in tranquility."

One of the lyric's most important characteristics is what is usually called "voice." Some voices, like George Herbert's or Sylvia Plath's or Rainer Maria Rilke's or Sappho's, are unmistakable in only a fragment. One's voice is almost as recognizable to our formidable neural hardware as is one's face. The very word "lyric," from the Greek *lyros*, lyre, implies the single personal singing voice to which the lyre was the normal accompaniment. Thus melody, by which personal tone is resolved into a form that can survive the speaker's absence or death, is essential to lyric; and some kind of form is necessary to act as a language, scale, or carrier-wave for that melody.

It is true that the lyric is, at present, in a state of crisis. But the production of lyric poetry, and its presence in the academy and in publication, has never been more dominant. The lyric mode has overwhelmed all the other genres of poetry, as a glance at almost any literary periodical will show. The poetry workshop, out of which most contemporary published verse flows, is almost always devoted to the articulation and branding of the poet's individual lyric voice, almost never to science, history, statecraft, other arts, technology, economics, war, or any of the other subjects that poets have graced with their insights over the last six thousand years or so. Arts once considered integral to poetry, such as rhetoric, logic, and grammar, are no longer taught to beginning poets, since lyric poetry not only does not seem to demand them but indeed often explicitly seems to reject them as artifices and obstacles to the honest flow of feeling.

How did this lyric dominance come about? Various reasons suggest themselves. Perhaps the most positive and encouraging one is that the individual has become increasingly important over the last two hundred years. Our economy needs individuals, as workers, consumers, and shareholders, rather than groups such as guilds, clans, religious communities, or hereditary aristocracies. The democratic vote turns the individual into the sovereign. Progress in arts, sciences, technology, and business relies on individual giftedness and innovation rather than on collective and traditional custom. Morally we have come to recognize that individual rights must be the foundation, if not the whole, of any ethical system and political constitution. The self has rightfully achieved its true dignity and valuation, and the lyric poem is the celebration of that self. The question we will have to face later is whether the individual self cut loose from its communal and past foundations is worth celebrating.

Addressing the question of lyric's dominance in terms of critical fashion, one could cite the examples and precepts of such poets as Poe, Wilde, Baudelaire, Rimbaud, and Mallarmé. The romantic and postromantic poets had certainly expanded the range and justified reputation of lyric, but they always hankered after other poetic genres that came less easily to their temperaments, and sometimes they achieved great successes in them. In England Coleridge with the narrative poem (*The Rime of the Ancient Mariner*), Wordsworth with the epic (*The Prelude*, notwithstanding its autobiographical subject), Byron with the satire (*Don Juan*), Keats with the romance (*The Eve of St. Agnes*), all successfully attempted non-lyric poetic works and implicitly acknowledged that the lyric flourished best in a rich matrix of other poetic forms and genres. We can similarly cite Victor Hugo in France and Goethe and Schiller in Germany, artists whose lyric poems were part of an oeuvre that included much more "objective" and disinterested forms. But Poe and Baudelaire and their ilk went much further, essentially dismissing poetic narrative, the longer poetic forms, logical and empirical argument, rhetorical persuasion, and objective, useful, and informative content as having no place in poetry. Poetry should be an absolutely original and subjective reverie; its purity and full force could only be found in its lyric integrity, unique imaginative vision, and personal interiority. It is from these sources that contemporary lyric flows.

But there have been major changes in the flow. A second stage in the ascendancy of lyric began when such poets as Mallarmé insisted that what lyric poetry gave up in terms of discursive rationality, it had to make up in terms of music. The state of poetic dreaminess needed an acoustic narcotic for its portal. The French admiration of Poe largely resulted from Poe's English verse sounding as good to the French ear as any French alexandrine verse, and Baudelaire's celebrated translations of him emphasized this point. Verlaine is a formidable metricist, as are Swinburne, Elizabeth Barrett Browning, and Dante Gabriel Rossetti, all major contributors to the new ideal of poetry as paradigmatically lyrical. But with the advent of the twentieth century, *vers libre* and free verse began to dominate. If argument, plot, informative substance, dramatic mimesis, and so on were all deemed obstacles to the free flow of subjective self-expression, surely the tricky artificial business of rhyme, meter, stanza, and so on were just as obstructive. Why should not they too be discarded? After all, as so many free verse poets from D. H. Lawrence, Eliot, and Pound to Charles Olson and William Carlos Williams have insisted, free verse takes as much, nay more, discipline and taste and exactness of ear as meter. Even when handled with technical mastery (perhaps especially so, they argued), meter too often trots mechanically along with only the simulacrum of personal speech rhythm, a substitute for, rather than an expression of, the subjective voice.

The third stage of the conquest of poetry by the lyric was the realization that without the need for deep knowledge and scholarship of the world, without the need for tedious technical mastery and virtuosity in versification, and with the requirement of only deep personal feeling and an expressive vocabulary, anyone could write poetry. If lyric needed only a human self, and poetry was lyric poetry, everybody was a potential poet. The results were the confessional poetry of the 1960s and 1970s (interrupted only by the political verse of Vietnam protest, an odd and temporary return to public poetry) and the current state of affairs, where there are perhaps 20,000 published poets in the United States of America, almost all of them lyricists.

Other reasons than literary critical ones might be suggested for the dominance of lyric. With romanticism came a hypostasizing of the arts and an emphasis on their purity and elevation. Artists became specialists in the art form in which their mysterious divine genius dictated to them. Mixed art forms came to be regarded as second-class. Connoisseurship and expertise led to specialization among audiences as well as among creators; a newly cultured middle class needed expert cicerones to instruct them in taste. J. J. Winckelmann's preference for the pure statuary of ancient Greece (so conveniently scrubbed by time of their original gaudy paint and religious ritual uses) is followed, as romanticism gave way to modernism, by the turn away from the narrative in painting, the demotion of the programmatic in serious music, and the eventual rejection, in architecture, of any organic or humanistic reference. In this context poetry itself was purged of the unpoetic as painting was of the unvisual, music of the unmusical, sculpture of the unsculptural, and architecture of the unarchitectonic and unfunctional. Anything that could be done by another form—storytelling by the novel, drama by theater, accurate description by photography, melody by popular music, argument by the essay—was purged from poetry, leaving the lyric naked in all its glory.

Another reason for the rise of lyric is as one of many consequences of the Newtonian revolution in the sciences and the subsequent recognition of the principles of thermodynamics. The Newtonian universe was a deterministic one. Pierre-Simon Laplace extrapolated Newton's demonstration of the predictability of physical trajectories and created from it a vision of the world in which every event was uniquely determined by the positions, vectors, and momenta of all particles in the universe at any given point in the event's past, including, presumably, all our decisions, experiences, thoughts, and feelings. Rudolf Clausius and Ludwig Boltzmann added the gloomy thought that not only is the universe (including ourselves) a piece of deterministic clockwork but the clock is running down: entropy or thermal disorder will steadily increase until a steady state is reached, the heat death of the universe. Much of the philosophical effort in the next century was devoted to dealing with the challenge that these concepts presented to any humanistic philosophy, from the work of Hegel and Kant in defining ethical and aesthetic realms independent of physical causality to that of Schopenhauer, Spengler, and Nietzsche in absorbing the dismal message into our moral and cultural understanding.

Poets, too, paid attention to these developments. (Poets in those days often followed science with more than a dilettante's interest.) In "Mock on, Mock on, Voltaire, Rousseau" and throughout the Prophetic Books and elsewhere, William Blake is clearly resisting the mechanistic determinism of the new natural philosophy. Goethe masterfully absorbs the new ideas into an organic philosophy that is in fact eerily prophetic of our current theories of emergent unpredictable self-organization, and in so doing he truly escapes the dilemma of natural order versus human freedom. We can see the pessimism of the new science clearly in such works as Tennyson's *Idylls of the King* and *In Memoriam* and in Arnold's "Dover Beach," and the pessimistic interpretation is the one that won out. The upshot of the poets' meditations could be paraphrased thus: "Out there in the physical world of objects in motion and collective racial drives, there can be no freedom, no transcendent meaning: it is all a dog-eat-dog struggle over diminishing resources of political and mechanical power. We dig up and burn the free energy of the world to power our civilization, merely hastening its decline. Only in the intimate recesses of the self, in the *thalamos* of the human heart, can freedom, meaning, and value be found. We are bound to a history and to bodies that are irreversible and are along for the ride. But at least in our lyric self-expression we can, if fruitlessly, defy and resist the universal downward slide. In this stance we choose to interpret nature not as objective events but as the mirror of our own feelings; we cannot after all know the *Ding an sich*, so we might as well take our subjective feelings about nature as our guide to reality." Since other genres of poetry seemed increasingly hostage to the physical, economic, and sociopolitical forces of necessity (heroic poetry merely the propaganda of power interests, philosophical poetry merely the ideology of the bourgeois ruling group [see Marx and Engels], religious poetry a comforting opiate), the lyric was the last stronghold of human values.

Of course these generalizations have huge exceptions, the largest being Goethe himself, who detected early the intellectual errors of the romanticism he helped to initiate. He clearly saw the flaws in any mechanistic natural philosophy in its own terms and, as a serious biologist, recognized the profound originality of natural growth and evolution. Religious poets like Hopkins and Dickinson took the new science as merely confirming the old distinction between matter and spirit (see Hopkins' "That Nature Is a Heraclitean Fire," "The Leaden Echo and the Golden Echo" or Dickinson's "Mine–by the Right of the White Election!," and "Because I could not stop for Death"), and their lyricism is not infected by any defensive pessimism about physical necessity. The Americans, until the world wars brought them under the spell of European pessimism, were able to reformulate the new science in terms of philosophical pragmatism and theological transcendentalism. But the main line of Western poetry has been dominated by the short lyric poem, usually celebrating an existential moment of private experience and by implication marking out a transient and indefensible space of free experience from a perceived public and physical world of necessity. Nature indeed figures largely in such poetry, but when it does, it is a nature not of science but of mysticism and empathetic union.

A further reason for the lyric's ideological dominance may well be political. In many parts of the world as the state hypertrophied into twentieth-century giantism, overwhelming the civil societies out of which the state grew, the realm of inner personal freedom shrank until it reached its final fallback positions, one of which was the lyric poem. This phenomenon is obvious in the totalitarian countries, where lyric poets were the last holdouts against the hegemony of the state. Their heroic defense of the free person makes a grand litany: Anna Ahkmatova, Boris Pasternak, Osip Mandelstam, Vladimir Mayakovsky, Marina Tsvetaeva, Joseph Brodsky, Paul Celan, Miklós Radnóti, Attila József, Mihály Babits, Czesław Miłosz, among others. Even in many of the free countries, state socialism was taking up more than half of the nation's economic activity, and the state's self-justifying politics, with its attendant propaganda, was permeating all forms of artistic expression. The lyric poem was, it seemed, one of the only places (together with abstractionist painting and music and the lovers' bed) where the free personal self could flourish. Much had to be sacrificed in this last stand, though. Poets came to mistrust any of the techniques—heroic and elevated language, "sentimental" and moral emotions, allegorical meanings, depictions of exemplary actions, logical suasion, and the devices of rhyme, meter, and trope—that had served the national anthems of the totalitarians who would have stolen their souls.

And there were risks, too, in this abandonment of the public territory to the state. If poets stuck to private reverie and the existential moment, the fortes of lyric, they were little threat to the commissars. Pasternak was tolerated by Stalin; Yevgeny Yevtushenko and Andrey Voznesensky even had their official personality cults in the Soviet Union. Indeed, the moral license they promoted in the private realm actually served the state's purposes well, since the loss of personal discipline in the private cultural sphere would lead both to a morally flabbier populace without the political steel needed to oppose tyranny and to a condition of personal and economic dependency that made the state increasingly indispensable. If this sounds like a wild assertion, consider the demographic and cultural collapse that followed *perestroika* in Russia. If every citizen lives the poets' bohemian life-style of vodka, free love, and existentialism, the state must take over the parental role to protect him from himself (as we now see Vladimir Putin doing).

In the Western democracies the turn to lyric served the state in another way. Without the political discipline of totalitarianism, the most pressing form of discipline that the individual experiences is the economic constraint of the marketplace. Most people raised in a traditional way, with religious, customary, and community reminders of their contractual duties as human beings, accept that discipline as more or less fair. But the lyric mode by its very nature foregrounds the feelings, desires, and interests of the self and looks with a jaded eye upon the requirements of society, the vulgar pressures of trade, and the injunctions of economic authority. The very contrarianism that made martyrs of the first generation of great poets under Stalin could make Western poets into enemies of the economic system, market capitalism, that supports their own democratic freedoms and balances the power of the state.

As the lyric became easier to write than to read, the pleasure of the form shifted from the reader to the writer: the 20,000 poets now write for perhaps 5,000 serious readers of contemporary poetry (judging by the print-runs of most major poetry collections in America). A whole industry (creative writing schools, workshops, poetry readings, prizes, residencies, arts councils, grants, and so on) has sprung up to help people with the urge to express themselves find the resources to call themselves poets. Since the industry cannot be supported by publication royalties or performance fees (supply so outpacing demand), it has become largely subsidized by the state through the universities and colleges. Industry members have naturally joined the constituency of those arguing for more state patronage of the arts, thus adding to the general tendency of the state to engross power into itself and away from civil society. Lyric poetry is in danger of becoming the state's preferred safety valve and consolation prize for the discontented.

How, then, can lyric be in a state of crisis if, as it seems, it has triumphed over its rivals and now rules the domain of poetry almost by definition? The account I have given may already suggest that the lyric's very success may be its problem. In redefining poetry as essentially and exclusively lyrical, poetry's friends denuded it of all the ways in which it might find common cause with the imperfect but durable institutions of civil society: the Church, the heroic customs of military patriotism and honor, the marketplace (so vitally included in the worlds of Chaucer and Shakespeare), the pieties of marriage and family, the law, the sciences, and so on. Artists and poets who felt that to accept the role of respectable citizen was to compromise and corrupt their art were often depriving themselves of the audience and patronage they needed to preserve their independence from the state. Bohemia is fatally vulnerable to its protectors and suppliers. And since poetry's very medium is the common coin of language, to alienate oneself from the rich vernacular fund of associations and values that civil society generates through idiom, jargon, craft terminology, popular science, and so on, even if in the search for a truly authentic and unique personal language, is to dry up the sources of imagery and symbol. It was Shakespeare who said that all his best was dressing old words new; he recognized his dependency upon the mother tongue and the subtle fallacies of originality.

As lyric came to dominate poetry, the realm of poetry itself shrank, leaving poetry's old functions as folk history, prayer, work-song, spiritual advice, entertainment, philosophical explanation, national epic, reasoned ideological suasion, comedy, tragedy, satire, mythmaking, biography, science, battle-hymn, and so on to other media. And since those other media did not possess poetry's huge prerogative of being the canonical language in which all groups in a society can communicate with one another, the specialization of poetry as lyric deprived society itself of the glue and ligaments by which it finds its higher unity. Where poetry still remains public and civic is in protest, but protest poetry, tragically, is almost always an attack more on the "hypocritical" institutions of civil society and thus more on the sentiments of possible new readers than on the real enemies of human freedom and meaning. The common marketplace supplies the mulch and manure out of which poetry grows, but poets seem more eager to chastise it for its neglect of poets than to persuade it that poetry can once more become its home, garden, and bond.

The reader might take these reflections as an attack on the lyric poem. This is very far from my intention. In the context of all the other genres and forms and functions and modes of poetry, lyric does indeed merit the high praise it has been given in the last three hundred years. For perhaps of all things in the world that are the most marvelous, the human self takes the prize. Of the genres that specifically celebrate it—comedy, tragedy, and lyric—lyric takes the most direct, searching, and immediate path to the mystery of selfhood. I remember that my first impulse toward becoming a poet (I was about nine years old) was to express and describe the astonishing miracle that I had just noticed, my own consciousness, my own power to represent the outside natural world in my inner self. The exploration of the self has been one of the greatest triumphs of Western civilization, leading to the recognition of the primary value of freedom and the great political institutions of democracy. Montaigne, Descartes, Shakespeare, Donne, Rembrandt, Whitman, Freud all helped to recognize, articulate, and construct that marvel that we hear in Radnóti's great poem "Foamy Sky":

Foamy Sky

The moon sways in a foamy sky.
How strange that I'm alive. A bland,
efficient death searches this age
and they turn white on whom it lays its hand.

Sometimes the year looks round and shrieks,

looks round and faints away.
What kind of autumn lies in wait,
what winter dulled with agony to grey?

The forest bled, and every hour
in that revolving time bled too.
The wind was scrawling numbers, huge,
and darkening in the unsettled snow.

I have seen certain things, such things
that now the air feels dense as earth.
A rustling tepid silence holds
me fast, as in that time before my birth.

I come to a standstill by this trunk.
It stirs its thick leaves angrily,
reaches a branch down—for my neck?
Now I am neither weak nor cowardly,

just tired. Unmoving. And the branch
searches my hair, terrified, mute:
such things one must forget, but I
have never yet been able to forget.

Foam gushes forth upon the moon.
A dark green venom streaks the sky.
I roll myself a cigarette,
am slowly, carefully, a living I.
                         8 June 1940

Radnóti is a paradigmatic figure in the history of the lyric, and he is worth a closer look. At the time he is writing, he will soon be drafted into his last slave-labor brigade, where he will eventually be shot into a mass grave (from which the notebook containing his last poems will astonishingly be recovered). He stands before us in this poem absolutely alive, an unmistakable subjectivity in a world absolutely devoted to its extermination. A few years after this poem Radnóti makes explicit the role of lyric poetry as he saw it and the threats it faced:

O Ancient Prisons

    O peace of ancient prisons, beautiful
        outdated sufferings, the poet's death,
images noble and heroical,
        which find their audience in measured breath—
how far away you are. Who dares to act
        slides into empty void. Fog drizzles down.
Reality is like an urn that's cracked
        and cannot hold its shape; and very soon
its rotten shards will shatter like a storm.
        What is his fate who, while he breathes, will so
speak of what *is* in measure and in form,
        and only thus he teaches how to know?

        He would teach more. But all things fall apart.
        He sits and gazes, helpless at his heart.
                27 March 1944

Radnóti was one of the few poets of his time who reversed the usual process of beginning as a formal poet of meter and rhyme and turning toward the modernist fashion of free verse in later years. He defiantly became a formal poet just when others were insisting that formal verse was an anachronism. The "ancient prisons," as he ironically calls them, are clearly the traditional strict forms of poetry (this one is itself a sonnet) to which he found his way after his youthful flirtation with free verse. Perhaps, he implies, those ancient prisons were not so bad. The Bastille contained seven prisoners when it fell. Well might the victims of serious professional totalitarian tyranny regret nostalgically the amateurish oppression of the old monarchies, associated by free-verse enthusiasts with the decadent conventions of meter and rhyme! Better the old prisons than the new.

    If, as Radnóti clearly implies in this poem, lyric was helpless against the secular forces of his century, if all that is left for us now is an empty void, a "heap of broken images," as Eliot put it, what is to be done? If the lyric's domination of poetry has not benefited either the lyric or poetry, what is it that the lyric has lost in the process, and what steps might be taken to begin to restore the lyric to its vital human and spiritual role?

Here we come to the nub of this essay, which is that the crisis of the lyric is at bottom the crisis of the self. The dominance of the lyric may fundamentally reflect the need to replace the structures that had maintained the self's integrity. Or rather, perhaps, to compensate for their loss by more and more heroic acts of self-revelation, until only the dregs of a boneless self remain to be sifted over. What were those structures? Paradoxically, I believe, they are the things in a human being that make him capable of tragedy, capable, in Shakespeare's words, of his own distress. They are also what make him capable of comedy, since his rigidities, as Bergson rightly claimed, make him prone to mechanical mishaps of either physical or mental varieties. The grandeur of the traditional lyric poem was that the self that was revealed in it was complete with unbreakable rules—rules of honor, prejudice, loyalty, passion, duty, submission, family solidarity, *duende*, blessing and curse, commitment, chivalry, professional formation. Lyric rose to dominance as those structures decayed; it was an increasingly desperate attempt to assert the value of an entity whose vital functions were shutting down.

It would be easy enough to find culprits for the decay of the conception of the self. The autonomy of the self, its freedom and self-determination, its ability to go to heaven or hell, have been under attack for at least two hundred years. One way of describing what happened would be that the soul was detached from the self and then declared a fable; but without the awful and steely bones of the soul, the self begins to lose its structure. At first it was the hard sciences that seemed to put a limit to the "heft," as Dickinson has it, of the human soul. But it was the humanities and the human and social sciences that more insidiously challenged its writ. When Nietzsche proclaimed the death of God, he knew that he was leaving in the language a huge God-shaped hole that would have to be filled, but it could not be filled by any conception of the self that he was capable of. Although Freud was one of the great heroes of the drama of the self, he could also be read as an explainer-away of the self as a mere scar-tissue protecting the id from the superego. Marx and Engels dismissed the bourgeois self as a sentimental false consciousness, manipulated by class interest. Evolutionary psychology was taken as a revelation of the self as a collection of survival and reproductive drives. And with Derrida, Lacan, and Foucault, the self degenerates into a function of social power.

Historically one could cite at least three major events that seemed to reduce the self to triviality: the carnage of the trenches in the First World War, the systematic regime of lies perpetrated by totalitarian state socialism, and, most important of all, the Holocaust (I owe this insight to my colleague Zsuzanna Ozsvath). The humane interiority of an Anne Frank or a Miklós Radnóti disappears into the black hole of grotesque meaninglessness (though its lovely and pathetic afterglow still blazes from the event horizon where it vanished). What is left is the horrible aimless picaresque storylessness of the darkest holocaust narratives, one senseless event after another.

We are living in the aftermath of these developments, but the contemporary lyric, which of all things one might call upon as the medicine, the *pharmakon*, of the wounded self, offers no healing. Its audience has largely given up on it, turning to the poetry of the past when possible, but shepherdless when confronting the major moral and spiritual issues of our time.

People do not read other people's lyric poems these days because they fear they will encounter someone whose inner dignity they cannot trust, someone who wishes to justify his failure by commiseration or drag the "hypocrite lecteur" into some kind of belittling contract or relieve himself of some of the formless stuff that flows from an unshaped mind and imagination or satisfy his spleen at his own neglect by some kind of insult. When one reads a lyric poem by Donne or Hopkins or Goethe or Radnóti or Borges (or Du Fu or Matsuo Basho or Hafez), one is encountering a self that is capable of making a religious confession, fighting a duel, pursuing for years an unrequited love, enduring torture and martyrdom, vowing (and keeping) celibacy in holy orders, accepting military discipline, laughing itself senseless, sacrificing itself in battle, going blind with scholarship, feeling the guilt of ruining a woman, risking itself on repeated dangerous sea voyages, serving a liege lord, speaking in prayer to God, keeping up an epistolary friendship, facing unmedicated surgery and death, taking up the authority of a father, and ruining itself for the sake of a principle. When such a self reveals itself, it is as if a great athlete were to unveil his body. But if a flabby, timid, divorced creative writing teacher, afraid of death, liberated from the tyranny of ritual discipline, whose deepest opinions come from the *New York Times*, who has never even had to struggle with the limits of rhyme and meter, and who has never had to fight or submit—if such a being strips himself, who wants to see?

It will be noticed that I have confined this diatribe to male poets. Many of these strictures do not apply to female poets, or at least to some female poets. The very nature of female sexuality, with its built-in tragic aura of childbirth, menopause, physical defenselessness against male violence, huge commitments and empathetic vulnerability, and the limitations on female freedom implied by the struggle between motherhood and career, gives women a natural dignity, a natural shame that makes lyric self-revelation interesting. Emily Dickinson's modest reserve makes her poetic nakedness the more shockingly and shamefully beautiful. Whatever one thinks of Plath or Sexton or Rich, their selves burn pretty brightly in their poems. But in these days it is indeed a burning. Poets who have through good or bad luck inherited a grand and dignifying curse can only exorcise it once, in a first slim volume, and are then condemned to a lifetime of self-plagiarism, playing over and over the worn grooves of pain or grievance. It is as if the economic and technological underpinning of modernism, which is the practice of digging old things up and burning them to fuel our engines, is reflected in the contemporary poet's mining of the capital of his own fate and experience. And technology, medicine, and the urge toward social justice are rapidly erasing the difference between the male and female conditions and so also the female advantage as regards existential dignity. If one's election by pain is as a racial minority, a kid from the wrong side of the tracks, or a shunned homosexual, the same problem, of the second book, always arises.

To write good lyric poetry, one must have a self worth writing about. This is not to commit the biographical fallacy, though it comes close. We should not read a lyric poem as a mere *roman à clef* of a sensational personality. If a poet were skillful enough to be able to reproduce perfectly the unselfconscious integrity of a hero, one might be happy to be deceived. But that sort of thing cannot be faked. Just as one can walk into a room and at once know that its taste is genuine or fake, so too with a lyric poem.

Our society feels the loss, though it does not know what it has lost. Paradoxically, the vast bulk of the middle class does indeed possess its own everyday dignity, as it goes through its family crises, its PTA politics, its church year, its births, marriages, and funerals, its patriotic celebrations, its small entrepreneurial business adventures, its sports championships, its active charitable work. But a culture needs poetry to articulate those passages and raise them into their proper realm of spiritual importance and memorable brilliance. In moments of great stress and emotion, ordinary people seek for the appropriate form of words, for the true poetic phrase. Lyric, however, bereft of the other poetic genres that gave it relevance and energized its vocabulary, cannot help. Where are the ballads and Pindaric odes and epithalamia and georgics and eclogues and epitaphs and epics that escort the lyric mode to the people?

The future of lyric is not as bleak as this analysis might imply. There has been a distinct change in the wind in the last few years that may portend a recovery of the dignity of the self and thus of the effectiveness and interest of the lyric poem. The New Formalist and New Narrative movements in poetry are providing now a body of practice and expertise, at least, in the ancient techniques of meter, form, poetic storytelling, and architectonic structure. There has been a definite turn away from the confessional mode in poetry and a renewal among younger poets of the ideals of craft and virtuosity. I have discussed these developments elsewhere (Turner "Reading" 8-15).

But these "in-house" improvements will be ineffective without deeper changes in the culture at large. Some of those changes will be demographic; the generation in which the crisis came to a head, the so-called boomers, will not last forever. The most recent generation, hardened in the fire of 9/11, shows some signs of a recommitment to the disciplines of religion, family, military duty, the marketplace, scholarship, technical expertise, and friendship. A new literate culture is emerging, based on electronic text, in which epistolary friendship and the intellectual salon are undergoing a revival, and a new conception of the public as a viable and honest human space is being created.

Perhaps more important still in the long run, there has been an epochal change in the fundamental conception of the physical universe—a change as important as the Newtonian one I discussed earlier in this essay. In fact it is a reversal of many of the ideas that dominated the Enlightenment and Industrial Revolution (without compromising the good science that was done in those periods but rather reinterpreting those ideas in the light of more information). Essentially, science no longer believes in one-line, deterministic cause and effect as the governing principle of all physical relations. Quantum physics postulates an infinity of possible world-lines at the most fundamental particulate level of existence, all of which can be and are chosen, at vanishing levels of probability, by a given physical system. It conceives of physical relations not as causes but as harmonic coordination. Biology postulates a world in which one cause, say, an existing species, can have many different branching effects (e.g., emerging subspecies, destined to found their own genera and families), many of them in competition with each other. Chaos and complexity science show that in any nonlinear dynamical system (and most events in the universe take place in systems of this kind) a better explanation of the outcomes of a given process is in terms of attractors, which "pull" effects into being, rather than in terms of causes, which "push" them. Aristotle's formal and final causes are being reinstated.

If, as the new science implies, the universe is not deterministic and thus not meaningless but rather free and creative, capable of generating organisms and ecosystems that imply their own emergent values, then the self need no longer be conceived of as the last refuge in a world of meaningless mechanism. Instead, the self is a free choosing entity among all the other free choosing entities of the universe, from quantum particles to social animals, and is at home in the world. It need not ensure its integrity by cutting itself off from the public world of knowledge and motive and retreating into a private undetermined world of whim and arbitrary or aleatory art. The self recovers its dignity as a determinant of the future among other determinants. Its subconscious motives and evolutionary provenance and socioeconomic nurture are not the limits but the grammar of its freedom and creativity. Goethe's sense of freedom as discipline, responsibility, and craft has been vindicated.

How may these changes find their due expression in lyric poetry and begin to revive this most important humanistic artform? The following pedagogical suggestion is not meant entirely seriously (the opposition to it as a serious proposal would be overwhelming!) but may be of value as a thought experiment.

The education of the poet has classically been conceived in terms of the mastery of a succession of poetic genres: first lyric, then pastoral poetry, then comedy and tragedy, and finally epic (with perhaps a coda of philosophical, mythological, religious, prophetic, or invocatory poetry in old age). We see Virgil, Dante, Chaucer, Shakespeare, Milton, and Goethe go through their own versions of this progression. One starts out expressing the native subjective passions of one's youth; then one adds the sketchy and stylized characterization of the pastoral nymph and shepherd (who are still mouthpieces for the poet); then one ventures forth into a cast of fully rounded dramatic characters who can challenge the poet's own intentions for their fate; and finally the poet submits himself to an objective historical world (even if the history, as it usually is, is mythic) and offers himself simply to serve the heroes, heroisms, and destinies of a whole society. The coda, if the poet lives that long, is a kind of distillation into simpler and subtler forms of what has been learned in the process. That education is one that starts from the subjective, the self, and travels on into the realm of the objective, the other.

What this sequence relied on, as now becomes obvious, was that the native youthful self of the poet was in fact already deeply imbued with the structures, disciplines, and moral spine inherited from his collective customary culture and from the existential and technological constraints of his world. He was already a formed being, a creature of duties, habits, prejudices, codes of honor, constraints, disappointments, and shames. Part of his poetic education was indeed a *liberation* from those structures and limits as new, more spiritual, spontaneous, individuated, and internalized disciplines took their place.

But as I have pointed out, such a given youthful self can no longer be assumed. A modern youth has not necessarily ever had to restrain his sexuality or battle a repressive family or village context for his beloved. He will not have had to consider or to fight a duel in which he could die. He will not usually have had to face the death of parents and the assumption of family responsibility or have the opportunity to become a priest or be conscripted into an army. He will not have been trained in a craft or have needed to bargain in a marketplace, nor often will he have had to work for a living. His life expectancy would be eighty, not thirty-five, years. There is little, if anything, he needs to be liberated from, except his own self (which has been hugely served already by a psychotherapeutic culture and a self-esteem-based educational system).

Such a being may indeed have as much, or more, potential than the prematurely aged youth of past eras. But any kind of structure in his character or personality cannot be assumed. My modest proposal is that the poetic education of such a person may in fact compensate for all the missing disciplines in his cultural upbringing. Let it be an ordeal—a delightful ordeal, certainly—in which instruction becomes in-struction, the internalization of structure.

If this is the case, then the sequence of genres in the poetic education needs to be pretty much reversed. It should start with philosophical, mythical, and religious ideas, the common property of the society. Then at once it should go to epic, to storytelling, to the forgetfulness of self that comes from the absorption in the adventures of an admired or even feared hero. Here training in meter and form are absolutely essential in order to preserve the poetic integrity of the long narrative and the memorability of the plot points. Likewise, a formidable scholarship in history, natural science, and political, economic, and military philosophy would be needed in order to body forth the social and natural world of the protagonist. The more dialogical world of tragedy should follow. Here all subjective partisanship must at some level be abandoned if the characters are to speak with any true life, and a variety of metrical forms is needed to express the varying dialects of the dramatis personae. Here, too, a passionate curiosity into the human heart is demanded, one which may be permitted to extend to the poet's own heart. Comedy, where the conflict of character comes to be experienced as funny and delightful (rather than threatening and vexing, as it is to the egocentric), should succeed tragedy. Then pastoral, in which the poet's self, now partly formed and disciplined, should take its first shy and modest steps in informing the fable and inspiring the conventional figures.

Only now will the poet be ready for the lyric, when the hardships of his poetic experience will perhaps have united with or even inspired the hardships of his adulthood and when he will have grown a self with crevices, hardpoints, intricacies, resistances, and habits that will make his subjectivity interesting to a reader. The vale of soul-making—the valley of the shadow of death—will have begun to do its necessary work. Only now will the poet have the imaginative experience of dealing with a public world that will give him insight into his reader's needs and expectations. Only now will he have a sense of the self that will make him valuable to his society.

This sequence is not as counterintuitive as it sounds. It may well recapitulate the actual historical emergence of poetry, in which the human species apprenticed itself to its own poetic vocation. It parallels the education of a traditional shaman, in which the strange schizy youth is taught to build his own drum and to submit himself to the myths of the tribe that he may the more richly transcend them on his flying journeys to the underworld and upperworld. Such a course of study would certainly discourage many people who should not be poets. Others, in rejecting its constraints and defining a counterstance to it, might find in the storm and stress of their rebellion the hardening discipline they need to make great lyric poetry.

WORKS CITED

INDEX

PERMISSIONS

Works Cited

Abbott, E. A. *A Shakespearean Grammar.* London: Macmillan, 1905.
Agamben, Giorgio. *Language and Death: The Place of Negativity.* Trans. Karen E. Pinkus and Michael Hardt. Minneapolis: U of Minnesota P, 1991.
Apollinaire, Guillaume. *Oeuvres poétiques.* Ed. Marcel Adéma and Michel Décaudin. Paris: Gallimard, 1959.
apRoberts, Ruth. "Old Testament Poetry: The Translatable Structure." *PMLA* 92 (1977):987-1004.
Auden, W. H. *Secondary Worlds.* Boston: Faber, 1968.
Bachelard, Gaston. *The Poetics of Space.* Trans. Maria Jolas. New York: Orion, 1964.
Bakhtin, Mikhail. *Problems of Dostoevsky's Poetics.* Trans. and ed. Caryl Emerson. Theory and History of Literature 8. Minneapolis: U of Minnesota P, 1984.
———, and P. N. Medvedev. *The Formal Method in Literary Scholarship: A Critical Introduction to Sociological Poetics.* Trans. Albert J. Wehrle. Cambridge, Mass.: Harvard UP, 1985.
Baldassari, Anne, et al. *Matisse Picasso.* New York: Museum of Modern Art, 2002.
Baldwin, T. W. *William Shakspere's Small Latin & Lesse Greeke.* 2 vols. Urbana: U of Illinois P, 1944.
Baugh, Edward. "Getting There." Brown and McDonald 9-10.
———. "Sometimes in the Middle of the Story." *A Tale from the Rainforest.* Kingston, Ja.: Sandberry, 1988. P. 52.
Belli, Carlos Germán. Introduction. *Asir la forma que se va.* 1979; rpr. in *Antología Personal.* Lima: CONCYTEC, 1988.
Bianchi, Martha Dickinson. "Emily Dickinson's Garden." *Emily Dickinson International Society Bulletin* 2 (1990):1.
Bingham, Millicent Todd. *Ancestor's Brocades: The Literary Discovery of Emily Dickinson.* New York: Harper, 1945.

Bishop, Elizabeth. *The Complete Poems, 1927-1979.* New York: Farrar, 1983.
———. *Exchanging Hats: The Paintings.* Ed. William Benton. New York: Farrar, 1996.
Bloom, Harold. *The Anxiety of Influence: A Theory of Poetry.* New York: Oxford UP, 1973.
———. Foreword. *Elizabeth Bishop and Her Art.* Ed. Lloyd Schwartz and Sybil Estess. Ann Arbor: U of Michigan P, 1983.
———. *Shakespeare and the Invention of the Human.* New York: Penguin, 1998.
———. *Wallace Stevens: The Poems of Our Climate.* Ithaca: Cornell UP, 1977.
Bois, Yve-Alain. *Matisse and Picasso.* Paris: Flammarion, 1999.
Bowra, C. M. *Early Greek Elegists.* Cambridge, Mass.: Harvard UP, 1938.
———. *Greek Lyric Poetry from Alcman to Simonides.* Oxford: Clarendon, 1961.
———. *Pindar.* Oxford: Clarendon, 1964.
Brandenburger, Adam, and Barry Nalebuff. *Co-opetition.* New York: Currency/Doubleday, 1996.
Brantley, Richard E. *Experience and Faith: The Late-Romantic Imagination of Emily Dickinson.* New York: Palgrave Macmillan, 2004.
Brathwaite, Edward Kamau. *The Arrivants: A New World Trilogy.* New York: Oxford UP, 1973.
———. *History of the Voice: The Development of Nation Language in Anglophone Caribbean Poetry.* London: New Beacon, 1984.
———. *MR.* New York: Savacou North, 2002.
Breiner, Laurence A. *An Introduction to West Indian Poetry.* New York: Cambridge UP, 1998.
Bromwich, David. "Elizabeth Bishop's Dream-Houses." *Raritan* 4 (1984):77-94.
Brown, Clarence. *Mandelstam.* Cambridge: Cambridge UP, 1973.
Brown, Stewart, and Ian McDonald, eds. *The Heinemann Book of Caribbean Poetry.* Oxford: Heinemann, 1992.
Brueggemann, Walter. *The Bible Makes Sense.* Atlanta: Knox, 1977.
———. *Praying the Psalms.* Winona, Minn.: St. Mary's, 1982.
———. *The Prophetic Imagination.* Philadelphia: Fortress, 1978.
Bunyan, John. *The Pilgrim's Progress from This World to That Which Is to Come.* Ed. James Blanton Wharey. 2nd rev. ed. Roger Sharrock. Oxford: Clarendon, 1960.

Burton, Reginald William Boteler. *Pindar's Pythian Odes: Essays in Interpretation*. Oxford: Oxford UP, 1962.

Cady, Edwin H., and Louis J. Budd, eds. *On Dickinson*. Durham, N.C.: Duke UP, 1990.

Calame, Claude. *Alcman*. Rome: Ateneo, 1983.

———. *Les Choeurs de jeunes filles en Grèce archaïque*. Rome: Ateneo e Bizzarri, 1977.

Calvin, John. *Institutes of the Christian Religion*. Trans. Henry Beveridge. 2 vols. bound as one. Grand Rapids, Mich.: Eerdmans, 1989.

Campbell, David A., ed. *Greek Lyric Poetry: A Selection of Early Greek Lyric, Elegiac and Iambic Poetry*. New York: St. Martin's, 1967.

Chamberlin, J. Edward. *Come Back to Me My Language: Poetry and the West Indies*. Urbana: U of Illinois P, 1993.

Cholokian, Ruben C. *The Troubadour Lyric: A Psycho-Critical Reading*. Manchester: Manchester UP, 1990.

Coleridge, Samuel Taylor. *Biographia Literaria. Samuel Taylor Coleridge: A Critical Edition of the Major Works*. Ed. H. J. Jackson. New York: Oxford UP, 1985.

Cook, Albert. *The Root of Things: A Study of Job and the Song of Songs*. Bloomington: Indiana UP, 1968.

Costello, Bonnie. *Elizabeth Bishop: Questions of Mastery*. Cambridge, Mass.: Harvard UP, 1991.

Cowan, Donald. *Unbinding Prometheus: Education for the Coming Age*. Dallas: Dallas Institute, 1988.

Cowan, Louise. "Allen Tate and the Garment of Dante." *Sewanee Review* 80 (1972):377-82.

———. *The Fugitive Group: A Literary History*. Baton Rouge: Louisiana State UP, 1959.

———. "Introduction: The Comic Terrain." *The Terrain of Comedy*. Ed. L. Cowan. Dallas: Dallas Institute, 1984. Pp. 1-18.

Crane, Hart. "Appendix I: General Aims and Theories." *Hart Crane: The Life of an American Poet*. By Philip Horton. New York: Norton, 1937. Pp. 321-27.

Crashaw, Richard. "The Weeper." *The Verse in English of Richard Crashaw*. New York: Grove, 1949. P. 33.

Curtius, E. R. *European Literature and the Latin Middle Ages*. Trans. Willard R. Trask. New York: Princeton UP, 1953.

Dante. *The Divine Comedy, Vol. III: Paradise.* Trans. Mark Musa.
    New York: Penguin, 1995.
———. *Inferno.* Trans. Charles Singleton. Princeton: Princeton UP, 1970.
———. *Paradiso.* Trans. Charles Singleton. Princeton: Princeton UP, 1975.
———. *Purgatorio.* Trans. Charles Singleton. Princeton: Princeton UP, 1973.
Davidson, Donald. "Meditation on Literary Fame." *Poems: 1922-1961.*
    Minneapolis: U of Minnesota P, 1966. Pp. 23-24.
———. "Poetry as Tradition." *Still Rebels, Still Yankees.* Baton Rouge:
    Louisiana State UP, 1972. Pp. 3-22.
Davidson, Donald. "What Metaphors Mean." *Critical Inquiry* 5.1 (1978):31-47.
Dickinson, Emily. *The Complete Poems of Emily Dickinson.* Ed. Thomas H.
    Johnson. Boston: Little, 1960.
———. *Emily Dickinson's Herbarium: A Facsimile Edition.* Cambridge, Mass.:
    Belknap, 2006.
———. *The Letters of Emily Dickinson.* Ed. Thomas H. Johnson. Cambridge,
    Mass.: Belknap, 1958.
Diehl, Ernst, ed. *Anthologia Lyrica Graeca.* Leipzig: Teubner, 1933-43.
Diehl, Joanne Feit. "Bishop's Sexual Poetics." *Elizabeth Bishop: The Geography
    of Gender.* Ed. Marilyn May Lombardi. Charlottesville: UP of
    Virginia, 1993. Pp. 17-45.
Doggett, Frank. "Romanticism's Singing Bird." *Studies in English
    Literature, 1500-1900* 14.4 (1974):547-61.
Donaldson, E. T. "The Myth of Courtly Love." *Ventures* 5 (1965):16-23.
Donatus. *Commentarii Vergiliani: Vita Vergiliana.* http://www.forumromnum.org
    /literature/donatus_vita.html.
Donne, John. *The Elegies and the Songs and Sonnets.* Ed. Helen
    Gardner. Oxford: Clarendon, 1965.
———. *John Donne: A Selection of His Poetry.* Ed. John Hayward.
    Baltimore: Penguin, 1950.
———. *John Donne: The Complete English Poems.* Ed. A. J. Smith.
    Harmondsworth: Penguin, 1971.
———. *The Songs and Sonnets of John Donne.* Ed. Theodore Redpath. Rev. ed.
    London: Methuen, 1983.
Doreski, C. K. *The Restraints of Language.* New York: Oxford UP, 1993.

Dressman, Michael R. "Empress of Calvary: Mystical Marriage in the Poems of Emily Dickinson." *South Atlantic Bulletin* 42.1 (Jan. 1977):39-43.

Dronke, Peter. *The Medieval Latin and Romance Lyric to AD 1300*. Cambridge: Cambridge UP, 1951.

———. *Medieval Latin and the Rise of the European Love Lyric*. Oxford: Clarendon, 1965.

———. *The Medieval Lyric*. London: Hutchinson, 1968.

Du Bois, W. E. B. *The Souls of Black Folk*. New York: Vintage, 1990.

Dubrow, Heather. "'Incertainties now crown themselves assur'd': The Politics of Plotting Shakespeare's Sonnets." *Shakespeare's Sonnets: Critical Essays*. Ed. James Schiffer. New York: Garland, 2000. Pp. 113-33.

Dunbar, Paul Laurence. "An Ante-Bellum Sermon." Gates and McKay 912-14.

———. "Representative American Negroes." *The Negro Problem: A Series of Articles by Representative Negroes of Today*. By Booker T. Washington et al. New York: James Pott, 1903. Pp. 187-209.

———. "Sympathy." Gates and McKay 922.

Duncan, Jeffrey L. "Joining Together/Putting Asunder: An Essay on Emily Dickinson's Poetry." *Missouri Review* 4.2 (Winter 1980-81):111-29.

Dupree, Robert S. *Allen Tate and the Augustinian Imagination: A Study of the Poetry*. Baton Rouge: Louisiana State UP, 1983.

Edmondson, Paul, and Stanley Wells. *Shakespeare's Sonnets*. New York: Oxford, 2004.

Edwards, Jonathan. "Images of Divine Things." *Typological Writings*. Ed. Wallace E. Anderson. New Haven: Yale UP, 1993.

Egan, Mary Joan. "Allusions to Keats in 'Autumn Refrain.'" *Wallace Stevens Journal* 9.2 (1985):98-100.

Eliot, T. S. "Eeldrop and Appleplex." *Little Review* (New York) 4.1 (May 1917):7-11 and 4.5 (Sept. 1917):16-19.

———. *Inventions of the March Hare*. Ed. Christopher Ricks. New York: Harcourt, 1996.

———. "The Love Song of J. Alfred Prufrock." *The Waste Land and Other Poems*. New York: Harbrace, 1934.

———. "On a Recent Piece of Criticism." *Purpose* 10 (Apr./June 1938): 91-92.

———. *Poetry and Drama*. Cambridge, Mass.: Harvard UP, 1951.

———. *The Sacred Wood*. New York: Barnes & Noble, 1960.
———. *Selected Prose*. Ed. Frank Kermode. New York: Harcourt, 1975.
———. *The Varieties of Metaphysical Poetry*. Ed. Ronald Schuchard. New York: Houghton Mifflin Harcourt, 1994.
Ellmann, Richard. *Yeats: The Man and the Masks*. New York: Dutton, 1973.
Emerson, Ralph Waldo. *The Collected Works of Ralph Waldo Emerson*. Ed. Robert E. Spiller. 7 vols. Cambridge, Mass.: Harvard UP, 1971.
Erne, Lucas. "Shakespeare's 'Ever-Fixed Mark': Theological Implications in Sonnet 116." *English Studies* 4 (2000):293-304.
Fain, John Tyree, and Thomas Daniel Young, eds. *The Literary Correspondence of Donald Davidson and Allen Tate*. Athens: U of Georgia P, 1974.
Farr, Judith. *The Gardens of Emily Dickinson*. Cambridge, Mass.: Harvard UP, 2004.
———. *The Passion of Emily Dickinson*. Cambridge, Mass.: Harvard UP, 1992.
———. Preface. Dickinson, *Emily Dickinson's Herbarium* 15-18.
Fergusson, Francis. Introduction. *Aristotle's Poetics*. By Aristotle. New York: Hill and Wang, 1961. Pp. 1-44.
Ferrante, Joan M. "Cortes'Amor in Medieval Texts." *Speculum* 55 (1980): 685-95.
Ferry, Anne. *All in War with Time: Love Poetry of Shakespeare, Donne, Jonson, Marvell*. Cambridge, Mass.: Harvard UP, 1975.
Finneran, Richard J. *The Collected Poems of W. B. Yeats*. 2nd ed. New York: Scribner, 1996.
Flam, Jack. *Matisse and Picasso: The Story of Their Rivalry and Friendship*. New York: Basic, 2003.
Frank, Donald K. *Naturalism and the Troubadour Ethic*. New York: Lang, 1988.
Fränkel, Hermann. *Early Greek Poetry and Philosophy*. Trans. Moses Hadas and James Willis. Oxford: Blackwell, 1975.
Freedman, David Noel. "Pottery, Poetry and Prophecy: An Essay on Biblical Poetry." *Journal of Biblical Literature* 96 (1977):5-26.
Freinkel, Lisa. *Reading Shakespeare's Will: The Theology of Figure from Augustine to the Sonnets*. New York: Columbia UP, 2002.
Friedrich, Paul. "Lyric Epiphany." *Language in Society* 30.2 (2001):217-47.

Frye, Northrop. *Anatomy of Criticism: Four Essays*. Princeton: Princeton UP, 1957.
The Fugitive: April, 1922—December, 1925. Rpr. Gloucester, Mass.: Smith, 1967.
Gardner, Helen. General Introduction. Donne *Elegies* iii-xvii.
Gates, Henry Louis, Jr., and Nellie McKay, eds. *The Norton Anthology of African American Literature*. New York: Norton, 2004.
Gelpi, Albert. *Emily Dickinson: The Mind of the Poet*. Cambridge, Mass.: Harvard UP, 1965.
Genette, Gérard. *The Architext: An Introduction*. Trans. Jane E. Lewin. Berkeley: U of California P, 1992.
Gentili, Bruno. *Poetry and Its Public in Ancient Greece*. Trans. A. T. Cole. Baltimore: Johns Hopkins UP, 1988.
Gilot, Françoise. *Matisse and Picasso: A Friendship in Art*. New York: Talese/Doubleday, 1990.
Girard, René. *Deceit, Desire, and the Novel: Self and Other in Literary Structure*. Trans. Yvonne Freccero. Baltimore: Johns Hopkins UP, 1965.
Goldin, Frederick, ed. and trans. *Lyrics of the Troubadours and Trouveres: An Anthology and a History*. Garden City: Anchor, 1973.
Goluboff, Benjamin. "'If Madonna Be': Emily Dickinson and Roman Catholicism." *New England Quarterly* 73 (2000):355-85.
Gottwald, Norman K. "Poetry, Hebrew." *Interpreter's Dictionary of the Bible*. Ed. George Arthur Buttrick. New York: Abingdon, 1962. P. 830.
Griffin, Jasper. "The Fourth Georgic, Vergil, and Rome." *Greece & Rome* 26 (1979):61-80.
Habegger, Alfred. *My Wars Are Laid away in Books: The Life of Emily Dickinson*. New York: Random, 2001.
Hall, Donald. *Poetry and Ambition: Essays, 1982-88*. Ann Arbor: U of Michigan P, 1988.
Hanna, Mary. "Book Review—A Retrospective." *Jamaica Gleaner*. 20 Aug. 2006. http://www.jamaica-gleaner.com/gleaner/20060820/arts/arts3.html.
Hardy, Barbara. *The Advantage of Lyric: Essays on Feeling in Poetry*. Bloomington: Athlone, 1977.
Harrison, R. K. *Introduction to the Old Testament*. Grand Rapids, Mich.: Eerdmans, 1971.

Harvey, Ruth. *The Troubadour Marcabru and Love*. London: U of London P, 1989.
Hawkins, Peter S., and Rachel Jacoff, eds. *The Poets' Dante*. New York: Farrar, 2001.
Heaney, Seamus. "Place, Pastness, Poems: A Triptych." *Salmagundi* 68-69 (1985-86):30-47.
———. *The Redress of Poetry*. New York: Noonday, 1996.
———. "The Sense of Place." *Preoccupations: Selected Prose 1968-1978*. London: Faber, 1980. Pp. 131-49.
Heidegger, Martin. *Poetry, Language, Thought*. Trans. Albert Hofstadter. New York: HarperCollins, 2001.
———. "The Question Concerning Technology." *The Question Concerning Technology and Other Essays*. Trans. William Lovitt. New York: Harper, 1977. Pp. 3-35.
Helsinger, Elizabeth K. *Ruskin and the Art of the Beholder*. Cambridge, Mass.: Harvard UP, 1982.
Heschel, Abraham J. *The Prophets*. 2 vols. New York: Harper, 2001.
Hill, R. T., and T. G. Bergin, eds. *Anthology of the Provençal Troubadours*. Rev. ed. 2 vols. New Haven: Yale UP, 1973.
Hirsch, Edward. *How to Read a Poem and Fall in Love with Poetry*. New York: Harcourt, 1999.
Hope, Jonathan. *Shakespeare's Grammar*. London: Thomas Learning, 2003.
Hopkins, Gerard Manley. *Further Letters of Gerard Manley Hopkins*. Ed. C. C. Abbott. Rev. ed. London: Oxford UP, 1955.
———. *Journals and Papers of Gerard Manley Hopkins*. Ed. Humphry House and Graham Storey. London: Oxford UP, 1959.
———. *The Letters of Gerard Manley Hopkins to Robert Bridges*. Ed. C. C. Abbott. London: Oxford UP, 1955.
———. *Poems of Gerard Manley Hopkins*. Ed. W. H. Gardner and N. H. MacKenzie. London: Oxford UP, 1970.
———. *The Sermons and Devotional Writings of Gerard Manley Hopkins*. Ed. Christopher Devlin. London: Oxford UP, 1959.
Horner, Matina. "Bright Women: Fail." *Psychology Today*, 3 Nov. 1969: 36-38, 62.
Hulme, T. E. "Romanticism and Classicism." *Criticism: The Foundations of*

Modern Literary Judgment. Ed. Mark Schorer, Josephine Miles, and Gordon McKenzie. Rev. ed. New York: Harcourt, 1958. Pp. 257-65.

Ingarden, Roman. *The Literary Work of Art: An Investigation on the Borderlines of Ontology, Logic, and Theory of Literature.* Trans. George G. Grabowicz. Evanston: Northwestern UP, 1973.

Ingram, Annie Merrill. "Victorian Flower Power: America's Floral Women in the Nineteenth Century." *Common-Place* 7.7 (2006). http://www.common-place.org/vol-07/no-01/ingram.

Jackson, Virginia. *Dickinson's Misery: A Theory of Lyric Reading.* Princeton: Princeton UP, 2005.

Johnson, James Weldon. Preface from *The Book of American Negro Poetry.* Gates and McKay 883-905.

Joseph, Sr. Miriam. *Shakespeare's Use of the Arts of Language.* New York: Columbia UP, 1947.

Joyce, James. *Critical Writings of James Joyce.* Ed. Ellsworth Mason and Richard Ellmann. New York: Viking, 1959.

Kalstone, David. *Becoming a Poet: Elizabeth Bishop with Marianne Moore and Robert Lowell.* New York: Farrar, 1989.

Keats, John. *Keats's Poetry and Prose.* Ed. Jeffrey N. Cox. New York: Norton, 2009.

Keil, C. F., and F. Delitzsch. *Biblical Commentary on the Old Testament.* Vol. 5. Grand Rapids, Mich.: Eerdmans, 1956.

Kendrick, Laura. *The Game of Love: Troubadour Word Play.* Berkeley: U of California P, 1988.

Kirby, David. "Countee Cullen's 'Heritage': A Black 'Waste Land.'" *South Atlantic Bulletin* 36.4 (Nov. 1971):14-20.

Kundera, Milan. "What Is a Novelist: How Great Writers Are Made." *New Yorker*, 9 Oct. 2006:40.

Lanciani, Rodolfo. *Pagan and Christian Rome.* New York: Houghton, 1892.

Landry, Hilton. "The Marriage of True Minds: Truth and Error in Sonnet 116." *Shakespeare Studies* 3 (1967):98-110.

Lefkowitz, Mary. *First-Person Fictions: Pindar's Poetic "I."* Oxford: Oxford UP, 1991.

———. "Who Sang Pindar's Victory Odes?" *American Journal of Philology* 109 (1988):1-11.

Léglu, Catherine. *Between Sequence and "Sirventes": Aspects of Parody in the Troubadour Lyric.* Oxford: European Humanities Research, 2000.

Leishman, J. B. *Themes and Variations in Shakespeare's Sonnets.* London: Hutchinson U Library, 1961.

Lewis, C. Day. *The Lyric Impulse.* Cambridge, Mass.: Harvard UP, 1965.

Lewis, C. S. *Allegory of Love.* New York: Oxford UP, 1958.

———. "Donne and Love Poetry in the Seventeenth Century." *Seventeenth-Century Studies Presented to Sir Herbert Grierson.* Ed. J. Dover Wilson. Oxford: Clarendon, 1938. Pp. 64-84.

Lewis, David Levering. Introduction. *The Portable Harlem Renaissance Reader.* New York: Penguin, 1994.

———. Preface to the Penguin Edition. *When Harlem Was in Vogue.* New York: Penguin, 1997.

Locke, Alain, ed. *The New Negro: Voices of the Harlem Renaissance.* 1925; rpr. New York: Simon & Schuster, 1997.

Louis, M. K. "Emily Dickinson's Sacrament of Starvation." *Nineteenth Century Literature* 43.3 (Dec. 1988):346-60.

Lundin, Roger. *Emily Dickinson and the Art of Belief.* Grand Rapids, Mich.: Eerdmans, 1998.

Mahood, M. M. *Shakespeare's Wordplay.* Methuen: London, 1957.

Maritain, Jacques. *Art and Scholasticism.* Trans. Joseph W. Evans. New York: Scribner, 1962.

———. *Creative Intuition in Art and Poetry.* New York: Pantheon, 1953.

———. *The Dream of Descartes.* Trans. Mabelle L. Andison. New York: Philosophical Library, 1944.

———. *Existence and the Existent.* Trans. Lewis Galantiere and Gerald B. Phelan. New York: Vintage/Random, 1966.

Maurer, Karl. "An Index of Pindar's Images for Poet, Poetry, Song." http://www.udallas.edu/classics/resources/PindarIndex.htm.

———. "*Notiora Fallaciora.* Exact, Non-Allusive Echoes in Latin Verse." *Studies in Latin Literature and Roman History.* Ed. Carl Deroux. Vol. 11. Brussels: Latomus, 2003. Pp. 121-56.

McDonald, Russ. *Shakespeare and the Arts of Language.* Oxford: Oxford UP, 2001.

McKay, Claude. "If We Must Die." Gates and McKay 1007.

McLeod, Glen. "Stevens and Surrealism: The Genesis of 'The Man with the Blue Guitar.'" *American Literature* 59.3 (1987):359-77.

Melville, Herman. *Moby-Dick*. Ed. Charles Child Walcutt. New York: Bantam, 1967.
Mendelson, Edward. *Early Auden*. New York: Viking, 1981.
Millier, Brett Candlish. *Elizabeth Bishop: Life and the Memory of It*. Berkeley: U of California P, 1993.
Miłosz, Czesław. Introduction. *A Book of Luminous Things: An International Anthology of Poetry*. Ed. Miłosz. New York: Harcourt, 1996. P. xvi.
———. *Miłosz's ABC's*. Trans. Madeline Levine. New York: Farrar, 2001.
Milton, John. *Complete Poems and Prose*. Ed. Merritt Y. Hughes. New York: Odyssey, 1957.
Mishkin, Tracy. *The Harlem and Irish Renaissances: Language, Identity, and Representation*. Gainesville: UP of Florida, 1998.
Mitchell, Domhnall. "A Little Taste, Time, and Means: Dickinson and Flowers." *Monarch of Perception*. Amherst: U of Massachusetts P, 2000. Pp. 112-53.
Morris, Mervyn. Introduction. Scott, *Uncle Time* n.p.
———. "Literary Evening, Jamaica." *Caribbean Voices*. Ed. John Figueroa. 2 vols. London: Evans Bros., 1966. 2:181.
———. *Making West Indian Literature*. Kingston, Ja.: Ian Randle, 2005.
———, ed. *Seven Jamaican Poets: An Anthology of Recent Poetry*. [Kingston?], Ja.: Bolivar, 1971.
Morrison, Toni. *The Bluest Eye*. New York: Plume, 1993.
Mullen, William. *Choreia: Pindar and Dance*. Princeton: Princeton UP, 1982.
Nagy, Gregory. *Pindar's Homer: The Lyric Possession of an Epic Past*. Baltimore: Johns Hopkins UP, 1997.
Nelson, Jeffrey. "Love's Logic Lost." *ANQ* 13.3 (2000):14-19.
Newman, F. X. *The Meaning of Courtly Love*. Albany: SUNY P, 1968.
Newman, John Henry, Cardinal. *Certain Difficulties Felt by Anglicans in Catholic Teaching*. http://www.Newmanreader.org.
The New Princeton Encyclopedia of Poetry and Poetics. Ed. Alex Preminger. Princeton: Princeton UP, 1993.
Oberhaus, Dorothy Huff. *Emily Dickinson's Fascicles: Method and Meaning*. University Park: Pennsylvania State UP, 1995.
Page, Sir Denys Lionel. *Poetae Melici Graeci*. Oxford: Clarendon, 1962.
Parker, Robert Dale. *The Unbeliever: The Poetry of Elizabeth Bishop*. Urbana: U of Illinois P, 1988.

Paterson, Linda. *Troubadours and Eloquence*. Oxford: Clarendon, 1975.
Pearce, Roy Harvey. "Toward Decreation: Stevens and the 'Theory of Poetry.'" *Wallace Stevens: A Celebration*. Ed. Frank Doggett and Robert Buttel. Princeton: Princeton UP, 1980. Pp. 286-307.
Philp, Geoffrey. "'Epitaph' by Dennis Scott: An Appreciation." *Geoffrey Philp's Blog Spot*. http://geoffreyphilp.blogspot.com/2007/05/epitaph-by-dennis-scott- appreciation.html.
———. "Happy Birthday Dennis Scott." *Geoffrey Philp's Blog Spot*. http://geoffreyphilp.blogspot.com/2006/12/happy-birthday-dennis-scott.html.
Pindar. *The Odes of Pindar*. Trans. C. M. Bowra. London: Penguin, 1969.
———. *Pindar: The Olympian and Pythian Odes*. Ed. Basil Gildersleeve. New York: Harper, 1885.
———. *Pindari Carmina cum Fragmentis*. Ed. C. M. Bowra. Oxford: Clarendon, 1935.
———. *Pindari Carmina cum Fragmentis*. Ed. Bruno Snell. Leipzig: Teubner, 1964.
Plato. *Republic*. Trans. Allan Bloom. New York: Basic Books, 1968.
———. *Symposium*. Trans. Walter Hamilton. New York: Penguin Classics, 1951.
Plutarch. "Lycurgus." *Plutarch's Lives*. Trans. John Dryden. Rev. and ed. A. H. Clough. Vol. 1. Boston: Little, Brown, 1895. Pp. 83-126.
Podlecki, Anthony. *The Early Greek Poets and Their Times*. Vancouver: U of British Columbia P, 1984.
Pound, Ezra. *The Cantos*. New York: New Directions, 1989.
———. *Collected Early Poems*. Ed. Michael John King. New York: New Directions, 1982.
———. *Collected Shorter Poems*. London: Faber and Faber, 1952.
———. *Patria Mia*. Chicago: Ralph Fletcher Seymour, 1950.
———. *Personae: The Collected Poems*. New York: New Directions, 1950.
———. *Selected Letters*. New York: Harcourt, 1971.
———. *Selected Prose 1909-1965*. Ed. William Cookson. New York: New Directions, 1975.
———. *The Spirit of Romance*. New York: New Directions, 1968.
Power, Sr. Mary James. *In the Name of the Bee*. 1943; rpr. New York: Biblo & Tannen, 1970.
Praz, Mario. "Donne's Relation to the Poetry of His Time." *A Garland for John*

Donne. Ed. Theodore Spencer. Cambridge, Mass.: Harvard UP, 1931. Pp. 51-72.

Press, Alan R., ed. and trans. *Anthology of Troubadour Lyric Poetry*. Austin: U of Texas P, 1971.

Puttenham, George. *The Arte of English Poesie*. Ed. Baxter Hathaway. Kent: Kent State UP, 1970.

Ramchand, Kenneth. "West Indian Poetry." *Breaklight*. Ed. Andrew Salkey. London: Hamilton, 1971.

Ransom, John Crowe. "The Future of Poetry." *The Fugitive*. 3.1 (1924). http://www.english.illinois.edu/MAPS/poets/m_r/ransom/future.htm.

———. *Selected Poems*. 3rd ed. New York: Knopf, 1991.

———. "Wanted: An Ontological Critic." *Selected Essays of John Crowe Ransom*. Ed. Thomas Daniel Young and John Hindle. Baton Rouge: Louisiana State UP, 1984.

Ricoeur, Paul. *The Rule of Metaphor: Multi-disciplinary Studies of the Creation of Meaning in Language*. Trans. Robert Czerny, with Kathleen McLaughlin and John Castello. Toronto: U of Toronto P, 1977.

Rilke, Rainer Maria. *Duino Elegies*. Trans. David Young. New York: Norton, 1978.

Robertson, D. W., Jr. *A Preface to Chaucer*. Princeton: Princeton UP, 1962.

Roessner, Jane. "The Coherence and the Context of Shakespeare's Sonnet 116." *JEGP* 81.3 (1982):331-46.

Rubin, William. *Picasso and Braque: Pioneering Cubism*. New York: Museum of Modern Art, 1989.

Ruskin, John. *Modern Painters, Vol. 3*. Vol. 4 of *The Works of John Ruskin*. Ed. E. T. Cook and Alexander Wedderburn. New York: Longmans Green, 1903-12.

Russ, Harry. Email to Dan Russ 6 Mar. 2007.

Schiffer, James. "Reading New Life into Shakespeare's Sonnets: A Survey of Criticism." *Shakespeare's Sonnets: Critical Essays*. Ed. Schiffer. New York: Garland, 2000. Pp. 3-71.

Scott, Dennis. *After-Image*. Leeds: Peepal Tree, 2008.

———. *Dreadwalk*. London: New Beacon, 1982.

———. *Strategies*. Kingston, Ja.: Sandberry, 1989.

———. *Uncle Time*. Pittsburgh: U of Pittsburgh P, 1973.

———. "Walcott on Walcott." Interview. *Caribbean Quarterly* 14.1-2

(1968):77-82.

Scott, R. B. Y. "Introduction to Proverbs." *The New Oxford Annotated Bible, Revised Standard Version*. Ed. Herbert G. May and Bruce M. Metzger. New York: Oxford UP, 1973. P. 769.

Sewall, Richard B. *The Life of Emily Dickinson*. 2 vols. New York: Farrar, 1974.

———. "Science and the Poet: Emily Dickinson's Herbarium and 'The Clue Divine.'" Dickinson, *Emily Dickinson's Herbarium* 19-34.

Seymour, A. J. "Editorial." *Kyk-Over-Al* 1.1 (1945):7.

Shakespeare, William. *Othello*. Ed. E. A. J. Honigmann. 3rd ed. London: Arden, 1997.

———. *Shakespeare's Poems*. Ed. Katherine Duncan-Jones. 3rd ed. London: Arden, 1997.

———. *Shakespeare's Sonnets*. Ed. Stephen Booth. New Haven: Yale UP, 1977.

———. *Shakespeare: The Complete Sonnets and Poems*. Ed. Colin Burrow. New York: Oxford UP, 2002.

———. *The Sonnets*. Ed. G. Blakemore Evans. Cambridge: Cambridge UP, 1996.

———. *The Sonnets*. Vol. 25 of *New Variorum Edition of Shakespeare*. Ed. Hyder Edward Rollins. Philadelphia: Lippincott, 1944.

Shurr, William. *The Marriage of Emily Dickinson: A Study of the Fascicles*. Lexington: UP of Kentucky, 1983.

Simon, Paul. "Under African Skies." *Graceland*. Rhino, 2004.

Snell, Bruno. *The Discovery of the Mind: The Greek Origins of European Thought*. Trans. T. G. Rosenmeyer. New York: Harper, 1953.

Sophocles. *Oedipus at Colonus*. *The Three Theban Plays*. Trans. Robert Fagles. New York: Penquin, 1982. Pp. 279-388.

Spiller, Michael. *The Development of the Sonnet: An Introduction*. London: Routledge, 1992.

Stevens, Wallace. *The Collected Poems of Wallace Stevens*. New York: Vintage/Random, 1990.

———. *The Letters of Wallace Stevens*. Ed. Holly Stevens. Berkeley: U of California P, 1966.

———. *The Necessary Angel: Essays on Reality and the Imagination*. New York: Random, 1951.

———. *The Palm at the End of the Mind*. Ed. Holly Stevens. New York:

Vintage/Random, 1990.

———. Wallace Stevens Concordance. http://www.wallacestevens.com/concordance/WSdb.cgi.

Stevenson, Anne. *Five Looks at Elizabeth Bishop*. Agenda/Bellew Poets on Poetry 1. London: Bellew, 1998.

Syme, Sir Ronald. *The Roman Revolution*. Oxford: Clarendon, 1939.

Synge, J. M. Preface. *The Playboy of the Western World: A Comedy in Three Acts*. Boston: J. W. Luce, 1911.

Tate, Allen. *Collected Poems 1919-1976*. New York: Farrar, 1977.

———. *Essays of Four Decades*. Wilmington, Del.: ISI, 1999.

———. *Poems*. Chicago: Swallow, 1960.

Tennyson, Alfred, Lord. "The Eagle (Fragment)." *The Norton Anthology of Poetry*. 3rd ed. New York: Norton, 1983. P. 713.

Thompson, Leonard L. *Introducing Biblical Literature: A More Fantastic Country*. Englewood Cliffs: Prentice-Hall, 1978.

Tocqueville, Alexis de. *Democracy in America*. Ed. and trans. Harvey C. Mansfield and Delba Winthrop. Chicago: U of Chicago P, 2000.

Trimpi, Wesley. "Whose Worth's Unknown, Although His Height Be Taken." *Order in Variety: Essays and Poems in Honor of Donald E. Stanford*. Ed. R. W. Crump. Newark: U of Delaware P, 1991.

Tripp, Raymond. *Duty, Body, and World in the Works of Emily Dickinson: Reorganizing the Estimate*. Studies in American Literature 32. Lewiston, N.Y.: Mellen, 2000.

Turner, Frederick. "Reading Contemporary American Poetry: A Personal View." *American Arts Quarterly* 21.2 (2004):8-15.

———."The State of Poetry." *American Arts Quarterly* 22.2 (2004):9-13.

U2. "40." *War*. Island, 1983.

Valency, Maurice. *In Praise of Love*. New York: Macmillan, 1958.

Vendler, Helen. *The Art of Shakespeare's Sonnets*. Cambridge, Mass.: Harvard UP, 1997.

———. "Stevens and Keats' 'To Autumn.'" *Wallace Stevens: A Celebration*. Ed. Frank Doggett and Robert Buttel. Princeton: Princeton UP, 1980. Pp. 286-307.

———. *Wallace Stevens: Words Chosen out of Desire*. Knoxville: U of Tennessee P, 1984.

Vickers, Brian. *In Defense of Rhetoric*. Oxford: Oxford UP, 1988.

Virgil. *Georgics*. Ed. R. A. B. Mynors. New York: Oxford UP, 1990.

———. *Virgil*. Trans. H. R. Fairclough. Rev. G. P. Goold. Loeb Classical Library 63-64. 2 vols. Cambridge: Harvard UP, 1999.

Voegelin, Eric. *The Drama of Humanity and Other Miscellaneous Papers, 1939-1985*. Ed. William Petropulos and Gilbert Weiss. Vol. 33 of *Collected Works of Eric Voegelin*. Columbia: U of Missouri P, 2004.

Walcott, Derek. *The Antilles: Fragments of Epic Memory*. New York: Farrar, 1993.

———. "Meanings." *Critical Perspectives on Derek Walcott*. Ed. Robert D. Hamner. Washington, D.C.: Three Continents, 1993. Pp. 45-50.

———. *Omeros*. New York: Farrar, 1990.

Washington, Booker T. "The Atlanta Exposition Address." Gates and McKay 594-97.

We Moderns 1920-1940. New York: Gotham Book Mart, 1940.

West, M. L. "The Singing of Homer and the Modes of Early Greek Music." *Journal of Hellenic Studies* 101 (1981):113-29.

Wilbur, Richard. "Sumptuous Destitution." *Emily Dickinson: A Collection of Critical Essays*. Ed. Richard Sewall. Englewood Cliffs: Prentice-Hall, 1964. Pp. 53-61.

Wright, George. *Shakespeare's Metrical Art*. Berkeley: U of California P, 1988.

Yeats, William Butler. *The Collected Poems of W. B. Yeats*. Ed. Richard J. Finneran. New York: Macmillan, 1989.

———. "Symbolism of Poetry." *Essays and Introductions*. New York: Macmillan, 1961.

———. *A Vision*. New York: Collier, 1965.

Yin, Joanna. "Garden, as Subject." *The Emily Dickinson Encyclopedia*. Ed. Jane Donahue Eberwein. Westport: Greenwood, 1998.

Zumthor, Paul. *Essai de poétique médiévale*. Paris: Seuil, 1972.

Index

A

Abraham, 35; bosom of, 244, 256
Absence, 200, 204, 205, 227-31, 343, 361; in reality (Stevens), 221, 226, 237
Absolute, 261
Abstraction, 221, 250, 257, 263, 270, 275-76, 278, 279-80, 336
Abstractionist painting, 366
Adam, 7, 8, 17, 18, 27, 39, 157, 167, 352
Admiration, as lyric stance, 341-42
Adorno, Theodor, 340
Aeneas, 9, 39, 96, 98-100, 212
Aeschylus, 212
Agamben, Giorgio, 93 n. 11
Agape, 278
Ahkmatova, Anna, 365
Alcaeus, 60
Alcman, *xi*, 47, 49, 50, 51, 54, 55, 56, 58, 60, 65, 71 n. 11, 72 n. 18
Alexander, Lewis, 307-8; "Enchantment," 307-8; "Medicine Dance" (section of "Enchantment"), 307-8
Allegory, as figurative drama, 324
Allegory, figures of, 316
American Indian, 250
Amherst, 154, 171, 182, 185; Amherst College, 154, 185
Amor, 264, 266
Amour courtois conventions, 91 n. 5, 113, 119. *See also* Fin amours.
Anagogical, 276, 282
Analogy, analogical, 219, 269-70, 273, 276, 277-80, 286-87, 288, 289, 354-55; *analogia entis* (analogy of being), 278; analogical eye, 289; analogical symbolism, 279
Ananias, 184-85
Angels, 121, 347; the angelic, 201; angelic fallacy, 277; angelic imagination, 15, 147, 279; anthropocentric angelism, 277
Anglicanism, 182
Antimetabole, 131
Aotis (dawn goddess), 51
Aphrodite, 234, 284
Apocalypse narratives, in Stevens, 225
Apollinaire, Guillaume, 266; *Zone*, 266
Apollo, 60, 151 n., 284
Apollonian, 38. *See also* Dionysian; Nietzsche.
Apophatic theology, 179
Aporia, 144
Apple of God's eye, 35-36
apRoberts, Ruth, 25
Apuleius, 146
Apulia, 67
Arcadia, Arcady, 49-50, 137
Archilochus, 60
Aristotle, *vii*, 5, 22, 26, 27, 72 n. 8, 137, 260, 375; *energeia*, *viii* (*see also* Being-at-work); *Poetics*, *vii*, 5, 105 n. 1
Arnold, Matthew, 34, 201-2, 226, 364; "Dover Beach," 364
Arp, Jean, 220
Art for art's sake, 87
Artifice of eternity, 138, 206, 230
Asclepiad (meter), 76 n. 53
Attar, Farid ud-Din, *x*
Attractors, 375
Aubade, 11, 227. *See also* Poetry, forms of.
Auden, W. H., 17, 27, 60, 155-56, 162, 167-68; "In Memory of W. B. Yeats," 17; *Secondary Worlds*, 155, 167-68
Aufidus River, 66-67
Augustine, Saint, *x*, 262, 331 n. 3; Augustinian metaphor, in Tate, 287; Augustinian vision, in Eliot, 263
Augustus Caesar (Octavian), 63, 65, 68, 283

Index

Auschwitz, 340
Avant-garde, 243, 260

B

Babits, Mihaly, 365
Babylonian Exile, *x*
Bachelard, Gaston, 200; *Poetics of Space, The*, 200
Back-to-Africa movement, 294
Bailey, Benjamin, 135
Bakhtin, Mikhail, *viii*, 201
Basho, Matsuo, 372
Bastille, 370
Bathsheba, 41
Baugh, Edward, 338-39; "Getting There," 339; "Sometimes in the Middle of the Story," 339
Baudelaire, Charles, 122, 250, 257, 263, 333 n. 15, 361-62, 372; Baudelairean, 259; "Au Lecteur," 372; "La Vie antérieure," 333 n. 15
Bay Psalms, 42
Beatific Vision, 270, 277, 278. *See also* Ontological splendor.
Beatrice, 7, 15, 136, 147, 149-50, 278, 285, 287
Beauty, the beautiful, 4-5, 7, 8, 17, 32, 33, 40, 82-85, 88, 90, 96, 98, 101-3, 122, 135, 141, 143, 144, 147-51, 153, 155, 161, 169, 171-72, 173, 176, 188, 194, 195, 209, 222, 224, 230, 231, 234, 251, 253, 255, 261, 264, 270, 293, 308, 335, 345-46, 348, 355, 373
Bede, Venerable, 15
being, *viii*, *ix*, 89, 200, 204, 206, 218, 220, 222, 224, 232-33, 236, 237, 266
Being, 10, 15, 86-87, 89-90, 93 n. 11, 215 n. 1

Being-at-work, 201
Bel-Argent, 339
Belli, Carlos Germán, 87-88, 93 n. 11; *Asir la forma que se va (Taking Hold of Form That Moves)*, 87-88
Bennett, Louise, 338
Beowulf, 39
Bergson, Henri, 371
Bernard of Clairvaux, Saint, *viii*, 7
Bible, The Book, Scripture, 21, 23, 25, 28, 33, 39, 168, 175, 187, 320, 326, 337, 352: Apocalypse, 190, 192; Beatitude, 336; Daniel, 345; Job, 25; Deuteronomy, 35; Ecclesiastes, 34; evangelists, 352; Exodus, 37, 209; Genesis, 3, 30; Gospel of John, 183; gospels, 352; Jeremiah, 174; Letter to the Hebrews, 187; Job, 29, 35, 40-41; Lamentations, 41; Old Testament, 125; Patriarchs, 37, 39; Pentateuch, 21, 23; Prophets, 29; Proverbs, 13, 24, 313, 317, 318, 320-29; Revelation, 184; Song of Songs, *viii*, 2, 29, 192; Tanakh, 39, 42; Torah, 22; Vulgate, 174; Wisdom books, 320. *See also* Psalms.
Bill Cosby Show, The, 340
Bird, birds, *x*, 7, 8, 11, 17, 30, 35, 36, 55, 59, 72 n. 20, 148, 171, 192, 204, 209, 211-12, 213-14, 219, 226-33, 238-39, 276, 312-13, 315, 326-28, 340-41, 351, 352, 353, 354; winged man, 340. *See also* Nightingale.
Birdsong, 7, 8, 55, 85, 148-49, 204, 226-33, 235, 238-39, 312-13, 352
Bishop, Elizabeth, *xi*, 83-85, 86, 90, 309-31; Bishop's notebook, 314, 320; despair, 312; "Drunkard, A," 333 n. 12; "End of March, The," 322; "Fish, The," 331; "Imaginary Iceberg," 313; *North*

& South, 313, 331; "One Art," 83-85.
"Unbeliever, The," 309-31: allegorical complexities in, 331; as allegorical text, 314; believer (character in), 319; cloud (character in), 315, 326; drinking (as metaphor), 312, 322; ecstasy in, 321; Epigraph, 316-31; Father Mapple, as Bunyanesque figure, 325; the precious, as opposed to the sublime, 329, 331, 332 n. 5; seagull (character in), 315, 326-28; Unbeliever (character in), 314-18, 320, 326-30
Black and brown bodies, 306-7
Blade Runner, 81
Blake, William, 1, 80, 156, 203, 220, 364; "Ah, Sunflower," 1; "Auguries of Innocence," 156; "London," 8-9; "Mock on, Mock on, Voltaire, Rousseau," 364; Prophetic Books, 364
Blessed time, blessed moment (time of blessedness), *ix*, 6, 7, 11, 12, 15, 17, 21, 123, 269, 336
Bloom, Harold, 98, 105 n. 2, 231, 234, 242, 315-16, 340; *Anxiety of Influence*, 242
Blues, 293, 298. See also Music.
Bohemia, 367
Bohemian life-style, 366
Boland, Eavan, 90
Bollingen Prize, 244
Boltzmann, Ludwig, 364
Book of American Negro Poetry, The, 297, 298, 302
Book of Common Prayer, 42
Book of Songs, *x*
Booth, Stephen, 96, 102
Borges, Jorge Luis, 372
Bowles, Samuel, 156-57, 190
Bowra, C. M., 54

Brabantio (*Othello*), 202
Braque, Georges, 267 n. 4
Brancusi, Constantin, 220
Brathwaite, Edward Kamau, 338, 355 n. 3
Breiner, Laurence, 336, 348
Bride of Christ, 190. See also Church, the.
Bridges, Robert, 171, 194
British Empire, 203, 344
Brodsky, Joseph, 68, 365
Brooke, Tucker, 97
Brown, Wayne, 338
Browning, Elizabeth Barrett, 192, 196 n. 16, 241, 362; *Aurora Leigh*, 241
Browning, Robert, 122, 134, 242, 257; Browningesque psychology, 251
Brueggemann, Walter, 23, 29, 39, 42-43
Bryant, William Cullen, 212; "To a Waterfowl," 212
Buddha, the, 250; Buddhist, 176, 263, 264
Bullard, Otis, 156
Bunyan, John, 311, 313, 317, 319-28. *Pilgrim's Progress*, 313-14, 318-20, 322-26, 327: as spiritual allegorical text, 314; Christian (character in), 319-20, 322; frontispiece, 319; Presumption (character in), 319-20; Simple (character in), 319-20; Sleeper(s), 319, 322; Sleeping Portrait, 319, 331 n. 2; Sloth (character in), 319-20
Byron, George Gordon, Lord, 362; "Child Harold," 327; *Don Juan*, 362
Byzantium, 206, 230-31

C

Caedmon, 15, 22, 42
Cahiers d'Art, 223
Callimachus, 60, 62, 74 n. 31, 75 n. 44
Calvin, John, 184, 189, 192

Canon of English literature, 242, 250, 257
Canonical language, 368
Capo Palinuro, 103
Caribbean poets, 90
Caribbean spirit, 352
Carpe diem, 2, 3, 306
Carrhae, battle of, 74 n. 35
Carroll, Lewis, 243
Carthusian monastery, 201
catachresis, 106 n. 18
Catholic, Catholicism, Roman Catholicism, 181-82, 188, 191, 194, 264, 280
Cato, 74 n. 32
Celan, Paul, 365
Ceres, 136
Chaos and complexity science, 374
Chaucer, Geoffrey, 367, 375
Cherokees, 209
Chiasmus, 24
Chilhowee, 208-9, 212
China, *x*, 264
Choral song, choral lyric, 46, 48, 50, 54
Christ, 126, 127, 128, 131, 133, 171, 176, 178, 182, 184-85, 188, 190, 191-92, 193-95, 280, 287; Christ as Bridegroom, 171, 178, 191-92, 194-95; Christ as (Divine) Lover, 193-95; Christ as romantic poet, 194-95
Christendom, 207
Christian: allegory, 225; ceremony, 181; culture, 192; experience, 126; saint (Stylite), 326
Church, the, 130, 178, 181-83, 188, 192, 194, 199, 282, 367
City, *x*, 6, 8-10, 39, 133, 141, 205, 259, 262, 264; holy city, 206. *See also* Dresden, Dublin, Harlem, Hiroshima, London, Troy.
City of God, 262-64

City of Man, 262, 264
Civil War, 207, 208, 270, 347, 360
Civilization, 275, 297
Clausius, Rudolf, 364
Clausulae, 47
Clifton, Lucille, 308
"Cloud of unknowing," 4, 15
Cocteau, Jean, 267 n. 4
Coleridge, Ernest Hartley, 187
Coleridge, Samuel Taylor, 15, 35, 95, 187-88, 218, 242, 329, 343, 362; Coleridgean, 86; "Kubla Khan," 218; *Rime of the Ancient Mariner, The*, 218, 329, 362
Coltrane, John, 42
Columella, 74 n. 32
Commonwealth Poetry Prize, 340
Communion, in Dickinson, 183-84; in Hopkins, 182-83
Conceit, 113
Confessional poetry, 363, 374
Confucius, 250; Confucian tradition, *x*; Confucianist, 264
Congregational church, Congregationalism, 184-85, 193
Contemplation, 327, 344, 346
Cook, Albert, 24
"Co-opetition," 241, 242-44, 257, 262
Corbière, Tristan, 257
Costello, Bonnie, 313-16
County Sligo, 203-4, 205
Cowan, Louise, *vii*, 26, 29, 93 n. 10, 208, 271, 289, 290 n. 1; "Allen Tate and the Garment of Dante," 289; *Fugitive Group, The*, 208, 271, 290 n. 1
Crane, Hart, 130, 272-74, 276, 312, 315-16; *Bridge, The*, 273-74
Crane, Louise, 333 n. 13
Crashaw, Richard, 310, 329-30; "Weeper, The," 329

Crassus, 74 n. 35
Crusoe, Robinson, 310
Cubism, 255, 267 n. 4
Cullen, Countée, 300-301, 304, 305-6; "Fruit of the Flower," 304; "Harlem Wine," 305; "Heritage," 300; "Heritage" as "Black *Waste Land*," 300; Herrick-like wit in, 306; "She of the Dancing Feet Sings," 306; "Tableau," 305; "To a Brown Boy," 306; "To a Brown Girl," 306
Cultural poetics, 201
Cultus, 121, 134 n. 3
Cupid, 146, 188

D

Dallas Institute of Humanities and Culture, xi
Dance, and lyric, 46, 141, 354. *See also* Scott, Dennis, dance as analogy to lyric.
Daniel, Arnaut, 77, 92 n. 6, 92 n. 8, 250; "En cest sonnet coind'e leri," 77
Dante, 7, 13, 15, 35, 39, 77, 86, 87, 89-90, 95, 105 n. 4, 111, 132, 135, 145-46, 151, 172, 206, 250, 257, 261, 269, 273-74, 276-82, 284-90, 375; Dantean mode, 281, 284; sacramental attitude, 274, 281; symbolic (analogical) imagination, 270, 276, 278, 281, 285-86, 287, 289-90; *Vita Nuova*, 86, 133, 135.
  Divine Comedy, The (Commedia): 86-87, 135, 269-70, 273, 274, 276, 281, 287; Bonagiunta da Lucca, 288; Brunetto Latini, 87;
  Canto 30, 278; Empyrean, 269; Eunoe, 286; Glaucus, 151 n.; Inferno, 151, 276, 282, 284-85; Jupiter, sphere of, 280; Love, 279, 288; Mount Purgatory, image of, 7, 288; *Paradiso*, paradise, 13, 95, 133, 145, 151, 151 n., 206, 269, 284-85; *Purgatorio*, 151, 278, 284, 286; Satan, 277; spiritual light, 276; Triune Circle, 277
Dantists, 289
Darwin, Charles, 181; Darwinism, 181
Daunus, 66, 67
David, 27, 35, 37, 41, 43 n. 2
Davidson, Donald (philosopher), 236
Davidson, Donald (poet-critic), 17, 207-12, 270-72, 275, 280, 282-84, 290 n. 1, 290 n. 2; "Lee in the Mountains," 208, 272; *Long Street, The*, 272; Mosaic tone in "Sanctuary," 209; "Randall, My Son," 208; "Sanctuary," 207-9; *Tall Men, The*, 272; *Tennessee, The*, 272
Débussy, Claude (De Bussy), 253
Decreation, 223-25, 230-32, 233, 237
Delphi, 60, 225
Derrida, Jacques, 371
Descartes, René, 200, 368; Cartesianism, 277; Cartesian dualism, 279
Desire, 111, 116-17, 130, 135, 193, 218, 284, 366
Dewey, John, 274
Dialect lyric poetry, 301-2, 338, 341, 342, 377
Diaspora, 21
Dickens, Charles, 207
Dickerman, Mrs. George S., 159
Dickinson, Austin, 167
Dickinson, Edward, 184
Dickinson, Emily, xi, 17, 153-69, 171-95, 234, 315-16, 332 n. 7, 332 n. 8, 365, 371, 373; botany as a religious vocation, 167-68; "Daisy," as symbolic name for Dickinson, 156; *Emily Dickinson's Fascicles*, 158; *Emily Dickinson's*

Herbarium, 153-55, 161, 162, 167; gardening as religious vocation, 167; "marriage group" poems, 189-90, 192-93, 196 n. 18; Master Letters, 164; renunciation in, 175, 176, 177, 183, 189. *Works:* "All the letters I can write" (#334), 158; "Art thou the thing I wanted" (#1282), 176-77; "Because I could not stop for Death" (#712), 365 ; "Bloom–is Result–to meet a Flower" (#1058), 161; "Brain–is wider than the Sky, The" (#632), 179; "Come slowly—Eden!," 190; "Daisy follows soft the Sun, The" (#106), 156-57; "Dandelion's pallid Tube, The" (#1519), 159; "Essential Oils–are wrung" (#675), 159, 160; "'Faith' is a fine invention" (#185), 164; "Gentian weaves her fringes, The" (#18), 164-65; "God gave a loaf to every Bird" (#791), 175; "God made a little Gentian" (#442), 165-66; "Here, where the Daisies fit my Head" (#1037), 158-59, 163; "'Hope' is the thing with feathers" (#254), 17; "How ruthless are the gentle" (#1439), 184; "I cautious, scanned my little life" (#178), 183; "I reckon–when I count it all" (#569), 186-87; "I'm 'wife'–I've finished that" (#199), 191; "Mine–by the Right of the White Election!" (#528), 365; "My life closed twice before its close" (#1732), 175; "My period had come for Prayer" (#564), 179-80; "Of God we ask one favor" (#1601), 174; "On a Columnar Self" (#789), 176; "One Blessing had I than the rest" (#756), 176; "Pit–but Heaven over It, A," 332, n.7; "Renunciation–is a piercing Virtue" (#745), 175; "Sepal, petal, and a thorn, A" (#19), 164; "So I pull my Stockings off" (#1201), 185-86; "Some keep the Sabbath going to Church" (#324), 166; "There is another sky" (#2), 167; "This is a Blossom of the Brain" (#945), 163; "This is my letter to the World" (#441), 162-63; "This was a poet–It is That" (#448), 160, 162; "Unable are the Loved to die" (#809), 186; "Victory comes late" (#690), 184; "Were nature mortal lady" (#1762), 173; "What Soft–Cherubic Creatures" (#401), 185-86; "Wife–at daybreak I shall be, A" (#461), 189-90; "Wild Nights! Wild Nights!" (#249), 190; "Word made Flesh is seldom, A" (#1651), 183

Dickinson Homestead, 167
Dickinson, Lavinia, 157, 159, 162
Didactic epic, 61
Diehl, Joanne, 177
Ding an sich, 219, 224-25, 237, 364. *See also* Thing.
Dionysian, 38, 148, 227. *See also* Apollonian; Nietzsche.
"Dissociation of sensibility," 274; "dissociated" poetry, 278. *See* Eliot, T. S.
"Disunity of the intellect," 276. *See* Tate, Allen.
Dithyrambic poetry, *vii*, 5, 65
Divine Essence, 269
Doctrine of the four senses, 278
Dolce stil nuovo, 86, 148. *See also* "Sweet new style."
Domingo, W. A., 300; "Gift of the Black Tropics, The," 300
Don Quixote, 39
Donatus, Aelius, 71 n. 6; *Vita Vergiliana*, 71 n. 6
Donne, John, *viii*, *xi*, 2, 8, 10, 11, 27, 29, 35, 36, 111-34, 135, 242, 250, 280,

313, 352-53, 355, 368, 372.
Works: "Air and Angels," 116, 121; *Anniversaries*, 122, 125-28; "Anniversary, The," 116; "Apparition, The," 119; "Bait, The," 115; "Batter My Heart" (Holy Sonnet XIV), 280; "Blossom, The," 118; "Break of Day," 119; "Broken Heart, The," 119; "Canonization, The," 10, 11, 116-17, 121; "Curse, The," 119; "Damp, The," 121; "Dream, The," 116; "Ecstasy, The," *viii*, 116; Elegies, 120; "Elegy XIX: To His Mistress Going to Bed," 2; "Expiration," 119; "Farewell to Love," 118, 121; "First Anniversary," 123-25, 127; "Flea, The," 130; "Funeral, The," 119, 121; "Good Friday, 1613. Riding Westward," 126, 128-29; "Good Morrow, The," 36, 116-17, 121; Holy Sonnet III, 128; Holy Sonnet XIII, 121; Holy Sonnet XVII, 126; Holy Sonnet XVIII, 128; *Holy Sonnets*, 126, 127; "Hymn to Christ, A," 127, 133; "Hymn to God my God," 127; "Hymn to God the Father, A," 131; "La Corona," 127, 129-32; "La Corona: Temple," 129; "Lecture upon the Shadow, A," 113, 116; "Legacy, The," 118; "Love's Alchemy," 118, 121; "Love's Diet," 118; "Love's Exchange," 118; "Love's Growth," 112, 116; "Love's Usury," 118-19, 121; "Lovers' Infiniteness, 116; "Negative Love," 116; "Nocturnal upon St. Lucy's Day," 11, 112, 119, 121; "Relic, The," 119-20, 121; Satires, 120; "Second Anniversary," 123, 125-26, 127; "Song" ("Go and catch a falling star"), 117-18; "Song" ("Sweetest love, I do not go"), 116; Songs and Sonnets, 120, 122; "Sun Rising, The," 116-17; "Twicknam Garden," 8, 119, 121; "Valediction: of my Name in the Window, A," 134 n. 3; Valedictory, valediction poems, 119, 121, 353; "Will, The," 118, 119; "Witchcraft by a Picture," 119, 134 n. 3; "Woman's Constancy," 117

Dorian poets, 49. *See also* Alcman; Polybius; Pindar.
Douglas, Gavin, 242
Dove, Rita, 308
"Dramma per musica," 260
Dresden, destruction of, 10. *See also* City.
Drury, Elizabeth, 122-26, 127. See Donne, *Anniversaries*.
Dryden, John, 16
du Bellay, Joachim, *x*
Du Fu, 372
Dublin, 296. *See also* City.
DuBois, W. E. B., 291-96, 300, 303, 345. *Works: Souls of Black Folk, The*, 291, 292, 300; "Sorrow Songs, The," (Chap. in *The Souls of Black Folk*), 292; "Talented Tenth," 291-92, 295, 296, 298, 301, 302
Duende, 371
Dunbar, Paul Laurence, 294, 301-3; "Ante-Bellum Sermon, An," 302-3
Dunbar, William, 3; "Lament for the Makers," 3
Dupree, Robert Scott, 284

E

Earthly Paradise, 7, 13, 167, 263-64. *See also* Eden, Garden, Garden of Eden.
Eberhart, Richard, 12; "Groundhog, The," 12
Eden, Edenic, 120, 157, 190-91, 211, 300. *See also* Earthly Paradise, the Fall, Garden, Garden of Eden.

Index   405

Egyptian sages, 320, 326
Ekphrasis, 144
Eleanor of Aquitaine, 91 n. 4
Eliot, T. S., 7, 9, 16, 122, 207, 220, 230, 241-66, 272, 273, 274, 289, 308, 312, 336-37, 341, 362, 370; *coup de goût*, 242; "ideal order," 247; "Old Possum," 247, 256, 262.
  Works: "At Graduation 1907," 258; "Ballade of the Fox Dinner," 258; "Eeldrop and Appleplex," 262; "First Caprice in North Cambridge," 258; *Four Quartets*, 261, 265; "Gerontion," 122; "Hollow Men, The," 262; "Humoresque (After J. Laforgue)," 258, 261; *Inventions of the March Hare*, 256-58; "Love Song of J. Alfred Prufrock, The," 122, 134, 230, 259, 266; "Opera," 258, 259; "Preludes," 9, 259; Prufrock (character), 122, 230, 266; *Prufrock and Other Observations*, 255; "Second Caprice in North Cambridge," 258, 259-60; "Tradition and the Individual Talent," 244-45, 308; "Ulysses, Order and Myth," 248; *Waste Land, The*, 16, 134, 244, 256, 273, 370
Ellmann, Richard, 203-4, 205
Emerson, Ralph Waldo, 155, 184, 234; Emersonian pantheism, 182, 195 n. 10; Emersonian Transcendentalism, 186, 189; "Experience," 234; "Nature," 155
Emotion in poetry, feeling, 222, 250, 257, 261, 265, 279, 359, 360, 361, 364, 366
Empathetic union, 365
Engels, Friedrich, 365, 371
England, 202, 203, 248
English lyric tradition (native), 126, 352
Enlightenment, the, 264, 267 n. 4, 374
Ennius, 48

Entelechy, 77, 86, 87, 89
Entropy, 364
Epic Cosmos, The, *xi*
Epistolary friendship, 374
Eros, 2, 5, 6, 15, 134, 141, 146, 188, 189, 191-92, 195, 234-35, 278
Eroticism, 191
Ethos, as rhetorical category, 105 n. 10
Eucharist, 178, 182-83, 189, 193. *See also* Communion, in Dickinson; Communion, in Hopkins.
Euphrosyne, 72 n. 18
Eve, 7, 8, 17, 18, 39, 157, 167
Existential moment, 365
Ex-stasis, 321
Ezekiel, 249

F

Fall, the, 6, 8, 10, 17, 39, 123, 125, 166-67. *See also* Eden, Garden, Garden of Eden.
Falstaff (*1Henry IV*, *2 Henry IV*, *Henry V*, *Merry Wives of Windsor*), 104, 105 n. 2
Fancy, 297
Farr, Judith, 153, 154, 166, 191
Fate, in tragedy, 6
Faulkner, William, 207, 271, 287, 292; Joe Christmas, 287; *Light in August*, 287; verities, the, 271
Feminist discourse, 359
Fergusson, Francis, 5
film *noir*, 80-81
Fin amours, 77, 79-80, 81, 86, 87, 91 n. 1, 91 n. 5, 92 n. 9; *fin amours* conventions, 79-81. *See also Amour courtois* conventions.
Final cause, 375
Finneran, Richard, 203
Flaubert, Gustave, 241, 244, 360
"Flood subject," in Dickinson, 154

Flora's Interpreter: or, the American Book of Flowers and Sentiments (Hale), 155
Flynt, Eudocia, 158
Focus, 337
Folk culture, relationship to high culture, 336; folk spirit, 297-98
Folk imagination, Synge's debt to, 297
Ford, Emily Fowler, 157
Ford, Ford Madox, 253
Formal cause, 375
Fortune, in comedy, 6
Foucault, Michel, 371
Frank, Anne, 371
Free verse (*vers libre*), 261, 362; free verse poets, 362
Freedman, David Noel, 23
French symbolists, 257, 259, 261, 272
Frenemy, 257. *See also* "Co-opetition."
Freud, Sigmund, 172, 242, 368, 371
Frost, Robert, 2, 6, 7-8, 47, 199, 202, 208, 212-15, 220, 335, 353, 356 n. 8; "momentary stay against confusion," 214. Works: "Birches," 7, 213; "Death of a Hired Hand," 214; "Directive," 199, 208, 215; "Dust of Snow," 2; "Exposed Nest, The," 213-14; "Fear, The," 212, 214; "Gift Outright, The," 335; "Home Burial," 212, 214; "Oven Bird, The," 8; "Servant to Servants, A," 212
Frye, Northrop, 27
Fugitive, The, 270-71, 290 n. 1
Fugitives, Fugitive poets, 270-72, 276, 281, 283-84, 290 n. 2
Futurism, 255

G

Gaelic, Yeats's use of, 203; Gaelic homeland, 205
García Márquez, Gabriel, 340; "Very Old Man with Enormous Wings, A," 340.
Garden, the, 2, 6, 10, 13, 14, 16, 17, 26, 38, 120, 156, 199, 234, 266; "happy garden state," 295. *See also* Eden, Garden of Eden.
Garden of Eden, 2, 6, 26, 38, 39, 120, 157. *See also* Eden, the Fall, Garden of Eden.
Garden of Eloquence (Peachem), 97
Gardner, Helen, 132
Garvey, Marcus, 294; Garveyism, 301
Gates, Henry Louis, 295
Ge, 71 n. 11
Gelpi, Albert, 185
Genres, 376; genre as inner state and movement, *viii*, 5, 26; genre as territory /terrain of imagination, *vii, x*, 6; genre, literary history of, *viii*
Genres of Literature, The, *vii*
Gilgamesh, 39
Girard, René, 178
Glyconic (meter), 76 n. 53
Goethe, Johann Wolfgang von, 360, 362, 364-65, 372, 375
Goodison, Lorna, 338
Gospel songs, 42, 293
Gottwald, Norman, 25
Grady, Henry, 207
Graham, Jorie, 12, 90; "San Sepolcro," 12
Grande Chartreuse, as poetic sanctuary, 201. *See also* Sanctuary.
Grant, Ulysses S., 208
Graves, Robert, 47
"Great Black Migration," 294
Great chain of being, 120
Greatness of soul, 231
Greek lyric, 45-60
Greek mythology, 228
Greek theater, 260
Greek tragedy, 47. *See also* Sophocles; Tragedy.
Greenwich Village, 294
Gregorian chant, 42
Gregory, Lady, 199
Grieving, 127, 352

Grimké, Angelina, 304; "The Black Finger," 304
Guarded style, 17, 208, 209
Guggenheim fellowship, 331 n. 3
Guianese people, 338

H

Hades, 57, 136
Hafez, 372
Hagia Sophia, 206. See also Sanctuary.
Hall, Donald, 90
Hamlet (*Hamlet*), 104, 105 n. 2, 261
Hammett, Dashiell, 80
Hardy, Barbara, 27
Hardy, Thomas, 17, 47, 181
Harlem, 294, 296, 301, 337. See also City.
Harlem and Irish Renaissances, The (Mishkin), 297
Harlem Renaissance, 291, 293, 296-98, 302, 304, 308
Harrison, R. K., 24-25
Harvard Advocate, 261
Harvard Library, 153
Hayden, Robert, 308, 340-41, 349; "Angle of Ascent," 340-41; "Middle Passage," 349
Heaney, Seamus, 90, 292, 294, 339; "Death of a Naturalist," 339
Heather Island, 203. See also Innisfree.
Hegel, Georg Wilhelm Friedrich, 364
Heidegger, Martin, 12, 141, 200-201, 202, 204-5, 210, 215 n. 1, 226; "Building Dwelling Thinking," 200; "Language," 200; "Origin of the Work of Art, The," 141; "Thing, The," 215 n. 1
Heidelberg, 200, 210. See also Place.
Hera, 57
Heracles, 52, 72 n. 15
Herbert, George, 310, 313, 314, 360
Herodotus, 262
Heschel, Abraham, 22-23, 35, 41

Hesiod, 45, 46, 48, 61, 62, 65, 72 n. 8, 75 n. 40; *Theogony*, 46, 62, 75 n. 40; *Works and Days*, 61, 62
Higginson, Thomas Wentworth, 156, 162, 163-64
Higher Criticism, 181
Hiroshima, destruction of, 10. See also City.
Hirsch, Edward, 88-89, 289
Hitchcock, Edward, 154, 156; "Resurrections of Spring, The," 154
"Hoard of destructions," 223-25, 233, 237. See also Decreation.
Hölderlin, Friedrich, 12
Holocaust, 371
Holy Spirit, 126, 180
Homelessness, 39-40, 312
Homer, 43 n. 2, 47, 48, 65, 82, 261, 352; Achilles, 3; Homeric epics, 25; *Iliad*, 3; *Odyssey*, 352; Odysseus, 39, 261
Hope, 17, 26, 37, 116, 156, 166, 177-79, 189, 192, 217, 255, 292-93
Hopkins, Amy, 193
Hopkins, Everard, 193
Hopkins, Gerard Manley, 2, 3, 11, 12, 17, 34, 171-95, 313, 365, 372; inscapes in 188.
Works: "As Kingfishers Catch Fire," 194; "At the Wedding March," 193; Caradoc (character in *St. Winifred's Well*), 177-78; "Carrion Comfort," 178; "God's Grandeur," 2, 11, 34; "Hurrahing in Harvest," 178, 194; "I Wake and Feel the Fell of Dark," 11, 194; "Leaden Echo and the Golden Echo, The," 173, 175, 365; "No Worst, There Is None," 12, 180; "Nondum," 180; "Spring and Fall: To a Young Child," 3; "Starlight Night, The," 194; *St. Winifred's Well*, 177-78; Terrible Sonnets, 178; "That Nature Is a Heraclitean Fire," 365; "Thou art indeed just, Lord," 174

Horace, 45, 59, 60, 64, 66, 67, 68, 75 n. 43, 75 n. 47, 251, 252; *Carmen saeculare*, 76 n. 52; *Ode 4*, 68; *Odes*, 66
Horismus, 97, 106 n. 12
Hortus conclusus, 166
Housman, A. E., 1, 252; "Into my heart an air that kills," 1; *Shropshire Lad, A*, 252
Houston, Sam, 208
Howard University, 299
Hughes, Langston, *xi*, 299-300, 303, 304-5, 306, 307.
  Works: "Dream Variation," 307; "I, Too," 304; "Negro Speaks of Rivers, The," 303, 307; "Our Land," 304-5; "Poem," 307; "Song," 307; "Weary Blues, The," 303; "Youth," 299-300
Hugo, Victor, 199, 362
Hulme, T. E., 17
Humpty Dumpty, 243
Hurston, Zora Neale, 302

I

Icarus, 341
"Ignoble arts of quietness," 63. See Poet as hero; Poetic experience.
I'll Take My Stand, 280
Illuminative Way (way of theologians), 279
Images in lyric poetry: of arrows, 59; of a beacon, 98, 100; of a bridegroom, 30, 191-95; of a charioteer (in Plato), 222, 235; of a herald/messenger, 57, 59, 67, 73 n. 27; of a mixing bowl, 57, 58; of a star, 98, 100; of a winged man, 340; of an island, 205; of starvation, 189
"Images of Divine Things" (Edwards), 156
Imagination, 150, 186-87, 188, 207, 212, 217, 219, 223, 224, 231, 232-33, 235-36, 237, 245, 264, 266, 269, 272, 277, 278, 310, 319, 320, 335, 336; divinity of, 186; imaginative vision, 362; primary imagination, 15, 343; symbolic (sacramental) imagination, 15, 269-70, 278-79, 286, 289; unifying capacity of, 278; verbal imagination, 247
Imagism, 250, 254, 258, 259; Imagists, 90
Imago dei, 5
Imitation, *vii*, 200, 236. *See also* Mimesis.
Imitation of an action, *viii*
Immortality, 67, 68, 103, 154, 159, 162, 166-67, 168, 231
Impersonality, 359
Incarnation, the, 127, 183, 188, 194
incarnation, 7, 136, 143, 144, 149, 194-95
India, 202, 264
Industrial Revolution, 374
Ingarden, Roman, 145; *Literary Work of Art, The*, 145
Innisfree (Inis Fraoigh), 203-7, 211. *See also* Place; Yeats.
Integrity of art, 250
Intellectual poetry, 257
Intellectual salon, 374
Intellectus, 124
Interiority, 362
International Poetry Forum Award, 340
Into Great Silence, 201-2
iPod, 199
Ireland, 201, 202, 203, 205, 212, 297
Irish literary renaissance, 293
Irony, 63, 66, 67, 113, 117, 122, 171, 175, 184, 202, 208-9, 211, 258, 259, 260, 261, 263, 271-72, 297, 370
Isaac, 35
Istanbul, 206
Italian lyric tradition, 126

J

Jacob, 35
Jamaica, 336-55
Jamaica College, 340
Jamaican poetry, 336-37, 338-39, 347
Jazz, 298, 303. *See also* Music.
Jeremiah, as source for Hopkins, 174

Index 409

Jericho, 348
Jerusalem, 38, 39
Jesuit Order, 171, 172, 182
Jesus, 40, 43 n. 3, 178
"Jesus-Christers," 286
Jim Crow Laws, 293
Johnson, Georgia Douglas, 304
Johnson, James Weldon, 296, 297-98, 300, 302-3; "Creation, The," 302-3
Johnson, Samuel, 112, 130, 331 n. 3
Jonson, Ben, 242, 256, 258
Jordan River, 29
Jowett, Benjamin, 181
Joy (wife of Dennis Scott), 352
Joyce, James, 113-14, 202, 247, 248, 356 n. 8; conditions of art, 113-14, 120, 133-34; Joycean dialectic, 341; Stephen Dedalus, 341; *Portrait of the Artist as a Young Man, The*, 341
József, Attila, 365
Judah, tribe of, 39, 40
Julius Caesar, 63

K

Kant, Immanuel, 364; Kantian notion of form, 86
Kavanagh, Patrick, 202
Keats, George, 136, 143, 146
Keats, Georgiana, 136, 146
Keats, John, 2, 11, 17, 104, 132, 135-51, 172, 188, 199-200, 204, 205, 229, 230, 231, 232-33, 235, 237, 240 n. 4, 240 n. 5, 251-52, 312, 352, 355, 362. Works: "Bright Star," 104; *Eve of St. Agnes, The*, 362; "Ode on a Grecian Urn," 2, 11, 135-45, 149; "Ode on Melancholy," 147; "Ode to a Nightingale," 132, 148-49, 204; "Ode to Psyche," 146, 188; "To Autumn," 150, 199-200, 233
Keats, Thomas, 143, 205

King James Version, KJV, 325, 337
Klee, Paul, *ix*; *Remembrance of a Garden*, *ix*
Kleos, 142
Kômos, 137, 139-40
Komunyakaa, Yusef, 308
Ku Klux Klan, 294
Kundera, Milan, 22, 35
Kyk-Over-Al, 338

L

L.A. Confidential, 81
L*A*N*G*U*A*G*E poets, 85, 90
Labyrinth, 354
Lacan, Jacques, 371
Ladder of analogy, 277
Laforgue, Jules, 250, 256-58, 259, 260
Land, connection of lyric to, 335, 341, 342, 348
Landor, Walter, 250
Landry, Hilton, 103
Language, 145, 172-184, 200, 204, 205, 207, 217, 219-20, 224-25, 229, 231, 239 n. 4, 257, 265, 276, 281, 302, 312-14, 325, 335, 336, 338, 339, 346, 349-50, 361, 367-68, 371; ear, language of, v. language of the eye, 312-13; elevated (heroic) language, 366; Hebrew, 324-25; Miltonic language, 204; neo-Rossettian language, 251; original language, 8, 12-13, 30-31
Language, figurative and literal, in Bishop, 313, 315, 316, 320, 322, 323-27, 331
Language of creation, 12-13, 30-31, 129-30, 167-68
Laplace, Pierre-Simon, 363
Lar, 212
Laura, 90, 96. *See also* Petrarch.
Law, civil, 199, 367
Law, highest, 199; God's perfect law, 21, 30-31, 32, 37-38, 125

Law of Moses, 22
Lawrence, D. H., 356 n. 8, 362
Lee, Robert E., 208
Lethe, 149
Lewis, C. Day, 26
Lewis, C. S., 91 n. 1, 91 n. 5, 134 n. 1;
    Allegory of Love, 91 n. 1, 91 n. 5
Lewis, David Levering, 294, 296-97, 301
Lewis, Wyndham, 253-55
Li Po, 250
Libitina, 66, 67
Limen, 236
Little magazines, 270
Locke, Alain, 296-98, 299-308.
    New Negro, The, 296-97, 299-
    308: "Negro Digs Up His Past, The,"
    300; *New Negro* as the Bible of the
    Harlem Renaissance, 301; "New Negro,
    The," 296, 299
Locke, John, 279
Locus amoenus, ix
Logopoeia, 336
Logos, 144. *See also* Word.
London, 8, 203, 205, 207, 243, 248. *See
    also* City.
London establishment writers, 242, 248
Longfellow, Henry Wadsworth, 246
Lorca, Frederico García, 348
Lough Gill, 203, 204
Louvre, 51
Love of place, 340, 342, 350-51
Lowell, Robert, 43 n. 2, 212, 332 n. 6
Lowth, Robert, 23, 24
Lucy, Saint (Santa Lucia), 287-89
Ludi saeculares, 76 n. 52
Lyre, *lyros*, 114, 221, 226, 360
Lyric: as dance, 46-47, 48, 51, 54; as
    imitation, *vii-viii*, 85, 103; as mode of
    knowledge, 270; as prayer, praise, 26,
    29-30, 32-34, 38, 44, 51; as song, 46-
    47, 48, 51, 54, 66, 86, 114, 125;
    containing seeds of genres, 14;
individual lyric voice, 359-61; lyric
    exterior form, 25; lyric genius, 363; lyric
    integrity, 362; lyric moments, 352; lyric
    novelist, 310; lyric nostalgia, 1, 6, 9, 17,
    218; lyric paradise, 264-65; lyric quest
    for oneness, 270, 277; lyric spirit, 349
Lyric longing, yearning, 1-2, 6, 13, 14, 17,
    21, 27, 34-35, 37, 39, 115, 145, 146,
    188, 218, 232, 240 n. 4. *See also* Lyric
    stages, anticipation.
Lyric stages, 10-12, 26, 135; anticipation,
    11, 26, 34-35, 38, 188, 239; consumma-
    tion, 11, 26, 29, 34, 38, 115, 138-42,
    144, 145, 188, 239; lamentation, 11-12,
    26, 34, 38, 40-41, 42, 49, 140, 233,
    292, 304-5, 346
Lyrical Ballads, 188
lyricism, 22, 360, 365

M

MacArthur grant, 201
MacDonald, George, 167-68
Mallarmé, Stéphane, 250, 257, 361, 362
Mandelstam, Osip, *x*, 73 n. 26, 73 n. 29,
    365; "Horseshoe Ode: A Pindaric Frag-
    ment," 73 n. 29; "Slate Ode," 73 n. 26
Manley, Edna, 337, 347
Marcabrun, 77
Mariette, Auguste, 51
Maritain, Jacques, 4, 15, 133, 150, 215 n.
    3, 277
Marketplace, the, 366, 367, 368
Marriage, matrimony, 172, 178, 189, 191,
    193-95; theology of, in Hopkins, 194-95
Marriage of Christ and Church, 178
Marvell, Andrew, 2, 3, 11; "Garden, The,"
    11, 266; "To His Coy Mistress," 2, 3
Marx, Karl, 263, 365, 371
Mary, 18, 180, 285-86, 287, 306; as Virgin
    Muse in Tate, 285-86
Mary Lyon's Seminary, 154

Matisse, Henri, 267 n. 4
Maurer, Karl, 87-88
Mayakovsky, Vladimir, 365
McKay, Claude, 294-95, 299, 300, 302-5, 307, 337.
  Works: "America," 303; "Baptism," 305; Constab Ballads, 337; Harlem Shadows, 294, 299; "If We Must Die," 295, 300, 303; "Like a Strong Tree," 307; Songs of Jamaica, 337; "Tropics in New York, The," 304; "White House, The" ("White Houses"), 303, 305
McNeill, Anthony, 338
Melancholy, 136, 147-48
Melody, and lyric, 360-61
Melos, 14, 137
Melville, Herman, ix, 39, 310, 313-14, 318, 320, 326-30, 333 n. 14, 333 n. 15, 334 n. 17, 334 n. 18, 347, 360; Battle Pieces, 360; "Berg, The," 314. Moby-Dick, 313, 325, 334 n. 18: "Castaway, The," 325, 329, 333 n. 14, 334 n. 18; Descartian vortices, 328; "Extracts," 325; Ishmael, 39, 327; "Mast-Head, The," 325-28; Pip, 310; Stylite, 326
Memory, 340, 343, 348, 349, 360
Mencken, H. L., 293; "Sahara of the Bozart, The," 293
Mendelson, Edward, 60
Messiah, 40
Metaphor, relationship to spirituality, 315
Metaphysical poets, 256, 314-15, 318
Metaphysical unity, 218. See Unity of Being.
Middle Passage, 349
Military patriotism, 367
Miller, Margaret, 333 n. 13
Miłosz, Czesław, 6, 88, 93 n. 11, 365
Milton, John, 84, 157, 242, 252, 375; "L'Allegro," 252
Mimesis, 5, 46, 103, 362
Minnesänger, 81
Mode, 113-14, 125; lyric mode, 135

Modernism, modernist movement, 233-34, 241-43, 245, 254, 257, 261-62, 266, 267 n. 4, 271-73, 276-78, 279-81, 284, 299, 312, 346, 363, 370, 373; high modernist, 341, 347; modernist dilemma, 278; modernist techniques, 272
Modernity, modern, 122, 139, 194, 202, 207, 217, 218, 222, 224-25, 226, 230, 231, 246, 262, 271, 273, 274, 276-77, 279-80, 289, 373; poetics of, 96
Modus tollens, 107 n. 24
Monroe, Harriet, 243, 256
Montaigne, Michel de, 368
Moore, Marianne, 312, 313, 320, 324
More, Anne, 131
Morris, Mervyn, 337-39, 346, 351, 353; "Literary Evening, Jamaica," 339; "Pond, The," 339
Morrison, Toni, 28, 345; Bluest Eye, The, 28; Claudia (The Bluest Eye), 28
Mortality, 2-4, 40, 135-36, 137, 142, 144, 150, 162-63, 166-67, 354-55
Moses, 35, 39, 125, 184, 302
Mount Holyoke, 157, 184
Mouvance, 91 n. 5
Mundus imaginalis, 142
Muppets, 81
Muse, muses, 50, 57, 58, 62, 65, 71 n. 8, 71 n.11, 75 n. 40, 75 n. 45, 284, 285, 309-10, 343, 345-46, 350; Calliope, 50; Melpomene, 66, 69
Muser, Frani Blough, 333 n. 13
Museum of Modern Art, 233
Music, 26, 46-47, 48, 60, 62, 82, 85, 86, 111, 114, 120, 130, 137, 139-40, 141, 205, 206, 219, 231, 232, 243, 258-59, 261, 263, 298, 312, 313, 336, 362, 363, 366; music of the spheres, 26
Mystery of divinity, 219, 269
Mystery of selfhood, 368
Mystical marriage, 172, 178, 190, 192
Mystical presence, 192. See also Eucharist;

Communion, in Hopkins.
Mysticism, 172, 365
Myth, 141

N

Nashville, 207, 270
National Association for the Advancement of Colored People, 294
National Negro Business League, 293-94
National Urban League, 294
Negation, 229
Negative capability, 143, 151
Negative sublime, 316
Negro dialect, 301-2
"Negro problem," 293
Negro Problem: A Series of Articles by Representative Negroes of Today, The, 292
Negro Renaissance, 299, 301
Negro spirituals, 35
Nemerov, Howard, 18; "Blue Swallows, The," 18
Neo-Marxist discourse, 359
Neruda, Pablo, 348
Nettleford, Rex, 338
New Czechoslovakia, 296
New England, 201, 202, 212
New Formalist movement, 374
New Hampshire, 201
New historicist discourse, 359
New Ireland, 296
New Jerusalem, 2
New Narrative movement, 374
New Negro, 296, 299
New Negro, The. See Locke, Alain.
New South, 207
New Troy, 9
New York Times, 372
Newman, John Henry, 181
Newtonian revolution, 363, 374
Nietzsche, Friedrich, 260, 364, 371

Nigeria, 202
Nightingale, 17, 136, 148-49, 204, 228-33, 235-37. *See also* Bird; Birdsong.
Nihilism, 224
Nobility, 217-18, 220, 222, 335
Nomos, 38
Noorda, Raymond, 267 n. 3
Norcross cousins, 156
Northern Star, 100
Nostalgia, 1, 201, 218, 281, 300
Nostos, 18, 204, 206, 261

O

Oberhaus, Dorothy Huff, 158
"Objective correlative," 257, 261. *See* Eliot, T. S.
Objectivity, 359, 362
O'Casey, Sean, 202
Odysseus, 261
Oedipus complex, 242
Oikos, 6
Old Garden Street Theater, 294
Old South, 271, 273
Olson, Charles, 362
Olympia, 58
Omphalos, 225
Onomatopoeia, 231
Ontological identity, 236. *See also* Metaphysical unity; Unity of Being.
Ontological splendor, 4, 5, 10, 13, 224-25, 227, 232; ontological haziness, 226
Opsis, 14, 137
Orage, A. R., 264
Original sin, 123. *See also* Fall, The.
Orthria (dawn goddess), 51
Othello (*Othello*), 202
Ouranos, 71 n. 11
Ovid, 121
Oxford, 181; Oxford Movement, 182
Ozsvath, Zsuzsanna, 371

P

Paideia, 143
Pali, 256
Palinurus, 96, 98-100, 103
Panhellenic games, 56
Paradise, 6, 157, 215, 262-63, 264, 265, 266. *See also* Eden, Garden of Eden.
Parallelism in biblical verse, 23-25, 35, 42
Paris, 244
Paris, Gaston, 91 n. 5
Parmenides, 218
Parnassus, 284
Paronomasia, 27
Parousia, 139
Partheneia, 50, 51
Parthenon, 54
Partisan Review, 311
Pasternak, Boris, 365-66
Pater, Walter, 181
Pathos, divine, 22-23, 35; human pathos, 302
Patmore, Coventry, 172
Paul, Saint, 178; Pauline language, 102, 106 n. 13
Penn, William, 342
Perestroika, 366
Peripateia, 143
Persephone, 57, 136
Persia, 262
Persona, as rhetorical category, 105 n. 10
Peter, Saint, 352
Petrarch, 77, 89-90, 96, 105 n. 4, 111, 121; Petrarchan commonplace, 116
Pharmakon, 372
Phelps, Amira, 154-55; *Familiar Lectures on Botany*, 154-55
Phi Beta Kappa poets, 301
Philomela, 136, 228. *See also* Bird; Birdsong; Nightingale.
Phoenix, the, 239. *See also* Bird.
Physis, 38

Picasso, Pablo, 220, 222-25, 233, 267 n. 4; "une somme de destructions," 223. *See also* "Hoard of destructions."
Pindar, 47, 48, 49, 50, 56, 60, 65, 67, 68, 75 n. 40, 75 n. 47
Pindaric odes, 373: Nemean 4, 72 n. 18, 76 n. 53; Nemean 5, 56; Nemean 6, 56; Nemean 7, 56; Nemean 8, 47, 73 n. 29; Olympian 2, 58-59; Olympian 3, 48; Olympian 6, 57; Olympian 7, 58; Olympian 8, 58; Olympian 11, 75 n. 53; Olympian 13, 56; Olympian 14, 57; Pythian 1, 45; Pythian 2, 56; Pythian 5, 57; Pythian 6, 59, 67
Pinsky, Robert, 289
Pisa, 263
Place, in lyric, 201, 204, 205, 264, 338-40, 343-44; place of absence, 221; sheltered place, 204, 211 *(see also* Sanctuary); "spacious places," 28, 39; spirit of place, 212; timeless places, 28; Wilderness (Virginia), 208
Plath, Sylvia, 11, 17, 360, 373; "Black Rook in Rainy Weather," 11
Plato, 13, 21-22, 35, 72 n. 8, 124, 222, 234, 235, 236-37; *Phaedrus*, 222. *Symposium*, 234-35: Diotima, 234-36; *Metis* (Invention), 234; *Penia* (Poverty), 234-36; *Poros* (Contrivance, Resourcefulness), 234-35
Platonic: cast of mind, 133; Christian tradition, 113; forms, 90; idealizations, 127; loomings, 201; representations, 200; theology, 127
Platonism, 124
Pliny, 74 n. 32
Plutarch, 71 n. 11; *Lycurgus*, 71 n. 11
Poe, Edgar Allan, 277-78, 361-62
Poet as hero, 248; poet as divine, 186-88
Poetic: atonement, 292; communion, 312; experience, 278; high diction, 347; inspiration, 343; knowledge, way of

knowing, 15, 86, 133-34, 201, 215; place of refuge, 206-7, 211; presence, 205-6; principle, 317; process, 345; sacred authority, 201; salvation, 261; sanctuary, 201, 207, 210; space, 199-200, 202, 204-5, 208, 210, 214-15; sparing, 201; universal, 201

Poetic Way (way of poets), 279, 281

Poetics of love, 96

Poetry as sacred, immortal, divine, 63, 65, 66, 68, 167-68, 172, 187-88

Poetry, forms of : ballad, 227, 272, 373; battle-hymn, 368; eclogue, 373; epigram, 111; epitaph, 373; epithalamion, 13, 193, 373; eulogy, 111; folk sermon, 302; French alexandrine verse, 362; georgic, 374; hymn, 26, 28, 51, 65, 173; meditation, 111, 346-47; ode, 227, 373; pastoral, 227; prayer, 367; Roman satire, 121; sestina, 81; sonnet, 81, 111, 173, 252, 295; sonnet sequence, 95, 105 n. 4; sorrow song, 292; tomb inscription, *ix*; villanelle, 81, 83-85, 86, 227; work-song, 367

Poetry, Hebrew, 22-23, 24-25, 41

Poets' Dante, The, 289

Poiesis, 83, 85, 114, 298, 301, 362

Polis, 6, 13, 67

Political verse, protest poetry, 363, 368

Polo, Marco, 250

Polybius, 49-50

Pope, Alexander, 16

Postcolonial discourse, 359

Postcolonial literatures, 202-3

Postmodernity, 199, 201

Pound, Ezra, 85, 91 n. 5, 202, 220, 241-66, 269, 273, 289, 318, 341, 345, 362; as voice of prophet Ezekiel, 249; *A Lume Spento*, 251; "Ballad of the Goodly Fere," 345; *Canzoni*, 251, 254; *Cathay*, 254; *coup de goût*, 242; Dioce, 262, 264 (*see also* City); Far East, interest in, 253; "From Chebar," 249, 252-53; "Hugh Selwyn Mauberly," 244, 248; known as the impresario, 242, 248; "In a Station of the Metro," 85; "L'Art," 251; *Lustra*, 253-55; "Mr. Housman's Message," 251; *Patria Mia*, 249; "Portrait d'une Femme," 252; "Redondillas, or Something of That Sort," 252; "Rest, The," 255; "Return, The," 252; *Ripostes*, 252, 254, 258; "Salutation the Second," 254; "Seafarer, The," 252; "Song in the Manner of Housman," 251; *Spirit of Romance, The*, 244, 269; "What I Feel about Walt Whitman," 246-47. *Cantos*, 249, 261: Canto XLVI, 263; Canto XLV (usura), 263; Canto LXXIV, 262; Canto LXXVI, 262-63; *compassione* in, 264, 266; Dantesque vision, 264; Inferno in, 263; "Notes for CXI," 264; "Notes for CXVII et seq.," 265; Odysseus as figure in, 261; paradise in, 263, 264, 265, 266; *Pisan Cantos, The*, 262-63

Prague, 296

Praxis, 5

Praz, Mario, 130

Presence/absence, 142-43, 200, 202

Pre-Socratics, 218

Prior, Matthew, 16

Procne, 228

Promised Land, *ix*, 37, 39, 40, 348

Propertius, 242, 250

Prophets, 218, 249

Prospect, *ix-xi*

Prospero (*The Tempest*), 1

Protestantism, 181, 207, 337

Provençal, 77, 82, 83, 91 n. 5

Provence, 77, 86

Provincialism, 242, 250-51, 253, 261, 293

Psalms, *xi*, 11, 21-43: Psalm 1, 23-24; Psalm 8, 32; Psalm 17, 35-36; Psalm 18, 36; Psalm 19, 30-31, 32; Psalm 22, 40-

Index 415

41; Psalm 23, 11; Psalm 27, 24; Psalm 42, 37; Psalm 51, 40-41; Psalm 90 (Psalm of Moses), 39-40; Psalm 100, *viii*; Psalm 107, 28; Psalm 119, 37-38; Psalm 124, 24; Psalm 137, 8, 13, 16, 21, 38-39, 40, 305; Psalm 146, 32-33; Psalm 147, 32-33; Psalm 148, 32-33; Psalm 149, 29, 33; Psalm 150, 32, 34; Psalms of ascent, 38
Psalter, 21, 28, 33, 34, 36, 38
Psyche, 136, 146-47, 188
psyche, 148, 204, 211, 212
Purgatorial realm, 286. *See also* Dante, *Divine Comedy*.
Puritan, Puritanism, 185, 207, 212
Puritanic strain, 207, 306
Putin, Vladimir, 366
Puttenham, George, 101

Q

Quantitative verse, 46-47. *See also* Stress-accented verse.
Quantum physics, 374
Quasimodo, 199
Queer discourse, 359
Quintilian, 252

R

Race-spirit, 299
Radnóti, Miklós, 365, 368-70, 371, 372; "Foamy Sky," 368-69; "O Ancient Prisons," 369-70
Ragtime, 298. *See also* Music.
Rampersad, Arnold, 300-301, 304
Ransom, John Crowe, 2, 3, 4, 12, 202, 207-12, 214, 215, 270-72, 283-84, 290 n. 2, 341.
  Works: "Antique Harvesters," 212; "Bells for John Whiteside's Daughter," 3-4, 209-10; "Old Mansion," 207, 210-11; "Piazza Piece," 2; "Prelude to an Evening," 207, 211, 214; *Selected Poems*, 211; "What Ducks Require," 211-12
Rastafarianism, 336, 337, 347; Rastafarian typology, 348
Ratio, 124
Real Presence, 182-83. *See also* Eucharist; Communion, in Hopkins.
Reconstruction, 207
Red Sea, 29
Redemption, 346
Redress of poetry, poetic redress, 291, 292-93, 295-96, 298-99, 300-301, 304, 307-8
Reformation, 112, 124, 184
Reggae music, 336
Religio, 315
Rembrandt, 368
Resurrection, 156, 176
Rhine River, 202
Rich, Adrienne, 373
Ricks, Christopher, 258
Rilke, Rainer Maria, 12, 144, 360; *Ninth Duino Elegy*, 144
Rimbaud, Arthur, 257, 361
Robinson, Edwin Arlington, 210; "Miniver Cheevy," 210
Roethke, Theodore, 12, 88; "In a dark time, the eye begins to see," 12
Roman à clef, 373
Roman lyric, 45-48, 60-70
Roman lyric tradition, 126
Rome, 100, 273
Roosevelt, Franklin D., 28
Root, Abiah, 154, 157
Rossetti, Christina, 192, 196 n. 19
Rossetti, Dante Gabriel, 192, 362; "Blessed Damozel, The," 192
Różewicz, Tadeusz, 89-90; "In the Midst of Life," 89
Rudel, Jaufre, 77, 92 n. 7, 92 n. 8
Ruskin, John, 187
Russ, Harry, 43 n. 2

S

Sacrament, 188-89, 194-95; natural sacrament, 189; sacramental sense of analogy, 281; sacramental sexuality, 193
Sanctuary, 199, 205, 206, 207, 209, 210, 212, 214-15. *See* Place.
Sanskrit, 256
Sappho, 60, 360
Saturae, 121
Saul, 41
Schiller, Friedrich von, 362
Schoenberg, Arnold, 267 n. 4
Scholastics, 114, 130, 132, 189, 196 n. 13
Schopenhauer, Arthur, 364; Schopenhauerian backdrop, 260
Scientism, 277
Scott, Dennis, 335-55; creole in poetry, 356 n. 10; dance as analogy to lyric, 351, 354, 355 n. 3; death as lyric enemy, 355. *After-Image*, 351-55: "After-Image," 353; "Beast," 353; "Butterfly Dream," 354; "Comfort of Crows, A," 354; "Cross Country," 352-53; "Day Six," 352; "Diary of a Counter-Revolutionary," 354; "Editor, The," 354-55; "Game," 354; "Goodbyesong," 354; "Helen," 352; "Icon," 354; "Manuscript," 353; "Minos," 354; "Nibblesong," 352; "On the Edge," 354; "Open," 351; "Poem against Magic: For Mella," 354; "Seedsong," 353-54; "Sound of Birds, A," 352; "Sunday Loving, The," 352-53; "Third World Blues," 351; "Tracksong," 352-53. *Dreadwalk*, 348-49: "More Poem," 348. *Strategies*, 349-51: "Crossing," 349; "Marrysong," 350-51, 353. *Uncle Time*, 340-41, 345-49: "At that frail and absent evening house," 343; "Bird of Passage," 340, 352, 356 n. 9; "Black Mass" poems, 347; "Black Mass: Recessional," 347; "Cotyledon," 343; "Endgame," 347; "Epitaph," 346-47, 356 n. 11; "Exile," 342; "Fisherman," 341; "Grampa," 341-42; "Homecoming," 342; "Nightflight," 343; "No sufferer," 347-48; "Pages from a Journal, 1834," 343-44; "Resurrections," 344-45; "Reunion, The," 349; "Sentry," 341; "Suddentree, The," 345-46; "Uncle Time," 342, 356 n. 10; "Visionary," 340
Scott, Sir Walter, 207, 251, 252; "Great Scott," 252
Scotus, John Duns, 188
Sentimentality, 231, 345, 366, 371; Victorian sentimentality, 186, 190
Sermon on the Mount, 168
Sewall, Richard, 153, 155-58, 161; "Science and the Poet," 157
Sexton, Anne, 373
Seymour, A. J., 338
Shakespeare Association, 107 n. 25
Shakespeare, William, xi, 2, 3, 4, 47, 82, 95-104, 242, 252, 337, 356 n. 8, 367, 368, 371, 375; *Hamlet*, 261; *Macbeth*, 34; *Othello*, 103. *Sonnets*: Cupid sonnets, 96; Dark Lady sonnets, 96, 104; Fair Youth sonnets, 96, 98, 100, 101-3; Rival Poet sonnets, 102; Sonnet 63, 101; Sonnet 65, 2, 3; Sonnet 76, 102; Sonnet 80, 102; Sonnet 116, 95-104; Sonnet 126, 100, 103; Sonnet 154, 104
Shalom, 26, 32, 35, 41-42. *See also* Paradise.
Shaman, 377
Shaw, George Bernard, 202
Shelley, Percy Bysshe, 11, 15, 251-52, 315-16; "Hymn to Intellectual Beauty," 15; "Ode to the West Wind," 11
Shurr, William, 190-91
Sidney, Sir Philip, 96; Astrophel, 96; Stella, 96

Silence, stillness, solitude, 205, 206, 232-33, 266
Simile, 24, 58, 351
Simon, Paul, 22
Simons, Hi, 224, 231, 233
Simonides, 47
"Simultaneous order," 246
Sinai, 39
Snopes, 207
Socrates, 43 n. 3, 222, 234-35
Solomon, 320
Solon, 60, 65
Somnus, 100
Song, singing, 67, 125, 141, 206, 230, 258, 259, 307, 310, 313, 321, 323, 325, 326-27, 331, 340, 348, 360. *See also* Lyric: as song.
Sophia, 14
Sophocles, 35, 160, 341; *Antigone*, 35; Colonus, 160; "Ode to Man," in *Antigone*, 35; Oedipus, 39, 160; Philoctetes, 341
Soul-making, 136, 143, 151. *See also* Vale of soul-making.
South, the, 201, 202, 207-12. *See also* Old South.
Southern Renascence, 270, 293
Spencer, Anne, 304, 307; "Lady, Lady," 307
Spengler, Oswald, 364
Spenser, Edmund, 96; *Amoretti*, 96
Spirit v. soul, 342
Spirituality, 313-15, 318; spiritualized sexual bond, 172, 190
Spirituals, 292, 293. *See also* Negro spirituals.
St. Elizabeth's Hospital, 244
St. Lucia, 338
Stalin, Josef, 366
Stevens, Wallace, *xi*, 11, 15, 104, 211, 217-39, 310, 312, 315-16; "force" in, 217, 220, 224 (*see also* Picasso, "hoard of destructions"; Weil, "the uncreated"); Stevensian topos, 323.
Works: "Anecdote of the Jar," 15, 228; "Autumn Refrain," 228-34, 236-37, 239 n. 4; "Bantams in Pine Woods," 227; "Bird with the Coppery, Keen Claws, The," 227; "Catching at Goodbye," 225; *Collected Poems, The*, 237, 240 n. 8; "Comedian as the Letter C, The," 219; "Credences of Summer," 236-37; Crispin (character in "The Comedian as the Letter C"), 219; "Dove in the Belly, The," 227; "Dry Birds Are Fluttering in Blue Leaves" (Part IV of "The Pure Good of Theory"), 227; "Extracts from Addresses to the Academy of Fine Ideas," 234; "Figure of the Youth as Virile Poet, The," 228; "Final Soliloquy of the Interior Paramour," 235; "Gray Stones and Gray Pigeons," 227; *Harmonium*, 227, 315; *Ideas of Order*, 228; "Idiom of the Hero, The," 234; "In a Bad Time," 234; "Long and Sluggish Lines," 220; "Looking Across the Fields and Watching the Birds Fly," 227; "Madame La Fleurie," 238; "Man with the Blue Guitar, The," 220-23, 225; "Noble Rider and the Sound of Words, The," 217, 220, 222; "Not Ideas about the Thing but the Thing Itself," 238, 323; "Of Bright and Blue Birds in the Gala Sun," 227; *Opus Posthumous*, 227, 240 n. 8; "Ordinary Evening in New Haven, An," 236-37, 240 n. 4; "Ordinary Women, The," 234; "Owl in the Sarcophagus, The," 227; *Palm at the End of the Mind, The*, 227, 240 n. 8; "Plain Sense of Things, The," 219-20, 230; "Planet on the Table, The," 238; "Prologues to What Is Possible," 237; "Rock, The" (section in *Collected Poems*), 237-38; "St. Armorer's Church from the

Outside," 233; "Sunday Morning," 104, 211, 226-27; "Thirteeen Ways of Looking at a Blackbird," 226; "To an Old Philosopher in Rome," 234, 238; "Wild Ducks, People, and Distances," 227; "World as Meditation, The," 11

Stevenson, Anne, 313

Stich (stichos), 23

Stoicism, 176, 212

Strauss, Richard, 253

Stravinsky, Igor, 260, 267 n. 4

Stress-accented verse, 47. *See also* Quantitative verse.

Subjectivity, 359-60

Sublime, 313-14, 316, 320, 327-28, 329-31, 332 n. 5, 336; egotistical sublime, 316

Suffering, sufferer, 310, 340, 346, 347, 355

Summers, Joseph, 314

"Sweet new style," 288. *See also Dolce stil nuovo.*

Swinburne, Algernon, 362

Symbolist Movement, The (Symons), 258

Synagogue, 38

Synge, J. M., 202, 297; *Playboy of the Western World, The*, 297

Systrophe, 97, 106 n. 12

T

Tabernacle, 39

Tarleton, Banastre, 208

Tate, Allen, *xi*, 9, 11, 15, 16, 147, 207, 209, 210, 269-89, 290 n. 2; Dantean sequence, 281; poetry of Fugitive years, 274.
Works: "Aeneas at Washington," 9-10, 282; *Allen Tate: Collected Poems 1919-1976*, 281; "Angelic Imagination, The," 273, 276, 277-79; "Buried Lake, The," 281, 283, 286, 287-89; "Cross, The," 280, 282; "Hart Crane," 273; "Ignis Fatuus," 274-76, 282; "Last Days of Alice," 280; "Maimed Man, The," 281, 282-86, 287, 289; "Mr. Pope," 16; "New Provincialism, The," 270; "Ode to the Confederate Dead," 11-12, 210, 272, 282; "Remarks on the Southern Religion," 280; "Seasons of the Soul," 276; "Swimmers, The," 281, 283, 286; "Symbolic Imagination, The," 273, 276, 278, 280-81, 287, 289; "Winter Mask," 276

Techne, 81, 85

Telos, 138, 141-42

Tempe, 137-38

Temple, the, 26, 38

Tennessee Valley Authority, 208-9

Tennyson, Alfred, Lord, 71 n. 6, 329-30, 364; "The Eagle," 329-30; *Idylls of the King*, 364; *In Memoriam*, 364

Tenth Muse, New World figure of, 339

Terrain of Comedy, The, xi

Terza rima, 281, 283

Thalamos, of the human heart, 364

Thanatos, 2, 141

Theocritus, 245, 247, 264

Theognis, 60, 65

Theron, 59

Thing, thing itself, *res*, 219, 221, 237, 240 n. 4, 254, 269, 287

"Thinginess," 16, 201

Thomas Aquinas, Saint, 4, 115, 133, 279

Thomas, Dylan, 3; "Do Not Go Gentle into That Good Night," 3; "Refusal to Mourn the Death, by Fire, of a Child in London, A," 3

Thomson, James, 259; *City of Dreadful Night, The*, 259

Thoreau, Henry David, 155, 167

Time, 2-3, 6, 97, 100, 101, 137, 138-45, 160-61, 221, 261

Tiresias, 261

Tocqueville, Alexis de, 335-36

Todd, Mabel Loomis, 157, 158, 162
Toomer, Jean, 296, 304, 307; *Cane*, 296; "Georgia Dusk," 307; "Song of the Son," 304
Torrence, Ridgeley, 294, 295, 296
Totalitarian state socialism, 371
Tottel's Miscellany, 105 n. 4
Toussaint Louverture, 339
Tower of Babel, 8
Tradition, traditional, 244-48, 256-57, 258-59, 261, 270-73, 309-10, 318, 324, 325, 337, 361, 366; traditional poetic forms, 261, 271, 370
Tragedy, tragedians, 260, 352, 367. See also Greek tragedy.
Tragic Abyss, The, xi
Transcendence, transcendent, 16, 21, 129, 207, 224, 228, 261, 270-71, 285, 326; transcendent equilibrium, 292; transcendent principle, 314; transcendent realm, 270
Transcendentalism, 365; transcendental exaltation, 213; transcendental ideal, 316; transcendental radio, 312. See also Emerson, Emersonian transcendentalism.
Transhumanize *(trasumanar,* Dante), 13, 145, 147, 148, 151, 151 n., 285
Tristan und Isolde, 258, 260
Trobar clus, 80. See Daniel, Arnaut.
Troubadour poets, 77, 78, 86, 91 n. 5, 121
Troy, 10, 100
Tryon, William, 208
Tsurayuki, Ki no, *x*
Tsvetaeva, Marina, 365
Tuckerman, Sarah, 159
Tunisia, *ix*
Turner, Frederick, *xi*
Twain, Mark, 246

U

U2, 42
"Uncreated, the," 223-24, 229, 230. See also Decreation; Weil.
Union (Civil War), 208
Union of lovers, 270, 352 n. 10
Unitive Way (way of mystics), 279
Unity of Being, 218-19, 236, 269, 277. See also Ontological splendor.
Universal Negro Improvement Association, 294
University of the West Indies (UWI), 337-38
Unmoved mover, 22
Uriah, 41

V

Vale of soul-making, 377. See also Soul-making.
Valency, Maurice, 91 n. 5
Vanderbilt University, 207, 270
Varro, 74 n. 32
Vassar College Library, 333 n. 13
Vendler, Helen, 98, 102, 104, 240 n. 5
Ventadorn, Bernard de, 77
Venus, 188
Verlaine, Paul, 258, 362
"Victorian Flower Power: America's Floral Women in the Nineteenth Century" (Ingram), 154-55
Virgil, Vergil, 7, 47, 48, 60-65, 68, 75 n. 43, 95, 96, 100, 107 n. 21, 242, 261, 273, 282, 283, 345, 375.
  Works: *Aeneid*, 64, 95, 96, 98, 283; *Eclogues*, 283; *Georgics*, 47, 48, 61-63, 65, 67, 71 n. 6, 74 n. 35, 107 n. 21, 345
Virginity, 172
Vision, 219: prophetic, 218, 220; unclouded prelapsarian, 224

Visionary mode, 220; visionary language, 220, 221, 226; visionary poet, 221; visionary tradition, 218
Voegelin, Eric, 71 n. 8, 75 n. 47
Vorticism, 255
Voznesensky, Andrey, 366

W

Wadsworth, Reverend Charles, 190
Wagner, Richard, 258, 260
Walcott, Derek, 90, 300, 338, 355 n. 3, 356 n. 11; "Far Cry from Africa, A" 300
Waltrip, Darrell, 267 n. 3
Warren, Robert Penn, 207, 270, 290 n. 2
Washington, Booker T., 291-92, 293-94; "Atlanta Exposition Address," 291
Weil, Simone, 223-25, 229-30, 223; *La Pesanteur et la grâce*, 233. *See also* Decreation; "Uncreated, the."
West, Cornel, 43 n. 3
West Indies, West Indian, 336, 343, 355; West Indian consciousness, 337; West Indian (Jamaican) English, 336-37; West Indian poetry, 336-39
"Wet style," 17
Whitman, Walt, 234, 242, 244-46, 250, 255, 261, 264, 312, 360, 368; as "pigheaded father," 242, 264; "barbaric yawp," 245
Wilbur, Richard, 176
Wilde, Oscar, 361
William Shakspere's Small Latin & Lesse Greeke (Baldwin), 98
William the Troubadour (William IX), *xi*, 78, 79, 81, 92 n. 6; "Farai un vers," 78-80, 81, 82, 85
Williams, William Carlos, 85, 220, 362; "Red Wheelbarrow, The," 85
Winckelmann, J. J., 363
Winfrey, Oprah, 84, 340
Wisdom (Primal Wisdom), 14, 135
Wonder, 346, 353, 355
Word, the, as Christ, *as logos*, 14, 129-30, 172, 187-88
Word, as information, 266, 346
Word, words, use of in poetry, 183, 220, 346-47, 351
Wordsworth, William, 27, 29, 35, 188, 203, 242, 315-16, 359-60, 362; *Prelude, The*, 362; "World Is Too Much with Us, The," 203. *See also Lyrical Ballads*.
World War I, Great War, 243, 256, 270, 371
Wright, James, 199; "Jewel, The," 199
Wright, Jay, 308
Wyatt, Sir Thomas, 11; "They Flee from Me," 11

Y

Yahweh, 22, 28, 40, 41, 43 n. 3
Yale School of Drama, 340
Yeats, William Butler, *xi*, 11, 12, 35, 82, 138, 199, 202-7, 212, 213, 230-32, 245, 247, 253, 254, 257, 264, 266, 297; Coole Park, 199.
Works: "Circus Animals' Desertion, The," 206-7; *Collected Poems*, 203; "Lake Isle of Innisfree, The," 203, 207, 213; "Lapis Lazuli," 204; "Sailing to Byzantium," 11, 203, 204, 206-7, 230-31; "Second Coming, The," 204; "Wild Swans at Coole, The," 11
Yevtushenko, Yevgeny, 366
Yin, Joanna, 166

Z

zeitgeist, 184
Zion, 347
Zumthor, Paul, 91 n. 5

PERMISSIONS

Excerpts from "The Oven Bird" and "The Exposed Nest" and the entirety of "Dust of Snow" from THE POETRY OF ROBERT FROST edited by Edward Connery Lathem. Copyright 1923, 1928, 1947, 1949 © 1969 by Henry Holt and Co., copyright 1936, 1942, 1947, 1951, 1956, 1962 by Robert Frost, copyright 1964, 1970, 1975 by Lesley Frost Ballantine. Reprinted by permission of Henry Holt & Co., LLC.

Excerpts from "Aeneas at Washington," "The Maimed Man," 'The Swimmers," "The Buried Lake" from COLLECTED POEMS 1919-1976 by Allen Tate. Copyright © 1977 by Allen Tate. Reprinted by permission of Farrar, Straus and Giroux, LLC.

"Bells for John Whiteside's Daughter," "Old Mansion," "Prelude to an Evening," "What Ducks Require" from SELECTED POEMS by John Crowe Ransom, copyright 1924 by Alfred A. Knopf, a division of Random House, Inc. and renewed 1952 by John Crowe Ransom. Used by permission of Alfred A. Knopf, a division of Random House, Inc.

Ll. 1-3, 6, 28-32, 36-40 from "BLACK ROOK IN RAINY WEATHER" from CROSSING THE WATER by SYLVIA PLATH. Copyright © 1960 by Ted Hughes. Reprinted by permission of HarperCollins Publishers.

Excerpt from "The Blue Swallows," from THE COLLECTED POEMS OF HOWARD NEMEROV, by Howard Nemerov, © 1977 by Howard Nemerov. All rights reserved. Reprinted by permission from The University of Chicago Press. Originally published in THE BLUE SWALLOWS, © 1967 by Howard Nemerov and the University of Chicago Press.

"The Unbeliever" and "One Art" from THE COMPLETE POEMS 1927-1979 by Elizabeth Bishop. Copyright © 1979, 1983 by Alice Helen Methfessel. Reprinted by permission of Farrar, Straus and Giroux, LLC.

Excerpt from "Introduction" to *Asir la forma que se va*, by Carlos Germán Belli, used by permission of the translator, Karl Maurer.

Excerpt from A BOOK OF LUMINOUS THINGS, AN INTERNATIONAL ANTHOLOGY OF POETRY, copyright © 1996 by Czesław Miłosz, reprinted by permission of Houghton Mifflin Harcourt Publishing Company. This material may not be reproduced in any form or by any means without the prior written permission of the publisher.

"In the Midst of Life," by Tadeusz Różewicz, is from MAGUIRE, ROBERT A., THE SURVIVOR AND OTHER POEMS BY TADEUSZ RÓŻEWICZ, © 1976 by Princeton University Press; 2004, renewed by PUP. Reprinted by permission of Princeton University Press.

Permissions   423

Excerpts from "Randall My Son," "Lee in the Mountains," and "Sanctuary" are from POEMS 1922-1961, by Donald Davidson, published by the University of Minnesota Press. Copyright 1934, 1938 by Donald Davidson.

"Autumn Refrain," "The Comedian as the Letter C," "Credences of Summer," "Final Soliloquy of the Interior Paramour," "The Man with the Blue Guitar," "Not Ideas about the Thing but the Thing Itself," "Prologues to What is Possible," "Sunday Morning" from THE COLLECTED POEMS OF WALLACE STEVENS by Wallace Stevens, copyright 1954 by Wallace Stevens and renewed 1982 by Holly Stevens. Used by permission of Alfred A. Knopf, a division of Random House, Inc.

Excerpts from "Sailing to Byzantium" reprinted with the permission of Scribner, a Division of Simon & Schuster, Inc., from THE COLLECTED WORKS OF W. B. YEATS, VOLUME I: THE POEMS, REVISED by W. B. Yeats, edited by Richard J. Finneran. Copyright © 1928 by The Macmillan Company, renewed 1956 by Georgie Yeats. All rights reserved.

Excerpts from INVENTIONS OF THE MARCH HARE: POEMS 1909-1917 by T. S. Eliot, text copyright © 1996 by Valerie Eliot, reprinted by permission of Houghton Mifflin Harcourt Publishing Company. This material may not be reproduced in any form or by any means without the prior written permission of the publisher.

"Opera," "First Caprice in North Cambridge," and excerpt from "Second Caprice in North Cambridge" are taken from INVENTIONS OF THE MARCH HARE: POEMS 1909-1917 by T. S. Eliot © 1996 by Valerie Eliot and reprinted by permission of Faber and Faber Ltd.

Excerpts from the essays "The Angelic Imagination" and "The Symbolic Imagination" from ESSAYS OF FOUR DECADES, by Allen Tate, are reprinted with the gracious permission of Mrs. Helen H. Tate.

Excerpts from "Bird of Passage," "Exile," "Homecoming," "Visionary," "Nightflight," "At that frail and absent evening house," "Uncle Time," "Pages from a Journal, 1834," "Grampa," "Resurrections," "No sufferer," and in their entirety "The Suddentree" and "Epitaph" from UNCLE TIME, by Dennis Scott, © 1973. Reprinted by permission of the University of Pittsburgh Press.

"More Poem" from *Dreadwalk* by Dennis Scott, published 1982 by New Beacon Books, Ltd.

Excerpt from "Crossing" and the entirety of "Marrysong" from STRATEGIES, by Dennis Scott, reprinted with the permission of Joy R. Scott, Executor of the Estate of Dennis C. Scott.

Excerpts from "Open," "Third World Blues," "Seedsong," "The Sunday Loving," "Beast," "Nibblesong," "A Comfort of Crows," "Poem against Magic: For Mella," "Goodbyesong," "Butterfly Dream," "The Editor," and the entire poem "Manuscript" by Dennis Scott reprinted from Scott's *After-Image* with the kind permission of Peepal Tree Press.

"Foamy Sky" and "O Ancient Prisons," from *Foamy Sky: The Major Poems of Miklós Radnóti*, by Miklós Radnóti (Corvina Press), reprinted with the gracious permission of translators Zsuzsanna Ozsvath and Frederick Turner.

www.ingramcontent.com/pod-product-compliance
Lightning Source LLC
Chambersburg PA
CBHW031307150426
43191CB00005B/108